ISBN: 9781091276130

Table of Contents

Chapter One

Property ownership (Salesperson 8%; Broker 10%)

A. Real versus personal property; conveyances

B. Land characteristics and legal descriptions
  1. Types of legal descriptions;
  Metes and bounds,
  Lot and block,
  government survey
  2. Measuring structures
  3. Livable, rentable, and usable area
  4. Land Measurement
  5. Mineral, air, and water rights

C. Encumbrances and effects on property ownership
  1. Liens
  2. Easements and licenses
  3. Encroachments
  4. Other potential encumbrances of title

D. Types of ownership
  1. Tenants in common
  2. Joint tenancy
  3. Common- interest ownership
    a) Timeshares
    b) Condominiums
    c) Co-ops
  4. Ownership in severalty/sole ownership
  5. Life Estate ownership
  6. Property ownership

Real Versus Personal Property; Conveyances

Real Property

Any land and things permanently attached to the land. It consists of minerals, oil, mines or quarries. When you own real estate, you own from the center of the earth and up unto infinity. You own air space above the land.

Land plus all improvements (things permanently attached to it), and also includes the bundle of rights—interests, benefits and rights inherent of ownership.

Examples of **real property** include buildings, fixtures attached to the building, fences, structures, fruit, nut and ornamental trees and bushes. Standing timber and a vineyard are real property.

The bundle of legal rights/sticks includes the rights of real estate ownership
- Possession
- Control
- Enjoyment
- Exclusion
- Disposition
- Encumbrance

When you own real estate, you own from the center of the earth up into infinity

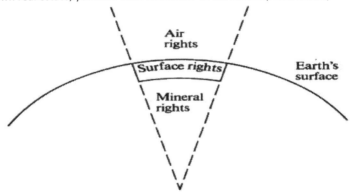

The land and all things permanently attached to it by either nature or by man (improvements). Can be sold or leased to others.

Surface rights = The land.
Subsurface rights = under the land

Mineral rights are property rights to exploit an area for the minerals it harbors.
Mineral rights can be separate from property ownership.

Subsurface rights may be leased.

Fixtures

- Those things attached to the structure that is attached to the land such as doors, water heaters, built-in air conditioners, sinks, faucets and ceiling lamps.
- Fixtures includes; buildings, standing timber, pear trees, apple trees, orange trees, fences, doors, faucets, plumbing fixtures, washer-less faucets, hot water heaters, fences, landscape shrubs and in-ground swimming pools.
- When articles of personal property, including landscaping, are permanently attached to the improvements or land they become **Fixtures**.
- Fixtures are personal property of the real estate owner, which is attached (**annexed**) to his real property. Fixtures are the Landlord's property.
- Legal tests of a **fixture**: overall test is the intention of the annexor.

The test for a fixture (MARIA)
1. Method of annexation
2. Agreement between the parties
3. Relationship of the parties – lessor/lessee
4. Intention of the annexor (If ivy growing in a free-standing pot attached to the front of a building, is it real property? NO)
5. Adaptation of the article to real estate

Fructus Naturales
The natural fruit of the land. Apple tree, orange tree, olive tree

Annexation - Annexed	Severance - Severed
Personal property that has been attached (annexed) to real property becomes real property. Such as doors, windows, moldings.....	A fixture severed from the real property becomes personal property. Such as doors, windows, moldings.....
	An item of real property may be changed to personal property. It is severed from the real property.

Types of Real Property
- Residential—single-family and multifamily
- Commercial—office space, shopping centers, stores, theaters, hotels, parking facilities
- Mixed-use—commercial and residential uses in the same building
- Industrial—warehouses, factories, land in industrial districts, power plants
- Agricultural—farms, timberland, ranches, orchards
- Special-purpose—schools, places of worship, cemeteries, government-held property

Personal Property
- Personal Property is movable. Things not permanently attached to the land are personal property. Personal property is movable.
- All property that does not fit the definition of real property.
- Personal property – "Personality" can be called **chattel**.
- **Chattel** is the French word for cattle. Cattle are movable.
- Personal property (**chattel**) includes movable items, such as a chair or a sofa.
- Personal Property is conveyed by **Bill of Sale**

Fructus Industrials
Crops cultivated yearly are personal property. (corn, peas, tomatoes)

A farmer is entitled to the fruits of his labor.
If a tenant farmer gets evicted, he is allowed to cultivate and harvest the crops. Emblements are personal property.

- Manufactured homes can be personal property unless permanently affixed to land.
- Bricks placed on the driveway before they are built into a patio are personal property.
- When an orange falls from its tree, it is personal property.
- A lease or stock ownership interest in real estate is truly a piece of paper that allows someone to have possession of real property. Both pieces of paper are movable. Thus, personal property.

Trade Fixtures
- An article owned by a tenant, attached to a rented space, used in conducting business. Example (Dining booths at a restaurant)
- Personal property attached by a commercial tenant to assist in a trade or business. If the tenant does not remove trade fixtures within a reasonable time after the lease expires, they become the property of the landlord.

Trade Fixtures - Attached shelves in a book store
Shelves are used for business

Trade Fixtures - Bowling Alley
A bowling alley is the most trade fixture business.

Trade Fixtures

Attached items used for business

Trade fixtures include personal property attached to the leased structure and used in the course of business   If removed by a tenant, the premises are returned to original condition before the lease expires.

If a trade fixture is left behind by tenant, the landlord will acquire this property by **accession.**
A trade fixture will transfer to the real property owner if the tenant leaves it behind after moving out of the leased property. When the landlord takes possession of the trade fixture left behind through **accession**, it becomes the landlord's real property.

Fixtures	Trade Fixtures
Landlord property	Tenant property
REAL property	PERSONAL property

	Real or Personal
A vineyard	
Grapes	
Orange tree	
wood fence between properties	

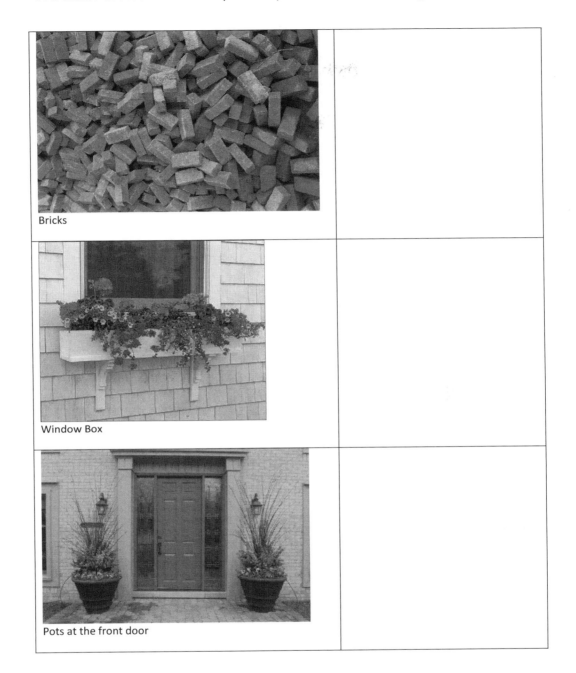

Bricks

Window Box

Pots at the front door

The Swansons received a crystal chandelier from their parents for their 10th wedding anniversary. The chandelier was personal property, but now that it is attached to the ceiling of their dining room, it is real property. The Swansons are planning on selling their home and want to take the chandelier with them. What are the Swanson's' options?	1) They could remove the chandelier from the ceiling and replace it with another lighting fixture PRIOR to listing their home for sale 2) They could leave the chandelier in place, put a tag on it stating "excluded from sale" AND state in the purchase and sale agreement that the chandelier be excluded from the sale.
The buyers of the Johnsons' home have written into the purchase and sale agreement that they would like the painting that hangs over the fireplace included with the sale of the property. The Johnsons are in agreement with this. What should the sellers do?	They should leave the painting with the home and supply the purchaser with a bill of sale for the personal property.
Pete Anderson leased a structure to start a restaurant business. He installed a kitchen with counters, an oven, a sink and a preparation area. He also installed various signs which advertised his restaurant, explained the origins of the cuisine and displayed a menu and prices. When Pete closed up his business was he able to take the fixtures with him?	It is the responsibility of the tenant to restore the property to its original condition.
Mary leased a structure to start a shop which specialized in dried herbs and spices. She installed shelving to hold the dry good, a checkout area with a cash register, a credit card machine and counters. She also partitioned off an area for storage and an area where deliveries could be accepted.	When Mary closed her business, she was able to take these fixture with her. Note: It is the responsibility of the tenant to restore the property to its original condition. Note: It is the responsibility of the tenant to restore the property to its original condition.
A woman rents space in a commercial building where she operates a bookstore. In the bookstore, she has installed a large reading table fastened to the walls and installed bookshelves that create aisles from the front of the store to the back. These shelves are bolted to both the ceiling and the floor. Which characterizes the contents of the bookstore?	The shelves and tables are trade fixtures and may properly be removed by the woman before her lease expires, and the tenant would be responsible to the landlord for any damage that their removal caused to the premises
In determining whether an item is real or person property, a court would NOT consider what?	The cost of an item when it was purchased
While moving into a newly purchased home, the buyer discovered that the seller had taken the ceiling fan that hung over the dining room table. The seller had not indicated that the ceiling fan would be removed and the contract did not address this issue. What is true about this?	Ceiling fans are usually considered real estate. The seller can be sued for specific performance. **Specific performance** is a unique remedy that may be available in some cases. It is considered an equitable remedy and is used when traditional monetary damages do not suffice to resolve a legal dispute. One of the traditional areas where this type of remedy is available is in real estate transactions.

A buyer purchased a parcel of land and immediately sold the mineral rights to an oil company. The buyer gave up what rights?	Subsurface Rights
A truckload of lumber that a homeowner purchased has been left in the driveway of use in building a porch. The lumber is considered _____.	Personal Property
A paint company purchases a large tract of scenic forest land and build several tin shacks there to store used turpentine and other items. What is true?	The company's action constitutes improvement of the property
A property owner's bundle of legal rights entitles the owner to do all of the following except	exclude utility meter readers
According to law, a trade fixture is usually treated as	personality
SOURCE	**https://quizlet.com/113095802/real-property-vs-personal-property-flash-cards/**

TRANSFER OF REAL ESTATE – Conveyance of Real Estate

When property transfers from the seller to the buyer,
UNLESS indicated. All real property must remain.

REAL PROPERTY NEEDS TO BE DELIVERED IN THE SAME CONDITION IT WAS IN WHEN THERE WAS THE MEETING OF THE MINDS.

Land Characteristics and Legal Descriptions

Land
- Land, sometimes referred to as dry land, is the solid surface of the Earth that is not permanently covered by water.
- The earth's surface extending downward to the center of the earth and upward to infinity, including things permanently attached by nature, such as trees and water.

Measurements

You will need to know these measurements.

1 yard	3 feet
1 mile	5,280 feet
1 sq. yard	9 sq. feet (3 ft. x 3 ft.)
1 acre	43,560 sq. feet
A section	1 sq. mile or 640 acres
1 sq. mile or 640 acres	5,280 ft. on each side
1 cubic yard	27 cubic feet (3 ft. x 3 ft. x 3 ft.)

Land Characteristics

Economic Characteristics of Land	Physical Characteristics of Land
Scarcity	Immobility
Improvements	Indestructibility
Permanence of investment	Permanence of investment
Location (situs – area preference)	Non-homogeneity, or uniqueness

14

Questions	Correct Answers
A city can easily estimate the tax base of the city ten years in advance. What characteristic allows them to do this?	Immobility
A City is able to fairly accurately project what their tax base will be in ten years because of	immobility. You can't pick up all the homes and businesses and move them out of the city.
A builder built two identical homes. One was on the ocean and the other was six miles inland. The house on the ocean sold for $200,000 more than the home six miles inland because of	situs (location / area preference)

Areas where land meets large bodies of water are called coastal zones.

Supply and Demand

The real estate market reflects principles of supply and demand, influenced by the uniqueness and immobility of parcels of real estate.

1. When the supply increases and demand remains stable, prices go down.
2. When demand increases and supply remains stable, prices go up.

A developer built his first home in a pre-planned community. The demand for his home design was constant. Which home most likely sold for the least?	The first one
A developer built his first home in a pre-planned community. The demand for his home design was constant. Which home most likely sold for the most?	The last one

Types of legal descriptions and measurement

OVERVIEW

Metes and Bounds	Rectangular / Governmental Survey System	Lot and Block
One of the oldest measures is "Metes and Bounds". It is described as a surveyor's description of a parcel of real property, using carefully measured distances, angles, and directions, which results in what is called a "legal description" of the land, as distinguished from merely a street address or parcel number. Such a metes and bounds description is required to be recorded in official county record on a subdivision map and in the deeds when the boundaries of a parcel or lot are first drawn.	This measure provided for the division of land into townships, sections, and quarter sections. This system utilizes township lines and range lines as a part of the description. An example would be: The E ½ of the NE ¼ Section 31, T6N, R6W. This would be a description of 80 acres. This system followed the Metes and Bounds surveys, and was established in 1785. Lot and Block	Subdivision Plat Map will overlay either the Metes and Bounds or the Rectangular Survey System. A sub-divider will break the land into lots, blocks and street addresses. Once completed, the new legal descriptions are recorded. It can overlay either main types of measurement. This map breaks up a large parcel of land into smaller parcels. A sub-divider would break down the individual lots with the Lot and Block numbers system using an engineer or surveyor. The new smaller lots are recorded to give constructive notice to the world.

In More Detail

Metes and Bounds

Metes and bounds is a measurement that tells a story (prose).

Typically, the system uses physical features of the local geography, along with directions and distances, to define and describe the boundaries of a parcel of land. The boundaries are described in a running prose style, working around the parcel in sequence, from a point of beginning, returning to the same point; compare with the oral ritual of beating the bounds. It may include references to other adjoining parcels (and their owners), and it, in turn, could also be referred to in later surveys. At the time the description is compiled, it may have been marked on the ground with permanent monuments placed where there were no suitable natural monuments.

A typical description for a small parcel of land would be: "beginning with a corner at the intersection of two stone walls near an apple tree on the north side of Muddy Creek road one mile above the junction of Muddy and Indian Creeks, north for 150 rods to the end of the stone wall bordering the road, then northwest along a line to a large standing rock on the corner of the property now or formerly belonging to John Smith, thence west 150 rods to the corner of a barn near a large oak tree, thence south to Muddy Creek road, thence down the side of the creek road to the starting point."

The most important feature is the Point of Beginning. (POB) The surveyor begins and ends at the **POINT OF BEGINNING (POB)**

Point of Beginning

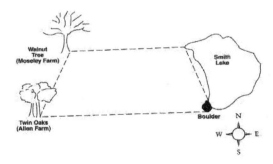

Metes.

The term "metes" refers to a boundary defined by the *measurement of each straight run,* specified by a **distance between the points**, and an orientation or direction.   More specific than bounds.

Bounds.

A more general boundary description such as along a certain watercourse, a stone wall, an adjoining public roadway, or an existing building.

The system is often used to define larger pieces of property (e.g. farms), and political subdivisions (e.g. town boundaries) where precise definition is not required or would be far too expensive, or previously designated boundaries can be incorporated into the description

The areas of the country that use Metes and Bounds are the original thirteen states, the older parts of the country and Texas.

Keywords for Metes and Bounds

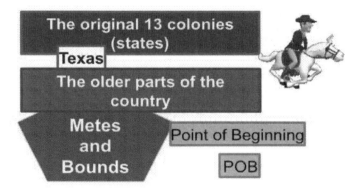

The parts of the country that use the metes and bounds are the 13 original states, the older parts of the country and Texas.

The Rectangular Survey System

The Rectangular Survey System was created to provide simplicity to interpreting and describing any piece of land, located on a map or on the ground, and where practicable, its units are in a rectangular grid form.

The Public Land Survey System (PLSS)

The Public Land Survey System (PLSS) is a way of subdividing and describing land in the United States. All lands in the public domain are subject to subdivision by this rectangular system of surveys, which is regulated by the U.S. Department of the Interior, Bureau of Land Management (BLM)

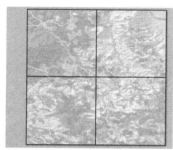

The Rectangular Survey System is a grid of lines based upon a true meridian and is originated from an *initial point*.

The surveyor establishes an initial point.

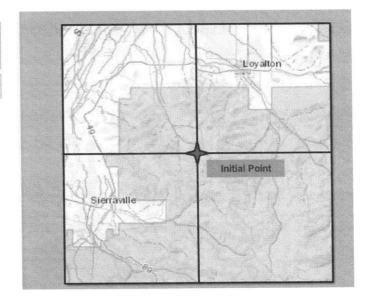

The Rectangular Survey System is basically a grid of lines based upon a true meridian and is originated from an initial point. To begin the grid, the surveyor establishes an initial point from which to begin surveying. From the initial point, the surveyor extends a north-south line called a **Principal Meridian** and a **Base Line** running east and west parallel to the equator.

From the initial point, the surveyor extends a north-south line called a *Principal Meridian* and a *Base Line* running east and west parallel to the equator.

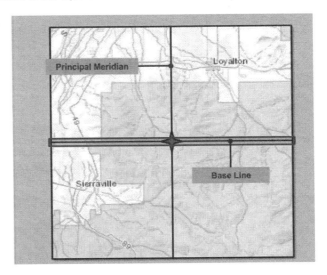

Along the north-south line, the surveyor establishes township lines north and south from the initial point. Each line is created at 6 nominal mile intervals. Along the east-west line, the surveyor establishes range lines east and west from the initial point also at 6 nominal mile intervals. Each of these 6 by 6 nominal mile squares is called a township.

Township Lines

Township Line	6	5	4	3	2	1
Township Line	7	8	9	10	11	12
Township Line	18	17	16	15	14	13
Township Line	19	20	21	22	23	24
Township Line	30	29	28	27	26	25
	31	32	33	34	35	36

Township lines run parallel to the Baseline

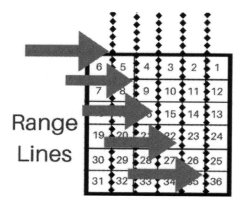

Range Lines

Range lines run parallel to the Meridian

Along the north-south line, the surveyor establishes *township lines* north and south from the initial point.

Each line is created at 6 *nominal mile intervals*.

Along the east-west line, the surveyor establishes *range lines* east and west from the initial point also at 6 nominal mile intervals.

Each of these 6 by 6 nominal mile squares is called a *township*.

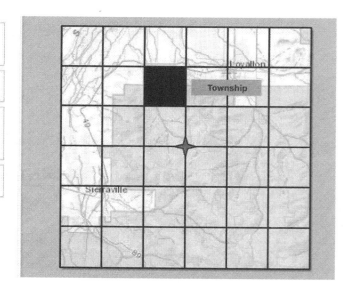

6	5	4	3	2	1
7	8	9	10	11	12
18	17	16	15	14	13
19	20	21	22	23	24
30	29	28	27	26	25
31	32	33	34	35	36

Each township is subdivided into 36 sections of one square nominal mile each.

Section numbering begins at number one in the upper right northeast.

Sections are numbered right to left and left to right down the rows until reaching the lower right southeast section.

Each township is further subdivided into thirty-six sections of one square nominal mile each. Section numbering begins at number one in the upper right northeast. Sections are numbered right to left and left to right down the rows until reaching the lower right southeast section. This wandering arrangement is based on how farmers plowed their land or "as the ox plows." The benefits of this numbering system guarantee that a section is always adjoined by its preceding and succeeding section. A section will never end up next to a confusingly numbered section in an adjoining township. Section 16 is set aside for schools.

Each township is subdivided into 36 sections of one square nominal mile each.

Section numbering begins at number one in the upper right northeast.

Sections are numbered right to left and left to right down the rows until reaching the lower right southeast section.

When describing portions of regular sections, *aliquot* parts, or exact divisions of the whole are used. Quarters are described in their relative position within the section.

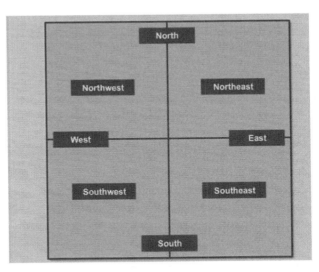

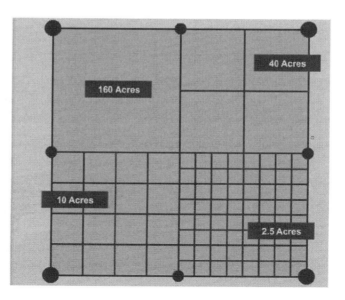

Along the township and range lines, **corner monuments** are set every nominal mile at all **section corners**.

Monuments, called **quarter corners**, are set at mid-point between each mile marker.

These monuments are called quarter corners because when connected, they form the legal boundaries that divide each section into quarters.

Quarter parts can be subdivided into quarters equal to 40 acres each. The 40 acre quarter-quarter is considered the standard land unit.

Quarters can then be subdivided into quarters equal to 10 acres each. These 10 acre quarters can be subdivided into quarters equal to 2 ½ acres each.

For various reasons, not all sections contain 640 acres, which is contrary to the plan of the rectangular system as shown here. The sections along the north tier and the west range of a regular township are often irregular sections and contain lots. These non-aliquot parts are designated by section and given a lot number. Though lots may contain more or less than 40 acres, they are considered a subdivision unit of a section.

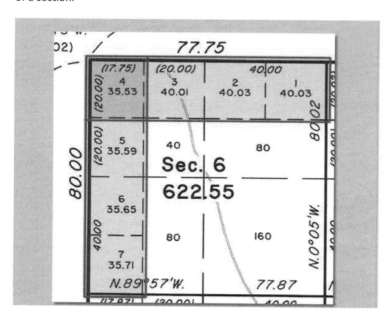

Not all sections contain 640 acres contrary to the plan of the rectangular system shown.

Sections along the north tier and west range of a regular township are often **irregular sections** and contain lots.

Lots:
- Designated by section
- Given a lot number
- May contain more or less than 40 acres
- Considered a subdivision unit of a section

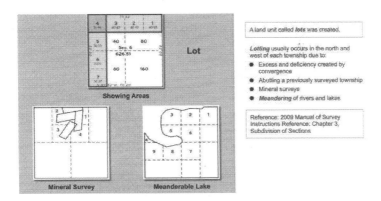

To compensate for loss in acreage to the convergence a land unit called **lots** was created. This is due to excess and deficiency in area created by convergence or because the township is abutting a previously surveyed township. **Lotting** also occurs when special surveys such as mineral surveys, and the meandering of rivers and lakes because the reduced land area around them cannot be described in aliquot parts. Lots are numbered similar to the 36 sections of a township. For various reasons, not all sections contain 640 acres, which is contrary to the plan of the rectangular system. The sections along the **north tier and the west range** of a regular township are often irregular sections and contain lots. Though lots may contain more or less than 40 acres, they are considered a subdivision unit of a section.

Correction lines are for the curvature of the earth.
There are four townships in a row. The fifth township shifts over. The line is called the **correction line**. It is for the **curvature of the earth**.

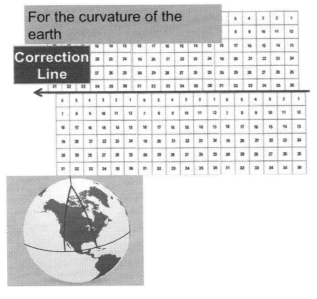

As a surveyor works north from the initial point, range lines do not continue in a straight line because of the curvature of the Earth's surface. If not corrected, the township on the baseline would contain more area than one further north.
Rectangular Survey System

Quick Mini Review

Match the letter to its term

[▼]	**Section**
[▼]	**Aliquot Part**
[▼]	**Section Corner**
[▼]	**Quarter Corner**
[▼]	**40-acre Quarter-Quarter**

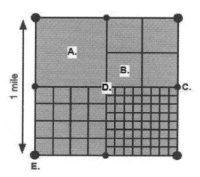

Correct Answers
A. Aliquot Part _____
B. 40- acre Quarter-Quarter _____
C. Quarter Corner _____
D. Section _____
E. Section Corner

NORTH

6	5	4	3	2	1
7	8	9	10	11	12
18	17	16	15	14	13
19	20	21	22	23	24
30	29	28	27	26	25
31	32	33	34	35	36

WEST (left) **EAST** (right)

SOUTH

If you are walking from section 6 to section 36, what direction are you walking?

SOUTHEAST

Sections are numbered right to left and left to right down the rows until reaching the lower right southeast section.

This wandering arrangement is based on how farmers plowed their land or **"as the ox plows"**.
The benefits of this numbering system guarantee that a section is always adjoined by its preceding and succeeding section.

A section will never end up next to a confusingly numbered section in an adjoining township.
Each township is subdivided into thirty-six sections of one square mile each.

There are 640 acres in one square mile.

Section numbering begins at number one in the upper right northeast.

There are 43560 square feet in one square acre. (**4** old ladies driving **35** in a **60**.)
Section 16 is set aside for Schools
Principle Meridians run North and South
Baselines run East and West

How many nominal miles wide and high is a Township versus a Section?
1. Township: 1 mile and Section: 6 miles
2. Township: 10 miles and Section: 4 miles
3. Township: 5 miles and Section: 1 mile
4. Township: 10 miles and Section: 5 miles

Correct answer:
Township: 6 miles and Section: 1 mile

True or False: When bodies of water are involved, such as a meandered river or lake,……. lots are used to define those areas that cannot be made into aliquot parts.

Correct Answer:
True

ARPENT – Louisiana
In Louisiana, parcels of land known as arpent sections or French arpent land grants also pre-date the PLSS, but are treated as PLSS sections.

An **arpent** is a French measurement of approximately 192 feet, and a square arpent (also referred to as an arpent) is about 0.84 acres.

French arpent land divisions are long narrow parcels of land usually found along the navigable streams of southern Louisiana, and also found along major waterways in other areas. This system of land subdivision was begun by French settlers in the 1700s, according to typical French practice at the time and was continued by both the Spanish and by the American government after the acquisition of the Louisiana Purchase.

This method of land division provided each land-owner with river frontage as well as land suitable for cultivation and habitation. These areas are given numbers just like standard sections, although the section numbers frequently exceed the normal upper limit of 36.

Lot and Block

Subdivision Plat – Lot and Block Numbers
Plat Map

Subdivision Plat Map will overlay either the Metes and Bounds or the Rectangular Survey System.

- A sub-divider will break the land into lots, blocks and street addresses. Once completed, the new legal descriptions are recorded.
- This map can overlay either main types of measurement.
- This map breaks up a large parcel of land into smaller parcels.
- A sub-divider would break down the individual lots with the Lot and Block numbers system using an engineer or surveyor.
- The new smaller lots are recorded to give constructive notice to the world.

The map must **identify:**
- Individual lots
- The block in which the lot is located
- A reference to a platted subdivision or similar
- A reference to find the cited plat map
- A description of the map's place of official recording

Usage of Legal Descriptions

In a real estate deed, a legal description of the real property being conveyed is required to be present. The deed can also include a reference to the recorded map, survey, or deed containing the legal description in order to meet this requirement.

Measuring Elevations

Datum

A datum is a fixed starting point of elevation.
A point of reference for measuring elevations.
The United States Geological Survey (USGS) uses mean (average) sea level in New York Harbor.

Benchmark

The term benchmark, or bench mark, originates from the chiseled horizontal marks that surveyors made in stone structures, into which an angle-iron could be placed to form a "bench" for a leveling rod, thus ensuring that a leveling rod could be accurately repositioned in the same place in the future. These marks were usually indicated with a chiseled arrow below the horizontal line.

Contour maps are used in hilly areas.

A topographic map showing the lay of the land of an area (works well for describing hilly terrain).

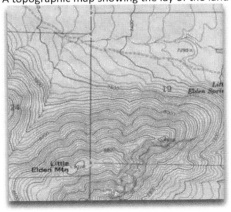

Air Rights

(also, known as air lots) are the those rights to ownership, not including surface rights or sub-surface rights, that allow you to use the open vertical space above a property.

Appurtenances

The rights, privileges, and improvements that go with a transfer of the land even though they may not be part of it. Examples are water rights, rights-of-way, and easements.

Monuments

Markers used as points of beginning or other corners in metes and bounds descriptions. May be artificial (iron stakes or other man-made) or natural (trees, river centerline) provided by nature.

Base Lines

East-west imaginary lines, crossing a principal meridian at a specific point, and forming boundaries of Townships in the Government Survey System of land description.

Benchmark

A reference point or marker placed by a surveyor and used to establish elevations and altitudes above sea level.

Correction Lines

Correction for curvature of the earth back to a full 6 miles made at every 4th township line in the Government Survey System of land description.

Datum

A point, line or surface from which a vertical height or depth is measured.

Permanence of Investment

One four Economic Characteristics of Real Estate. Refers to the long payback period and stable nature of real estate investment. Requires future projections on usage. Zoning can stabilize value as investors can predict future use.

Economic Characteristics of Real Estate

Four: 1) Scarcity; 2) Improvement; 3) Location; 4) Permanence of Investment.

Governmental Survey System

(a/k/a Rectangular Survey System) One of 3 major methods of land description. Used for large parcels in non-urban areas. Based on principle meridians and baselines which form Quadrangles, Townships, Sections and fractions of sections.

Legal Description

A description of property more accurate than street addresses and required in contracts, deeds or other real property transfers. The 3 major methods of legal descriptions are metes and bounds; governmental survey system; or subdivision (lot, block and tract).

Lot, Block and Tract

One of the 3 major methods of land description that identifies a parcel by reference to a recorded plat map, using a lot number within a specific block which lies within a specific tract.

Metes and Bounds

One of three major methods of land description. Used most often to describe irregular parcels using azimuth and bearing measurements. Metes are a measure of length and bounds are boundaries.

Mile

A distance in a straight line measuring 5,280 feet.

Point of Beginning (POB)

The starting point, usually a monument, in a metes and bounds land description. For the legal description to be complete, it must return to the POB.

Principal Meridian

The main imaginary lines that run north and south, crossing a base line at a specific point. There are 36 principal meridians in the US.

Range

A six-mile wide strip of land or townships which run north and south of a baseline, and numbered east or west of a principal meridian. Used in the Governmental Survey System.

Real Estate

Land plus all improvements (things permanently attached to it), running from the center of the earth up through the sky.

Plat

The legal description in map form of a subdivision. It contains lot and block numbers and show dimensions of each parcel. Used mostly in urban/suburban areas. Plat maps are "recorded" by filing with the county clerk and recorder

Rectangular Survey System

Synonym for Government Survey System

Sections

One of 36 sub-units within a township that is one mile square in the Governmental Survey System

Tier

A six-mile wide horizontal row of townships running and numbered north or south of a baseline in the Governmental Survey System).

Township

A 6 mile-square parcel of land in the Governmental Survey System. Contains 36 1 mile-square Sections.

16th Section Lands

The Land Ordinance of 1785 established the practice of setting aside section number 16 in each township for the maintenance of public schools. The United States Congress established the Mississippi Territory in 1798. In 1803, Congress enacted laws providing for the sale of all land south of the State of Tennessee, and made provision for the reservation of Section Sixteen in each township for the support of public schools. Congressional action granting statehood to Mississippi in 1817 also called for the survey of land in the state and further provided for the reservation of Section Sixteen in each township for the support of public schools. Sixteenth Section Land is also known as Public School Trust Land.

Block

A square or portion of a city or town enclosed by streets, whether partially or wholly occupied by buildings or containing only vacant lots.

Dryland

Land which is above the mean or ordinary high tide line; fast lands or uplands.

Easement

A non-possessory interest in public trust tidelands created by a grant or agreement which confers the limited right, liberty and privilege to use said public trust tidelands for a specific purpose and during a specific time.

Global Positioning System (GPS)

A method of determining the legal boundaries of a parcel of property which utilizes a system of coordinates established by satellite.

Legal Description

The part of a conveyance, advertisement of sale, etc. which identifies the land or premises intended to be affected.

Lot

Any portion, piece, division or parcel of land.

Mean High Water

The arithmetic mean of all the high waters occurring in a particular nineteen-year tidal epoch period or for a shorter period of time after corrections are applied to the short-term observations to reduce these values to the equivalent nineteen-year value.

Mineral Acres

Acres where the mineral interests have been retained in whole or in part.

Parcel

A description of property, formally set forth in a conveyance, together with the boundaries thereof, in order to easily identify it.

Parcel Number

The number assigned by a county to a parcel of property for identification purposes.

Plat Book

A book of maps, available in the county chancery clerk's office, of land subdivided into lots, with street, alleys, etc.

Reclamation

The process of restoring land which has become submerged or artificially altered fast land to its original botanical and/or geological condition.

Section/Township/Range

Section — A division or parcel of land, on the government survey, comprising one square mile or 640 acres.

Township – a division of land six miles square, containing thirty-six sections. Range – one of the divisions of a state, a row or tier of townships as appearing on a map.

Site

A parcel of land controlled by a state agency, the site name being determined by reasonable convenience, common usage, or physical location.

Subdivision

Division into smaller parts.

Submerged Land or Submerged Water Bottoms

Lands which remain covered by waters, where the tides ebb and flow, at ordinary low tides.

Tidelands

Those lands which are daily covered and uncovered by water by the action of the tides, up to the mean line of the ordinary high tides.

Township

The public land survey system established during the founding of the nation called for surveying all lands in six-mile square blocks. Each six-mile square block is called a township. Each township is divided into 36 one-mile square blocks called sections. The sections in a township are numbered 1 through 36 beginning in the northeast corner of the township. Numbering of sections in a Township runs east to west across the first row of sections, then west to east across the second and alternately thereafter so that section 36 is in the southeast corner of the section.

Upland

Land which is above the mean high tide line; dry land or fast land.

Living Area

Livable Area

The American National Standards Institute (ANSI) guidelines on how to calculate a home's square footage are considered the standard, but there are no official laws that govern this process. In addition, some Multiple Listing Services (MLS) report all finished and unfinished square footage as one number, adding to the confusion. As a result, buyers and their agents often have to investigate.

Residential Square Footage Guidelines
1 foot = 12 inches
1yard = 3 feet
1 sq. yard = 9 sq. feet (3 ft. x 3 ft.)
1 cubic yard = 27 cubic feet (3 ft. x 3 ft. x 3 ft.)

Measuring Structures

When reporting square footage, real estate agents should carefully follow these Guidelines or any other standards that are comparable to them, including those approved by the American National Standards Institute, Inc. (ANSI).

Living Area Criteria

Living area (sometimes referred to as "heated living area" or "heated square footage") is space that is intended for human occupancy and is:

1. Heated by a conventional heating system or systems (forced air, radiant, solar, etc.) that are permanently installed in the dwelling (not a portable heater) which generates heat sufficient to make the space suitable for year-round occupancy;

2. Finished, with walls, floors and ceilings of materials generally accepted for interior construction (e.g., painted drywall/sheet rock or paneled walls, carpeted or hardwood flooring, etc.) and with a ceiling height of at least seven feet, except under beams, ducts, etc. where the height must be at least six feet four inches [Note: In rooms with sloped ceilings (e.g., finished attics, bonus rooms, etc.) you may also include as living area the portion of the room with a ceiling height of at least five feet if at least one-half of the finished area of the room has a ceiling height of at least seven feet.]; and

3. Directly accessible from other living area (through a door or by a heated hallway or stairway). Real estate appraisers and lenders generally adhere to more detailed criteria in arriving at the living area or "gross living area" of residential dwellings. This normally includes distinguishing **"above-grade"** from **"below-grade"** area, which is also required by many multiple listing services.

Real estate agents are permitted to report square footage of the dwelling as the total "living area" without a separate distinction between "above-grade" and "below-grade" areas.

"Above-Grade" is defined as space on any level of a dwelling which has living area and no earth adjacent to any exterior wall on that level.

"Below-Grade" is space on any level which has living area, is accessible by interior stairs, and has earth adjacent to any exterior wall on that level.

Living area (sometimes referred to as "heated living area" or "heated square footage") is space that is intended for human occupancy.

Basements & Attics
- Regardless of whether or not they are finished, basements do not typically count towards a home's gross living area.
- Since they are below the grade of the rest of the home, basements can't be included in the total square footage.
- Professionals may note the size of a finished basement.
- Attics may be counted in a home's total square footage if they are finished.

The amount of living area dwellings is based upon exterior measurements except for condominiums, which use interior measurements.

A tape measure that indicates linear footage in "tenths of a foot" will greatly simplify your calculations. When measuring a structure, you should measure to the nearest tenth of a foot.

Real estate agents are expected to be able to accurately calculate the square footage of most dwellings. An agent is expected to use reasonable skill, care and diligence when calculating square footage.

What is a good management technique to protect yourself from false accusations?
Maintain a written record.

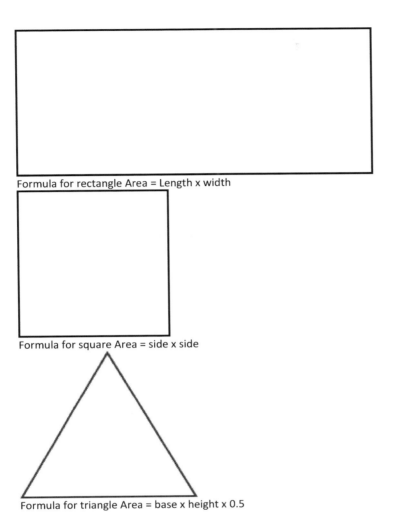

Formula for rectangle Area = Length x width

Formula for square Area = side x side

Formula for triangle Area = base x height x 0.5

Measuring Structures

Knowing how to measure square footage can be very useful for real estate rental and sale purposes, and it can also help you ace your next geometry test. To measure the square footage of a space, separate the space into manageable parts, find the square footage of all those different parts (usually by multiplying length times width), and add the square footage of all separate parts together to find the square footage of the overall space.

Find the Square Footage of a Space

Break down the area into manageable parts.
if you're having trouble finding the square footage, then it's probably because you're not working with a neat area with just one length and one width.
The space might have squares jutting off in different places and could be shaped erratically.
All you have to do is split up the space into even squares or rectangles.
To find the square footage, or the area, of the entire space, you'll need to find the square footage of the individual spaces and then add them all together.

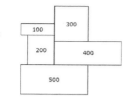

Draw faint lines separating the different sections.
Measure the length and width of the spaces.

Add the square footages of the spaces.
Once you find the sum of the square footages of the spaces, you'll know the square footage of the entire space.

Rentable and Usable Area

In architecture, construction, and real estate, floor area, floor space, or floor space are the areas measured as square feet.

Gross leasable area (GLA) is the amount of floor space available to be rented in a commercial property.

It is the gross leasable area in the total floor area designed for tenant occupancy and exclusive use, including any basements, mezzanines, or upper floors.

It is typically expressed in **square foot**.

Gross leasable area is the area for which tenants pay rent, and thus the area that produces income for the property owner.

The Building Owners and Managers Association has established a standard for measuring floor area and calculating gross leasable area and loss factor.

RENTABLE AREA
means the tenant's USABLE AREA and its proportionate share of FLOOR COMMON AREA and

BUILDING COMMON AREA. - **FLOOR COMMON AREA**
refers to areas common to all the tenants of a floor, such as corridors, elevator lobbies, washrooms, janitor closets, telecommunications and utility areas.

Mineral, Air, and Water Rights

Riparian	Littoral	Prior Appropriation
Small river or stream.	Large body of water and tidal waters. Navigable	With prior appropriation, the first person to take water for a beneficial purpose has the right to continue with the use of taking of the water.
The rights of an adjacent landowner to a creek, stream, pond or adjacent small body of water. It gives all owners of land contiguous to the same body of surface water equal reasonable rights to the water whether a landowner uses the water or not. A landowner cannot deny another landowner downstream from the water by rerouting the water or damming it. If the water right is attached (appurtenant) to the land, it runs with the deed and transfers to the next owner.	Tidal Water Littoral rights give the homeowner shoreline rights.	Other landowners may take water as long as it does not infringe on the first user. "Fist in time of use." Prior Appropriation is used where water is scarce or limited.
Riparian Owners own the real estate up to the middle of the river or stream	The land in between the high tide and low tide is set aside for the use and enjoyment of the public.	Government Granted Western States where water is scarce.

If the water right is attached (appurtenant) to the land, it runs with the deed and transfers to the next owner.

In More Detail

Riparian Rights
Riparian rights include such things as the right to access for swimming, boating and fishing; the right to wharf out to a point of navigability; the right to erect structures such as docks, piers, and boat lifts; the right to use the water for domestic purposes; the right to accretions caused by water level fluctuations; the right to exclusive use if the water body is non-navigable. Riparian rights also depend upon "reasonable use" as it relates to other riparian owners to ensure that the rights of one riparian owner are weighed fairly and equitably with the rights of adjacent riparian owners.

Riparian right, in property law, doctrine pertaining to properties adjacent to a waterway that
(a) governs the use of surface water and
(b) gives all owners of land contiguous to streams, lakes, and ponds equal rights to the water, whether the right is exercised or not.

The riparian right is **usufructuary**, meaning that the landowner does not own the water itself but instead enjoys a right to use the water and its surface.

Riparian water rights, therefore, occur as a result of landownership.

A landowner who owns land that physically touches a river, stream, pond, or lake has an equal right to the use of water from that source.

The water may be used as it passes through the property of the land owner, but it cannot be unreasonably detained or diverted, and it must be returned to the stream from which it was obtained. The use of riparian water rights is generally regulated by **"reasonable use."** Reasonable use allows for the consumptive use of water, but what actually constitutes reasonable use has varied widely from state to state and continues to evolve.

Riparian water rights cannot be lost through non-use and are indefinite in duration. Therefore, a riparian landowner does not lose their riparian right by not putting the water to use. However, the courts tend to provide greater protection for existing uses, than for potential future uses.

Riparian rights can, however, be lost through prescription. Prescription is a process of involuntary transfer from one party to another. Under prescription, a party making open use of water for the proper time period (usually 20 years) gains title to the water right superior to that of the original holder.

Littoral Rights
Littoral rights are rights concerning properties that about static water like an ocean, bay, delta, sea or lake.
Littoral rights are usually concerned with the use and enjoyment of the shore.

The land between low water and high water is reserved for the use of the public by state law and is regulated by the state.

Prior Appropriation
Doctrine of Prior Appropriation
The theory governing water rights in many states which holds that the right to divert the un-appropriated waters of any natural stream (surface or underground) to beneficial use shall never be denied.

Priority is determined by time of claim and follows the order of domestic, agricultural, manufacturing and recreational.

Western United States

The prior appropriation doctrine, or "first in time - first in right", developed in the western United States in response to the scarcity of water in the region.

The doctrine evolved during the California gold rush when miners in California needed to divert water from the stream to locations where it was needed to process ore.

Customs and principles relating to water diversion developed in the mining camps, and disputes were resolved by simple priority rule.

Non-Use
Unlike a riparian right, an appropriative right exists without regard to the relationship between the land and water.

An appropriative right depends upon continued use of the water and may be lost through non-use.

Unlike riparian rights, these rights can generally be sold or transferred, and long-term storage is not only permissible but common.

Four Essential Elements
1. Intent
2. Diversion
3. Beneficial Use
4. Priority

Intent
In all states with the prior appropriation doctrine, the acquisition of water requires that the appropriator demonstrate an intent to appropriate the water, divert the water, and apply it to beneficial use.

Diversion
A point of diversion is an essential element of a consumptive use water right.

Beneficial Use
Beneficial use is perhaps the most important characteristic in defining a prior appropriation water right. Beneficial use is used to determine whether a certain use of water will be recognized and protected by law against later appropriations. The justification for beneficial use criteria is to prevent waste. Since water is a scarce resource in the west, states must determine what uses of water are acceptable. Beneficial uses of water have been the subject of great debate, and each western state has an evolving system for evaluating what uses of water are considered "beneficial."

Priority
The first appropriator on a water source has the right to use all the water in the system necessary to fulfill his water right. A junior appropriator cannot use water to satisfy his water right if it will injure the senior appropriator. A senior appropriator may "place a call" on the river. A call requires that the

institution which manages the water source shut down a junior diverter in order to satisfy the senior right. Senior appropriators, however, cannot change any component of the water right if it will injure a junior appropriator. Therefore, if a senior wants to change his place of use and this change will adversely affect a junior's interest, the junior can stop the senior from changing the water right.

Any change of a water right (time of use, place of use, purpose of use, point of diversion, etc.) cannot cause harm to another water user, regardless of priority.

Accretion

The process of increasing land through deposits of mud or sand (alluvion) by the action of water. The opposite of erosion.

Alluvion

The mud or soil that is carried by a river or stream and adds to the volume of land over time in a process called accretion.

Avulsion

The loss of land when it is washed away by a sudden act of nature. Contrasted to erosion, the loss of land over a long period of time.

Erosion

A gradual loss of soil due to nature—winds, rainfall, currents, etc.

Flood plain

Low area adjacent to waterways and subject to flooding if inundated.

Groundwater

Non-flowing water below the surface. (Such as groundwater aquifers)

Reliction

An increase of land due to the gradual recession of water from its normal level.

Special common-law right held by owners of land adjacent to rivers, lakes, or oceans and restriction the rights of land ownership

Well Permit

Authorization to use well water for single family residences. The permit will state the amount and uses (no watering of garden etc.).

Wetland

A wetland is an area of ground that is saturated with water either permanently or seasonally

Encumbrances and Effects on Property Ownership

Encumbrance are Private Limitations on Property Use
An encumbrance is a right or interest in a piece of real estate that belongs to someone other than the property owner. Because someone else holds an interest in your property, that right is a limit or restriction on your use of the property. Encumbrances generally are considered private limitations; however, the government can make a claim on your property for unpaid taxes, which also is considered an encumbrance. *

Encumbrance means "something burdensome" or something that bothers something. Encumbrances can be classified in several ways. They may be financial (ex: liens) or non-financial (ex: easements, private restrictions).

An encumbrance is a right to, interest in, or legal liability on real property that does not prohibit passing title to the property but that diminishes its value. Alternatively, they may be divided into those that affect title or those that affect the use or physical condition of the encumbered property (ex: restrictions, easements, encroachments).

Liens
When a lien is attached to real estate, it can limit ownership.
The property can be sold against your will to pay off the debt.
A lien refers to non-possessory security interests.

Liens affect the title.

Priority of liens*
This refers to who gets paid first when property is sold against the owner's wishes to satisfy a number of different debts. It also is referred to as the position of the person being paid, such as the "mortgage is in first position after taxes."

The first person paid from a court-ordered sale of a piece of real estate is the government. Real estate taxes take first position in the payment of liens. If several liens are attached to the property and one is for unpaid real estate taxes, the real estate taxes are paid first, including any special assessments, or special taxes above and beyond the general real estate tax.

Payment of general and special assessment taxes takes priority over all other liens, regardless of when the liens were attached.

Other than real estate tax liens, all other liens usually are paid off in the order that they were recorded in the appropriate local office of public records — the county clerk's office or some other office of public records.

Voluntary Liens	Involuntary Liens
A lien voluntarily placed on a property by a property owner. A voluntary lien is where the property owner willingly takes some action that enables the placement of a lien against the property. A mortgage is the most common example of a voluntary lien. mortgage trust deed chattel mortgage	A lien placed on the property without the consent of the property owner. An involuntary lien is placed on the property against the owner's will. Judgments. Inheritance taxes and mechanics liens are examples of involuntary liens Tax liens, imposed to secure payment of a tax "Weed liens" and "Demolition liens Homeowner Association Mechanics lien Judgments Specific Liens Specific liens are liens specifically on a single

	property. General Liens General liens could be liens on everything you own

One other characteristic of a lien is identifying how many separate pieces of real estate it can be attached to.

Specific Liens	General Liens
A specific lien attached to only one property. A general lien attached to a number of properties. * Mortgage liens and Trust Deeds Property taxes Ad Valorem taxes, meaning according to value. Special Assessments: A special assessment is an added tax that is paid for by the people who benefit from an improvement. Mechanics liens	A general lien is on may properties A judgment Inheritance Liens Income Tax liens

Equitable Liens - Court Ordered	Statutory Liens – Automatic
These are liens that are imposed by the court in order to maintain a certain degree of fairness or "equity" in the situation surrounding the property. They usually arise when one person holds possession of property for another person. These situations can often be quite complex, and may involve multiple parties and state laws.	A statutory lien is a lien arising solely because of a statute. It is essentially a lien that is created automatically by operation of a statute or law (meaning it doesn't require any subsequent judicial action such as a lawsuit or court judgment).

Various Types of Liens

Tax lien.
These are liens afforded to the IRS (by federal law) or state and local taxing authorities (by state law) for unpaid tax obligations.

Landlord's lien.
Your landlord may have a statutory lien on your personal property located in the house or apartment if you don't pay your rent.

Mechanic's lien.
These liens are afforded to laborers, contractors, or suppliers on your real property if you don't pay for the construction or materials used to improve the property.

Vendor's lien.
If you are buying real property but fail to pay the full purchase price, the seller is afforded a lien on the property.

Mechanic's lien
Mechanic's liens on the title to real property are exclusively the result of legislation. Each state has its own laws regarding the creation and enforcement of these liens, but, overall, there are some similar elements among them.
Mechanic's Liens are for the benefit of those who have supplied labor or materials that improve the property. In the realm of real property, it is called by various names, including, generically, construction lien. It is also called a materialman's lien or supplier's lien when referring to those supplying materials, a laborer's lien when referring to those supplying labor, and a design professional's lien when referring to architects or designers who contribute to a work of improvement.
When a mechanic's lien is filed for the non-payment of labor or materials used to improve a property, the effective date of the lien is the date the improvement, work or materials were furnished.

Mortgage lien

A security interest in real property held by a lender as a security for a debt, usually a loan of money. A mortgage in itself is not a debt, it is the lender's security for a debt. It is a transfer of an interest in land (or the equivalent) from the owner to the mortgage lender, on the condition that this interest will be returned to the owner when the terms of the mortgage have been satisfied or performed. In other words, the mortgage is a security for the loan that the lender makes to the borrower.

Tax lien

Imposed to secure payment of a tax

Taxes take priority over all liens.

After taxes, liens are paid in the order they were recorded.

A property tax bill or an unpaid mortgage bill may affect ownership.

Ad valorem tax lien (ad valorem = according to value) This is your property taxes paid once a year.

Taxes are to meet the demand of the government.

Ad valorem are specific, involuntary, statutory liens.

Special assessments lien (improvement taxes)

Only the people who benefit from the improvement pay the special assessments.

Judgment lien

Imposed to secure payment of a judgment

Homeowner Association (HOA) lien

For unpaid assessments, fines, late charges, interest, costs, and attorney fees.

Weed liens" and "Demolition lien

Assessed by the government to rectify a property from being a nuisance and public hazard

Lis pendens – lawsuit pending

a lawsuit has been filed

A foreclosure can wipe out a lis pendens.

Easements

Easement Appurtenant

Appurtenant means "in addition to" or "belonging to"

Easement is most like a "right of way".

Easements **"run with the land"**, meaning that when a real estate owner sells the property, the easement automatically transfers with the property deed.

An easement is **annexed** to ownership. It is a right to use another's land.

There must be **at least two properties** to have an easement appurtenant.

An easement **is recorded** and in your deed.

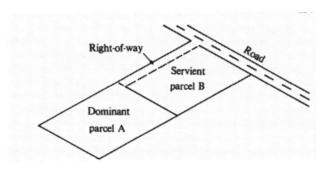

Servient Tenement	Dominant Tenement
The burdened land. The tenement on which the easement is placed. The easement on the servient tenement is an encumbrance.	The tenement that benefits from the easement. Easements are for **Ingress and Egress** In and Exit In an easement appurtenant, the two tracts of land can be contiguous or noncontiguous.

In an easement appurtenant, the two tracts of land can be contiguous or noncontiguous.

Noncontiguous:

Things not side by side.

In an easement appurtenant, the two tracts of land can be contiguous or noncontiguous.

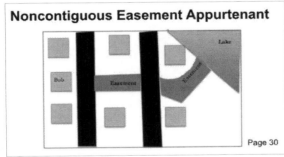

Noncontiguous Easement Appurtenant

Page 30

*Bob owns his home in a lake front community in addition to a **non-contiguous easement appurtenant** for access to the lake. **Or** Bob owns his home in addition to a "right of way" over his neighbor's property in order to access the lake. (For ingress and egress.)

TYPES OF EASEMENTS

Easement in Gross

Frequently for utilities Utility Company Access. There is no dominant tenement. All of the homes up against a Gross Easement are Servient Tenements.

Easement in Gross

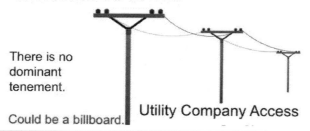

There is no dominant tenement.

Could be a billboard. **Utility Company Access**

Party Wall Easement	A wall that straddles the property line of adjacent properties with different owners. The wall facing the person is the responsibility or that person. If the entire wall falls down, the Homeowner's Association takes responsibility.
Easement by Necessity	Land locked property. It is because owners must have ingress to and egress from their land.
Easement by Prescription – Prescriptive Easement ## Easement by Prescription Continuous Visible Open Notorious This will be in the form of a time factor question! Based on the principles of Adverse Possession.	Continuous usage, without the owner's approval. It's usage that is visible, open and notorious. It's based on the principles of **Adverse Possession**. It's when someone has been using another's property for a long period of time. *Bob was driving over the northeast corner of Al's property for 10 years. Al knew about it but didn't like it. Al never said anything to Bob. One day, Al decided he wanted to build a home for his daughter on that portion of land that Bob has been driving over. Al asked Bob to stop using his property. Bob took Al to court and was granted permission to continue to drive over Al's property. Al's intention to build his daughter a new home on that section of land had to be abandoned. Bob was granted an PRESCRIPTIVE EASEMENT.

Easement by Condemnation
Acquired for a public purpose; requires compensation for loss in property value.

Encroachment
An encroachment is an improvement over onto another's property
The best way to find an encroachment is to hire a surveyor.
Bob's garage extended onto Sally's property. It is an **encroachment**.
If many years go by and nothing is done to remove the overextending garage, Bob may be granted a **prescriptive easement**.

Adverse Possession
A way of taking title to another person's property by the open, continuous, notorious and hostile use of another person's property for a statutory period of time.

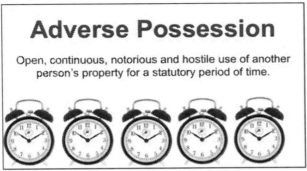

Creating an Easement
- By express grant in a deed from the owner of the property.
- By express reservation by the grantor in a deed of conveyance.
- By use.
- By implication.

Terminating an Easement
- When the purpose for which it was created no longer exists.
- MERGING OF TITLES
- By release of the right of easement to the owner of the servient tenement.
- By abandonment
- By the non-use of a prescriptive easement by its owner.
- By adverse possession
- By destruction of the servient tenement (for instance, party wall).
- By court decision of a quiet title action against someone claiming an easement.
- By excessive use (possibly a change in land use).
- When the Dominant Tenement Easement user releases the easement in favor of the owner of the Servient Tenement

Tacking is a factor that allows for the addition of the times during which several different owners continuously engage in the same use. So, if five different successive owners use your property for the prescribed period of time — for example, your state's ten-year requirement — the latest owner's request for an easement can be granted by the court. *

License
A license is a temporary right to use the land of another.
A revocable right to use another's land for a specific reason.

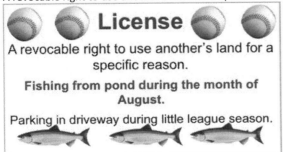

Deed restrictions
A deed restriction is a limitation on the use of your property that appears in the deed to your property and is put there by another person. The Deed Restriction is considered a private agreement, because no one forces you to buy the particular property governed by it and if you do buy it.

Deed restrictions also are referred to as covenants, conditions, and restriction (CCRs), or sometimes restrictive covenants.

Sometimes a deed restriction and public law cover the same issue but have different degrees of limitation. In that case, **the more restrictive or limiting of the two applies.**

Types of Ownership – Freehold Estates

Estate
One's legal interest in property – either freehold or non-freehold.

Deed
A written instrument that conveys title to real estate or an interest in real estate once it has been executed and delivered.
Essential Elements of a Deed
In writing, competent grantor, named grantee, recital of consideration, words of conveyance, habendum (type of ownership), unambiguous legal description, signature of the grantor, and effective delivery and acceptance.

Bundle of Rights
The rights of ownership associated with real property, including the right to use, enjoy, encumber, exclude and alienate, whether by deed, lease or devise by will.

Ownership in severalty	1. Tenancy in common	2. Joint tenancy	Tenancy by the entirety
Title held by one individual. Sole rights to ownership. Sole discretion to transfer part or all ownership rights to another person. May be a single individual or an artificial person, such as a corporation.	Each tenant holds an undivided fractional interest. Co-owners have unity of possession and right to occupy. Each interest can be sold, conveyed, mortgaged, or transferred; interest passes by will when a co-owner dies.	Four unities (PITT): possession interest time title—same document The right of survivorship; upon the death of a joint tenant, JTWROS Termination death conveyance of a joint tenant's interest through partition, which can be brought to force division or sale of property.	Some states Husband and Wife only Rights of survivorship Termination Death of either spouse; survivor becomes owner in severalty. Agreement between both parties (new deed). Court ordered sale.

Ownership in Severalty/ Sole Ownership
Title held by one individual.
Sole rights to ownership.
Sole discretion to transfer part or all ownership rights to another person.
May be a single individual or an artificial person, such as a corporation.
Ownership by a sole person (individual, corporation, partnership).

Co-ownership, title held by two or more individuals.
Termination of co-ownership by suit for partition.
The court may physically divide the property, or order it sold and divide the proceeds among the disputing owners. It is sometimes described as a **forced sale**.

Tenancy in Common – Tenants in Common
Each tenant holds an undivided fractional interest.
Co-owners have unity of possession and right to occupy.
Each interest can be sold, conveyed, mortgaged, or transferred;
interest passes by will when a co-owner dies.

Tenancy in common is a form of concurrent estate in which each owner, referred to as a tenant in common, is regarded by the law as owning separate and distinct shares of the same property.

Tenancy in Common owners own percentages in an **undivided property** rather than particular units or apartments, and their deeds show only their ownership percentages.
This form of ownership is most common where the co-owners are not married or have contributed different amounts to the purchase of the property.

Tenants in common have no right of survivorship, meaning that if one tenant in common dies, that tenant's interest in the property will be part of his or her estate and pass by to that owner's devisees or heirs, either by intestate succession or will.

Also, as each tenant in common has an interest in the property, they may, in the absence of any restriction agreed to between all the tenants in common, sell or otherwise deal with the interest in the property (e.g. mortgage it) during their lifetime, like any other property interest.

Partition:
Partition in Kind is the physical division of the land. The court decides how to split up the land between co-tenants so each receives a portion equal to their share. If the court is unable to equitably split up the land, then partition by sale will be used.
In partition by sale, the court forces the sale of the property and each co-tenant receives their share of the profits.

Where any party to a tenancy in common wishes to terminate (usually termed "destroy") the interest, he or she may obtain a partition of the property This is a division of the land into distinctly owned lots, if such division is legally permitted under zoning and other local land use restrictions. Where such division is not permitted, a forced sale of the property is the only alternative, followed by a division of the proceeds.

Joint tenancy
Four unities (PITT):
1. possession
2. interest
3. time
4. title—same document

A form of co-ownership in which one fee simple title is undivided and shared equally among two or more owners with an automatic right-of-survivorship. Four unities–time, title, interest and possession–are required to create joint tenancy.
The type of co-ownership does not affect the right of co-owners to sell their fractional interest in the property to others during their lifetimes, but it does affect their power to the property upon their death to their devisees. However, any joint tenant can change this by severing the joint tenancy. This occurs whenever a joint tenant transfers his or her fractional interest in the property.

A joint tenancy or joint tenancy with **right of survivorship JTWROS** is a type of concurrent estate in which co-owners have a right of survivorship, meaning that if one owner dies, that owner's interest in the property will pass to the surviving owner or owners by operation of law, and avoiding probate. The deceased owner's interest in the property simply evaporates and cannot be inherited by his or her heirs. Under this type of ownership, the last owner living owns all the property, and on his or her death the property will form part of their estate. Unlike a tenancy in common, where co-owners may have unequal interests in a property, joint co-owners have an equal share in the property.

It is important to note, however, that claims against the deceased owner's estate may, under certain circumstances, be satisfied by the portion of ownership previously owned by the deceased, but now owned by the survivor or survivors. In other words, the deceased's liabilities can sometimes remain attached to the property.

This form of ownership is common between spouses, parent and child, and in any other situation where parties want ownership to pass immediately and automatically to the survivor. For bank and brokerage accounts held in this fashion, the acronym JTWROS is commonly appended to the account name as evidence of the owners' intent.

In order to **terminate a joint tenancy**, one of the four unities must be destroyed. (PARTITION) You may do this by conveying your joint tenancy interest to any third person. This can be done through gift or sale. Upon termination, a tenancy in common is formed between the third person and the remaining co-tenant(s). A joint tenant may transfer their interest unilaterally and without the knowledge or consent of the co-tenant(s).

Right of Survivorship
A key feature of joint tenancy whereby the deceased joint tenant's ownership rights automatically pass to the surviving joint tenant(s).

Tenancy by the entirety
A legal form of co-ownership in some states between only lawfully married husband and wife giving both spouses equal, undivided interest in the whole property. Upon the death of one party, the remaining spouse has a right of survivorship. While living, both parties must sign to sell the property.
Some states only
Husband and Wife only
Rights of survivorship
Joint Tenancy with Marriage

Community Property
Property acquired during a marriage and considered equally owned. Property acquired before the marriage or with separate funds during the marriage is considered separate property. Only used in 10 states.

Dower
The life estate interest of a wife in the real property of her deceased husband.

Curtesy
The life estate interest of a husband in the real property of his deceased wife.

Undivided Interest
An ownership interest in a percentage of a property, including use/possession of the total property

Common- Interest Ownership

Time-shares	Condominiums	Town house – Garden Home	Co-ops – cooperative
Interval Ownership A timeshare owner owns property along with others owners.	The owner holds fee simple title to the airspace of a unit as well as an undivided share in the common elements.	A form of ownership in which houses share common vertical walls.	A corporation owns the real estate and the inhabitants own stock in the corporation.
Timeshares are most often a vacation home.			A purchaser of stock becomes a shareholder in the corporation and receives a proprietary lease.
The use of the estate is limited to the timeshare interest.	Common elements are owned by condominium unit owners as tenants in common.	Titles to individual units include a fractional interest in common areas.	
Title is held as Tenancy in Common	Condominium units may be mortgaged; default on payment does not affect other unit owners.	Common elements are owned by unit owners as tenants in common.	The IRS treats a cooperative the same as real estate for tax purposes.
Time-share ownership permits multiple purchasers to buy interests in real estate, a form of ownership most commonly found with resort property.	It is possible to hold title as "In Severalty" and "In Common" when owning a condominium.	Maintenance of common elements are funded by fees charged to each unit owner.	Personal property but has a real property condition disclosure if there are 4 or less transferring.
		It is possible to hold title as "In Severalty" and "In Common" when owning a condominium	

Typically, common interest communities have:
A Single Developer – one who initially regulates the community

Planned Unit Development – PUD
A community planned with a variety of individual ownership interests such as residential and shared interests of common recreation areas.

Subdivider
One who partitions a large parcel of land for resale as individual lots.

The development of an entire community. Includes, homes, stores, schools, business, parks and a Home Owners Association.

A Board, Governing Body or Association – When the developer leaves, a board usually takes over and governs the community. The board's duties include:
Enforcing any covenants or restrictions against the residents
Collects fees for maintaining and improving the common areas of the community
Levy fines if any resident does not follow the regulations of the community

Laws or Regulations – While states do have laws regarding common interest communities, these communities are usually governed by their own documents. You can usually find the common interest community's regulations in these documents:
The master deed from the developer
The bylaws of the community, which usually include duties and powers of the governing body

The constitution of the association or community

Time-shares

Interval Ownership

A timeshare owner owns property along with others owners.

Timeshares are most often a vacation home.

The use of the estate is limited to the timeshare interest.

Title is held as Tenancy in Common

Time-share ownership permits multiple purchasers to buy interests in real estate, a form of ownership most commonly found with resort property.

Timesharing

Ownership or right-to use interest by multiple owners of undivided interests in a single real property for a specified period of time. Usually a resort condominium or hotel. The time period may be fixed or variable.

Condominiums

In a condominium community, people literally own their own units and the air space within the unit. The people who purchase a condominium have legal title to the unit. They share ownership and obligations for the common areas with the other condominium owners. Often, the condominium owners pay a periodic fee for the repair and maintenance of the common areas. The association or board does not actually own anything and is merely the regulatory body of the community.

A condo is an estate in real property consisting in an individual interest in airspace within a unit and an undivided common interest in the common areas, such as the land, parking areas, elevators, stairways, etc.

The owner holds fee simple title to the airspace of a unit as well as an undivided share in the common elements.

Common elements are owned by condominium unit owners as tenants in common.

Condominium units may be mortgaged;
default on payment does not affect other unit owners.
It is possible to hold title as "In Severalty" and "In Common" when owning a condominium.

Common Elements

The areas in a condominium project or PUD where all owners share an undivided interest and full possession, such as the common area hallways, swimming pool and clubhouse.

Limited Common Elements

Those areas in a common interest community reserved for exclusive use by a particular owner, such as decks, storage areas or parking spaces.

CC&R stands for "Covenants, Conditions and Restrictions."

The term refers to any document, contract, or agreement that restricts the usage and enjoyment of real property. It is an agreement between property owners or between a property owner and an association. CC&R's are frequently imposed in order to:

Allow property owners to enhance or maintain the property's value
Allow property owners to make the enhancements in such a way that does not damage, destroy, injure, annoy, distract, or offend adjacent property and property owners
Covenants, conditions and restrictions are regularly used in connection with organizations such as condominiums and homeowner's associations. They are particularly useful in situations such as condominiums, where the property of each individual owner is in very close proximity to another's. CC&R's can also dictate the rights of property owners in relation to the condo or homeowner's association.

Town House – Garden Home

A form of ownership in which houses share common vertical walls.
Titles to individual units include a fractional interest in common areas.

Co-ops – Cooperative

In a cooperative, a corporation or association owns the building and the land. The individual pays rents for the maintenance and repair of the common areas in the building. The rents are also usually equivalent to mortgage payments for the property and property taxes. In the cooperative, the "buyer" owns nothing. The "buyer" is essentially the tenant with the association acting as the landlord.

The people living there have a proprietary lease.

A form of multi-unit residential ownership in which a corporation owns property and the shareholders own stock and proprietary "leases" to individual units.

A corporation owns the real estate and the inhabitants own stock in the corporation.

A purchaser of stock becomes a shareholder in the corporation and receives a proprietary lease.

The IRS treats a cooperative the same as real estate for tax purposes. Personal property but has a real property condition disclosure if there are 4 or less transferring.

Non-freehold Estate
Less than freehold. A non-ownership or leasehold estate, that a tenant possesses in real property.

Leasehold Estate
Personal property interest of a tenant giving the right to occupy according to lease terms. Less than a freehold estate.

Freehold *OWN*
Estate for an indeterminable time.
Real property ownership that are for an indefinite duration. (e.g. fee simple, life estate)
A Freehold estate of real property is when the owner has immediate rights (bundle of rights) to the property for an undefined amount of time.

Fee Simple Estate / Fee Simple Absolute

The most complete and absolute ownership of real property. It is freely transferable, has an indefinite duration and may be left to heirs. All other estates are created from a fee simple estate.
Can be inherited.
Highest interest in ownership.
The highest form of ownership in real estate.

Fee Simple Defeasible
Also, called a Qualified Fee. Ownership estate in which fee simple title may be "defeated" by either
a) "determinable" (so long as the specific use in the deed continues) or

b). a condition subsequent (so long as a certain condition in the deed is not violated.)
Highest form of ownership with a condition.
If the condition is violated the property will revert back to the original grantor

Condition Subsequent
A requirement of a defeasible fee whereby the grantee's title depends on a specific condition. If the condition is not met, the grantor must make a statement to this effect and retake the property within a reasonable time period. The estate does not automatically terminate upon violation of the condition of ownership, the owner must go through the court to assert this right.

Fee Simple Determinable
An estate that may be "defeated" by failure of a condition determined in the deed, whereupon title automatically reverts to the grantor.

Contingent Remainder
A known future interest in real property, provided some condition specified in the deed occurs.

Life Estate
A Life Estate is a **Freehold Estate**
Life estate is based on the lifetime of the person granted the estate.
Life tenant is entitled to possession of the property.
A life estate holder is not beholden to the future owners.
At the life estate owner's death, the property will pass to the remainder man or revert to the original grantor.
The property returns to the grantor (or the grantor's heirs).
An interest in real property limited to the duration of someone's life, either the grantor or other designated person.

Pur Autrie Vie
A life estate based on the life of another.
A life estate based on the duration of the life of a person and other than the grantor. (from French "for other life")

Remainder Estate
A life estate that goes to a named third-party when the life tenant dies, also known as a vested remainder interest.

Remainderman
The person who takes ownership when the life estate owner dies. He is said to hold the property for the remainder of the property existence.

Reversionary Interest
an interest retained by the creator of a life estate if no remainderman is named

Property ownership held in `

Bequest
Personal property left to someone in a will.

Codicil
An addition to a will.

Trustor
A person who creates a trust.

Executor/ Executrix
Male/Female

A person named to carry out the instructions and requests of a deceased person's will.

Trust
Fiduciary arrangement where an owner (trustor) conveys property or money to a third party (trustee) who administers the trust for the benefit of another person (beneficiary).

Nuncupative Will
An oral will made by the testator in front of witnesses just prior to death.

Probate
An official court process to determine whether a will is valid, whether assets exist, and to dispose of assets and debts.

Inter Vivos Trust
A trust under which property is transferred by a living trustor to a trustee with instructions for management of assets and for distribution of income.

Differs from a testamentary trust created by will and effective upon death.

Trust property is typically tied into an estate planning strategy used to facilitate the transfer of assets and to reduce tax liability. Some trusts can also protect assets in the event of a bankruptcy or lawsuit.

The trustee is required to manage the trust property in accordance with the trustor's wishes and in the beneficiary's best interests.

A trustee can be an individual or a financial institution such as a bank. A trustor sometimes called a "settlor" or "grantor" can also serve as a trustee managing assets for the benefit of another individual such as a son or daughter.

Regardless of the role a trustee plays, the individual or organization must abide by specific rules and laws that govern the functioning of whichever type of trust is established.

What Are the Benefits of a Trust?
While there are many different kinds of trusts with unique features and benefits for each, some of the common benefits of a trust include reduced estate taxes, allocation of assets into the desired hands, avoiding court fees and probate, protection from creditors, or even protection of assets among family members themselves (for conflicts or underage recipients).

Parts of a Trust
A Trust is composed of three parties
- the trustor
- trustee
- beneficiary

But what are these three parts and how do they operate?

1. **Trustor**
   The trustor is the person who grants the trustee control over their assets, estate, or property, and who creates the agreement.
2. **Trustee**
   The trustee is responsible for managing the trust that the grantor (trustor) has appointed them over. They are the person who is in charge of managing the property or assets the trustor gives them to keep, and are titled in the agreement.
3. **Beneficiary**
   The beneficiary or beneficiaries are the people who received the benefits of the trust agreement. They are given the property or assets by the trustee from the trustor according to the terms of the agreement.

Trusts are often used to manage property, assets, or estates being held for a minor or person incapable of being financially accountable until that person be deemed able to manage the assets themselves.

Administrator's Deed
Used to transfer title of real property by the personal representative of a deceased owner

Main Types of Trusts
While the basic structure of a trust remains pretty much the same, there are several different types of trusts with different purposes and specifics.

Living Trust
A living trust, sometimes known as an **inter-vivos trust**, is one made by a trustor (grantor) during his or her lifetime, with assets or property intended for the individual's use during their lifetime. This type of trust allows the trustor to benefit from the trust while alive, but passes the assets and property on to a beneficiary (using a trustee) upon their death.

Testamentary Trust
A testamentary trust, often called a will trust, is an agreement made for the benefit of a beneficiary once the trustor has died, and details how the assets must be endowed after their death. This type of trust is often instituted by an executor, who will manage the trust after their will and testament has been created. And, a testamentary trust is irrevocable (cannot be changed or altered).

Revocable Trust
A revocable trust is a trust that is able to be changed, terminated, or otherwise altered during the trustor's lifetime by the trustor themselves. It is often set up to transfer assets outside of probate. In this case, all three parts of the arrangement (the trustor, trustee and beneficiary) are often the same person who can manage their own assets, but will be given over to a successor trustee and other beneficiaries upon the original trustor's death.

Irrevocable Trust
On the contrary, an irrevocable trust is one that a trustor (grantor) cannot change or alter during his or her lifetime or that cannot be revoked after his or her death. Because this type of trust contains assets that cannot be moved back into the possession of the trustor, irrevocable trusts are often more tax efficient – with little to no estate taxes at all. For this reason, irrevocable trusts are often the most popular as they transfer assets completely out of the trustor's name and into the next generation or beneficiary's name. However, a living trust can be either revocable or irrevocable based on its specifications.

Funded or Unfunded Trust
In the case of a funded trust, it means that property has been put inside for the trust. An unfunded trust is simply the trust.

Credit Shelter Trust
A credit shelter trust, also known as a bypass trust or a family trust, is a trust fund that allows the trustor to grant the recipients an amount of assets or funds up to the estate-tax exemption. Basically, this allows the trustor to give a spouse or family member the remainder of the estate tax free. These kinds of trusts are often very popular due to how the estate remains tax free forever, even if it grows in size.

Insurance Trust
An insurance trust allows the trustor to combine their life insurance policy within the trust, keeping it free from taxation on the estate itself. This kind of trust is irrevocable and doesn't allow the trustor to change or borrow against the life policy itself, but allows the life policy to help pay for post-death expenses on the estate.

A charitable trust
is a trust that has a charity or non-profit organization as the beneficiary. In normal cases, this type of trust would be built up during the trustor's lifetime and, upon their passing, be doled out to a charity or organization of the trustor's choosing, avoiding or reducing estate taxes or gift taxes. A charitable trust

could also be part of a normal trust, wherein the trustor's children or inheritors would receive part of the trust upon their passing, with the remainder of the estate going to the charity.

Blind Trust

A blind trust is a trust that is handled solely by the trustees without the beneficiaries' knowledge. These trusts are often used to avoid any conflicts between the trustees and beneficiaries or between beneficiaries.

Land Trusts: Additionally, trusts can be used for privacy (to keep wills private) or a good way to hide ownership)

A land trust is a nonprofit organization that actively works to conserve land by undertaking or assisting in land or conservation easement acquisition, or by its stewardship of such land or easements. Land trusts work with landowners and the community to conserve land by accepting donations of land, purchasing land, negotiating private, voluntary conservation agreements on land, and stewarding conserved land through the generations to come. A distinguishing characteristic of owning property by land trust is the identity of the legal owner is kept confidential

Still, one of the main benefits of setting up a trust remains the avoidance of high estate taxes or gift taxes.

Ownership by Business Entities

General Partnership
- A business organizational form in which all general partners actively participate in ownership and management and are liable for all debt and actions.
- All partners are general partners who participate in the partnership and share full liability

Limited Partnership
- The general partner provides the management.
- The limited partners are only liable to the extent of their investment.
- A business organizational form in which general partner(s) are liable for all debts and actions and limited partners carry no liability beyond the amount of their investment.

S corporations
- Corporations that elect to pass corporate income, losses, deductions, and credits through to their shareholders for federal tax purposes.
- Shareholders of S corporations report the flow-through of income and losses on their personal tax returns and are assessed tax at their individual income tax rates.
- This allows S corporations to avoid double taxation on the corporate income. S corporations are responsible for tax on certain built-in gains and passive income at the entity level.

Corporations
- A legal entity created under state law, consisting of an association of one or more individuals but existing separately from such individuals. Managed by its board of directors, the liability of each shareholder is limited to his/her investment
- A legal entity or A person.
- Exist in perpetuity (forever) until formally dissolved
- Managed and operated by board of directors.
- Provide its shareholders with limited liability.
- Corporate profits are usually subject to double taxation unless a S corporation.

Limited Liability Companies (LLC)
- Members have the limited liability of a corporation, plus the tax advantages of a partnership.
- One person can be an LLC.
- A form of business organization treated like a limited partnership from a federal tax point of view and an "S" corporation from a liability point of view.

Joint Venture
- A form of business organization in which two or more individuals come together for a business purpose and share in the profits or losses of the venture.
- It is treated like a partnership for tax purposes.

Syndication
- A process for two or more people coming together to operate an investment, such as partnerships, corporations, etc. ***It is not a form of ownership***. *Mom and pops Shops*

Real Estate Investment Trusts (R.E.I.T.S.)
- Money funds through which small investors participate in large real estate projects through ownership of certificates. REITS are created and managed by brokerage companies.

Quiz by Broker Tina Perkins, CDEI, Senior Instructor

1. What is the owner of a life estate in property entitled to?
   a. Future real estate taxes.
   b. Possession of the property.
   c. Refunds on rent when the property passes to the remainder man.
   d. A Reversionary Right.

2. Three brothers own a hotel and took title as tenants in common. After many years, one brother decided to sell his interest. He may legally?
   a. Sell if there is a majority vote.
   b. Not sell because tenancy in common cannot be sold or willed.
   c. Sell because tenancy in common has an undivided interest that is transferable.
   d. Not sell because of JTWROS.

3. Which of the following is false?
   a. Fixtures are personal property.
   b. When a homeowner tears down an old rotted fence and places the boards on the curb, those fence boards are then real property.
   c. Trade fixtures are personal property.
   d. A water heater that is installed in a home is a fixture.

4. Which of the following would not be a specific lien?
   a. A voluntary mortgage
   b. IRS judgment
   c. Taxes on real estate
   d. A mechanic's lien

5. After purchasing a piece of landlocked property, the buyer tried unsuccessfully to obtain access to the nearest road. He would be granted access by way of?
   a. Appurtenant easement
   b. Easement in gross
   c. Easement by necessity
   d. Adverse possession

6. Which of the following is an example of an encroachment?
   a. A storage shed that butts up to your neighbor's fence.
   b. An easement by prescription.
   c. A fence built beyond a property boundary and onto a neighbor's property.
   d. A Dominant Tenement

7. A woman owned a life estate. Using a standard lease, she leased the property for 5 years. She died shortly after. What is the status of the lease?
   a. Valid only as long as she was living.
   b. Legal and valid for 5 years.
   c. Not valid because a life estate cannot be leased.
   d. Valid as long as an heir agrees to honor the lease.

8. A pool contractor installed a pool and hot tub for the owner of a newly purchased estate. When presented with the final bill, the owner refused to pay. 30 days after the work was completed, the contractor drove by the house and saw a 'For Sale' sign in the yard. What should the contractor do?
   a. File a mechanic's lien with notification of Lis Pendens.
   b. Begin demolition of the pool.
   c. Sue the listing agent.
   d. File a formal complaint with the city.

9. Tenants in common:

    a.   JTWROS
    b.   May have unequal shares.
    c.   Cannot will (testate) their interest in the property.
    d.   Ownership by severalty

10. An electrician rewired an entire house for a customer. To ensure he receives payment for the work, he filed a lien. The lien can be considered all of the following except?
    a.   Mechanic's lien
    b.   A specific lien
    c.   A voluntary lien
    d.   An encumbrance

11. A garage was built 30 years ago. It extended 6 inches onto a neighbor's lot. This encroachment is an example of which of the following?
    a.   A dominant easement
    b.   A servient tenement
    c.   A license
    d.   Adverse possession

12. Two neighbors own contiguous parcels. One has granted the other an easement appurtenant for ingress and egress. If one of the neighbors decides to sell, which of the following statements is true?
    a.   The dominant and servient tenement status does not change.
    b.   The easement appurtenant expires.
    c.   The buyer will have to pay and receive an additional deed for the easement.
    d.   The seller cannot sell as long as there is an easement on the property.

13. Bob and Steve purchased a vineyard as joint tenants. Bob died testate, how does Steve now own the property?
    a.   Joint tenants
    b.   In severalty
    c.   Tenancy in common with the new owner.
    d.   Ownership is determined by Bob's will.

14. A couple owns their house as tenants by entirety. The husband dies and his will states that all of his holdings are to go to his son. What is the status of the ownership in the house?
    a.   The son and wife own the house together.
    b.   The son has sole ownership of the property.
    c.   The son and wife take ownership as tenants in common.
    d.   The son has no interest in the property.

15. Three sisters take title to an income producing property in unequal shares. What does this mean?
    a.   Common law property
    b.   Ownership in entirety
    c.   They are joint tenants
    d.   They have title as tenants in common.

16. Legal property descriptions may not be based on which of the following?
    a.   The government survey system
    b.   The rectangular survey system
    c.   A street address
    d.   A previous survey

17. A land description that has a POB and ends at the POB and is based on directions, minutes and linear measurements is based on?
    a.   Metes and bounds
    b.   Benchmark metal markers

    c.   Datum
    d.   Townships

18. In the rectangular survey system, the principal meridians run?
    a. East and west
    b. North and South
    c. Along the correction lines
    d. Government survey system

19. You and your brother own a house. Your brother would like to sell his interest in the house to your aunt. What type of ownership do you and your brother have in the property?
    a. By entirety
    b. Tenancy for years
    c. Tenancy in common
    d. Life tenancy

20. Tenancy by entirety can only be held by?
    a. Joint tenants
    b. Husband and wife
    c. A life tenant
    d. Lis Pendens

21. Which of the following would be considered a fixture?
    a. Chattel
    b. Personal property
    c. A storage shed
    d. A water softener

22. Within the same township if you travel from section 8 to section 26, what direction are you travelling?
    a. Southwest
    b. Northeast
    c. North
    d. Southeast

23. Susan holds a life estate interest in a property. Her interest is?
    a. An interest that can be sold
    b. A remainderman
    c. Limited to her life
    d. Tenancy at will

24. A man and wife who own their property as tenants by entirety. All of the following is correct except?
    a. Both have a right of survivorship.
    b. The parties must be husband and wife.
    c. Each can sell or will their half of the ownership.
    d. Both parties must sign the deed.

25. The county library holds title to its land and building with the condition that if it ever changes for the access to the building and books, title will revert back to the original owner. This type of ownership is which of the following?
    a. Fee simple
    b. Defeasible fee
    c. Remainderman
    d. Revisionary

26. Which of the follow is considered personal property?
    a. Subsurface rights

       b.   Chattels
       c.   Air rights
       d.   Water rights

27. Fee simple ownership as tenancy in common with people who don't know each other could be which of the following?
       a.   JTWROS
       b.   Time Share estate
       c.   Life estate
       d.   Fee simple defeasible

ANSWERS

1. What is the owner of a life estate in property entitled to?
Possession of the property.

2. Three brothers own a hotel and took title as tenants in common. After many years, one brother decided to sell his interest. He may legally?
Sell because tenancy in common has an undivided interest that is transferable.

3. Which of the following is false?.
When a homeowner tears down an old rotted fence and places the boards on the curb, those fence boards are then real property.

4. Which of the following would not be a specific lien?
IRS judgment

5. After purchasing a piece of landlocked property, the buyer tried unsuccessfully to obtain access to the nearest road. He would be granted access by way of?
Easement by necessity

6. Which of the following is an example of an encroachment?
A fence built beyond a property boundary and onto a neighbor's property.

7. A woman owned a life estate. Using a standard lease, she leased the property for 5 years. She died shortly after. What is the status of the lease?
Valid only as long as she was living.

8. A pool contractor installed a pool and hot tub for the owner of a newly purchased estate. When presented with the final bill, the owner refused to pay. 30 days after the work was completed, the contractor drove by the house and saw a 'For Sale' sign in the yard. What should the contractor do?
File a mechanic's lien with notification of Lis Pendens.

9. Tenants in common:
May have unequal shares.

10. An electrician rewired an entire house for a customer. To ensure he receives payment for the work, he filed a lien. The lien can be considered all of the following except?
A voluntary lien

11. A garage was built 30 years ago. It extended 6 inches onto a neighbor's lot. This encroachment is an example of which of the following?
Adverse possession

12. Two neighbors own contiguous parcels. One has granted the other an easement appurtenant for ingress and egress. If one of the neighbors decides to sell, which of the following statements is true?

    The dominant and servient tenement status does not change.

13. Bob and Steve purchased a vineyard as joint tenants. Bob died testate, how does Steve now own the property?

    In severalty

14. A couple owns their house as tenants by entirety. The husband dies and his will states that all of his holdings are to go to his son. What is the status of the ownership in the house?

    The son has no interest in the property.

15. Three sisters take title to an income producing property in unequal shares. What does this mean?

    They have title as tenants in common.

16. Legal property descriptions may not be based on which of the following?

    A street address

17. A land description that has a POB and ends at the POB and is based on directions, minutes and linear measurements is based on?

    Metes and bounds

18. In the rectangular survey system, the principal meridians run?

    North and South

19. You and your brother own a house. Your brother would like to sell his interest in the house to your aunt. What type of ownership do you and your brother have in the property?

    Tenancy in common

20. Tenancy by entirety can only be held by?

    Husband and wife

21. Which of the following would be considered a fixture?

    A water softener

22. Within the same township if you travel from section 8 to section 26, what direction are you travelling?

    Southeast

23. Susan holds a life estate interest in a property. Her interest is?

    Limited to her life

24. A man and wife who own their property as tenants by entirety. All of the following is correct except?.

    Each can sell or will their half of the ownership.

    .

25. The county library holds title to its land and building with the condition that if it ever changes for the access to the building and books, title will revert back to the original owner. This type of ownership is which of the following?

    Defeasible fee

26. Which of the follow is considered personal property?

    Chattels

27. Fee simple ownership as tenancy in common with people who don't know each other could be which of the following?

   Time Share estate

Chapter 2

Land use controls and regulations (Salesperson 5%; Broker 5%)

Government rights in land
1. Property taxes and special assessments
2. Eminent domain, condemnation, escheat

Government controls
1. Zoning and master plans
2. Building codes
3. Regulation of special land types
4. Flood zones
5. Wet lands
6. Regulation of environmental hazards

Types of hazards
1. Abatement and mitigation
2. Restrictions on contaminated property

Private Controls
1. Deed conditions or restrictions
2. Covenants, conditions, and restrictions (CC&Rs)

Government Rights in Land

Government Control on Real Property (PETE)

1. **P**olice Power – Protect the health, safety and general welfare of the public (i.e. zoning),
2. **E**minent Domain
3. **T**axation
4. **E**scheat

Public controls based in police power

- The police power of the states is the inherent authority to create the regulations necessary to protect the public health, safety and welfare.
- Government rights protect public health, safety, morals and welfare by stipulating ordinances for zoning and building codes.

Police Power

- The constitutional authority and inherent power of the state to adopt and enforce laws and regulations.
- Government rights protect public health, safety, morals and welfare by stipulating ordinances for zoning and building codes.

Taxation

- The main source of revenue for cities and counties for things like schools and road maintenance.

Taxes are to meet the public needs of government.

There are two distinct forms of taxation:

- (**ad valorem tax**) relies upon the <u>fair market value</u> of the property. T
- (**special assessment**) relies upon a special enhancement called a "benefit or improvement" for its justification.

Al Valorem - According to Value (Latin for "according to value")

- **Property Tax**
- A tax based on the assessed value of real property; *100% deductible on income tax.*
- Taxes take priority.
- A **house tax** or **millage rate** is an ad valorem tax on the value of real estate. The tax is levied by the governing authority of the jurisdiction in which the house is located.

Special Assessment - Improvement Tax

- **Special assessment** is the term used to designate a unique charge that government can assess against real estate parcels for certain public projects.
- This charge is levied in a specific geographic area known as **a special assessment district** (SAD). A special assessment may only be levied against parcels of real estate which have been identified as having received a direct and unique "benefit" from the public project.
- Only those who benefitted from an improvement pay the special assessment.
- The most universally known special assessments are charges levied against lands when drinking water lines are installed; when sewer lines are installed; or when streets are paved with concrete or some other impervious surface. However, special assessment tax levies can be made for other purposes including police or fire protection, parking structures, street lighting and many of the other purposes permitted by state and local government statutes.
- Creates a priority lien on the affected property usually second only to ad valorem property tax

Calculating taxes due

You can calculate taxes due using one of the following three methods, depending on how the municipality calculates taxes or how the exam question is asked.

1. **Mills:** This method bases the tax rate on so many tenths of a penny (or mills) in taxes for each dollar of assessed value.

2. **Dollars per hundred:** This method bases the tax rate on so many dollars of tax for each $100 of assessed value.
3. **Dollars per thousand:** This method bases the tax rate on so many dollars of tax per $1,000 of assessed value. You need to be familiar with all three methods for exam purposes.

Math Covered in Chapter 11

Tax Liens
When property taxes or special assessments remain unpaid, they become a specific lien against the property which takes priority over other liens.

Tax Sale
The sale of real property to satisfy unpaid property tax liens.

Transfer Tax
A tax charged by the state to transfer an interest in real estate which helps establish an accurate value for tax assessment purposes.

County Assessor
A county official (or sometimes the county treasurer in small counties) who determines the assessed valuation of real property.

County Board of Equalization
The county commissioners, when meeting to review the assessment of all taxable property in the county, and hear appeals from protests filed with the county assessor. The state board of equalization meets each year to determine if each county has assessed at the percentage of actual value prescribed by law.

County Treasurer
A county official who collects the taxes and determines the budget for schools, road maintenance, etc.

The Taxpayer Relief Act of 1997
Passed by Congress to greatly reduce the tax on the gain to be realized on the sale of real estate, especially for residential real estate.

Building Code
Standard established by local or state government to protect the public by regulating building and construction methods, including plumbing, electrical and fire.

Eminent Domain, Condemnation, Escheat
Only the government can eminent domain. The government can take privately owned property for the good of the public.

Eminent Domain
The government takes your property for the use of the public.
The owner is paid Just Compensation
Through **Condemnation.**

Condemnation is compensation to the property owner. Known as "Just Compensation". Can a condo complex eminent domain three houses adjacent to its parking lot to expand their parking? NO

Escheat
Government right to take title to the land if the owner dies leaving no heirs and no will.
If a person dies without a will and no heirs can be found, the state will take possession of that person's property. The reason is that land cannot be ownerless.

Reverse Condemnation
The homeowner is forcing the government to use Eminent Domain to take his property.
Only the homeowner can file for reverse condemnation

A man at the end of an expanded airport runway could attempt Reverse Condemnation.

Inverse condemnation

a term used in the law to describe a situation in which the government takes private property but fails to pay the compensation required by the 5th Amendment of the Constitution, so the property's owner has to sue to obtain the required just compensation.
Government Controls on Land

Zoning and Master Plans

Zoning implements the city's master plan.

Master Plan

The general or master plan of a locality will provide the purpose for the zoning and land use ordinances the locality employs. Generally, a zoning ordinance must conform to the general plan of the locality

A comprehensive growth plan that guides the long-term zoning, use, and development of a community.

Zoning and Land Use Laws

Zoning ordinances are regulations for land use within cities and counties. Zoning categorizes and separates different land uses into districts within a city and county. Land use laws and regulations govern the way that land can be used in any given area. These laws are usually maintained by local governments and by municipal codes. Local governments typically provide separate districts for residential, business, and industrial uses.

Zoning Laws, Planning, and Land Use

- Laws created by city and county governments to control the use of land. Zoning laws are enacted in the exercise of police powers
- Zoning is a local government's attempt at creating uniform neighborhoods and land uses in certain areas, by controlling how you can use your property and what you can build on your property.
- Zoning categorizes and separates differing land uses into distinct districts within a municipality.
- Typically, a local government will provide separate districts for residential, business and industrial uses.
- Zoning includes various laws falling under the police power
- Zoning is the process of dividing land into zones (e.g. residential, industrial) in which certain land uses are permitted or prohibited.
- The type of zone determines whether planning /permission for a given development is granted.
- Zoning may specify a variety of outright and conditional uses of land. It may also indicate the size and dimensions of land area as well as the form and scale of buildings. These guidelines are set in order to guide urban growth and development.
- Cities and local municipalities are allowed to decide their own zoning through **State**

Enabling Acts or Rights.

- If a public control and a deed restriction conflict, the more restrictive of the two takes precedence.

Planning Department

Provides the municipality with the goals and objectives for its future development.

Most municipalities have a specific **Planning or Zoning Department** that will propose zoning ordinances and oversee zoning and land use hearings.

These departments will also make decisions regarding variances (see below), conditional use permits and other issues that may implicate a zoning or land use ordinance. Generally, the department will have a **public hearing** (first step to zoning or making a change in zoning) where the individual or group whose land is affected will be able to present their case. The hearing also allows for public comment on the case.

The general plan usually provides different possibilities for those whose land use may not comply with the zoning ordinance for their district:

Variance: If your use of land or proposed building does not entirely conform to existing zoning and land use laws, you can apply for a variance. Typically, the landowner must show that she will experience a substantial financial hardship if she does not receive a variance.

- A request for a deviation from the Zoning Code. An example would be a homeowner allowed to build a fence closer to a lot line than the zoning allows.
- A permanent exception granted to either build a new structure or conduct a new use that would not be permitted under the current zoning.
- Most zoning systems have a procedure for granting variances (exceptions to the zoning rules), usually because of some perceived hardship due to the particular nature of the property in question.

Non-Conforming Use: Generally, new zoning laws cannot force an existing structure or use to change. Thus, a building or use that exists before a zoning ordinance is passed cannot be illegal and does not need to be changed. The zoning department considers this a non-conforming use.

- A nonconforming use is a use of property that was allowed under the zoning regulations at the time the use was established, but which, due to changes in local regulations, is no longer a permitted use.
- Local governments and the courts are reluctant to order an owner to discontinue an activity immediately or demolish a building that was lawful until the enactment of the ordinance that made the use illegal. Therefore, the use is usually permitted and is recognized as a nonconforming use.

Conditional Use Permit

Special permission for a use to exist where the current zoning would not normally allow it. For example, it may allow a preschool in a residential neighborhood

A zoning exception which allows the property owner use of his land in a way not otherwise permitted within the particular zoning district. For instance, a medical clinic was granted a zoning variance to build in a neighborhood zoned for residential properties.

Legal nonconforming use

A legal nonconforming use or structure is a use or structure that was legally built under previous regulations but does not meet existing standards

Grandfather Clause

A phrase indicating permission to continue doing something that was once permissible but is now not allowed. In zoning, it permits a nonconforming use. For example, an existing auto repair shop being allowed to remain in a shopping area that is being revitalized.

Most Common Uses Found in Zoning Ordinances

Spot Zoning

An isolated use of a small parcel or area, zoned inconsistently with a larger surrounding use.

Downzoning

Changing the zoning to a more restricted use, such as from multi-family to single family which will restrict the density

Rezoning of an area that would be less dense in population. An example would be a neighborhood that downzoned from multi-unit residential zoning to single family residences only.

The multi-unit residential properties are **grandfathered in**, meaning that the new zoning does not apply to them. Usually, if the building burns down or gets destroyed, the new zoning would apply to the new construction.

Upzoning

A change in zoning to a less restricted use such as from single family to multi-family use.

Buffer Zone

A strip of land separating two parcels that are zoned differently, such as undeveloped land separating a shopping center from a residential neighborhood.

For use in nature conservation, a buffer zone is often created to enhance the protection of areas under management for their biodiversity importance.

The buffer zone of a protected area may be situated around the periphery of the region or may be a connecting zone within it which links two or more protected areas.

Use Districts: These dictate the type of use permitted within the zone. These consist of residential, commercial, industrial, and agricultural.

Height Districts: Building heights are a type of land use regulation. These regulations restrict the height of buildings within any given area.

Setback

The distance which a building or other structure is set back from a street or road, a river or other stream, a shore or flood plain, or any other place which is deemed to need protection.

Setbacks are generally set in municipal ordinances or zoning.

Density zoning

Ordinances restrict the average number of houses per acre that can be built within a particular subdivision.

Bulk Zoning

A method used to control density and overcrowding by restricting setbacks, building height, or ratio of open area.

Aesthetic Zoning

Zoning that requires that new structures match an existing architectural style.

Incentive Zoning

Provides an incentive to a developer to provide a specific unplanned feature as a tradeoff for being allowed something normally not permitted.

Cluster Zoning

An area where residential density is described overall but the developer is allowed flexibility in placing the residences in groups interspersed with open space.

Conservation Zoning

Open zoning where the intent is to keep the parcel in its natural or agricultural state.

Conservation Easement

An area where development would not be permitted so as to leave the natural habitat untouched.

Cumulative Uses: Cumulative zoning is a method of zoning where any use that is permitted in a higher use, less intensive zone is also permissible in a lower use, more intensive zone. Uses are generally ranked on a hierarchy of uses ranging from single family residential (highest) to heavy industrial (lowest). Higher uses are usually permitted in lower districts. When all or some higher uses are prohibited in lower zones, the zone is referred to as **non-cumulative or exclusive.**

Noncumulative Zoning

Zoning that permits only one use with no exception.

Inclusionary Zoning

Specifies inclusions within a development, such as a playground or that a percentage of homes must be affordable for low-income families.

Exclusionary zoning

Exclusionary zoning is any zoning ordinance which has a purpose, effect or result of achieving a form of economic or racial segregation. An exclusionary zoning ordinance can cause economic segregation by restricting land usage to high-cost, low population density residential development. These restrictions can effectively prevent low to moderate income families and individuals from moving into an area. In turn, minority groups with low income levels may also be excluded from living in certain areas.

Floating Zones: Floating zones are found where a noncompliant use is permitted within a specific zoning area.

Holding Zones: To restrict development in certain areas before there has been an opportunity to zone or plan it, the planning department within a municipality may temporarily zone the land for low intensity uses.

Regulation of Environmental Hazards
Regulation of special land types

Flood zones
The National Flood Insurance Program (NFIP)
- The program enables property owners in participating communities to purchase insurance protection, administered by the government, against losses from flooding, and requires flood insurance for all loans or lines of credit that are secured by existing buildings, manufactured homes, or buildings under construction, that are located in a community that participates in the NFIP.
- This insurance is designed to provide an insurance alternative to disaster assistance to meet the escalating costs of repairing damage to buildings and their contents caused by floods.

EPA
EPA regulates the production and distribution of commercial and industrial chemicals in order to ensure that chemicals made available for sale and use in the United States do not harm human health or the environment.

Hazardous waste that is improperly managed poses a serious threat to human health and the environment.

The Resource Conservation and Recovery Act (RCRA), passed in **1976**, was established to set up a framework for the proper management of hazardous waste.

The Toxic Substances Control Act of 1976
- Provides EPA with authority to require reporting, record-keeping and testing requirements, and restrictions relating to chemical substances and/or mixtures.
- Certain substances are generally excluded from TSCA, including, among others, food, drugs, cosmetics and pesticides.
- TSCA addresses the production, importation, use, and disposal of specific chemicals including polychlorinated biphenyls (PCBs), asbestos, radon and lead-based paint.

CERCLA – The Comprehensive Environmental Response, Compensation, and Liability Act (1980)
*This law, also known as **Superfund**,* was enacted to address abandoned hazardous waste sites in the U.S. The law has subsequently been amended, by the **Superfund Amendments and Reauthorization Act of 1986 (SARA)**, and the **Small Business Liability Relief and Brownfields Revitalization Act of 2002**.

- administered and enforced by the EPA.
- established a Superfund to clean up uncontrolled hazardous waste sites
- identifies potential *responsible parties* (PRPs)
- established liability as follows:
    - Strict liability where the landowner has no defense to the responsibility for cleanup
    - Joint and several liabilities in which each of several landowners is responsible for the entire cleanup
    - Retroactive liability where the present owner and previous owners are responsible
- established prohibitions and requirements concerning closed and abandoned hazardous waste sites;
- provided for liability of persons responsible for releases of hazardous waste at these sites; and
- established a trust fund to provide for cleanup when no responsible party could be identified.
- The law authorizes two kinds of response actions:

Short-term removals, where actions may be taken to address releases or threatened releases requiring prompt response.

Long-term remedial response actions, that permanently and significantly reduce the dangers associated with releases or threats of releases of hazardous substances that are serious, but not immediately life threatening.
These actions can be conducted only at sites listed on EPA's National Priorities List (NPL).

SARA – Superfund Amendments and Reauthorization Act of 1986
- stressed the importance of permanent remedies and innovative treatment technologies in cleaning up hazardous waste sites
- required Superfund actions to consider the standards and requirements found in other State and Federal environmental laws and regulations
- provided new enforcement authorities and settlement tools
- increased State involvement in every phase of the Superfund program
- increased the focus on human health problems posed by hazardous waste site;
- encouraged greater citizen participation in making decisions on how sites should be cleaned up
- increased the size of the trust fund to $8.5 billion *(innocent landowner immunity)*

Brownfields Revitalization and Environmental Restoration Act – 2001 and 2002
- *Helps rejuvenate deserted, defunct and derelict toxic industrial waste sites.*
- A former industrial or commercial site where future use is affected by real or perceived environmental contamination.
- Restrictions on Sale or Development of Contaminated Property

Definition of a Brownfield Site
- Real property, the expansion, redevelopment, or reuse of which may be complicated by the presence or potential presence of a hazardous substance, pollutant, or contaminant.
- Cleaning up and reinvesting in these properties protects the environment, reduces blight, and takes development pressures off greenspaces and working lands.
- It is estimated that there are more than 450,000 brownfields in the U.S.
- Cleaning up and reinvesting in these properties increases local tax bases, facilitates job growth, utilizes existing infrastructure, takes development pressures off of undeveloped, open land, and both improves and protects the environment.

How does EPA's Brownfields and Land Revitalization Program Stimulate Cleanup and Redevelopment?
Since its inception in 1995, EPA's Brownfields Program has grown into a proven, results-oriented program that has changed the way contaminated property is perceived, addressed, and managed. EPA's Brownfields Program is designed to empower states, communities, and other stakeholders in economic redevelopment to work together in a timely manner to prevent, assess, safely clean up, and sustainably *reuse brownfields*.

Land Revitalization
Land revitalization puts previously contaminated properties back into productive use. Reusing cleaned up sites protects public health and the environment by preventing sprawl, preserving green space and reinvigorating communities. EPA's Land Revitalization Program ensures that reuse considerations are integrated into all of EPA's cleanup decisions including cleanups affecting brownfields, underground storage tanks, and Superfund redevelopment.

Land Revitalization Programs at EPA:
Brownfields Program is designed to empower communities to work together to clean up and sustainably reuse Brownfields areas.
Superfund Redevelopment ensures that every Superfund site has the tools necessary to return the country's most hazardous sites into productive use.
Underground Storage Tanks supports the cleanup and reuse of abandoned properties that were contaminated with petroleum from underground storage tanks.
Cleanups at Federal Facilities works with other federal entities to facilitate faster, more effective, and less costly cleanup and reuse of federal facilities.
Resource Conservation and Recovery Act (RCRA) Brownfields helps facilities in need of corrective action to locate opportunities for reuse.
Mothballed brownfields are properties that the owners are not willing to transfer or put to productive reuse.

Environmental liability issues for real estate professionals
Discovery of environmental hazards includes; questioning the owner, and recommending an environmental audit (environmental site assessment).

Disclosure of environmental hazards
State laws cover disclosure of known material facts regarding property condition.

Environmental Impact Statement (EIS)
- Under United States environmental law, is a document required by the National Environmental Policy Act (NEPA) for certain actions "significantly affecting the quality of the human environment".
- An EIS is a tool for decision making. It describes the positive and negative environmental effects of a *proposed action*, and it usually also lists one or more alternative actions that may be chosen instead of the action described in the EIS.

Types of Hazards

Lead
- Lead can be found in pipes, pipe solder, paints, air, and
- Lead-based paint is found in many of the housing units built before 1978.
- Lead accumulates in the body and can damage the brain, nervous system, kidneys, and blood.
- The Lead-Based Paint Hazard Reduction Act of 1992 requires disclosure of known lead-based paint hazards to potential buyers or renters.
- Real estate licensees provide buyers and lessees with "Protect Your Family from Lead in Your Home," a pamphlet created by EPA, HUD, and the U.S. Consumer Product Safety
- Lead poisoning can cause permanent damage to the brain and many other organs and causes reduced intelligence and behavioral problems. Lead can also cause abnormal fetal development in pregnant women.
- HUD and EPA require the disclosure of known information on lead-based paint and lead-based paint hazards before the sale or lease of most housing built before 1978.
- Before ratification of a contract for housing sale or lease:
- Sellers and landlords must disclose known lead-based paint and lead-based paint hazards and provide available reports to buyers or renters.
- Sellers and landlords must give buyers and renters the pamphlet, developed by EPA, HUD, and the Consumer Product Safety Commission (CPSC), titled Protect Your Family from Lead in Your Home.
- Home buyers will get a 10-day period to conduct a lead-based paint inspection or risk assessment at their own expense. The rule gives the two parties flexibility to negotiate key terms of the evaluation.
- Sales contracts and leasing agreements must include certain notification and disclosure language.
- This rule does not require any testing or removal of lead-based paint by sellers or landlords.
- This rule does not invalidate leasing and sales contracts.
- Buyers sign a disclosure acknowledging the possibility of lead based paint.
- Sellers do not have to remove it.
- Lead can cause mental retardation

Radon
- Is easily mitigated
- Costs: @ 1200-2000
- an odorless, tasteless, radioactive gas produced by the natural decay of radioactive substances in the ground and is found throughout the United States.
- Radon gas may cause lung cancer.
- The number two reason people get lung cancer and the number one reason people who don't smoke get lung cancer.
- Testing for radon in buildings is not a federal requirement.

Asbestos
- Banned in 1978

- A material used for many years for insulation of heat pipes and ducts. Also, used in roofing and floor products. When asbestos ages it can become airborne.
- a mineral composed of fibers that have fireproofing and insulating qualities.
- Asbestos is a health hazard when fibers break down and are inhaled.
- Asbestos has been banned for use in insulation since
- Encapsulation can prevent asbestos fibers from becoming airborne.
- Asbestos is a mineral fiber that occurs in rock and soil.
- Airborne asbestos is called friable.
- The best way to handle asbestos is to encapsulate it.
- Prolonged inhalation of asbestos fibers can cause serious and fatal illnesses including lung cancer, mesothelioma, and asbestosis (a type of
- pneumoconiosis).
- Because of its fiber strength and heat resistance asbestos has been used in a variety of building construction materials for insulation and as a fire retardant.
- Asbestos has also been used in a wide range of manufactured goods, mostly in building materials (roofing shingles, ceiling and floor tiles, paper products, and asbestos cement products), friction products (automobile clutch, brake, and transmission parts), heat-resistant fabrics, packaging, gaskets, and coatings.

Where asbestos may be found:
- Attic and wall insulation produced containing vermiculite
- Vinyl floor tiles and the backing on vinyl sheet flooring and adhesives
- Roofing and siding shingles
- Textured paint and patching compounds used on wall and ceilings
- Walls and floors around wood-burning stoves protected with asbestos paper, millboard, or cement sheets
- Hot water and steam pipes coated with asbestos material or covered with an asbestos blanket or tape
- Oil and coal furnaces and door gaskets with asbestos insulation
- Heat-resistant fabrics
- Automobile clutches and brakes

Three of the major health effects associated with asbestos exposure are:
1. lung cancer
2. mesothelioma, a rare form of cancer that is found in the thin lining of the lung, chest and the
3. abdomen and heart asbestosis, a serious progressive, long-term, non-cancer disease of the lungs.

Formaldehyde
- a hazardous air pollutant in the Clean Air Act Amendments of 1990
- used for building and household products, such as urea-formaldehyde foam insulation (UFFI
- may cause respiratory problems, eye and skin irritations, and possibly cancer.
- It is made by using a pump set and hose with a mixing gun to mix the foaming agent, resin and compressed air.

The fully expanded foam is pumped into areas in need of insulation.

It becomes firm within minutes but cures within a week.

UFFI is generally found in homes built before the 1970s, often in basements, crawl spaces, attics, and unfinished attics

Real estate licensees should check state formaldehyde disclosure requirements, and appraisers should note the presence of formaldehyde

Carbon monoxide (CO)
- a colorless, odorless gas that is by-product of fuel burning
- is produced by furnaces, water heaters, space heaters (including kerosene heaters), fireplaces, and wood stoves
- may cause carbon monoxide poisoning, which can result in death unless the gas is properly vented
- is detectable with available carbon monoxide detectors, which may be required by state law

Polychlorinated biphenyls (PCBs)
- may be found in electrical equipment
- PCBs are suspected of causing health problems.
- The manufacture of PCBs has been banned in 1979
- The commercial distribution of PCBs has been banned
- Some PCB products are still functioning.
- In general individuals are exposed to PCBs overwhelmingly through food, much less so by breathing contaminated air, and least by skin contact.
- Once exposed, some PCBs may change to other chemicals inside the body.
- These chemicals or unchanged PCBs can be excreted in feces or may remain in a person's body for years, with half-lives estimated at 10–15 years.
- PCBs collect in body fat and milk fat.
- PCBs are present in fish and waterfowl of contaminated aquifers.

Chlorofluorocarbons (CFCs)
- used in refrigerators, aerosol sprays, paints, solvents, and foam applications
- Use stopped in 1978
- have been replaced by available environmentally friendly substitutes for home appliances

Mold
- May cause allergic reactions. Mold can be found around wet areas
- Black Mold – Stachybotrys Chartarum
- Molds are part of the natural environment, and can be found everywhere, indoors and outdoors.
- Mold is not usually a problem, unless it begins growing indoors.
- Allergic reactions to mold are common.
- They can be immediate or delayed.
- Molds can cause asthma attacks in people with asthma who are allergic to mold. In addition, mold exposure can irritate the eyes, skin, nose, throat, and lungs of both mold-allergic and non-allergic people.

Real estate licensees should recommend a mold inspection if mold is evident or suspected because of water problems.

EMFs – Electronic Magnetic Fields
- Electrical circulating currents
- Suspected of causing cancer.
- Electromagnetic fields (EMF) are a combination of electric and magnetic fields of energy that surround any electrical device that is plugged in and turned on.
- Scientific experiments have not clearly shown whether or not exposure to EMF increases cancer risk.
- Scientists continue to conduct research on the issue.
- The strength of electromagnetic fields fades with distance from the source.
- Limiting the amount of time spent around a source and increasing the distance from a source reduces exposure
- EMFs are found near power lines and other electronic devices such as smart meters.
- Electric and magnetic fields become weaker as you move further away from them.
- The fields from power lines and electrical devices have a much lower frequency than other types of EMF, such as microwaves or radio waves.
- EMF from power lines is considered to be extremely low frequency.

Groundwater Contamination
- Found under the earth's surface and forms the water table.
- The Safe Drinking Water Act (SDWA) of 1974 regulates the public drinking water supply.
- On property transfers, any water source other than a municipal supply should be tested, as should any septic system.

Underground storage tanks (USTs)

- May contain petroleum products, industrial chemicals, and other substances
- are a concern because the leakage may imperil both public and private water sources
- USTs are subject to federal law and state law, which is sometimes stronger than federal law.
- The EPA regulates the federal UST program.
- When a property purchase is being considered, a careful inspection of any property on which USTs are suspected should be conducted.
- UST owners include marketers who sell gasoline to the public (such as service stations and convenience stores) and non-marketers who use tanks solely for their own needs (such as fleet service operators and local governments).
- The greatest potential hazard from a leaking UST is that the petroleum or other hazardous substance can seep into the soil and contaminate groundwater, the source of drinking water for nearly half of all Americans.
- A leaking UST can present other health and environmental risks, including the potential for fire and explosion.

Leaking Underground Storage Tanks (LUSTs)

- Leaking underground storage tanks can pollute ground water.
- Leaking tanks must be removed along with all the polluted material.
- **Waste disposal sites**
- May be owned by municipalities, be part of commercial enterprises, or be found on farms and other rural properties.
- Disposal sites built on the wrong type of soil can leak into ground water.
- They are lined to prevent seepage
- They are capped with soil for aesthetic reasons
- Vented to release gases created by decomposing

Abatement, Mitigation, and Clean-up Requirements

- If a property is contaminated, CERCLA (Superfund) imposes mitigation, abatement and cleanup requirements on those responsible for the contamination or on owners of that property.
- The federal EPA has the authority to clean up hazardous waste sites and charge the owners of the property for the clean-up.

Environmental Impact Statement

A statement required by The National Environmental Policy Act of 1969 prior to development of a site that may have an affect or impact on the environment.

Private Controls

Home Owners Association
- An organizational framework set up for self-governance by owners through adoption and enforcement of bylaws
- Homeowner's Dues are associated with ownership for the upkeep of the buildings and common areas
- Maintenance of common elements are funded by fees charged to each unit owner.

Deed Restriction
Provisions placed in a deed to control future use of the property.
Violation of a deed restriction could be jail, a fine or both.

Restrictive Covenants
Rules or private agreements, usually stated in a deed or lease, that restrict things like lot size and architectural controls.

Bylaws
Rules and structure for administering homeowners' association.

Covenants, Conditions & Restrictions (CC&R's)
Private, voluntary rules (intended to be beneficial) used in homeowner associations and PUD's; also deed restrictions that control property use, architectural changes, landscaping, and whether or not animals are permitted, etc.

Common Elements
The areas in a condominium project or PUD where all owners share an undivided interest and full possession, such as the common area hallways, swimming pool and clubhouse.

Limited Common Elements
Those areas in a common interest community reserved for exclusive use by a particular owner, such as decks, storage areas or parking spaces.

Homogeneity
Similarity; Neighborhoods that have homogeneity of houses and people are generally stable in value

Conformity Principle – Basis for Home Owners Associations
A property that conforms to its surrounding properties in style, age, size, appearance tends to maximize value.

Master Deed
Describes the physical location of the common and individual elements (units) of a condominium.

Homestead
A tract of land owned and occupied as the family home. In many states a portion of the area or value of this land is protected or exempt from judgments for debt

Homestead rights
Protects the equity in a residence from a judgment by unsecured creditors.

Subdivider
One who partitions a large parcel of land for resale as individual lots.

Attractive Nuisance
An item or property which might attract the curious (children) to their detriment, e.g. a swimming pool, construction site, abandoned appliances, etc. Owners generally have direct liability for attractive nuisances that are not secured.

Amenities
Features that increase the value of property.

QUIZ by Broker Tina Perkins, CDEI, Senior Instruction

28. The city acquires a tract of land for a highway. What power will they exercise?
    a.   EPA
    b.   Zoning
    c.   Police Powers
    d.   Eminent Domain

29. An example of police power is?
    a.   Laches
    b.   Flood Zone Regulation
    c.   Lis pendens
    d.   Environmental protection laws

30. A mortgage company is operating out of a building that has recently been rezoned residential. The building was grandfathered in. The mortgage county is operating under which of the following?
    a.   A variance
    b.   A non-conforming use
    c.   Down zoning
    d.   PUD

31. Which hazard enters the house through the basement?
    a.   Carbon monoxide
    b.   Radon
    c.   UFFI
    d.   Asbestos

32. What mineral was used for insulation on heating ducts?
    a.   Asbestos
    b.   Friable
    c.   Radon
    d.   Portland cement

33. Banned from use in the 1970's, this material was pumped between the walls for insulation:
    a.   Lead
    b.   Encapsulation
    c.   Urea formaldehyde foam
    d.   Xenon

34. Ground water contamination could come from the following except?
    a.   Underground gas storage tanks
    b.   Waste disposal sites
    c.   Insecticides used on crops
    d.   Cement

35. Regarding building codes, all of the following could be requirements except?
    a.   Electrical wiring standards
    b.   Fire prevention standards
    c.   Sanitary equipment
    d.   Square footage of space per apartment unit

36. Strict liability under the superfund means?
    a.   The polluting party is responsible to an injured party without excuse.
    b.   Each owner is personally responsible for only their portion of ownership.
    c.   Liability cannot extend to past owners. (retroactive)
    d.   Absolute Laches

37. What term refers to what happens to asbestos when it ages, disintegrates and become airborne?
    a. Oxidation
    b. Friable
    c. Encapsulation
    d. Black mold

38. What best describes a buffer zone?
    a. A commercial building between a shopping center and a neighborhood
    b. A condo building between an industrial park and a row of townhomes
    c. A green space between a subdivision and an office park
    d. Downzoning a commercial space to a brown field

39. Which of the following is not a police power?
    a. City planning specifications
    b. EPA
    c. Building code enforcement
    d. Deed restrictions

40. A café which was "grandfathered in" when the neighborhood was downsized, recently burned to the ground. What would the owners need to obtain in order to rebuild?
    a. A conditional use permit
    b. A zoning variance
    c. Condemnation
    d. Escheat

41. Eminent Domain is the government's right to take property for the betterment of the public. The property owner receives just compensation. Which of the following provides for the monetary compensation to the owner of the property?
    a. Taxation
    b. Condemnation
    c. Police Power
    d. Enabling acts

42. Airborne asbestos fibers are known as?
    a. Peeling
    b. Friable
    c. Radon
    d. Encapsulation

43. A certified inspector should check around potentially wet areas such as showers, toilets and basements for which hazard?
    a. Radon
    b. Condemnation
    c. UFFI
    d. Mold

44. Black mold is an environmental concern and in known as/to:
    a. Common mold emits carbon monoxide
    b. No disclosure needed
    c. Stachybotrys chartarum in sufficient concentrations can cause severe health issues
    d. EPA has not yet set guidelines for remediation in public buildings

---

ANSWERS

1. The city acquires a tract of land for a highway. What power will they exercise?
   Eminent Domain

2.   An example of police power is?
     Environmental protection laws

3.   A mortgage company is operating out of a building that has recently been rezoned residential. The building was grandfathered in. The mortgage county is operating under which of the following?
     A non-conforming use

4.   Which hazard enters the house through the basement?
     Radon

5.   What mineral was used for insulation on heating ducts?
     Asbestos

6.   Banned from use in the 1970's, this material was pumped between the walls for insulation:
     Urea formaldehyde foam

7.   Ground water contamination could come from the following except?
     Cement

8.   Regarding building codes, all of the following could be requirements except?
     Square footage of space per apartment unit

9.   Strict liability under the superfund means?
     The polluting party is responsible to an injured party without excuse.

10. What term refers to what happens to asbestos when it ages, disintegrates and become airborne?
     Friable

11. What best describes a buffer zone?
     A green space between a subdivision and an office park

12. Which of the following is not a police power?
     Deed restrictions

13. A café which was "grandfathered in" when the neighborhood was downsized, recently burned to the ground. What would the owners need to obtain in order to rebuild?
     A conditional use permit

14. Eminent Domain is the government's right to take property for the betterment of the public. The property owner receives just compensation. Which of the following provides for the monetary compensation to the owner of the property?
     Condemnation

15. Airborne asbestos fibers are known as?
     Friable

16. A certified inspector should check around potentially wet areas such as showers, toilets and basements for which hazard?
     Mold

17. Black mold is an environmental concern and in known as/to:
     Stachybotrys chartarum in sufficient concentrations can cause severe health issues

Chapter 3

Valuation and Market Analysis (Salesperson 7%; Broker 7%)

Valuation and market analysis (Salesperson 7%; Broker 7%)

1. Appraisals
    1. Purpose and use of appraisals for valuation
    2. General steps in appraisal process
    3. Situations requiring appraisal by certified appraiser
2. Estimating Value
    1. Effect of economic principles and property characteristics
    2. Sales or market comparison approach
    3. Cost approach
    4. Income analysis approach
3. Competitive/Comparative Market Analysis
    1. Selecting comparables
    2. Adjusting comparables

Understanding the Appraisal

Professional real estate appraisers perform a useful function in society and offer a variety of services to their clients. They develop opinions of several types of property value and assist in various decisions about real estate.

Value in Appraisal
An appraisal is an opinion of a professional appraiser.

Market Value / Open Market Value	Market Price
The most probable selling price in an open market with an arm's length transaction. The future worth	the actual selling price.

Standards for the appraisal profession are set forth in the **Uniform Standards of Professional Appraisal Practice (USPAP)** developed by the **Appraisal Standards Board of The Appraisal Foundation. ***

USPAP specifies the procedures to be followed in developing and communicating an appraisal and the ethical rules for appraisal practice.

As defined in USPAP, **an appraisal is the act or process of developing an opinion of value.** The valuation process is a systematic procedure the appraiser follows to answer a client's question about real property value.

The most common type of appraisal assignment is the development of an opinion of **market value**.

The Intended Use of an Appraisal
1. To facilitate the transfer of ownership of real property
2. To help prospective sellers determine acceptable selling prices or prospective buyers decide on offering prices
3. To establish a basis for the exchange or reorganization of real property or for merging the ownership of multiple properties

Many appraisal assignments relate to financing and credit.
1. To assist the underwriter in establishing a value of security for a mortgage loan
2. To provide an investor with a sound basis for the purchase of real estate mortgages, bonds or other types of securities

Other appraisals are requested to help resolve legal or tax issues.
1. To estimate the market value of a property in eminent domain proceedings
2. To estimate the market value of a property in contract disputes or as part of a portfolio
3. To estimate the market value of partnership interests
4. To estimate damages created by environmental contamination
5. To estimate assessed value
6. To determine gift or inheritance taxes
7. To estimate the value of the real property component of an estate

Appraisals are also used in investment counseling and decision-making.
1. To set rent schedules and lease provisions
2. To determine the feasibility of a construction or renovation program
3. To aid in corporate mergers, issuance of stock or revision of book value
4. To estimate liquidation value for forced-sale or auction proceedings
5. To counsel a client on investment matters, including goals, alternatives, resources, constraints and timing
6. To advise zoning boards, courts and planners, among others, regarding the probable effects of proposed actions

7.   To arbitrate between adversaries

Appraisals for the Lending Industry
1.   Many appraisals are performed for lending purposes.
2.   Property owners should be aware that current federal lending regulations* require the lender to "initiate" the appraisal.
3.   The lender must have the first contact with the appraiser and oversee the appraisal process.
4.   According to these regulations, the lender must be the client and the appraiser must be engaged by the lending institution.
5.   Any property owner who wants to use the appraisal for lending purposes should communicate this need to the lender and have the lender engage the appraiser.
6.   This avoids the possibility of the lender rejecting the appraisal or requiring a new appraisal because the appraisal was not initiated by the bank.
7.   According to federal lending laws, any bank can use an appraisal prepared for another bank, as long as the initiating bank reviews the appraisal and finds it to be acceptable.

The Valuation Process

Although characteristics of properties differ widely, all appraisal problems can be solved through the systematic application of the valuation process.

In the valuation process the problem is identified, the work necessary to solve the problem is planned and relevant data is collected, verified and analyzed to form an **opinion of value.**

The valuation process is accomplished by following specific steps, the number of which depends on the nature of the appraisal assignment and the data available to complete it.
1.   Identification of the Problem
2.   Scope of Work Determination
3.   Data Collection and Property Description
4.   Data Analysis
5.   Site Value Opinion
6.   Application of the Approaches to Value
7.   Reconciliation of Value Indications and
8.   Final Opinion of Value
9.   Report of Defined Value

1. Identification of the Problem
The first step in the valuation process is to identify the problem.
This sets the parameters of the assignment and eliminates any ambiguity about the nature of the assignment.

In this step, the appraiser identifies the client and intended users of the appraisal, the intended use of the appraisal, the purpose of the assignment, the effective date of the opinion, the relevant property characteristics and the assignment conditions (extraordinary assumptions or hypothetical conditions).

2. Scope of Work Determination
The scope of work is the amount and type of information researched and the analyses applied in an assignment.

After the problem to be solved is clearly identified, the appraiser must next determine the appropriate scope of work to solve the problem.
The scope of work must be clearly disclosed in the appraisal report.

3. Data Collection and Property Description
In this step the appraiser gathers general data on the market area and specific data on the subject and comparable properties.

The appraiser collects general data related to property values in an area to understand the economic climate in which properties compete and the interacting forces that cause values to increase, decrease or remain stable.

Specific data are details about the property being appraised (the subject property) and comparable properties that have been sold or leased in the local market.

Land and building descriptions are specific data that help an appraiser to select comparable sales and rentals.

4. Data Analysis
In the analysis of general data, national, regional and local trends are emphasized. **Supply and demand** data are studied to understand the competitive position of the property in its market. In an analysis of specific data, a set of properties most like the subject property is studied.

The analysis of comparable properties helps an appraiser extract specific sale prices, rental terms, incomes and expenses, rates of return on investments, construction costs, economic life estimates and rates of depreciation. These figures are used in the calculations that result in indications of value for the subject property.

Highest and best use is a critical step in the development of a market value opinion. In highest and best use analysis, the appraiser considers the use of the land as though it were vacant and the use of the property as it is improved. To qualify as the highest and best use, a use must satisfy four criteria: it must be legally permissible, physically possible, financially feasible and maximally productive. The highest and best use is selected from various alternative uses.

Market analysis provides the basis for an appraiser's conclusions about the highest and best use of a subject property, and the remainder of the valuation process follows from these conclusions.

5. Site Value Opinion
A land value opinion is formed through the application of a variety of methods that are derived in varying degrees from the three approaches to value.

The most reliable procedure for arriving at a land value estimate is sales comparison.

Sales of similar vacant parcels are analyzed, compared and related to the land being appraised. If sufficient sales are not available for comparison or the value opinion indicated by sales comparison needs substantiation, the appraiser may use another procedure such as extraction, allocation, the land residual technique, ground rent capitalization, or subdivision development analysis.

6. Application of the Approaches to Value
The appraiser begins to derive an opinion of property value using one or more of the three approaches to value.

The approaches employed depend on the type of property, the use of the appraisal and the quality and quantity of the data available for analysis.

7. Reconciliation of Value Indications and Final Opinion of Value
In reconciliation, the appraiser analyzes alternative conclusions and selects a final *opinion of value* from among two or more indications of value. A thorough review of the entire valuation process may precede reconciliation.

In reconciliation, an appraiser draws upon his or her experience, expertise and professional judgment to resolve differences among the value indications derived from the application of the approaches.

The appraiser weighs the relative significance, applicability and defensibility of each approach and relies most heavily on those most appropriate to the intended use of the appraisal. The conclusion drawn is based on the appropriateness, accuracy and quantity of all the evidence in the appraisal.

8. Final Opinion of Value

When a final opinion of value has been derived, the immediate objective of the valuation process has been accomplished. However, an appraisal assignment is not completed until the conclusions and findings have been stated in a report and communicated to the client.

9. Report of Defined Value

The type, format, length and contents of a written appraisal report may vary depending on the requirements of the client and the scope of work criteria.
☐

The **Uniform Standards of Professional Appraisal Practice** set forth the requirements for appraisal reports, which may be presented in one of three written formats:
1. self-contained reports,
2. summary reports, and
3. restricted-use reports.

A **self-contained appraisal report** provides comprehensive coverage of appropriate information contained within the report itself with minimal reference to files outside the report. In general, a self-contained report fully describes the data and analyses used in the assignment.

A **summary appraisal report** summarizes the data and analyses used in the assignment.

A **restricted-use appraisal report** simply states the conclusions of the appraisal; this type of report may be provided only when the client is the sole user of the report.

The appraisal file for a summary or restricted-use appraisal report contains backup data and/or analyses that would be presented in a self-contained appraisal report.
☐

All appraisal reports will specify the following items:
- The identity of the client and any other intended users
- The intended use of the report
- The purpose of the assignment (type of value)
- The effective date of the opinion
- The real estate being appraised
- The real property interest being valued
- Any assignment conditions (extraordinary assumptions and hypothetical conditions) affecting the appraisal
- The scope of work—i.e., the extent of the process of collecting, confirming and reporting data
- Any usual valuation approaches that may have been excluded
- The highest and best use of the real estate when such an opinion is necessary and appropriate
- The information considered, appraisal procedures followed and reasoning applied
- A signed certification in accordance with USPAP Standards Rule 2-3

License Levels

- Appraiser Trainee:

Someone who is qualified to appraise those properties, which the supervising certified appraiser is qualified to appraise.

- Licensed Real Property Appraiser:

Someone who is qualified to appraise non-complex one to four units having a transaction value less than $1,000,000 and complex one to four residential units having a transaction value less than $250,000. This classification does not include the appraisal of subdivisions.

- Certified Residential Real Property Appraiser:

Someone who is qualified to appraise one to four residential units without regard to value or complexity. This classification does not include the appraisal of subdivisions. To be a state certified residential appraiser qualified to do appraisals for federally related transactions, a state must have requirements that meet or exceed this minimum standard.

- Certified General Real Property Appraiser:

Someone who is qualified to appraise all types of real property. To be a state certified general appraiser qualified to do appraisals for federally related transactions, a state must have requirements that meet or exceed this minimum standard.

Reports for the Different Types of Properties

Uniform Residential Appraisal Report
This report form is designed to report an appraisal of a one-unit property or a one-unit property with an accessory unit; including a unit in a **planned unit development (PUD).**

Individual Condominium Unit Appraisal Report
This report form is designed to report an appraisal of a unit in a condominium project or a condominium unit in a planned unit development (PUD). This report form is not designed to report an appraisal of a manufactured home or a unit in a cooperative project.

Individual Cooperative Interest Appraisal Report
This report form is designed to report an appraisal of the cooperative interest (the cooperative shares or other evidence of an ownership interest in the cooperative corporation and the accompanying occupancy rights) in a cooperative project or the cooperative interest in a planned unit development (PUD). This form is not designed to report an appraisal of a manufactured home or a unit in a condominium project.

Land Appraisal Report
Land

Estimating Value
Effect of economic principles and property characteristics

Value Influences
The analysis of *social, economic, governmental and environmental forces* provides an understanding of the dynamics of change and helps identify value trends.

The value of a property is affected by certain economic principles.

The Economic Principles Affecting Valuation

Anticipation A woman decided not to sell her property because she found out about a large shopping center that will be built nearby. She believes that the value of her property will increase due to the new development. She plans to sell when the construction is complete and the stores are open. She is basing her decision on **anticipation**.	Buyers buy properties for future benefits. The principle says that value rises using anticipated benefits (money or amenities) to be gained from a property in the future. For example…You purchase a home with a pool for $190,000. A similar home without pool sells for $140,000. Effectively you pay $30,000 for anticipated benefits of the pool, not its cost.
Supply and Demand **Factors Affecting Supply:** Labor force Construction costs Government controls at all levels Government fiscal and monetary policies **Factors Affecting Demand:** Population Demographics—the make-up of the population including mobility, financial stability, and size and nature of family unit Employment and wage levels—where and how money is spent; perceived job security	The scarcity of a commodity influences its value by creating a greater demand for the item. For example, as the supply of ocean facing property diminishes its value increases to meet the demand. Demand is also affected by desire. If there is an oversupply of apartments in a given area, the demand will reduce. The values and rents will go down.
Substitution	The value of a property tends to be set at the cost of an equally desirable substitute property. In theory, no one should pay more for a property than what it would cost to obtain a site by purchase and sale and to construct a building of equal appeal and utility.
Balance	This principle refers to the relationship between cost, added cost and the value it returns. For each dollar invested, the value should increase by more than one dollar.
Progression The smallest house in the neighborhood benefits from PROGRESSION.	*The idea behind this principle is, the price of a property escalates with an increased perceived value of a location. For example, if you are selling an old house, but the surrounding homes in the area are renovated and thereby have increased in value, the price of your property will also be pulled up because of its location*
Regression The largest house in a neighborhood suffers from REGRESSION.	This is the opposite of progression principle. The price of a property decreases with a reduced perceived

	value of a site. For example, even if you have the best house in a neighborhood of storm- hit homes, the value of your property will go down.	The value of a property is affected by certain economic principles.

Against this background, the appraiser investigates the characteristics of the **subject property** that might impact the property's value.

The appraiser also investigates the nature of the market for that property, competitive properties, and the buyers and sellers who constitute the market for that property type.

The principles of **supply and demand, substitution, balance and externalities** help explain shifts in value.

Four independent economic factors—
1. utility,
2. scarcity,
3. desire, and
4. effective purchasing power—

must be present to create value in a particular item or collection of items.

Professional appraisal standards specifically require the study of all value influences.
Change and anticipation are fundamental, and appraisers apply these principles and related concepts that influence value in their analyses.

Principles of Value
Economic rules that impact the value of real property, including principles of anticipation, change, competition, conformity, contribution, highest and best use, increasing and diminishing returns, **plottage**, progression and regression, supply and demand, substitution.

Conformity Principle
A property that conforms to its surrounding properties in style, age, size, appearance tends to maximize value.

Homogeneity
Similarity; Neighborhoods that have homogeneity of houses and people are generally stable in value.

Heterogeneity
No two are alike. Opposite of homogeneity

Contribution
A value principle holding that an amenity or improvement is worth the value it adds, not what it costs.

Competition Principle
A principle of value stating that Competition drives down profit, whereas excess.
Profit generates competition.

Highest and Best Use Principle
That use determined by an appraiser of a commercial property that would bring the highest net return on investment to the owner. May not be the same as the present use, depending on development in the surrounding area.

Increasing & Diminishing Returns Principle
The cost of improving a property increases its value (law of increasing returns) only to a certain point; over-improving an obsolete property, or improvements that do not add to value are examples of the law of decreasing returns

Assemblage
Consolidating two or more parcels to create a larger building site in order to create a greater return. The resultant increase in value is known as plottage.

Plottage
Increased value resulting from assemblage (the combining of adjacent lots into one larger lot)

Site Valuation
Determining the value of the vacant land alone.

Situs
Preference for one location over another without basis in objective fact or knowledge. It is said that the most important consideration in buying real estate is location, location, location.

Subjective Value
What a specific person might be willing to pay for a property because of a perceived direct benefit not shared with others. Contrasts with objective value. Example; the property is next to a friend or relative.

Utility Value
The value to a specific owner also known as subjective value.

Objective Value
The price an informed buyer might be willing to pay for a property absent a specific personal interest in the property. Contrasts with subjective value.

Arm's length
A term indicating parties to a transaction are acting independently and with full bargaining knowledge and position.

Less than Arm's Length
A sale to a family member is not "arm's length" and may therefore impact market value or have tax consequences. Not used for appraisals.

Capital Improvement
An improvement that extends the life of a property, as opposed to maintenance. Capital improvements are not included in computing the operating expenses of a property. Example: New siding or roofing, but not painting or ceiling fans.

Depreciation (appraisal)
Loss of property value due to any physical, functional or external condition.

Observed Condition Method
Method used by an appraiser to determine depreciation by subtracting observed physical deterioration, functional obsolescence and external obsolescence figures from the replacement cost. * see replacement cost below.

Book Value
The value **including accumulated depreciation** as reflected in the financial records of the owner. Normally lower than market value.

Incurable Depreciation
Loss of property value that cannot be fixed due to excessive cost or external factors.

Economic Life
The approximate length of time a building can be used profitably.

Effective Age

Age of an improvement taking into consideration all forms of depreciation. A building may be 10 years old, but due to poor maintenance have an effective age of 20 years.

Straight Line Method of Depreciation
A method of depreciation that is computed by dividing the adjusted basis of a property by the number of years of estimated remaining useful life. The cost of the property is thus deducted in equal annual installments

Age-life Table (Depreciation)
Method of determining depreciation based on the relationship of a property's condition and its economic life. Example: Effective age (based on condition) is 10 yrs. and estimated remaining economic life is 30 yrs. 10 + 30 = 40 yrs. economic life: 10 / 40 = 25% depreciation today.

Physical Deterioration
Ordinary wear and tear, age, and breakage.

Curable Depreciation
Depreciation that is not cost-prohibitive to repair.

Deferred Maintenance
Postponement of curable repairs; leads to further deterioration.

Amenities
Features that increase the value of property.

Change Principle
Changes in social and economic conditions have a constant impact on property value and must be considered in an appraisal.

Economies of Scale (The more you make the less it costs)
Incremental increases in production require relatively less increase in resources, resulting in overall increased earning potential.

Depth Tables
Charts intended to standardize lot values based on increase in lot depth, based on the front of a lot having greater value than the rear. Used by county assessors to assist in applying uniform assessments.

Depreciation
The loss of value in an improvement over time. Does not apply to land!
the cost of the structure divided by it's economic life equals the annual amount of depreciation.

Accrued Depreciation
The sum of depreciation from all causes: deterioration, obsolescence or changes in the neighborhood. (physical, deterioration, functional obsolescence and economic obsolescence.

Economic life
the period during which the structure is expected to remain useful in its original use.

Depreciation
Wasting Assets. Land does not depreciate. Only the improvements (buildings) depreciate.

Straight-line Method of Depreciation is the simplest and most often used method.
The value of the property is depreciated over a number of years.

Curable Depreciation
Correcting the defect of a home does NOT exceed the increase in property value.

Incurable Depreciation

Cost to improve exceeds property value.

Functional Obsolescence	Economic (External) Obsolescence
Loss of value from poorly designed features. WALL mount AC and baseboard heating. Curable and incurable (Building features are not easily corrected) poor design or style; inefficient floor plan; excessive ceiling height lack of modern facilities out-of-date equipment (over improvement), or inadequacy (under improvement)	Loss of value due to factors external to property. Tornado, polluted air from nearby factory. Incurable. proximity to negative environmental influences zoning restrictions adverse influences of supply and demand changes in neighborhood social or economic factors changes in locational demands

Physical Deterioration
Loss of value from wear and tear on property. Curable and Incurable
wear and tear from normal use
negligent care or lack of maintenance
damage from dry rot, pests, etc.
wear and tear from the elements (wind, rain, etc.)

Neighborhood Stages
Growth, Stability, Decline and Revitalization

Approaches to Value
Participants in the real estate market commonly think of value in three ways:

1. The current cost of **reproducing or replacing** a building, minus an estimate for depreciation, plus the value of the land (and entrepreneurial incentive, if applicable)
2. The value indicated by recent sales of **comparable properties** in the market
3. The value that the property's **net earning power** will support

These different viewpoints form the basis of the three approaches that appraisers use to value property

1. **cost approach**
2. **sales comparison `approach**
3. **income capitalization approaches**

One or more of these approaches may not be applicable to a given assignment or may be less significant because of the nature of the property, the appraisal problem or the data available.
The approaches to value are applied within the context of the valuation process.

The Appraisal Foundation (TAF)
The primary standards body; its Appraisal Standards Board (ASB) promulgates and updates best practices as codified in the Uniform Standards of Professional Appraisal Practice (USPAP), while its Appraisal Qualifications Board (AQB) promulgates minimum standards for appraiser certification and licensing.

Uniform Standards of Professional Appraisal Practice – **USPAP**
The quality control standards for real estate appraisers.

The Financial Institutions Reform, Recovery, and Enforcement Act of 1989 (FIRREA)
Demanded all the states to develop systems for licensing and certifying real estate appraisers.
FIRREA gives both Freddie Mac and Fannie Mae additional responsibility to support mortgages for low- and moderate-income families .

Cost Approach
The cost approach is based on the understanding that market participants relate value to cost. In the cost approach, the value of a property is derived by adding the estimated value of the land to the current cost of constructing a reproduction or replacement for the improvements and then subtracting the amount of depreciation in the structures from all causes.

Entrepreneurial profit and/or incentive may be included in the value indication.

The current cost to construct the improvements can be obtained from cost estimators, cost manuals, builders and contractors. Depreciation is of three different types (physical deterioration, functional obsolescence and external obsolescence) and is measured through market research and the application of specific procedures.

Land value is estimated separately in the cost approach.

This approach is particularly useful in valuing new or nearly new improvements and properties that are not frequently exchanged in the market. Cost approach techniques can also be employed to derive information needed in the sales comparison and income capitalization approaches to value, such as an adjustment for the cost to cure items of deferred maintenance.

An approach to determining value based on adding the cost of the land (as if vacant) (+) the current replacement cost of improvements (-) accrued depreciation.

Replacement Cost
Cost to replace a structure to similar utility using current materials and modern construction methods. Estimating replacement cost methods include square-foot, unit-in-place, quantity-survey or index.

Reproduction Cost
Cost to reproduce a structure exactly, using identical original materials and methods.
Sets the highest level of value.

Quantity Survey Method
The most complex, technical, time consuming and accurate method of determining replacement/reproduction cost by considering not only materials and labor, but regulatory costs, survey, taxes, profit, etc.
Applied primarily to historical structures.

Square-Foot Method
The most common and easiest method of determining replacement cost based on cost-per-square-foot of a comparable, recently constructed building multiplied by the square footage of the subject property

Unit-in-Place Method
A method of determining replacement cost based primarily on cost of materials per square foot or yard (or other unit of measurement) plus labor, profit etc.
Less technical and involved than the quantity survey method.

Development Method
The estimated value after development less the *cost of development equals the approximate **value of the land.**

Abstraction (Abstractive Method)
Estimating the value of land by deducting the *value of the improvements from the overall price of the property.

Accrued Depreciation (Cost Approach)
The difference between a property's estimated reproduction cost (cost approach to value) and current market value.
It is the sum of depreciation from all causes.

Sales Comparison Approach
The sales comparison approach is most useful when a number of similar properties have recently been sold or are currently for sale in the subject property's market.

Using this approach, an appraiser develops a value indication by comparing the subject property with similar properties, called **comparable sales**.

The sale prices of the properties that are judged to be most comparable tend to indicate a range in which the value indication for the subject property will fall.

The appraiser estimates the degree of similarity or difference between the subject property and the comparable sales by considering various elements of comparison:
- Real property rights conveyed
- Financing terms
- Conditions of sale
- Expenditures made immediately after purchase
- Market conditions
- Location
- Physical characteristics
- Economic characteristics
- Use/zoning
- Non-realty components of value

Dollar or percentage adjustments may be applied to the known sale price of each comparable property to derive a range of value indications for the subject property.

Through this comparative procedure, the appraiser ultimately arrives at an opinion of value.

Based on the principal of substitution.
Most appropriate for residential property, and sets the upper limit of value as it is concerned with most recent sales. Formerly known as market data approach.

Comparables
Similar properties in the vicinity of the subject (property being appraised) in the direct sales comparison approach to value.

An appraiser will compare the comps to the subject, and make adjustments to the comparables accordingly.

Cash Concept
The amount an individual would be willing to pay for the property in cash. (direct sales comparison approach)

CMA - Comparative Market Analysis is based on the Sales Comparison Approach
A CMA is a tool for real estate professionals. It helps the seller to determine a listing range.

Income Capitalization Approach
Income-producing real estate is typically purchased as an investment, and **earning power** is the critical element affecting property value from an investor's point of view.

- value is measured as the present value of the future benefits of property ownership.

Gross Rent Multiplier	Gross Income Multiplier
A rough calculation to determine value of an income producing property. GRM is the average sales price of similar	Is an appraisal method which relates the sales price of a property to its **yearly rental income** Sales Price / Gross Income = GIM

properties divided by the **monthly gross rent.** Monthly rents	Yearly Rents minus expenses

Rate of Return – Cap Rate Capitalization Rate
The rate of return.
An estimate of the rate of return an investor will demand on the investment of capital in a property.
The yield of an investment, expressed as a percentage that the investor expects to make over the term of ownership.

Yield
Annualized amount of return to an investor; expressed as a percentage of the original investment.

Operating Expenses
Fixed expenses, variable expenses, and replacement reserves of operating and maintaining a property.

Expenses do NOT include debt service (value is the same whether mortgaged or purchased with cash), capital improvements or depreciation. *Loans are considered incidental.*

Net Operating Income (NOI)
Projected income from a property, NOT including depreciation or cost of financing.

Effective Gross Income
Estimated income from a property after vacancy and collection loss is subtracted from gross income.

Residual Method
An appraisal process used in the income approach to estimate the value of the building by itself by deducting the value of the land.

Automatic Valuation Method

Zillow and Truli\

An AVM is a residential valuation report that can be obtained in a matter of seconds. It is a technology-driven report.
The product of an automated valuation technology comes from analysis of public record data and computer decision logic combined to provide a calculated estimate of a probable selling price of a residential property.
An AVM generally uses a combination of two types of evaluation, a hedonic model and a repeat sales index.
The results of each are weighted, analyzed and then reported as a final estimate of value based on a requested date.

Broker Price Option (BPO)
Often used by lenders in conjunction with loan portfolio valuation, loss mitigation, short sales, or collections.

Comparative Market Analysis (CMA)
Used by a broker or salesperson in attempting to find a listing price range.
It's a scaled-down version of the appraisers sales comparison approach. It is NOT an appraisal.
A CMA is an estimate of a home's value done by a real estate broker to establish a listing or offer price.
This service is usually offered free of charge and without obligation.
A CMA should only be used as a reference for deciding at what price you should list or buy a home.
A tool for real estate professionals.
It is NOT an appraisal.
It does NOT indicate value

Quiz by Broker Tina Perkins, CDEI, Senior Instructor

45. All of the following characteristics add to value in a property except?
    a. Supply and Demand
    b. Situs
    c. Depreciation
    d. Disposition

46. All of the following are principles of market value except?
    a. Both buyer and seller must be well informed.
    b. Market value is the average price that a property will bring.
    c. Both parties must be free from duress.
    d. Consideration must be made in cash or the equivalent.

47. There are several houses in the area that you desire to purchase. All of the homes are extremely similar. You choose the one with the lowest asking price. You are most likely basing your decision on?
    a. Depreciation
    b. Substitution
    c. Highest and best use
    d. Obsolescence

48. A developer built a luxury neighborhood where he sold the last lot in the subdivision for a much higher price than the first lot sold, why?
    a. Conformity
    b. Depreciation
    c. Zoning
    d. Supply and Demand

49. An appraiser has been given an assignment to appraise a post office, which approach would the appraiser use?
    a. Cost Approach
    b. Supply and Demand
    c. Income Approach
    d. Market/Data Approach

50. Which of the following is an example of locational obsolescence?
    a. A poor floor plan
    b. Escheat
    c. New zoning allowing for a decrease in lot size in a newly developed subdivision
    d. Conditions under which the property was sold

51. All of the following are examples of economic obsolescence except?
    a. Poor city planning
    b. A major industry closing
    c. Conflicting zoning in a neighborhood
    d. Four-bedroom house with a single bath

52. Depreciation applies to?
    a. A high-rise apartment complex
    b. Land
    c. Both the land and a farm
    d. ROI

53. The most important thing an appraiser will consider when using the market data approach to valuation is?
    a. The original cost of the property
    b. Date of sale

      c. Taxes
      d. PETE

54. The gross rent multiplier (GRM) is used for?
      a. CMA
      b. Income approach for a café
      c. Cost approach
      d. Income approach for a single-family home

55. Step 1 – established the gross income from rents
Step 2 – deduct loss for vacancies and collection losses prior to paying utilities to arrive at?
      a. bottom company dollar
      b. gross income
      c. effective net income
      d. effective gross income

56. When estimating the value using the income approach, what is the first step an appraiser would use?
      a. State the problem and then determine the annual potential gross income.
      b. Determine ROI
      c. Figure all expenditures
      d. Project occupancy

57. Flight patterns were changed and now airplanes fly directly over a subdivision. What term best describes the loss in value to this subdivision?
      a. Physical obsolescence
      b. Functional obsolescence
      c. External/economic obsolescence
      d. Condemnation

58. In a market data or sales comparison approach to value, which of the following would be considered?
      a. Conditions which the property was sold.
      b. GRM
      c. GIM
      d. Annual net income

ANSWERS

1. All of the following characteristics add to value in a property except?
      a. Depreciation

2. All of the following are principles of market value except?
      Market value is the average price that a property will bring.

3. There are several houses in the area that you desire to purchase. All of the homes are extremely similar. You choose the one with the lowest asking price. You are most likely basing your decision on?
      Substitution

4. A developer built a luxury neighborhood where he sold the last lot in the subdivision for a much higher price than the first lot sold, why?
      Supply and Demand

5. An appraiser has been given an assignment to appraise a post office, which approach would the appraiser use?

Cost Approach

6.   Which of the following is an example of locational obsolescence?
     New zoning allowing for a decrease in lot size in a newly developed subdivision

7.   All of the following are examples of economic obsolescence except?
     Four-bedroom house with a single bath

8.   Depreciation applies to?
     A high-rise apartment complex

9.   The most important thing an appraiser will consider when using the market data approach to valuation is?
     Date of sale

10. The gross rent multiplier (GRM) is used for?
     Income approach for a single-family home

11. Step 1 – established the gross income from rents
     Step 2 – deduct loss for vacancies and collection losses prior to paying utilities to arrive at?
     effective net income

12. When estimating the value using the income approach, what is the first step an appraiser would use?
     a.   **State the problem and then determine the annual potential gross income.**

13. Flight patterns were changed and now airplanes fly directly over a subdivision. What term best describes the loss in value to this subdivision?
     External/economic obsolescence

14. In a market data or sales comparison approach to value, which of the following would be considered?
     Conditions which the property was sold.

Chapter 4

Financing (Salesperson 10%; Broker 8%)

Basic concepts and terminology
1. Points
2. LTV
3. PMI
4. Interest
5. PITI

Financing instruments (mortgage, promissory note,
1. Types of loans
   - Conventional loans
   - FHA Insured loans
   - VA guaranteed loans
   - USDA/rural loan programs
   - Amortized loans
   - Adjustable-rate mortgage loans
   - Bridge loans
2. Owner financing (installment and land contract/contract for deed)

Financing and lending
3. Lending process application through closing
4. Financing and credit laws and rules
5. Truth in lending
6. RESPA
7. Equal Credit Opportunity
8. CFPB/TRID rules on financing and risky loan features

Underwriting
1. Debt ratios
2. Credit scoring
3. Credit history

Basic Concepts and Terminology

Trick to Remember

Or or or is the GIVOR
Ee ee ee is the gimee gimee gimee the property

Or or or is the GIVOR	Ee ee ee is the gimee gimee gimee the property
Vendor	Vendee
Optionor	Optionee
Lessor	Lessee
Grantor	Grantee
Mortgagor = borrower The Mortgagor is the GIVOR of the payment	Mortgagee = lender If the Mortgagee doesn't give the payment, the Mortgagee says: gimee, gimee, gimee the propertee

Primary Mortgage market
It's You going to your bank. First point of contact.

Secondary Mortgage market
Banks buying and selling loans to each other. In this market, formal appraisals are also done.

Points
Discount Point; 1% of the loan amount.
One percent of the loan amount.
Are often used for buy-downs, where they may be called Discount Points.
A percentage of the principal loan amount charged by the lender.
Each point is equal to 1% of the loan amount.
A fee paid by the borrow to lower the interest rate on a loan
Increases the lender yield
A financing technique used to reduce the monthly payments of a loan

AKA: Discount Points
An up-front lender charge to increase the yield or lower the interest rate on a loan. 1 discount point = 1% of the loan amount. Typically, it takes about 8 points to lower the loan rate 1 percent.

Buying Down Interest
Paying discount points up front (by either buyer or seller) to receive a lower interest rate. Usually 1 point (1% of the loan amount) will decrease the interest rate 1/8 of 1 percent.

mortgage insurance.

PMI - PRIVATE MORTGAGE INSURANCE
In the case of conventional loans, you will need to pay for Private Mortgage Insurance. Many lenders require it so that they are protected from huge losses in the event of a borrower defaulting on a mortgage.
Insures the lender against default of any amount of the mortgage above 80% LTV. PMI companies (such as Mortgage Guaranty Insurance Corp – MGIC) require the borrower to qualify separately from the lender before they are willing to insure the loan.

M.I.P. Mortgage Insurance Premium
In order to qualify for an FHA-approved loan, you will be required to pay a mortgage insurance premium. This insurance protects lenders from incurring a loss in case you are unable to make monthly payments

Charged up-front and annually (in each monthly loan payment) to insure the lender against default on that portion of a loan above the borrower's equity.

P.I.T.I.
Principal, Interest, Taxes and Insurance.

LTV – Loan to Value
The relationship between the amount of the mortgage loan and the value of the real estate being pledged as collateral.
The amount of money borrowed compared to the value (or price) of the property.
The amount of a first mortgage divided by the lesser of (1) the appraised value of the property or (2) the purchase price of the property.

Problems with a High LTV (Above 80%)
1. Loan could be denied
2. Lender could increase the cost of the loan to the borrower
3. Lender could require that the borrower pay for private mortgage insurance (PMI)

Interest
The charge for borrowing money

Annual Percentage Rate (APR): How much a loan costs over the loan term expressed as a rate. The APR includes the interest rate, points, broker fees and certain other credit charges a borrower is required to pay. This is not the interest rate that is used in setting your monthly payment

Impound Account
A trust account to reserve funds for a specific purpose—e.g. the lender will accrue funds to pay property taxes and homeowners insurance when they become due.

Financing instruments – mortgage, promissory note,

Mortgage
- A two-party security instrument for a promissory note that pledges the property in the event of loan default and creates personal liability for the borrower.
- Automatically released when paid off. Mortgage foreclosure must be pursued through the courts.

    mortgagee
    The lender; receives the mortgage from the borrower in exchange for the loan.
    mortgagor
    The borrower; gives the mortgage to the lender in exchange for the loan

Promissory Note
- The written evidence of and promise to repay a debt.
- Terms of the note usually include: Names of note holder and borrower, total amount to be repaid, interest rate, payment intervals and amounts.
- A note alone is unsecured (without collateral) unless accompanied by a security instrument, which in real estate is a deed of trust or mortgage.

Seller Financing
- The seller loans the buyer the money to purchase the property.
- Seller gets a note instead of cash.

Deed of Trust
- A three-party security instrument for a promissory note that conveys "naked title", and gives the trustee a right and process to foreclose without resort to courts in the event of default.
- The 3 parties are: the borrower (trustor), the trustee, and the lender (beneficiary of the trust).

- A 3-party security instrument for a promissory note that transfers title from the trustor (borrower) to a trustee (third party) to be held for the benefit of the beneficiary (lender). Must be released when the loan is paid off.
    1. **Trustor**
    The borrower in a deed of trust.
    2. **Trustee**
    The third party
    3. **Beneficiary**
    A person who is to receive payment under a deed of trust or the person for whom a trust operates.
    4. **Release of a Deed of Trust**
    Issued by the public trustee when shown a note signed by the lender "paid in full," accompanied by the original or copy of the deed of trust, and a "release of deed of trust" application signed by the lender.
    5. **Naked Title**
    Legal title only without the bundle of rights associated with ownership; Example: Title held by a trustee under a deed of trust.

Usual Elements of Deeds of Trust and Mortgages
- Date,
- parties,
- redemption,
- description of the indebtedness,
- amount,
- maturity date,
- method of repayment of the principal amount,
- interest rate and
- time of payment, and
- conditions of default as to principal and interest.

Maturity Date
The due date of the loan. (30 years for most residential loans).

"Or More" Clause
A contract provision that allows prepayment without penalty.

Prepayment
By making prepayments on a home loan, you are paying off your principal loan earlier than the amortization schedule, and reducing the total amount you pay in interest towards the mortgage.

Prepayment penalty
the amount set by the creditor as a penalty to the debtor for paying off a debt before it matures

Satisfaction
Payment of a debt or obligation such as a judgment.

Alienation (Due-on-Sale) Clause
A provision in a loan that makes the balance due and payable immediately upon a sale or transfer of ownership.

Acceleration Clause
A provision in a note, mortgage or deed of trust that makes the entire loan amount due immediately (accelerates all future payments to now) in the event of **default.**

Default Clause
- A provision in a deed of trust that allows a **junior lienholder** (e.g., 2nd deed of trust) to cure any higher priority lien(s);

- Absolutely essential to protect a junior lienholder from being wiped out
- by the foreclosure of the prior lien.

Partial Release Clause
- Partial release is a mortgage provision allowing some of the pledged collateral to be released from the mortgage contract if certain conditions are met.
- In other words, the partial release allows some of your collateral can be taken off the mortgage once a certain amount of the loan has been paid.
- The application process could require submitting a **survey map** to show which part of the property is to be released and what will remain with the lender's as the mortgage continues to be paid.
- Found in Blanket mortgages

WHAREHOUSING

How Fannie Mae and Freddie Mac Work

Banks lend money to people who want to buy a house. These loans, called mortgages, can be significant, as much as $300,000 or more, and borrowers typically have 15 to 30 years to repay them. With so many people needing mortgages, and with such long periods of time passing before these large debts are repaid, banks could run out of money to loan.

This is where Fannie Mae and Freddie Mac come in.

1. Fannie and Freddie work with lenders, not borrowers.
2. They buy mortgages from banks, which allows the banks to turn a quick profit and gives them the capital necessary to lend again. In general,
    *   Fannie buys mortgages from private commercial banks, like Chase and Bank of America
    *   Freddie buys mortgages from smaller banks, a.k.a., thrifts

Mortgage debt that Fannie and Freddie buy is then sold to investors as **mortgage-backed securities (MBS).**

*   Fannie and Freddie guarantee the loans that are bundled into the mortgage-backed securities they sell to investors.

In other words, if a borrower defaults on the mortgage, Fannie or Freddie will pay the investor (the ultimate owner of the mortgage debt) instead of the borrower.

In order for Fannie and Freddie to be able to provide a guarantee, they require originating banks (the banks that originally lend the money directly to the borrower) to make sure they check the creditworthiness of the borrower.

Originating banks have to follow certain rules and guidelines (e.g., at least 20% down payment or the requirement to pay mortgage insurance premiums); documented proof of income and ability to repay; documented appraisal of the home by a professional and neutral third party; and so on. These rules and guidelines are meant to reduce the likelihood of a default on the loan.

When all parts of the whole are functioning as they should, more people are able to afford to buy a home, debts are repaid, and investors make money.

Besides Fannie Mae and Freddie Mac, there is **Ginnie Mae.**

Unlike Fannie and Freddie, **Ginnie is wholly owned by the U.S. government as a public entity**, and all mortgage-backed securities that it sells to investors are <u>explicitly backed</u> by the U.S. government. In contrast, the securities bought from Fannie and Freddie are <u>implicitly backed.</u>

Fannie Mae	Freddie Mac	Ginnie Mae FHA – VA - HUD LOANS
government-sponsored enterprise (**GSE**),	government-sponsored enterprise (**GSE**),	wholly owned by the U.S. government as a public entity

implicitly backed.	explicitly backed
"implied or understood though not plainly or directly expressed." Something is, therefore, implicit when it is not directly stated but is either suggested Since Fannie Mae and Freddie Mac are **government-sponsored agencies**, their guarantee is implicitly backed by the full faith and	"to fully and clearly express something, leaving nothing implied." Something is explicit when it is cleared stated and spelled out and there is no room for confusion, as in the writing of

trust of the United States government.	a contract or statute.

Neither the certificates nor interest on the certificates are guaranteed by the United States, and they do not constitute a debt or obligation of the United States or any of its agencies or instrumentalities Conventional Loans **Conforming vs. Non-Conforming Loans** Fannie Mae and Freddie Mac directly affect conventional lending for home buying. When dealing with conventional loans, (NON GOVERNMRNT INSURED LOANS) there are two main kinds: **conforming** and **non-conforming**.	Guaranteed by the United States Department of Housing and Urban Development (HUD) Guarantees Veterans Affairs / VA loans and Federal Housing Administration / FHA loan

Conforming loans are also sometimes called "qualified mortgages," or QM.

Conforming loans are those which adhere to Fannie and Freddie's guidelines. That is, conforming conventional loans only go to those borrowers who are most likely to pay back their loans — i.e., those who make 20% down payments, have a good credit score, a reliable income, etc. They also do not exceed a certain amount

A non-conforming loan is a loan that a bank makes that does *not* adhere to Fannie and Freddie's guidelines.
- The loan is either made to less creditworthy borrowers or for a larger amount than Fannie and Freddie recommend (see **jumbo mortgage**).
- Non-conforming loans are usually higher interest loans to make up for the amount of risk inherently involved in the investment of them;
- non-conforming loans are common when it comes to buying a condo.

Conventional Loan
Conventional loans are provided by lenders who are not insured by the FHA or VA. These mortgages have an added risk, and therefore require higher down payments.
A loan with no government insurance or guarantee, secured by real estate.

Jumbo Loan
A jumbo loan is a mortgage with an amount that exceeds the limits set by Fannie Mae and Freddie Mac. A jumbo loan is a good option if you're looking to buy an expensive, luxury home, can afford a large down payment, and have a great credit score.

Historically, investing in Ginnie Mae's bonds is safer than investing in those bought from Fannie Mae and Freddie Mac

Tandem Plan
1938: The National Housing Act: Fannie Mae is created as a public entity to further facilitate the flow of capital in the housing market. It is only *allowed to buy government-insured mortgages — FHA loans.*

Freddie Mac was created to provide further competition in the secondary mortgage market.

The Housing and Community Development Act of 1992 requires Fannie Mae and Freddie Mac, to attempt to make housing more affordable.

Affordable housing goals are set, with both are required to have at least 30% of their mortgage purchases come from mortgages taken out by low- to moderate-income families and individuals.

FHA Insured loans

FHA EXCLUSIVITY
When applying for a mortgage, it's important to note that the FHA will insure your home loan only if you plan on purchasing or refinancing a property that serves as your primary residence.

The Federal Housing Administration, generally known as "FHA", provides mortgage insurance on loans made by FHA-approved lenders throughout the United States and its territories.
FHA insures mortgages on single family and multifamily homes including manufactured homes and hospitals.

It is the largest insurer of mortgages in the world.

What is FHA Mortgage Insurance?
FHA mortgage insurance provides lenders with protection against losses as the result of homeowners defaulting on their mortgage loans. The lenders bear less risk because FHA will pay a claim to the lender in the event of a homeowner's default. Loans must meet certain requirements established by FHA to qualify for insurance.

How is FHA funded?
FHA is the only government agency that operates entirely from its self-generated income and costs the taxpayers nothing. The proceeds from the mortgage insurance paid by the homeowners are captured in an account that is used to operate the program entirely. FHA provides a huge economic stimulation to the country in the form of home and community development, which trickles down to local communities in the form of jobs, building suppliers, tax bases, schools, and other forms of revenue.

FHA Loan Limits
Limits based on location
Here's what home buyers and mortgage shoppers need to know: 2019 FHA limits vary from one county to the next. They are based on the Home Price Index (HPI) and get updated — or at least *reviewed* — every year.

In high-cost areas across the United States, FHA's loan limit "ceiling" was increased to $726,525 for 2019. The housing agency also increased its "floor" to $314,827. These changes are the result of rising home values.

VA Guarantee Home Loans

VA helps Service members, Veterans, and eligible surviving spouses become homeowners. As part of our mission to serve you, we provide a home loan guaranty benefit and other housing-related programs to help you buy, build, repair, retain, or adapt a home for your own personal occupancy.

VA Home Loans are provided by private lenders, such as banks and mortgage companies. VA guarantees a portion of the loan, enabling the lender to provide you with more favorable terms.

Home Loan Eligibility
- You must have satisfactory credit, sufficient income, and a valid Certificate of Eligibility (COE) to be eligible for a VA-guaranteed home loan. The home must be for your own personal occupancy.
- A home loans can be used to:
- Buy a home, a condominium unit in a VA-approved project
- Build a home
- Simultaneously purchase and improve a home
- Improve a home by installing energy-related features or making energy efficient improvements
- Buy a manufactured home and/or lot
- To refinance an existing VA-guaranteed or direct loan for the purpose of a lower interest rate
- To refinance an existing mortgage loan or other indebtedness secured by a lien of record on a residence owned and occupied by the veteran as a home

VA Home Loan Guarantee
- The guarantee VA provides to lenders allows them to provide eligible persons with more favorable terms, including:
- No down-payment unless required by the lender or the purchase price is more than the reasonable value of the property
- No private mortgage insurance premium requirement

VA rules limit the amount you can be charged for closing costs
Closing costs *may* be paid by the seller

The lender can't charge you a penalty fee if you pay the loan off early
VA may be able to provide you some assistance if you run into difficulty making payments

You should also know that:
You don't have to be a first-time home buyer
You can reuse the benefit

VA-backed loans are assumable, as long as the person assuming the loan qualifies (They do not have to be a veteran or qualified non -veteran)

Interest Rate Reduction Refinance Loan (IRRRL): also, called the Streamline Refinance Loan can help you obtain a lower interest rate by refinancing your existing VA loan

Native American Direct Loan (NADL) Program: helps eligible Native American Veterans finance the purchase, construction, or improvement of homes on Federal Trust Land, or reduce the interest rate on a VA loan.

Adapted Housing Grants: help Veterans with a permanent and total service-connected disability purchase or build an adapted home or to modify an existing home to account for their disability

Eligibility Requirements
Your length of service or service commitment, duty status and character of service determine your eligibility for specific home loan benefits.

Qualifications

A veteran
A qualified non veteran
An unmarried surviving spouse
National Guard Members and Reservists with six years of service

VA Loan Assumption rules

VA must approve the buyer and assumption agreement.
Original borrower remains liable for the loan, unless VA approves a **release of liability**.
Non-veterans may assume the loan.

Certificate of Eligibility

Proof to a lender that a veteran may apply for a VA-guaranteed home loan. Obtained by most lenders from the VA electronically or by the veteran submitting a Department of Defense Form (DD 214) Active Duty discharge document to the

Certificate of Reasonable Value (CRV)

A statement of value issued by the Department of Veterans Affairs after appraisal by a VA approved lender. If the CRV does not match or exceed the contract purchase price, the veteran applicant may void the contract, or may choose to pay any excess in cash at closing.

USDA/rural loan programs

The USDA Loan is a mortgage option available to some rural and suburban homebuyers. USDA Home Loans are issued by qualified lenders and guaranteed by the United States Department of Agriculture (USDA).

USDA Home Loans are particularly favorable to those living in rural or low-income areas.

USDA Loans offer **$0 money down**, lenient eligibility requirements and competitive interest rates – due to the loan being guaranteed by the USDA.

USDA mortgages stand alone as the only mainstream zero money down program available to borrowers that have not served in the military.

Eligible borrowers will be hard pressed to find a home loan program that offers more favorable terms.

Farm Service Agency (FSA)
Farm Ownership Loans
"we keep America's agriculture growing."

No current or previous farm ownership requirements and 100 percent financing available

FSA direct farm ownership loans are a valuable resource to help farmers and ranchers become owner-operators of family farms, improve and expand current operations, increase agricultural productivity, and assist with land tenure to save farmland for future generations.

All FSA direct loans are financed and serviced by the Agency through local Farm Loan Officers and Farm Loan Managers. The funding comes from Congressional appropriations as part of the USDA budget.

Rural Housing Service

USDA's Rural Housing Service offers a variety of programs to build or improve housing and essential community facilities in rural areas.
We offer loans, grants and loan guarantees for single- and multi-family housing, child care centers, fire and police stations, hospitals, libraries, nursing homes, schools, first responder vehicles and equipment, housing for farm laborers and much more.

We also provide technical assistance loans and grants in partnership with non-profit organizations, Indian tribes, state and federal government agencies, and local communities.

We and our partners are working together to ensure that rural America continues to be a great place to live, work and raise a family.

Mortgages

Amortized loans
direct reduction loan
Fixed payment. The amount of principle paid increases and the amount of interest paid decreases over time. The monthly payment stays the same.
It reverses over time.

The amount applied to the interest decreases with each payment.
The amount applied to the principal increases with each payment.
Amortization: Paying off a loan over a period of time and at the interest rate specified in the loan documents. The amortization of a loan includes the payment of interest and a part of the amount borrowed in each mortgage payment. For instance, on a 30-year fixed-rate mortgage, the amortization period is 30 years.

Partially Amortized
A loan that is partially amortized while the rest f the balance is paid at the end of the loan term. Also known as a balloon payment

Interest Only Loan- Term Loan
A five- or ten-year interest-only period is typical.

After this time, the principal balance is amortized for the remaining term.

Interest-only loans represent a somewhat higher risk for lenders, and therefore are subject to a slightly higher interest rate.

Negative Amortization Mortgage
The quickest way to go underwater
Occurs in loans in which the periodic payment does not cover the amount of interest due for that loan period. The unpaid accrued interest is then capitalized monthly into the outstanding principal balance. The result of this is that the loan balance (or principal) increases by the amount of the unpaid interest on a monthly basis.

All NegAM home loans eventually require full repayment of principal and interest according to the original term of the mortgage and note signed by the borrower.

Most loans only allow NegAM to happen for no more than 5 years

Reverse Mortgages
Home Equity Conversion Mortgages for Seniors (HECM)
Homeowner must be 62 years or older. Turning the equity in a primary residence into cash free income.

A reverse mortgage is a special type of home loan that lets you convert a portion of the equity in your home into cash.

The equity that you built up over years of making mortgage payments can be paid to you. However, unlike a traditional home equity loan or second mortgage, HECM borrowers do not have to repay the HECM loan until the borrowers no longer use the home as their principal residence or fail to meet the obligations of the mortgage.

You can also use a HECM to purchase a primary residence if you are able to use cash on hand to pay the difference between the HECM proceeds and the sales price plus closing costs for the property you are purchasing.

Balloon payment mortgages
A large and final payment set at a pre-determined date.
A partially amortized loan and other loan forms where the balance is not paid off by the end of the term.

BLANKET MORTGAGE
A *blanket mortgage* is a loan that covers more than one piece of property. It sometimes is used to finance a subdivision development. Say, for example, that a builder buys six lots on which he plans to build houses and sell them.

The builder may want to use a blanket mortgage to finance the purchase, because it usually comes with a *partial release provision*. A *partial release* is a provision that allows the lien to be removed separately from each parcel as it is sold to a buyer and the bank is paid a portion of the loan amount.

Partial Release Clause
Used by sub-dividers and developers with a blanket loan. Sub dividers will get one large loan on a large parcel. The loan is called a Blanket Mortgage.

PACKAGE MORTGAGE
A *package mortgage* is a loan that covers real estate and personal property being sold with the real estate. The buyer of a house in which furniture is being included in the sale may want to apply for a package loan. For example, this loan can be used to purchase a furnished vacation home.

CONSTRUCTION LOAN
A *construction loan* is made to finance a construction project. A typical case is when someone who owns property hires a builder to build a house. Money from the loan is released to the builder at certain points as the project progresses. At the end of the project, the loan generally is converted to a conventional mortgage.

Wraparound Loans
A wraparound mortgage, more commonly known as a "wrap", is a form of secondary financing for the purchase of real property.
The seller extends to the buyer a junior mortgage which wraps around and exists in addition to any superior mortgages already secured by the property.
Under a wrap, a seller accepts a secured promissory note from the buyer for the amount due on the underlying mortgage plus an amount up to the remaining purchase money balance.

Bridge Loans
A sum of money lent by a bank to cover an interval between two transactions, typically the buying of one house and the selling of another.

Home equity loans
A home equity loan is a type of loan in which the borrower uses the equity of his or her home as collateral.

Participation Mortgage. Loan where the lender participates in the development and/or selling of the property.

PURCHASE MONEY MORTGAGE
The mortgage that a seller takes back as part of the sale price of a property.

*State government sets rates for interest that cannot be exceeded — called the **usury rate**.*

These seller mortgages may not be subject to the usury limits that are set by state law, so you need to verify that information in your state.

Mortgages made by lenders (not sellers) are subject to these limits.

SALE LEASEBACK

A *sale leaseback* isn't a mortgage, but can be a source of project financing and a means of obtaining the equity in a property. Usually used in commercial property situations, an owner-occupant uses a sale leaseback to sell the building but agrees to remain in the building under a lease. The new owner has a tenant and the old owner has gotten his money out of the building to use.

SHARED EQUITY MORTGAGE

The *shared equity mortgage* allows for a share of the profit on the property to be given to someone else in return for help purchasing the property. A relative, investor, or lending institution may agree to provide funds for a down payment or help with the mortgage payment. When the property is sold, a predetermined share of the profit is given to the person who provided the financial help.

TEMPORARY LOAN

A *temporary loan,* also called *interim financing, bridge loan, swing loan,* or *gap loan,* is used when funds are needed for short periods of time to complete a real estate transaction. A typical situation where a temporary loan may be used is when a seller is selling one house and plans to use the proceeds from the sale to buy another house.

Refinance – The payoff of an existing mortgage loan with a new mortgage loan using the same property as security. Homeowners may refinance to get cash drawn from existing home equity or to obtain a new mortgage loan with a better interest rate and/or payment terms.

Subprime Mortgage

Some lenders grant subprime mortgages to borrowers with low credit scores who don't usually qualify for most other home loans. These loans tend to have very high interest rates to protect lenders in the event that the borrower defaults.

Joint Loan

When you enter a mortgage agreement with a co-borrower who is equally responsible to repay the loan, it is called a joint loan. Having another credit score and income contributing the loan application can help qualify for a home loan.

Cosigner

A co-signer can help you qualify for mortgages by signing the loan application with you. Co-signers have no interest in owning the property, but their credit score, income, and assets will count towards getting you a lower interest rates.

Co-Borrower

By having co-borrowers join your loan application, their income, assets, and credit score can help you qualify for a loan and get lower interest rates. Co-borrowers are equally liable to pay back the loan.

Adjustable rate mortgages (ARMs) – Adjustable rate mortgages (ARMs) usually start with a lower interest rate than a fixed rate mortgage, therefore lowering monthly payments. This allows the borrower to qualify for a larger mortgage than would be possible with a fixed-rate mortgage. The interest rate on an ARM is adjusted periodically based on an **index** that reflects changing market interest rates. When the interest rate is adjusted, the monthly payment goes up or down.

Underwater Mortgage

A mortgage where the balance of the loan is higher than whats the property is worth.

Financing and Lending
Lending process application through closing

Borrower
A mortgage borrower is someone who takes out a home loan to purchase a property. When that person borrows the money, they are making a commitment to pay back that amount in full, on time, and with interest. THE MORTGAGOR

Lender
Your lender is the person or institution granting you a mortgage loan. Lenders loan you money to buy a home, with the understanding that you will make regular payments, with interest, to pay off the loan. THE MORTGAGEE

Loan Officer
The loan officer works at the lending institution where you've applied for a mortgage at. They are responsible for matching a mortgage program to your needs and processing your loan application.

Prequalification
Before shopping for a home, you should have an idea of how much you can afford to spend. With a prequalification, you can get an initial estimate of the mortgage amount a lender will loan you.

Pre-Approval
Getting pre-approved gives you more credibility as a buyer, since a lender has certified that you are likely to qualify for a mortgage loan based on a preliminary assessment.

Loan Application
To get the mortgage process underway, you have to fill out and submit a loan application to your lender. The application form and its supporting documents are used to determine your eligibility for the home mortgage.

Loan Approval
Your loan is approved when the lenders officially grant you a mortgage, based on the information you proved in your loan application.

Loan Balance / principle
Your loan balance is the amount you still owe on the mortgage principal, which is the original sum you borrowed. A portion of your monthly payments go towards paying off the balance.

Loan Calculator
Using a loan calculator, you can determine your monthly payments for a fixed-rate mortgage. Input your loan amount, interest, and term in the loan calculator to see how much you need to pay every month.

Loan Guidelines
In order to be approved for a mortgage, all borrowers must meet certain guidelines. When it comes to FHA loans, the guidelines are a little more lenient and easier for first-time buyers to meet.

Credit Report
Credit reports are detailed accounts of a person's credit history and payment habits. Lenders use this report to determine whether or not a borrower is liable to default on a home loan.

Disclosure
During the mortgage transaction process, you will be given disclosure documents that provide different details about the home loan agreement.

Mortgage Closing
When buying a home, the mortgage closing on a home is the final step in the transaction between you and the seller. This settlement meeting is when property title is handed over to the new homeowner, and funds are transferred to the seller in exchange.

Origination Fee

A lot of work goes into processing a mortgage transaction. As the one borrowing money, you will be required to pay an origination fee to cover the costs of putting the mortgage in place.
Charged by the lender for initiating the loan processing. Typically, 1% of the loan amount.

Discount Points

Discount points are considered a form of prepaid interest on your home loan. These "points" are a percentage of your loan paid up front that consequently lowers the mortgage's interest rate.

Down Payment

The down payment on your house is the amount you pay the lender upfront in order to secure the loan. The amount differs based on what you can afford, and the loan requirements that vary according to the lender.

Monthly Payment

Monthly payments are made to pay off a mortgage loan. The amount goes towards paying the principal balance and interest, and is determined according to the down payment, term, interest rate and cost of the property.

Second Mortgage

Second mortgages are loans taken out on property that is already being used as collateral for a home loan. These loans can be in the form of a home equity loan, or home equity line of credit.

Finance Charge

Sum total of all loan fees charged by the lender.

APR

The annual percentage rate is the cost of borrowing money from the lender, shown as a percentage of your mortgage amount. The APR includes the interest rate as well as all other fees that are paid over the life of the loan.
Rate that includes the principal plus all of the costs of obtaining the loan—closing costs, origination fee, and discount points, etc. Gives a higher interest rate than that calculated on the principal alone, and is required by T-I-L – Truth in Lending. Side-by-side APR's allow true comparative loan shopping.

Good Faith Estimate

The Good Faith Estimate is a document that offers potential homebuyers basic information about their home loan, with an estimate of the costs that go into acquiring one.

Escrow

Your escrow account is set up by your lender in order to collect funds that go toward paying property taxes and home insurance.

Financing and credit laws and rules

Fair lending – The prohibition against unlawful discrimination in lending. The Fair Housing Act prohibits discrimination on the basis of race, color, religion, national origin, sex, familial status, or disability. In addition, the Equal Credit Opportunity Act (*which is not administrated by HUD*) prohibits discrimination because of age, receipt of public assistance, marital status, and the good faith exercise of rights under the Consumer Protection Act.

Equal Credit Opportunity Act (ECOA) – Federal law requiring creditors to make credit equally available without discrimination based on race, color, religion, national origin, age, sex, marital status, or because all or part of the applicant's income is derived from any public assistance program, or because the applicant has, in good faith, exercised any right under the Consumer Credit Protection Act.

When You Apply For Credit, Creditors May Not...
- Discourage you from applying or reject your application because of your race, color, religion, national origin, sex, marital status, age, or because you receive public assistance.
- Consider your race, sex, or national origin, although you may be asked to disclose this information if you want to. It helps federal agencies enforce anti-discrimination laws. A creditor may consider your immigration status and whether you have the right to stay in the country long enough to repay the debt.
- Impose different terms or conditions, like a higher interest rate or higher fees, on a loan based on your race, color, religion, national origin, sex, marital status, age, or because you receive public assistance.
- Ask if you're widowed or divorced. A creditor may use only the terms: married, unmarried, or separated.
- Ask about your marital status if you're applying for a separate, unsecured account. A creditor may ask you to provide this information if you live in "community property" states: Arizona, California, Idaho, Louisiana, Nevada, New Mexico, Texas, Washington, and Wisconsin. A creditor in any state may ask for this information if you apply for a joint account or one secured by property.

Ask for information about your spouse, except:
- if your spouse is applying with you;
- if your spouse will be allowed to use the account;
- if you are relying on your spouse's income or on alimony or child support income from a former spouse;
- if you live in a community property state.
- Ask about your plans for having or raising children, but they can ask questions about expenses related to your dependents.
- Ask if you get alimony, child support, or separate maintenance payments, unless they tell you first that you don't have to provide this information if you aren't relying on these payments to get credit.

A creditor may ask if you have to pay alimony, child support, or separate maintenance payments.

When Deciding To Grant You Credit Or When Setting The Terms Of Credit, Creditors May Not...
- Consider your race, color, religion, national origin, sex, marital status or whether you get public assistance.
- **Consider your age, unless:**
  1. you're too young to sign contracts, generally under 18;
  2. you're at least 62, and the creditor will favor you because of your age;
  3. it's used to determine the meaning of other factors important to creditworthiness. For example, a creditor could use your age to determine if your income might drop because you're about to retire;
  4. it's used in a valid credit scoring system that favors applicants 62 and older. A credit scoring system assigns points to answers you give on credit applications. For example, your length of employment might be scored differently depending on your age.

Consider whether you have a telephone account in your name.
A creditor may consider whether you have a phone.

When Evaluating Your Income, Creditors May Not…
- Refuse to consider reliable public assistance income the same way as other income.
- Discount income because of your sex or marital status. For example, a creditor cannot count a man's salary at 100 percent and a woman at 75 percent. A creditor may not assume a woman of childbearing age will stop working to raise children.
- Discount or refuse to consider income because it comes from part-time employment, Social Security, pensions, or annuities.
- Refuse to consider reliable alimony, child support, or separate maintenance payments. A creditor may ask you for proof that you receive this income consistently.

You Also Have The Right To…
- Have credit in your birth name (Mary Smith), your first and your spouse's last name (Mary Jones), or your first name and a combined last name (Mary Smith Jones).
- Get credit without a cosigner, if you meet the creditor's standards.
- Have a cosigner other than your spouse, if one is necessary.
- Keep your own accounts after you change your name, marital status, reach a certain age, or retire, unless the creditor has evidence that you're not willing or able to pay.
- Know whether your application was accepted or rejected within **30 days** of filing a complete application.
- Know why your application was rejected. The creditor must tell you the specific reason for the rejection or that you are entitled to learn the reason if you ask within 60 days. An acceptable reason might be: "your income was too low" or "you haven't been employed long enough." An unacceptable reason might be "you didn't meet our minimum standards." That information isn't specific enough.
- Learn the specific reason you were offered less favorable terms than you applied for, but only if you reject these terms. For example, if the lender offers you a smaller loan or a higher interest rate, and you don't accept the offer, you have the right to know why those terms were offered.
- Find out why your account was closed or why the terms of the account were made less favorable, unless the account was inactive or you failed to make payments as agreed.

Fair Credit Reporting Act (FCRA) – A consumer protection law that regulates the disclosure of consumer credit reports by consumer credit reporting agencies and establishes procedures for correcting mistakes on one's credit record. FCRA can be found in 15 U.S. Code section 1681, et seq.

Truth in Lending Act TILA
Federal legislation, originally part of the 1969 Consumer Credit Protection Act and others; Implemented by the Federal Reserve Board as Regulation Z. T-I-L requires meaningful credit information be disclosed to a borrower, including representing interest as an annual percentage rate (APR).
Truth In Lending Act (TILA) – A federal law designed to protect consumers in credit transactions by requiring clear disclosure of key terms of the lending arrangement and all costs.

Regulation Z (Reg. Z)
Regulation Z (Truth in Lending Act) requires the lender at the time of loan application to disclose who the lender is, the payment schedule for the loan, prepayment clauses (if any), late payment charges, insurance required, filing fees, collateral that will be required, required deposits, assumability, balloon payment if any, total sales price, adjustable rate features if any, and an itemization of the amount financed.

Trigger Terms
5 items in advertising that, if used, trigger full financial disclosure in the advertisement.
They are
1. down payment amount or percent,
2. number of payments,

3. payment amount,
4. period of repayment (life of loan), and
5. finance charge (interest rate) or lack thereof.

Right of Rescission.
The right of a borrower to rescind a consumer loan (non-1st mortgage) in which real estate is used for collateral. **3 days for most, 5 days for time shares.**

RESPA
RESPA (Real Estate Settlement Procedures Act)
A federal disclosure act that requires lender to give borrowers a good-faith estimate of the settlement costs and an information booklet. Also requires use of a HUD-1 Settlement Statement at closing and prohibits payment of any unearned fees in connection with a real estate transaction. RESPA is administered by HUD.

Good Faith Estimate (GFE)
- An estimate required by RESPA within 3 days of loan application of all closing costs. Must be within specified accuracy when compared with actual closing costs.
- Is an estimate of charges or range of charges that a prospective borrower is likely to incur in connection with financing a home.

CFPB/TRID rules on financing and risky loan features
The lender must provide a Loan Estimate to the consumer, either by delivering by hand or placing in the mail, no later than **three business days** of the receipt of an application. An application is considered received when the consumer provides the following information:
§ Consumer's name,
§ Consumer's income,
§ Consumer's Social Security number to obtain a credit report,
§ Address of the property,
§ Estimate of the value of the property, and
§ The mortgage loan amount sought.

Revised Loan Estimate
When there is a changed circumstance after the Loan Estimate has been provided, the creditor can revise the Loan Estimate **within three business days**. A revised Loan Estimate generally can be provided no later than **seven business days** before consummation.

Closing Disclosure
Out of the numerous documents that you will come across during the mortgage process, your Closing Disclosure is one of the most important. This 5-page document specifies the terms of your home loan, such as your monthly payments, interest rates, and closing costs.

Usury
Charging interest above the rate set by law.

Bait-and-Switch
An illegal (Truth-in-Lending) advertising gimmick that offers property that is not really available in order to trick buyers into a different property. Typically, offers low-priced property, but really has only higher-priced properties available.

Predatory lending – The use of abusive and exploitive lending practices that extracts the equity out of a homeowner's home and/or increase indebtedness. This type of lending violates federal fair lending laws if it targets members of protected classes for harsher treatment and conditions.

Redlining – The refusal to offer credit or insurance in certain neighborhoods.

Reverse redlining – A practice in which lenders specifically market high cost or predatory loans to potential customers based on factors such as race or ethnicity. Reverse redlining is a form of discrimination not because it excludes minorities and other vulnerable populations, but because it targets and exploits them by offering loans with abusive terms and conditions.

Foreclosure – The legal proceedings initiated by a lender to repossess the collateral for the mortgage loan that is in default.

Loan term – The loan term is the length of time before the mortgage loan is due to be repaid in full. Most mortgage loans have 15, 20, or 30-year terms.

Underwriting

The process of evaluating a mortgage loan application to determine the risk involved for the lender. Underwriting involves an analysis of the borrower's creditworthiness and the quality of the property.

Underwriter

Person in a lending institution who determines if a borrower qualifies for a loan.

Debt to income ratio – the ratio of debt payments to income, including both a borrower's housing debt and other debts. Lenders calculate this ratio during the mortgage loan underwriting process and use the result as one major factor in determining whether a borrower qualifies for a mortgage loan. **A higher ratio means a greater debt burden** and generally indicates a greater risk of default.

Debt Ratio

The debt ratio shows your long-term and short-term debt as a percentage of your total assets. The lower your debt-ratio, the better your chances are of qualifying for a mortgage.

Qualification Ratio

The ratio of the borrower's monthly mortgage payment to monthly income (Front-end, usually 28%); or the ratio of the monthly payment plus all other monthly long term expenses to monthly income (Back-end, usually 36%).

Back-end Ratio

A loan qualification ratio, typically requiring projected monthly principal, interest, taxes and insurance (PITI), plus all other long-term monthly debt to be within 36% of gross monthly income. See front-end ratio.

Front-end Ratio

A loan qualifying ratio, typically requiring the principal, interest, taxes and insurance (PITI) of the proposed loan to be within 29% of gross monthly income. See back-end ratio.

Capacity

The borrower's income and indebtedness. Used to calculate the loan-to-value (LTV) ratio.

Credit Report

Credit reports are detailed accounts of a person's credit history and payment habits. Lenders use this report to determine whether or not a borrower is liable to default on a home loan.

Credit History

When applying for a mortgage, lenders will be looking at your credit history, which is a compilation of your borrowing and payment habits. It shows the lender how likely you are to repay the loan they grant you.

FICO Score

Your FICO score is a number that represents your creditworthiness. One of the most widely accepted credit scores, this number comes from an algorithm developed by Fair, Isaac and Company in the 1950. FICO debuted as a general-purpose score in 1989.

Credit Report

Credit reports are detailed accounts of a person's credit history and payment habits. Lenders use this report to determine whether or not a borrower is liable to default on a home loan.

Credit Score
Your credit score is a number that represents your creditworthiness to lenders who are determining whether to grant you a loan. FICO scores are the most widely accepted credit scores.

Character
The history of how a borrower has paid obligations in the past. Known as Credit Scores

Bankruptcy
Declaring bankruptcy means that you have submitted an application to a court that admits you are unable to pay back your debts. Filing for bankruptcy ruins your credit, which leads to problems when applying for loans in the future.

Collateral – An item of value that a lender can take as compensation if a borrower fails to repay a mortgage loan as scheduled. Borrowers generally are required to secure a mortgage loan with real or personal property as collateral. On mortgage loans, the property that the borrower purchases usually serve as the collateral.

Quiz by Broker Tina Perkins, CDEI, Senior Instructor

59. Which of the following statements regarding real estate financing is false?
    a. The mortgage is considered a voluntary lien
    b. The mortgagor is the buyer
    c. The mortgagee is the lender
    d. A promissory note is security for the mortgage

60. All of the following about a promissory note are true except?
    a. It is a negotiable document
    b. Is considered proof of the debt
    c. The instrument by which the purchaser agrees to repay the loan
    d. Is evidence of title to the property

61. Of the following, which allows for payments of interest only with a balloon payment of principal at maturity?
    a. ARM
    b. Fully amortized
    c. Straight
    d. Reverse

62. The secondary money market has the following participants except?
    a. FHLMC
    b. Fannie Mae
    c. FDIC
    d. GNMA

63. With a conventional loan, all of the following are correct except?
    a. It requires anywhere from 5-20% down
    b. The LTV typically does not exceed 80% without PMI
    c. It is never insured by a private agency
    d. It can be fully amortized

64. Which of the following is not true of the FHA (Federal Housing Administration)?
    a. In most cases mortgage insurance is charged
    b. The lender is insured against loss
    c. Debt to income ratios follow strict guidelines
    d. The FHA provides the money for the mortgage

65. What is not true of a VA loan?
    a. It is a government guaranteed loan
    b. It is available for eligible veterans
    c. The loan is insured
    d. Little or no money down is required

66. Hypothecation means?
    a. TILA
    b. Retaining possession of the property while making payments
    c. A mortgage amount higher than the property is worth
    d. A partial release clause

67. Regarding FHA loans, which of the following is false?
    a. Down payments can go as low as 3.5% down payment
    b. Buyers must fit the criteria for FHA loan approval
    c. FHA mortgages require a higher down payment than a VA loan
    d. FHA mortgages are not assumable

68. Which of the following may not be a requirement of an FHA loan?

a. Pay PMI if the buyer puts less than 20% down.
b. The buyer must meet credit criteria
c. Work with an FHA approved lender
d. Make a 15% down payment

69. Complete disclosure of the total cost of credit on a loan is required by?
    a. Trigger terms
    b. Regulation Z
    c. FECO act
    d. Federal Fair Housing Act of 1968

70. Funds for a VA loan are provided by which of the following?
    a. FNMA
    b. The VA department
    c. Freddie Mac
    d. Approved lenders

71. Usury laws prohibit which of the following?
    a. Life insurance companies providing mortgages
    b. Hypothecation
    c. Subordination agreements
    d. Charging interest rates higher than allowed by law

72. A retired Air Force officer purchased a home using his VA loan. Several years later he sold the property and with the lender's approval the buyer assumed the loan. The buyer defaulted on the loan 6 months later. What is the responsibility of the retired Air Force officer?
    a. Responsible for the PMI payments
    b. Required to pay the origination fees
    c. No longer responsible for anything regarding the property or the loan
    d. Under VA loan requirements, he is responsible till the loan is paid in full

73. When a bank charges 2 discount points on a $60,000 loan, how much will the purchaser have to pay?
    a. $600
    b. $1200
    c. $200
    d. None of the above

74. Truth in lending is a disclosure of the true cost of a loan and contains?
    a. FDIC
    b. RESPA
    c. Ginnie Mae
    d. Trigger terms

75. According to Truth in Lending, your bank must disclose which of the following?
    a. Equity
    b. Subordination agreements
    c. APR
    d. Underwater mortgage requirements

76. When a buyer has a poor credit history, the bank will charge a higher interest rate due to the risk of the loan not being paid back. This is an example of a?
    a. Term loan
    b. Subprime loan
    c. Straight loan
    d. ARM loan

77. A down payment for an FHA loan can go as low as?

      a.   20%

      b.   5%

      c.   3.5%

      d.   No down payment is required

78. A loan program that allows older homeowners to use part of the equity in their property as tax free income without having to sell is known as?
    a. Purchase and lease back
    b. Blanket mortgage
    c. Subordination loan
    d. Reverse mortgage

79. When a property is not worth the amount of mortgage owed on it, the mortgage on that property is referred to as being a?
    a. Wraparound mortgage
    b. Option to purchase
    c. Underwater mortgage
    d. Laches

80. After an accepted offer, the buyer was unable to obtain a mortgage. Both parties agreed to cancel the contract. Who does the earnest money deposit belong to?
    a. The seller for compensation of the failed transaction
    b. The listing agent for their marketing efforts
    c. The purchaser is entitled to the entire amount of the earnest money.
    d. The selling agent since they produced the buyer

ANSWERS

1. Which of the following statements regarding real estate financing is false?
   A promissory note is security for the mortgage

2. All of the following about a promissory note are true except?
   Is evidence of title to the property

3. Of the following, which allows for payments of interest only with a balloon payment of principal at maturity?
   Straight

4. The secondary money market has the following participants except?
   FDIC

5. With a conventional loan, all of the following are correct except?
   It requires anywhere from 5-20% down

6. Which of the following is not true of the FHA (Federal Housing Administration)?
   The FHA provides the money for the mortgage

7. What is not true of a VA loan?
   The loan is insured

8. Hypothecation means?
   Retaining possession of the property while making payments

9. Regarding FHA loans, which of the following is false?
   FHA mortgages are not assumable

10. Which of the following may not be a requirement of an FHA loan?

Make a 15% down payment

11. Complete disclosure of the total cost of credit on a loan is required by?
    Regulation Z

12. Funds for a VA loan are provided by which of the following?
    Approved lenders

13. Usury laws prohibit which of the following?
    Charging interest rates higher than allowed by law

14. A retired Air Force officer purchased a home using his VA loan. Several years later he sold the property and with the lender's approval the buyer assumed the loan. The buyer defaulted on the loan 6 months later. What is the responsibility of the retired Air Force officer?
    No longer responsible for anything regarding the property or the loan

15. When a bank charges 2 discount points on a $60,000 loan, how much will the purchaser have to pay?
    $1200

16. Truth in lending is a disclosure of the true cost of a loan and contains?
    Trigger terms

17. According to Truth in Lending, your bank must disclose which of the following?
    APR

18. When a buyer has a poor credit history, the bank will charge a higher interest rate due to the risk of the loan not being paid back. This is an example of a?
    Subprime loan

19. A down payment for an FHA loan can go as low as?
    3.5%

20. A loan program that allows older homeowners to use part of the equity in their property as tax free income without having to sell is known as?
    Reverse mortgage

21. When a property is not worth the amount of mortgage owed on it, the mortgage on that property is referred to as being a?
    Underwater mortgage

Chapter 5

General Principles of Agency (Salesperson 13%; Broker 11%)

1. Agency and non-agency relationships
    1. Types of agents and agencies
    2. Other brokerage relationships (non- agents)
        1. Transactional
        2. Facilitators
    3. Agent's duties to clients
        1. Fiduciary responsibilities
        2. Traditional agency duties (COALD)
        3. Powers of attorney and other delegation of authority
    4. Creation of agency and non-agency agreements; disclosure of conflict of interest
        1. Agency and agency agreements
            1. Key elements of different types of listing contracts
            2. Key elements of buyer brokerage/tenant representation contracts
        2. Disclosure when acting as principal or other conflict of interest
    5. Responsibilities of agent to customers and third parties, including disclosure, honesty, integrity, accounting for money
    6. Termination of agency
        1. Expiration
        2. Completion/performance
        3. Termination by force of law
        4. Destruction of property/death of principal
        5. Mutual agreement

Introduction to the Brokerage

Agency and non-agency relationships

Agency
The fiduciary relationship that results when one party (principal) gives another party (agent) the authority to act on the principal's behalf to transact business.
Agency is created by **Delegated Authority and Consent to Act.**

Actual Authority
That expressed or implied authority conferred upon an agent by the principal.

Agent
The one who acts for a principle in an agency relationship.

Real Estate Broker
Any licensed person, firm, partnership, association, or corporation who, in consideration of valuable compensation or with the intention of receiving such compensation, acts as a special agent for parties in the sale or lease of real estate.

Real Estate Salesman
One who is employed by a real estate broker, usually as an independent contractor.

Associate Broker – Affiliate Broker
A salesperson with a broker's license.

Types of agents

Special Agent
One authorized by the principal to perform a narrow or specific task. A listing broker employed to sell one home is a special agent. Opposite of General Agent

General Agent
An agent given a wide scope of authority to handle a variety of things. A property manager is a general agent because of the wide range of activity necessary to rent and maintain the property. Opposite of Special Agent

Designated Agent
A practice under law in some states, in which the employing broker 'designates' a licensee as the exclusive company representative (agent or facilitator/transaction broker) to a seller, buyer landlord or tenant; This enables another licensee in the same firm to be designated to the other side of the transaction without creating dual agency.

Universal Agent
Holds Power of Attorney

Seller Agent
An agent employed by the Seller.

Buyer Agent
Works with buyers

Cooperating Broker
One working with or representing the buyer or tenant; Cooperates with the listing broker by providing a prospective buyer/tenant for the listed property.

Other brokerage relationships (non-agents)

Facilitator-Transaction broker

Could be the closing attorney

A facilitator may assist buyer and seller in the same transaction without creating dual agency.

Agent's duties to clients

PRESENT ALL OFFERS TO THE SELLER

Principal

The person appointing an agent in an agency relationship.

Fiduciary responsibilities

Fiduciary

That special relationship of trust and confidence forged by agency whereby the agent puts the principal's interests ahead of his or her own interest. Fiduciary duties owed to a principal are the same as duties of an agent.

Traditional agency duties (ColdAC)

Duties of an Agent

Fiduciary duties that are inherent in an agency relationship include reasonable Care, Obedience to lawful instructions, Accounting, Loyalty and Disclosure. **(C.O.A.L.D.)**

- Confidentiality
- Obedience
- Loyalty
- Disclosure
- Accountability
- Care

A listing Broker has earned his commission when he brings a **"Ready, willing, and able" buyer**

A Ready Willing and Able Buyer is One who is prepared to buy property on the seller's terms and is ready to take positive steps to consummate the transaction.

Confidentiality

A duty of an agent to maintain the trusted confidence and secrets of a principal. Neither agent nor non-agent transaction brokers may reveal anything that would weaken the principal's or client's position.

Obedience

A fiduciary duty of an agent to obey the lawful instructions of the principal.

Loyalty

The fiduciary duty of an agent to act at all times solely in the best interests of the principal to the exclusion of all other interests, especially the broker's own self-interest

Disclosure

A duty of an agent to principle to discover and reveal information that might adversely affect the principal's position. Also, an affirmative duty of every real estate licensee to reveal adverse material facts about property condition, inability of either party to complete the contract, non-availability of hazard insurance, inclusion in a flood plain, Megan's law, etc.

Accounting / Accountability

The agent must account for all funds entrusted to her and not *commingle* (combine) client/customer funds with her personal and/or business funds.

Care(Reasonable) and Diligence

The duty of an agent to discover and share relevant facts that a real estate licensee could readily discover—such as zoning changes, school closing, new roads, etc.

Powers of attorney and other delegation of authority

Power of Attorney
A written document appointing an "attorney-in-fact" to act independently and with signature authority on behalf of another person in matters specified. May be either specific (e.g., attend a closing and sign on behalf of a seller) or general (e.g., manage extensive business and personal matters).

Universal Agent
Holds Power of Attorney

General Power of Attorney
Appointment of an attorney-in-fact with signature authority and with wide-ranging discretion in handling the delegated matters in the appointment.

Attorney in Fact
A person named in a written power of attorney document to act on behalf of the person who signs the document, called the principal. The attorney-in-fact's power and responsibilities depend on the specific powers granted in the power of attorney document. An attorney-in-fact is an agent of the principal. One authorized to act independently (and sign for) another person for either a specific or general purpose or power. A real estate broker is NOT an attorney-in-fact unless specifically appointed separately from the listing agreement.

REALTOR®
REALTOR® is a federally registered collective membership mark which identifies a real estate professional who is member of the NATIONAL ASSOCIATION OF REALTORS® and subscribes to its strict Code of Ethics.

Although the **National Association of Realtors** is the most popular, there are several real estate industry groups other than REALTORs®⍰
National Association of Real Estate Brokers

What is a Realtist
A NAREB member is called a REALTIST and represents all professional disciplines within the real estate industry. Realtists promote the highest standards of professional integrity and follow a strict code of real estate industry ethics. We have a special charge to make certain that communities of color are treated with dignity and respect.

Both Realtors® and Realtists subscribe to a CODE OF ETHICS

Creation of Agency and Non-agency Agreements; Disclosure of Conflict of Interest

AGENCY LAW
Agency law is the law that governs the relationship between a client and an agent, in this case a buyer or seller and you their real estate agent. Every state has its own version of how it defines this relationship.

Express agency:
Express agency is where the agency relationship is created through an agreement in which the agent and the principal state their intentions to enter into an agency relationship, that the agent will represent the principal. The parties state or express their intentions in words, either orally or in writing. Whether an oral agreement establishing an agency relationship is binding varies from state to state.

Implied agency:
Implied agency establishes an agency relationship through the actions of the two parties. Although nothing formal has been said or written down, the agent and the principal *act* as if they have an agency relationship. Creating an implied agency may not have been what the two parties intended, but an agency relationship can be created anyway.

Agency by estoppel:
An *agency by estoppel* is created when a principal doesn't stop an agent from going beyond the agent's normal duties, which thus gives the impression that an agency relationship has been established.

Agency by ratification:
An *agency by ratification* is created by accepting circumstances that created the agency after the fact. Suppose a real estate agent, without authorization and without ever speaking to the seller, negotiates a deal for a house that's for sale by the seller. One day the agent arrives with a completed contract simply awaiting the seller's signature and acceptance of the deal.

Agency coupled with an interest: An *agency coupled with an interest* is a situation in which an agent has some kind of interest in the property that's being sold.

Agency and agency agreements

SINGLE Agency
Representation of only one party in a real estate transaction.

DUAL Agency
Agent represents both Buyer and Seller with the written expressed acceptance of both the Buyer and Seller. (Or, licensees in the same firm representing both parties.)
Undisclosed dual agency is always fraudulent.
Dual agency is illegal in some states

The Seller's Agreement with the Listing Broker
The typical real estate transaction involves several steps.
First, if the seller chooses to hire a real estate broker rather than selling the home on his or her own, the seller contracts with a "listing broker."

Once the seller has selected a listing broker, they enter into a contractual relationship called a "listing agreement" by which the broker agrees to market and sell the home in exchange for a set fee, typically in the form of a percentage commission.

The commission "rate" is the percentage of the home sales price that the broker retains as a commission.

Commission "fees" are the total dollar amount paid by consumers for real estate brokerage services.

Commission fees may also be flat fees, hourly fees or a combination of fees.

This contract often specifies the commission the homeowner will pay the listing broker if the home is sold within a specified period of time, how the home is to be listed in the MLS, and, as discussed below, the share of the commission to be offered by the listing broker to a so-called "cooperating broker," who works with the buyer.

The listing broker typically markets the home, both within his or her brokerage firm and to other brokers in the community, by uploading the listing data, including the offer of compensation to cooperating brokers, into the MLS database so that the information can be disseminated to cooperating brokers, who in turn can inform potential buyers of the listing.

Key elements of different types of listing contracts

There are three principal types of listing agreements.

1. In an **"exclusive right to sell"** contract, the listing broker receives a payment if the home is sold during the listing period, regardless of who finds a buyer for the home.
2. In an **"exclusive agency"** agreement, the listing broker receives payment if any broker finds the buyer, but does not receive payment if the seller finds the buyer.
3. In an **"open listing,"** a broker has a nonexclusive right to sell the home and receive payment, but other brokers or the seller may also sell the home without any payment to the listing broker.

Net listing:
This type of agreement may be illegal in your state. The agent gets to keep everything he can get that's more than the sale price the owner wants.

Key elements of buyer brokerage/tenant representation contracts

The Buyer's Relationship with the Cooperating Broker
The broker who works with the buyer is often referred to as the "cooperating broker" "or "buyer's broker."

Cooperating brokers typically attempt to find housing from the available stock that match buyers' preferences, show prospective buyers homes for sale, provide them information about comparable home sales that have occurred in the area, assist prospective buyers in becoming pre-qualified for a certain level of financing, advise them on making offers, and assist in closing the transaction.

Buyers typically do not pay their brokers directly. But, agents can charge buyers for their real estate services if agreed upon.

Mostly, listing brokers compensate cooperating brokers according to the terms stated in the MLS listing, which usually specifies an unconditional offer of compensation to any broker that is the "procuring cause" of the sale.

"procuring cause" – The person who is responsible for the transaction moving forward.

The Buyer's Offer, Contingencies, and Closing in a Typical Transaction

Once a buyer makes an offer on a home, the listing broker may help the seller evaluate offers and formulate counteroffers and may negotiate directly with the buyer or buyer's broker.

If the seller accepts the offer, the home is "under contract," and, pursuant to contracts containing typical contingencies, several things must occur during a stated time period before the transaction closes, such as home inspections, appraisals, securing buyer financing, assuring the title to the home is clear, and conducting necessary repairs.

If a seller makes a counter offer, it VOIDS the original offer. Not until there is a MEETING OF THE MINDS will the transaction be under contract.

Both listing and cooperating brokers typically work together to assure that all contingencies are satisfied, allowing the closing to occur as scheduled.

Many other actors are necessary to assure a successful closing, including the mortgage lender, the insurance agent, the home inspector, the termite inspector, the surveyor, the appraiser, the closing attorney (in some states), the title company, and the escrow agent.

Once all contingencies have been satisfied, the parties proceed to closing, where they exchange purchase money and title to the home.

Buyers Broker / Agent Agreements

An agent employed by and owing fiduciary duties to the Buyer.

- **Exclusive right-to-represent contracts**
most common buyer-broker agreement
the buyer may *not* retain more than one broker to assist him or her
sets forth the commission amount to be paid to the broker, which is owed even if the buyer finds the house herself or another broker does so.
- **Nonexclusive right-to-represent contracts**
compensation to be paid to the broker if the broker finds the house or rental the buyer or tenant decides to buy or rent.
- **Nonexclusive/OPEN**
The client can hire as many agents as he/she wants. To get paid, the agent has to be the procuring cause.

Disclosure when acting as principal or other conflict of interest

- When a licensee is advertising their own property for sale, purchase or exchange the licensee must indicate that he or she is licensed.
- The disclosure of licensee's status must be made in all forms of advertising including the "for sale" sign.
- In addition to disclosing their licensed status in all advertisements, licensees are required to disclose their licensed status on all real estate contracts in which they have an ownership interest.
- Disclose agent owned properties. Disclose when you are in a transaction with a relative. Disclose – Disclose – Disclose

Disclose when you are the buyer, the seller, the renter, the landlord.

Responsibilities of agent to customers and third parties, including disclosure, honesty, integrity, accounting for money

Disclosure of Agency and Agency Agreements

You must disclose to the party that you don't represent, that you represent someone else.

A customer is not represented.
A customer is due fair and honest dealings.

Caveat emptor
A Latin phrase meaning, "let the buyer beware."

Inside the brokerage

Subagent
An agent of an agent.

Salespersons are agents of their broker and sub agents to the client.

Responsible Broker – Broker in Charge
All salespeople work under one broker. The Broker is responsible for the salespeople's real estate activities. He is also responsible for all client funds.
All the salesperson's listings belong to the broker. All real estate activities of salespeople (good or bad) belong to the broker.

The Broker and the Agents/Salespersons have an employment contract in which defines what is expected of each party.
If the Broker in the deal dies, all deals and listings die. The Agents/salespersons would need to move to another responsible Broker and execute all new contracts and disclosures because one of the parties in the transaction have changed.

If an Agent/salespersons die, it has no effect on any listings or transactions.

A Broker cannot pay another Responsible Broker's Agent unless the deal on which the Broker is paying was generated while the Agent was under the direct supervision of that responsible Broker.

An Agent/Salesperson cannot accept any payment or bonus unless it is from the responsible Broker to which their license is held. If a client or customer gives an

Agent/salesperson a bonus, the Agent/Salesperson must turn that bonus over to her responsible Broker.

A responsible Broker is responsible for the real estate activities of his agents/Salespersons.
The responsible broker is responsible for all client and customer deposits.

Termination of Agency

When a real estate agency is in effect, the parties to the contract have different opportunities to terminate their arrangement.

The following represent the various ways that an agency contract can be terminated:

1. **Mutual Agreement (Rescission)** – If a principal and an agent mutually agree to form an agency contract, they can mutually agree to terminate the contract. This is called rescission.

2. **Expiration Date** – All listing agreements must have an expiration date. When that date is reached, the principal and agent have mutually agreed in advance that the listing agreement is over.

3. **Completion** – Fulfillment of the Purpose – If the goal of the agreement is reached, the agent has Tendered Performance. The agent has completed his/her requirement under the agreement.

4. **Revocation by the Principal** – The principal can unilaterally (one-sided) revoke the agent's authority to represent the principal. This can be done if no injury is caused to agent/broker.
       a. Broker Costs – If the broker has spent advertising money and is actively seeking a sale, the seller/principal may have to pay damages for breach of contract to the broker.
       b. Broker Interest – If a listing agreement is an *"agency coupled with an interest*, the seller/principal cannot unilaterally terminate the listing agreement. The seller is obligated until expiration date of agreement.

5. **Termination by force of law**

6. **Destruction of property/death of principal**

7. **Other potential grounds for termination or rescission include:**
   - Illegality
   - Mistake of Fact / Non-Facts

- Agent's lack of authority
- Fundamental breaches / Discharge by breach
- Pre-contractual misrepresentations
- Renunciation / Refusal to perform
- Inequality of bargaining power
- Duress and undue influence

Quiz by Broker Tina Perkins, CDEI, Senior Instructor

1. A seller had her house listed. Her agent received an offer on the property in which she presented to the seller. While the seller was considering the offer, the agent received a second offer on the property. According to the agent's office policy, the agent does not present the second offer until the seller has accepted or rejected the first offer. In this scenario, the agent's actions are?
   a. Allowed to give the seller time to thoroughly consider the first offer
   b. Allowed if the first offer was on a written state contract
   c. Not allowed as all offers are to be presented to the seller upon the agent receiving them
   d. Allowed only if the seller rejects the first offer in writing

2. An agent had an exclusive right to sell listing agreement with a client on a home listed for $100,000. The agent knew that the seller would actually take $92,000 for the house due to the seller being under duress. During an open house, a buyer came to view the property. The potential buyer loved the house but could not afford more than $90,000. The agent encouraged the buyer to submit an offer. The agent also informed the buyer to offer $90k because she knew the seller would accept $92,000. Did the agent violate her agency relationship with the seller?
   a. No, getting it sold is all that matters.
   b. Yes, regardless of intent, an agent can never reveal the lowest amount a seller will take for a property.
   c. Yes, the agent should have had a dual agency agreement signed prior to informing the buyer the lowest amount the seller would take.
   d. No, the buyer was ready, willing and able to meet the terms of the contract.

3. What is a requirement of a universal agent?
   a. A written buyer's agency agreement
   b. An executed exclusive right to sell agreement
   c. An independent contractor agreement
   d. An executed power of attorney agreement

4. A seller signed an exclusive right to sell listing agreement. All of the following are true except?
   a. Fiduciary duties are owed to the seller.
   b. The broker owns the listing.
   c. If the salesperson dies, the contract is null and void.
   d. If the broker dies, the listing agreement is terminated.

5. Typically, a real estate agent is considered to be a?
   a. Special agent
   b. Universal agent
   c. General agent
   d. A transactional broker

6. Each statement is true regarding a real estate broker except?
   a. All offers received by the listing broker must be presented to the client.
   b. Blind ads are allowed if the broker approves them.
   c. A set place of business must be maintained by the broker.
   d. A broker's commission is negotiable.

7. You have listed your neighbor's home. Which of the following describes your relationship with your neighbor?
   a. You are a subagent of your neighbor.
   b. Your neighbor is your principal.
   c. The seller is your customer.
   d. The relationship is considered interpleader.

8. You are acting in the capacity of a mediator in a transaction without representing either the buyer or the seller. You would be acting as a/an?
   a. Broker
   b. Cooperative broker
   c. Exclusive buyer's agency broker
   d. Transactional broker

9. One of the responsibilities of a broker to their customer is?
   a. Acting in the capacity of a general agent
   b. Accepting offers on their behalf
   c. Accountability of funds received
   d. Providing funds for the mortgage

10. The listing broker owes fiduciary duties (COLDAC) to?
    a. Customer
    b. Buyer
    c. Principal
    d. Mortgage broker

11. After listing a property, the broker can?
    a. Offer legal advice on how to take title to the buyer
    b. Accept an offer on behalf of the seller
    c. Advertise the seller's property
    d. Reject an offer for the seller's property

12. Which of the following is a violation of a broker's fiduciary duties to a client?
    a. The broker charges no commission
    b. A broker places the client's interest above theirs.
    c. A broker tells a buyer the lowest price the principal will accept.
    d. A broker tells a buyer the highest price a principal will accept.

13. A fiduciary is all of the following except?
    a. A person who owes confidentiality forever to their client
    b. A person who must follow all legal instructions of their principal
    c. Is a broker in a real estate transaction
    d. A neutral third party

14. A salesperson working under a responsible broker is allowed to?
    a. Work as an independent contractor
    b. Receive payment directly from the seller
    c. Place a 'For Sale' sign in a yard without identifying the brokerage
    d. Act as a dual agent without everyone agreeing to it in writing

15. A general agent is best described as?
    a. One who has power of attorney
    b. Has authority to represent the principal in a specific transaction
    c. One who manages an apartment complex
    d. One who acts as a transactional broker

16. When presenting an offer to purchase to a client, the real estate agent is responsible for?
    a. Detailing the pros and cons of the offer to the seller
    b. Giving legal advice on how to take title
    c. Accepting the offer on behalf of the client
    d. Performing the title abstract

17. After listing a friend's home, the commission the broker is to receive should be determined by?
    a. Law
    b. Commission set by the Real Estate Commission

    c.   Their office policy

    d.   Negotiations with her friend

18. A salesperson has earned a commission in the sale of a property. Who is responsible for paying the salesperson?
    a.   Their responsible broker
    b.   The closing attorney
    c.   The other agent's responsible broker
    d.   The mortgage company

19. After receiving an EMD (earnest money deposit) on an accepted offer to purchase, a broker is to?
    a.   Deposit the money directly into their escrow/trust account
    b.   Deposit the money into their business account
    c.   Pay the past due office rent with it
    d.   Deposit into their personal savings account

20. Regarding their legal responsibilities to a prospective customer (buyer):
    a.   The agent must not use deceit.
    b.   The agent must help them get the lowest price on one of the agent's current listings.
    c.   The agent is a mediator only and has no responsibility to the customer.
    d.   Hold their actual EMD check in the customer's file till closing.

ANSWERS

1. A seller had her house listed. Her agent received an offer on the property in which she presented to the seller. While the seller was considering the offer, the agent received a second offer on the property. According to the agent's office policy, the agent does not present the second offer until the seller has accepted or rejected the first offer. In this scenario, the agent's actions are?
Not allowed as all offers are to be presented to the seller upon the agent receiving them

2. An agent had an exclusive right to sell listing agreement with a client on a home listed for $100,000. The agent knew that the seller would actually take $92,000 for the house due to the seller being under duress. During an open house, a buyer came to view the property. The potential buyer loved the house but could not afford more than $90,000. The agent encouraged the buyer to submit an offer. The agent also informed the buyer to offer $90k because she knew the seller would accept $92,000. Did the agent violate her agency relationship with the seller?
Yes, regardless of intent, an agent can never reveal the lowest amount a seller will take for a property.

3. What is a requirement of a universal agent?
An executed power of attorney agreement

4. A seller signed an exclusive right to sell listing agreement. All of the following are true except?
If the salesperson dies, the contract is null and void.

5. Typically, a real estate agent is considered to be a?
Special agent

6. Each statement is true regarding a real estate broker except?
Blind ads are allowed if the broker approves them.

7. You have listed your neighbor's home. Which of the following describes your relationship with your neighbor?
    Your neighbor is your principal.

8. You are acting in the capacity of a mediator in a transaction without representing either the buyer or the seller. You would be acting as a/an?
    Transactional broker

9. One of the responsibilities of a broker to their customer is?
    Accountability of funds received

10. The listing broker owes fiduciary duties (COLDAC) to?
    Principal

11. After listing a property, the broker can?
    Advertise the seller's property

12. Which of the following is a violation of a broker's fiduciary duties to a client?
    A broker tells a buyer the lowest price the principal will accept.

13. A fiduciary is all of the following except?
    A neutral third party

14. A salesperson working under a responsible broker is allowed to?
    Work as an independent contractor

15. A general agent is best described as?
    One who manages an apartment complex

16. When presenting an offer to purchase to a client, the real estate agent is responsible for?
    Detailing the pros and cons of the offer to the seller

17. After listing a friend's home, the commission the broker is to receive should be determined by?
    Negotiations with her friend

18. A salesperson has earned a commission in the sale of a property. Who is responsible for paying the salesperson?
    Their responsible broker

19. After receiving an EMD (earnest money deposit) on an accepted offer to purchase, a broker is to?
    Deposit the money directly into their escrow/trust account

20. Regarding their legal responsibilities to a prospective customer (buyer):
    The agent must not use deceit.

Chapter 6

Property disclosures (Salesperson 6%; Broker 7%)

1. Property condition
   a. Property condition that may warrant inspections and surveys
   b. Proposed uses or changes in uses that should trigger inquiry about public or private land use controls

2. Environmental issues requiring disclosure

3. Government disclosure requirements (LEAD)

4. Material facts and defect disclosure

Property Condition

Material fact

A fact that a reasonable person would recognize as important. In other words, it is a fact, the suppression of which would reasonably result in a different decision.

Nonmaterial fact

Homicide, suicide felony on the property, HIV AND AIDS - Things that do not affect the physical condition of the property or the surrounding area. Varies state to state

"Falsified evidence"

Falsification of a material fact that would cause a party to a contract to refrain from entering into the contract may be grounds for rescission.

Property condition that may warrant inspections and surveys

- Slipping hill
- UST
- wood rot
- noisy pipes
- easements
- encroachments
- lawsuits
- Destruction, damage, or material alteration of property
- Not fit for occupancy
- Fire
- Meth house
- Sinking foundation'
- Bad electrical
- Sewer well
- Plumbing problems

Proposed uses or changes in uses that should trigger inquiry about public or private land use controls
- Freeway addition
- Zoning Changes
- Airport Expansion
- Special assessments
- New highway in backyard
- Railroads

Stigmatized Property

- Properties that have been the scenes of murders, suicides, or are alleged to be haunted, are stigmatized.
- When in doubt, licensees should make full disclosure.

Red Flag Issues

- A red flag issue is "something wrong with the property that you would like to inspect further".
- Examples would be a brown spot on the ceiling, musty mold smells or several cracks in a driveway going up or down a hill.
- A professional should inspect all red flags.

Blighted

Considered blighted property when the Secretary of State's field inspection confirms a complaint that the property is in a deteriorated or impaired condition and presents a hazard to public health, safety or welfare.

Restrictive Covenants If restrictive covenants exist for the property being sold, the purchasers must be presented with a copy before the buyer signs the purchase contract.

Pest Infestation An agent is responsible to look for animal feces, strange odors, dead bugs and anything that will indicate an infestation. The findings may create a red flag issue. In that case, a professional should be called to investigate.

Structural issues such as roof, gutters, downspouts, doors, windows, and foundation – Disclose anything you find may constitute a material fact.

Zoning and Planning Information – There are zoning maps available. It is the duty of the agent to investigate the zoning of a property.

Boundaries of School/Utility/Taxation Districts, Flight paths – Disclose everything. Section 16 of every township is set aside for schools. Disclose any special assessments added to the tax base.

Encroachments must be disclosed. Hire a profession to survey the property or look toward public records for the measurement.

Local Taxes and Special Assessments, Other Liens neighborhoods in the same city may have different tax amounts due to special assessments.

A special assessment is an added tax to the property owner. An example of a special assessment would be if a school district needed a new school; the city would go ahead and build it and then tax the homes in that district with a special assessment. Only the people who benefit from an improvement will pay the special assessments.

Property Condition Disclosure Statement (PCDS)
A document required by law which reveals specific information. Must be filled out by the seller.
Property Owner's Role Regarding Property Condition
- The Seller will provide the buyer with a written property condition disclosure.
- The Seller must identify all material facts relating to the property and its surrounding area.
- Seller must identify latent defects if aware of defect

Licensee's Role Regarding Property Condition
- A licensee is not responsible to identify latent defects.
- If the agent is aware of a latent defect, he must disclose it.
- The agent must disclose what is readily seen.

Latent Defect
A defect that is not visible or apparent; a hidden defect that would not be discovered in a reasonably thorough inspection of property.

Record Keeping
Sellers and lessors must retain a copy of the disclosures for no less than three years from the date of sale or the date the leasing period begins.

Accuracy of Representation of Lot or Improvement Size, Encroachments or Easements Affecting Use
Hire a professional to measure the property and its improvements.
Information may be gained from recorded instruments.

CLUE
Comprehensive Loss Underwriting Exchange –
It gives insurance companies and buyers a 7-year history of the property.

Environmental Issues Requiring Disclosure

Radon Gas
A naturally occurring radioactive gas that emanates from rocks; it is odorless, colorless and tasteless but has been identified as a cancer-causing agent.

Asbestos
A fibrous material that was once very common in many building materials because of its insulating and heat-resistant value. (Now banned in most places for most uses, and subject to strict EPA regulations. Airborne asbestos is called friable.

Underground Storage Tanks
May contain household heating oil or industrial fuel or chemicals (vents out of ground, basement pipe leading nowhere)

Groundwater Contamination
Happens near groundwater. Leaking tanks/septic systems or mini landfills or pesticides

Pest Infestation
Termites, Carpenter Ants

Lead
Found in dust, paint, pipes, soil, drinking water. Lead can cause mental retardation.

Mold
Caused by moisture and lack of air circulation

Disclosure
A duty of an agent to principal to discover and reveal information that might adversely affect the principal's position.

Government Disclosure Requirements (LEAD)
THE LEAD DISCLOSURE RULE

Congress passed the Residential Lead-Based Paint Hazard Reduction Act of 1992, also known as Title X, to protect families from exposure to lead from paint, dust, and soil.

It directed HUD and EPA to require the disclosure of known information on lead-based paint and lead-based paint hazards before the sale or lease of most housing built before 1978.

Homebuyers and Renters: Know Your Rights Before You Buy or Lease

Many homes and condominiums built before 1978 have lead-based paint. Paint that has chipped or is deteriorating, or on surfaces that rub together such as windows and doors, creates lead dust which can pose serious health hazards to occupants and visitors. Homebuyers and renters have important rights to know about whether lead is present — before signing contracts or leases.

Homebuyers

Federal law requires that before being obligated under a contract to buy housing built prior to 1978, buyers must receive the following from the home seller:

An EPA-approved information pamphlet on identifying and controlling lead-based paint hazards titled *Protect Your Family From Lead In Your Home*

Any known information concerning the presence of lead-based paint or lead-based paint hazards in the home or building.

For multi-unit buildings, this requirement includes records and reports concerning common areas and other units when such information was obtained as a result of a building-wide evaluation.

An attachment to the contract, or language inserted in the contract, that includes a "Lead Warning Statement" and confirms that the seller has complied with all notification requirements.

A 10-day period to conduct a paint inspection or risk assessment for lead-based paint or lead-based paint hazards.

Parties may mutually agree, in writing, to lengthen or shorten the time period for inspection. Homebuyers may waive this inspection opportunity.

If you have a concern about possible lead-based paint, then get a lead inspection from a certified inspector before buying.

For the Buyer or Tenant

IMPORTANT – Lead From Paint, Dust, and Soil in and Around Your Home Can Be Dangerous if Not Managed Properly

• Children under 6 years old are most at risk for lead poisoning in your home.
• Lead exposure can harm young children and babies even before they are born.
• Homes, schools, and child care facilities built before 1978 are likely to contain lead-based paint.
• Even children who seem healthy may have dangerous levels of lead in their bodies.
• Disturbing surfaces with lead-based paint or removing lead-based paint improperly can increase the danger to your family.
• People can get lead into their bodies by breathing or swallowing lead dust, or by eating soil or paint chips containing lead.
• People have many options for reducing lead hazards. Generally, lead-based paint that is in good condition is not a hazard

Before renting or buying a pre-1978 home or apartment, federal law requires:

• Sellers must disclose known information on lead-based paint or lead based paint hazards before selling a house.

• Real estate sales contracts must include a specific warning statement about lead-based paint. **Buyers have up to 10 days to check for lead.**

• Landlords must disclose known information on lead-based paint and lead-based paint hazards before leases take effect. Leases must include a specific warning statement about lead-based paint.

Simple Steps to Protect Your Family from Lead Hazards

If you think your home has lead-based paint:

• Don't try to remove lead-based paint yourself.

• Always keep painted surfaces in good condition to minimize deterioration.

• Get your home checked for lead hazards. Find a certified inspector or risk assessor at epa.gov/lead.

• Regularly clean floors, window sills, and other surfaces.

• Take precautions to avoid exposure to lead dust when remodeling.

• When renovating, repairing, or painting, hire only EPA- or state approved Lead-Safe certified renovation firms.

• Before buying, renting, or renovating your home, have it checked for lead-based paint.

• Consult your health care provider about testing your children for lead. Your pediatrician can check for lead with a simple blood test.

• Wash children's hands, bottles, pacifiers, and toys often.

• Make sure children eat healthy, low-fat foods high in iron, calcium, and vitamin C.

• Remove shoes or wipe soil off shoes before entering your house.

Lead Gets into the Body in Many Ways

Adults and children can get lead into their bodies if they:

• Breathe in lead dust (especially during activities such as renovations, repairs, or painting that disturb painted surfaces).

• Swallow lead dust that has settled on food, food preparation surfaces, and other places.

• Eat paint chips or soil that contains lead.

Lead is especially dangerous to children under the age of 6.

• At this age, children's brains and nervous systems are more sensitive to the damaging effects of lead.

• Children's growing bodies absorb more lead.

• Babies and young children often put their hands and other objects in their mouths. These objects can have lead dust on them.

Women of childbearing age should know that lead is dangerous to a developing fetus.

• Women with a high lead level in their system before or during pregnancy risk exposing the fetus to lead through the placenta during fetal development.

Lead in Drinking Water

The most common sources of lead in drinking water are lead pipes, faucets, and fixtures.

Lead pipes are more likely to be found in older cities and homes built before 1986.

You can't smell or taste lead in drinking water.

To find out for certain if you have lead in drinking water, have your water tested.

Remember older homes with a private well can also have plumbing materials that contain lead.

Important Steps You Can Take to Reduce Lead in Drinking Water

• Use only cold water for drinking, cooking and making baby formula.

Remember, boiling water does not remove lead from water.

• Before drinking, flush your home's pipes by running the tap, taking a shower, doing laundry, or doing a load of dishes.

• Regularly clean your faucet's screen (also known as an aerator).

• If you use a filter certified to remove lead, don't forget to read the directions to learn when to change the cartridge. Using a filter after it has expired can make it less effective at removing lead. Contact your water company to determine if the pipe that connects your home to the water main (called a service line) is made from lead. Your area's water company can also provide information about the lead levels in your system's drinking water.

Other Sources of Lead

•Lead smelters or other industries that release lead into the air.

• Your job. If you work with lead, you could bring it home on your body or clothes. Shower and change clothes before coming home. Launder your work clothes separately from the rest of your family's clothes.

• Hobbies that use lead, such as making pottery or stained glass, or refinishing furniture. Call your local health department for information about hobbies that may use lead.

• Old toys and furniture may have been painted with lead-containing paint. Older toys and other children's products may have parts that contain lead.

• Food and liquids cooked or stored in lead crystal or lead-glazed pottery or porcelain may contain lead.

• Folk remedies, such as "greta" and "azarcon," used to treat an upset stomach.

Health Effects of Lead

Lead affects the body in many ways. It is important to know that even exposure to low levels of lead can severely harm children.

In children, exposure to lead can cause:

• Nervous system and kidney damage
• Learning disabilities, attention-deficit disorder, and decreased intelligence
• Speech, language, and behavior problems
• Poor muscle coordination
• Decreased muscle and bone growth
• Hearing damage

While low-lead exposure is most common, exposure to high amounts of lead can have devastating effects on children, including seizures, unconsciousness, and in some cases, death. Although children are especially susceptible to lead exposure, lead can be dangerous for adults, too.

In adults, exposure to lead can cause:

• Harm to a developing fetus
• Increased chance of high blood pressure during pregnancy
• Fertility problems (in men and women)
• High blood pressure
• Digestive problems
• Nerve disorders
• Memory and concentration problems
• Muscle and joint pain

Renovating, Repairing or Painting a Home with Lead-Based Paint

If you hire a contractor to conduct renovation, repair, or painting (RRP) projects in your pre-1978 home or childcare facility (such as pre-school and kindergarten), your contractor must:

• Be a Lead-Safe Certified firm approved by EPA or an EPA-authorized state program
• Use qualified trained individuals (Lead-Safe Certified renovators) who follow specific lead-safe work practices to prevent lead contamination
• Provide a copy of EPA's lead hazard information document, The Lead-Safe Certified Guide to Renovate Right RRP contractors working in pre-1978 homes and childcare facilities must follow lead-safe work practices that:
• Contain the work area. The area must be contained so that dust and debris do not escape from the work area. Warning signs must be put up, and plastic or other impermeable material and tape must be used.
• Avoid renovation methods that generate large amounts of lead-contaminated dust.

Some methods generate so much lead contaminated dust that their use is prohibited.

They are:
• Open-flame burning or torching
• Sanding, grinding, planning, needle gunning, or blasting with power tools and equipment not equipped with a shroud and HEPA vacuum attachment
• Using a heat gun at temperatures greater than 1100°F
• Clean up thoroughly.

The work area should be cleaned up daily.

When all the work is done, the area must be cleaned up using special cleaning methods.
• Dispose of waste properly. Collect and seal waste in a heavy-duty bag or sheeting.
When transported, ensure that waste is contained to prevent release of dust and debris.

Where Lead-Based Paint Is Found
In general, the older your home or childcare facility, the more likely it has lead-based paint.
Many homes, including private, federally-assisted, federally owned housing, and childcare facilities built before 1978 have lead-based paint. In 1978, the federal government banned consumer uses of lead-containing paint.

Learn how to determine if paint is lead-based:
In homes and childcare facilities in the city, country, or suburbs,
• In private and public single-family homes and apartments,
• On surfaces, inside and outside of the house, and
• In soil around a home. (Soil can pick up lead from exterior paint or other sources, such as past use of leaded gas in cars.)

Identifying Lead-Based Paint and Lead-Based Paint Hazards
Deteriorating lead-based paint (peeling, chipping, chalking, cracking, or damaged paint) is a hazard and needs immediate attention.

Lead-based paint may also be a hazard when found on surfaces that children can chew or that get a lot of wear and tear, such as:
• On windows and window sills
• Doors and door frames
• Stairs, railings, banisters, and porches

Lead-based paint is usually not a hazard if it is in good condition and if it is not on an impact or friction surface like a window.
Lead dust can form when lead-based paint is scraped, sanded, or heated.
Lead dust also forms when painted surfaces containing lead bump or rub together.
Lead paint chips and dust can get on surfaces and objects that people touch.
Settled lead dust can reenter the air when the home is vacuumed or swept, or when people walk through it.

EPA currently defines the following levels of lead in dust as hazardous:
• 40 micrograms per square foot ($\mu g/ft^2$) and higher for floors, including carpeted floors
• 250 $\mu g/ft^2$ and higher for interior window sills Lead in soil can be a hazard when children play in bare soil or when people bring soil into the house on their shoes. EPA currently defines the following levels of lead in soil as hazardous:
• 400 parts per million (ppm) and higher in play areas of bare soil
• 1,200 ppm (average) and higher in bare soil in the remainder of the yard Remember, lead from paint chips—which you can see—and lead dust—which you may not be able to see—both can be hazards.
The only way to find out if paint, dust, or soil lead hazards exist is to test for them.

Reducing Lead Hazards
Disturbing lead-based paint or removing lead improperly can increase the hazard to your family by spreading even more lead dust around the house.
• In addition to day-to-day cleaning and good nutrition, you can temporarily reduce lead-based paint hazards by taking actions, such as repairing damaged painted surfaces and planting grass to cover lead contaminated soil. These actions are not permanent solutions and will need ongoing attention.
• You can minimize exposure to lead when renovating, repairing, or painting by hiring an EPA- or state certified renovator who is trained in the use of lead-safe work practices. If you are a do-it-yourselfer, learn how to use lead–safe work practices in your home.
• To remove lead hazards permanently, you should hire a certified lead abatement contractor. Abatement (or permanent hazard elimination) methods include removing, sealing, or enclosing lead-based paint with special materials. Just painting over the hazard with regular paint is not permanent control. Always use a certified contractor who is trained to address lead hazards safely.

• Hire a Lead-Safe Certified firm to perform renovation, repair, or painting (RRP) projects that disturb painted surfaces.
• To correct lead hazards permanently, hire a certified lead abatement professional. This will ensure your contractor knows how to work safely and has the proper equipment to clean up thoroughly. Certified contractors will employ qualified workers and follow strict safety rules as set by their state or by the federal government.

Checking Your Home for Lead

You can get your home tested for lead in several different ways:
• A lead-based paint inspection tells you if your home has lead based paint and where it is located. It won't tell you whether your home currently has lead hazards. A trained and certified testing professional, called a lead-based paint inspector, will conduct a paint inspection using methods, such as:
• Portable x-ray fluorescence (XRF) machine
• Lab tests of paint samples
• A risk assessment tells you if your home currently has any lead hazards from lead in paint, dust, or soil. It also tells you what actions to take to address any hazards. A trained and certified testing professional, called a risk assessor, will:
• Sample paint that is deteriorated on doors, windows, floors, stairs, and walls
• Sample dust near painted surfaces and sample bare soil in the yard
• Get lab tests of paint, dust, and soil samples
• A combination inspection and risk assessment tells you if your home has any lead-based paint and if your home has any lead hazards, and where both are located.
Be sure to read the report provided to you after your inspection or risk assessment is completed, and ask questions about anything you do not understand.

In preparing for renovation, repair, or painting work in a pre-1978 home, Lead-Safe Certified renovators may:

• Take paint chip samples to determine if lead-based paint is present in the area planned for renovation and send them to an EPA-recognized lead lab for analysis. In housing receiving federal assistance, the person collecting these samples must be a certified lead-based paint inspector or risk assessor
• Use EPA-recognized tests kits to determine if lead-based paint is absent (but not in housing receiving federal assistance)
• Presume that lead-based paint is present and use lead-safe work practices
There are state and federal programs in place to ensure that testing is done safely, reliably, and effectively.

What You Can Do Now to Protect Your Family

If you suspect that your house has lead-based paint hazards, you can take some immediate steps to reduce your family's risk:
• If you rent, notify your landlord of peeling or chipping paint.
• Keep painted surfaces clean and free of dust. Clean floors, window frames, window sills, and other surfaces weekly. Use a mop or sponge with warm water and a general all-purpose cleaner. (Remember: never mix ammonia and bleach products together because they can form a dangerous gas.)
• Carefully clean up paint chips immediately without creating dust.
• Thoroughly rinse sponges and mop heads often during cleaning of dirty or dusty areas, and again afterward.
• Wash your hands and your children's hands often, especially before they eat and before nap time and bed time.
• Keep play areas clean. Wash bottles, pacifiers, toys, and stuffed animals regularly.
• Keep children from chewing window sills or other painted surfaces, or eating soil.
• When renovating, repairing, or painting, hire only EPA- or state approved Lead-Safe Certified renovation firms (see page 12).
• Clean or remove shoes before entering your home to avoid tracking in lead from soil.
• Make sure children eat nutritious, low-fat meals high in iron, and calcium, such as spinach and dairy products.
Children with good diets absorb less lead.

For the Property Owner – What is Required?

Before ratification of a contract for housing sale or lease, sellers and landlords must:
Give an EPA-approved information pamphlet on identifying and controlling lead-based paint hazards ("Protect Your Family From Lead In Your Home" pamphlet, currently available in English, Spanish, Vietnamese, Russian, Arabic, Somali).

Disclose any known information concerning lead-based paint or lead-based paint hazards. The seller or landlord must also disclose information such as the location of the lead-based paint and/or lead-based paint hazards, and the condition of the painted surfaces.

Provide any records and reports on lead-based paint and/or lead-based paint hazards which are available to the seller or landlord (for multi-unit buildings, this requirement includes records and reports concerning common areas and other units, when such information was obtained as a result of a building-wide evaluation).

Include an attachment to the contract or lease (or language inserted in the lease itself) which includes a Lead Warning Statement and confirms that the seller or landlord has complied with all notification requirements. This attachment is to be provided in the same language used in the rest of the contract. Sellers or landlords, and agents, as well as homebuyers or tenants, must sign and date the attachment.

Sellers must provide homebuyers a **10-day period** to conduct a paint inspection or risk assessment for lead-based paint or lead-based paint hazards. Parties may mutually agree, in writing, to lengthen or shorten the time period for inspection. Homebuyers may waive this inspection opportunity.

Types of Housing Covered?
Most private housing, public housing, Federally owned housing, and housing receiving Federal assistance are affected by this rule.

TYPE OF HOUSING NOT COVERED !
! Housing built after 1977 (Congress chose not to cover post-1977 housing because the CPSC banned the use of lead-based paint for residential use in 1978).
! Zero-bedroom units, such as efficiencies, lofts, and dormitories.
! Leases for less than 100 days, such as vacation houses or short-term rentals.
! Housing for the elderly (unless children live there).
! Housing for the handicapped (unless children live there)
! Rental housing that has been inspected by a certified inspector and found to be free of lead-based paint.
! Foreclosure sales.

Effective Dates
The regulations became effective on September 6, 1996 for transactions involving owners of more than 4 residential dwellings and on December 6, 1996 for transactions involving owners of 1 to 4 residential dwellings.

Recordkeeping
Sellers and lessors must retain a copy of the disclosures for no less than **three years** from the date of sale or the date the leasing period begins.

SELLER/LANDLORD DISCLOSURE

Material Facts and Defect Disclosure
Licensee has a duty to disclose any adverse material fact about the physical condition of the property

Full seller disclosure
Sellers must disclose everything even if not asked.

Megan's Law

A federal law requiring residence registration of convicted sexual predators, in effect creating a stigmatized property. Real Estate licensees should direct buyers/tenants to the source of such registration lists as opposed to providing the information personally.

Latent Defects
A defect that is not visible or apparent; a hidden defect that would not be discovered in a reasonably thorough inspection of property.

Red Flag Issues
A red flag issue is an indication that a property may have a problem that may require a closer inspection. A Red flag issues could include ceiling stains or odors.

Home warranties
FHA/VA requires it with new construction
-covers material/work for defects for new construction

What is a home warranty?

A home warranty is an annual service contract that covers the repair or replacement of important appliances and systems components that break down over time.

Homeowners Insurance covers things that *might* happen.	Home Warranty covers things that will happen.
Theft	HVAC stops running
Fire damage	Water leaks
Storm damage	Dishwasher stops running
Floods	Toilet overflows

Homeowner's insurance protects your home from things that might happen — like fires, theft or natural disasters.

A home warranty helps protect your budget from the expense of repairing or replacing covered home systems components or appliances when they break down.

What do home warranty plans cover?

Our home warranties cover the parts and components of major home systems and appliances. From HVAC systems to kitchen appliances, our plans help cover damage caused by everyday wear and tear

Home Inspection
Done to find true property condition report. Only for systems, major elements of building

Quiz by Broker Tina Perkins, CDEI, Senior Instructor

1. Who is responsible for completing the Property Condition Disclosure Statement?
   a. The listing agent
   b. The seller
   c. The home inspector
   d. The appraiser

2. All of the following could describe a latent defect except?
   a. A buried gas storage tank
   b. Hidden rotting structural beams
   c. A large crack in the fireplace
   d. Failing copper water pipes in the concrete

3. A seller had a fire in their kitchen one year ago. The burned joists were treated and sealed. Will the seller have to disclose these repairs?
   a. No, since they were repaired.
   b. The seller cannot sell without replacing the joists.
   c. Only if the home inspector discovers them and lists it as a defect in the home inspection.
   d. Yes, known latent defects still must be disclosed.

4. A buyer hired an agent under an exclusive buyer's agency agreement. The buyer client wanted to submit an offer on a house that had been stigmatized by a recent murder-suicide. What is the agent's ethical responsibility to her client?
   a. Not say anything; it doesn't affect the structure of the property.
   b. Remain silent to protect the seller.
   c. Disclose it only if the home inspector finds proof of damage.
   d. Disclose it prior to signing any offer to purchase.

5. Red flag issues are all of the following except?
   a. Huge amounts of dead insects
   b. Mildew smells
   c. A large cracked window
   d. Water damage to hardwood flooring near a kitchen

6. Regarding home inspections, all of the following are correct except?
   a. Home inspections should be conducted by a licensed home inspector.
   b. A detailed report should list safety concern items.
   c. The buyer needs not be present during the inspection process.
   d. The home inspection could be a contingency in the offer to purchase.

7. Which of the following would not be considered a latent defect?
   a. A roof missing several rows of shingles
   b. A fuse junction box rewired without a permit
   c. An improperly installed septic tank
   d. A cracked living room floor under carpet

8. Megan's Law requires which of the following?
   a. The home inspector be licensed.
   b. Lawful disclosure of a stigmatized property
   c. Disclosure of toxic mold
   d. The disclosure of where to find the information on convicted sex offenders in a community.

ANSWERS

151

1. Who is responsible for completing the Property Condition Disclosure Statement?
   The seller

2. All of the following could describe a latent defect except?
   large crack in the fireplace

3. A seller had a fire in their kitchen one year ago. The burned joists were treated and sealed. Will the seller have to disclose these repairs?
   Yes, known latent defects still must be disclosed.

4. A buyer hired an agent under an exclusive buyer's agency agreement. The buyer client wanted to submit an offer on a house that had been stigmatized by a recent murder-suicide. What is the agent's ethical responsibility to her client?
   Disclose it prior to signing any offer to purchase.

5. Red flag issues are all of the following except?
   A large cracked window

6. Regarding home inspections, all of the following are correct except?
   The buyer needs not be present during the inspection process.

7. Which of the following would not be considered a latent defect?
   A roof missing several rows of shingles

8. Megan's Law requires which of the following?
   The disclosure of where to find the information on convicted sex offenders in a community.

Chapter 7

Contracts (Salesperson 17%; Broker 18%)

1. General knowledge of contract law
    1. Requirements for validity
    2. Factors affecting enforceability of contracts
    3. Void, voidable, unenforceable contracts
    4. Rights and obligations of parties to a contract
    5. Executory and executed contracts
    6. Notice, delivery and acceptance of contracts
    7. Breach of contract and remedies for breach
    8. Termination, rescission and cancellation of contracts
    9. Electronic signature and paperless transactions
    10. Bilateral vs. unilateral contracts (option agreements)
2. Contract Clauses, including amendments and addenda
3. Offers/purchase agreements
    1. General requirements
    2. When offer becomes binding
    3. Contingencies
    4. Time is of the essence
4. Counteroffers/multiple offers
    1. Counteroffers
    2. Multiple offers

General Knowledge of Contract Law

Everything in real estate has to be in writing according to the Statute of Frauds

Contract
a voluntary, legally enforceable promise between two competent parties to perform some legal act in exchange for consideration

Covenant
A binding agreement or promise.

Implied Agreement
Shown by actions

Expressed
"Said" or in writing

Requirements for validity

Essential Elements of a Contract
Competent Parties, Mutual Assent (*Meeting of the Minds*), Legal Purpose and Consideration

Mutual Assent or Agreement
An essential element of a contract.

Legal Purpose
An essential element of a valid contract. A contract for an illegal purpose is void.

Consideration
Anything of value that induces one to enter into a contract.

Factors affecting enforceability of contracts

Menace
The threat of duress used to force a party to sign a contract. The injured party may void a contract signed under duress or menace.

Misrepresentation
An untrue statement of material fact that induces a party to act. It may be intentional (fraud) or unintentional. A contract so signed is voidable by the injured party.

Mistake
An error of fact by both parties that may cause a contract to be voidable. Example: A contract's legal description depicts a different lot than the buyer was shown.

Fraud – VOID
Intentional deception or misrepresentation – a material misstatement of fact.

Undue Influence
Strong urging that overwhelms a person so they no longer act of their own accord. Contracts signed as a result of undue influence are voidable.

Void, voidable, unenforceable contracts

Valid Contract
A contract that is enforceable by all parties to the contract in a court of law.

Voidable Contract

A flawed contract in which the innocent party has the power to either void or enforce, but that remains valid unless voided. Example: A minor (not legally competent) may enforce the contract even though the adult party cannot force the minor to perform.

Void
having no legal force or binding effect, not enforceable

Rights and obligations of parties to a contract

Contractual Intent
Inference that both parties are acting in good faith.

Executory and executed contracts

Execute
To sign a document; or to carry out a promised act or contract.

Executed Contract
One that has been fully performed. The closing executes the real estate purchase contract.

Executory Contract
One that has not yet been fully performed. (Example: when you are "under contract" you have an executory contract.)

Notice, delivery and acceptance of contracts

Actual Notice
That truly seen, heard, or read or observed and not presumed. Contrasts with constructive (legal) notice.

Acceptance
Any language or action that indicates an agreement forming a contract has been reached. An offer is just an offer until acceptance.

Acknowledgment
Written declaration by a person who signs a document that he or she is actually who he or she claims to be. Acknowledgements are witnessed by a notary public or other authorized official.

Breach of contract and remedies for breach

Breach of Contract
A violation or default of the terms and/or conditions stated in a contract

Default
Breach or violation of an agreement.

Specific Performance and or Damages
A contract remedy permitting either party to force the other to perform the contract and/or sue for damages. Buy-Sell contracts are often "specific performance" against the seller. Opposite of liquidated damages.

Liquidated Damages
Those damages specified by contract in advance (usually loss of earnest money) if the buyer defaults. If specified, liquidated damages are the seller's only remedy against the buyer.

Exemplary Damages
Damages above and beyond the actual cost of the loss, assessed to punish or set an example for others.

Punitive Damages

Additional charges intended to "punish" above and beyond compensatory damages which are intended to return the parties to their original positions before the contract.

Termination, rescission and cancellation of contracts
- **performance** – all parties fulfilled
- **assignment and delegation** – someone takes over for one party
- **death**
- **impossibility of performance** – not legal
- **mutual agreement** or **Mutual Rescission** – Agreement by both parties to abandon an executory contract.
- **novation** – new contract replaces old one
- **operation of law** – some legal issue cancels contract
- **partial performance** – accept incomplete work as fulfillment
- **substantial performanc**e – most of work is done

Rescind
To take back or annul. Until an offer is accepted and becomes a contract, the offering party may rescind the offer without penalty.

Rescission
Ending of a contract with the return of the parties to their original position.

Revocation
To recall or withdraw; such as withdrawal of an offer prior to acceptance by the offeree, or offeror

Bilateral vs. unilateral contracts (option agreements)

Bilateral Contract
A promise for a promise, e.g. real estate purchase contracts. Buyer promises to buy, seller promises to relinquish title.

Option
A **unilateral contract** in which the optionor (property owner) promises to sell if and when the optionee (prospective buyer) chooses to buy – at a price and before a date set in the option contract

Contract Clauses, including amendments and addenda

Amendment
a minor change in a document.

Addenda
literally "something added," from Latin **addendum**

Hold Harmless Clause
A provision in a contract that protects a party from damage or harm arising from the transaction.

Electronic signature and paperless transactions

The Electronic Signatures in Global and National Commerce Act (E-Sign Act),
Signed into law on June 30, 2000, provides a general rule of validity for electronic records and signatures for transactions in or affecting interstate or foreign commerce.

The E-Sign Act allows the use of electronic records to satisfy any statute, regulation, or rule of law requiring that such information be provided in writing, if the consumer has affirmatively consented to such use and has not withdrawn such consent.

Summary of Major Provisions Consumer Disclosures Prior Consent, Notice of Availability of Paper Records

Prior to obtaining their consent, financial institutions must provide the consumer, a clear and conspicuous statement informing the consumer:

- of any right or option to have the record provided or made available on paper or in a non-electronic form, and the right to withdraw consent, including any conditions, consequences, and fees in the event of such withdrawal;

- whether the consent applies only to the particular transaction that triggered the disclosure or to identified categories of records that may be provided during the course of the parties' relationship;

- describing the procedures, the consumer must use to withdraw consent and to update information needed to contact the consumer electronically; and

- informing the consumer how the consumer may nonetheless request a paper copy of a record and whether any fee will be charged for that copy.

Prior to consenting to the use of an electronic record, a consumer must be provided with a statement of the hardware and software requirements for access to and retention of electronic records.

- If the consumer consents electronically, or confirms his or her consent electronically, it must be in a manner that reasonably demonstrates the consumer can access information in the electronic form that will be used to provide the information that is the subject of the consent.

- If a change in the hardware or software requirements need to access or retain electronic records creates a material risk that the consumer will not be able to access or retain subsequent electronic records subject to the consent, a financial institution must: provide the consumer with a statement of the revised hardware and software requirements for access to and retention of electronic records, and

- the right to withdraw consent without the imposition of any condition, consequence, or fee for such withdrawal; and

- again, comply with the requirements of subparagraph

Oral communications or a recording of an oral communication shall not qualify as an electronic record.

Record Retention

The E-Sign Act requires a financial institution to maintain electronic records accurately reflecting the information contained in applicable contracts, notices or disclosures and that they remain accessible to all persons who are legally entitled to access for the period required by law in a form that is capable of being accurately reproduced for later reference.

If the consumer uses electronic means to open an account or request a service, the disclosures must be provided before the account is opened or the service is requested.
In response to a consumer request, disclosures should be made available in a reasonable amount of time and may be electronic if the consumer agrees.

There are exceptions to the consumer consent requirement for electronically providing certain types of disclosures when the consumer is using electronic means such as a home computer.
Disclosures should be maintained on the website for a reasonable amount of time for consumers to access, view, and retain the disclosures.

Definitions

"Consumer" – The term "consumer" means an individual who obtains, through a transaction, products or services which are used primarily for personal, family, or household purposes, and also means the legal representative of such an individual.

"Electronic" – The term "electronic" means relating to technology having electrical, digital, magnetic, wireless, optical, electromagnetic, or similar capabilities.

"Electronic Agent" – The term "electronic agent" means a computer program or an electronic or other automated means used independently to initiate an action to respond to electronic records or performances in whole or in part without review or action by an individual at the time or the action or response.

"Electronic Record" – The term "electronic record" means a contract or other record created, generated, sent, communicated, received, or stored by electronic means.

"Electronic Signature" – The term "electronic signature" means an electronic sound, symbol, or process, attached to or logically associated with a contract or other record and executed or adopted by a person with the intent to sign the record.

"Federal Regulatory Agency" – The term "Federal regulatory agency" means an agency as that term is defined in section 552(f) of Title 5, United States code.

"Information" – The term "information" means data, text, images, sounds, codes, computer programs, software, databases, or the like.

"Person" – The term "person" means an individual, corporation, business trust, estate, trust, partnership, limited liability company, association, joint venture, governmental agency, public corporation or any other legal or commercial entity.

"Record" – The term "record" means information, that is inscribed on a tangible medium or that is stored in an electronic or other medium and is retrievable in perceivable form.

"Requirement" – The term "requirement" includes a prohibition.

"Self-Regulatory Organization" – The term "self-regulatory organization" means an organization or entity that is not a Federal regulatory agency or a State, but that is under the supervision of a Federal regulatory agency and is authorized under Federal law to adopt and administer rules applicable to its members that are enforced by such organization or entity, by a Federal regulatory agency, or by another self-regulatory organization.

"State" – The term "State" includes the District of Columbia and the territories and possessions of the United States.

"Transaction" – the term "transaction" means an action or set of actions relating to the conduct of business, consumer, or commercial affairs between two or more persons, including any of the following types of conduct:
1. the sale, lease, exchange, licensing, or other disposition of
      (i) personal property, including goods and intangibles,
      (ii) services, and
      (iii) any combination thereof; and
2. the sale, lease, exchange, or other disposition of any interest in real property, or any combination thereof.

Offers/Purchase Agreements

Acknowledgment
Written declaration by a person who signs a document that he or she is actually who he or she claims to be. Acknowledgements are witnessed by a notary public or other authorized official.

General requirements

Essential Elements of a Contract
Competent Parties, Mutual Assent (Meeting of the Minds), Legal Purpose and Consideration

When offer becomes binding

A meeting of the minds.
The parties agree to all provisions of the contract.

Acceptance
- Communication to an offeror that the recipient (offeree) finds the terms and conditions of an offer acceptable. Turns an offer into a binding contract.
- Any language or action that indicates an agreement forming a contract has been reached. *An offer is just an offer until acceptance*.

Contingencies

Contingency
A condition in a contract that requires completion of something before the contract will be binding.

Hold Harmless Clause
A provision in a contract that protects a party from damage or harm arising from the transaction.

Time is of the essence
A contract clause requiring adherence to contract deadlines.

Counteroffers/Multiple Offers

Counteroffers

- Legally, a rejection of the original offer; a new offer. In form, a counter usually states that the first offer is accepted "except for the following changes…" thus incorporating (merging) the first contract.
- Not binding on the buyer (who is now the offeree) until accepted.
- A counter offer voids the original offer.

Multiple offers

An agent should advise the seller to respond to one offer at a time.

QUIZ by Broker Tina Perkins, CDEI, Senior Instructor

1. A contract shown by the actions of the parties would be a/an?
    a. Unilateral
    b. Implied
    c. Bilateral
    d. Executed

2. Of the following, what is not necessary for a contract to be valid?
    a. An earnest money deposit
    b. Consideration
    c. Offer and acceptance (mutual assent)
    d. Legally competent parties

3. When a person that is 17 years of age signs a lease, it is?
    a. Bilateral
    b. Void
    c. An option
    d. Voidable

4. Everything in real estate has to be in writing according to the?
    a. The REALTOR association
    b. The Real Estate Commission
    c. Statute of Frauds
    d. The office policy of the responsible broker

5. A broker presented an offer to her seller. The Seller rejected it. The broker presented a second offer. Prior to the seller accepting or countering the second offer, the buyer calls the agent and rescinds the offer. At this point in time, there is?
    a. An expressed contract
    b. An option
    c. A bilateral contract
    d. No contract

6. On a For Sale By Owner, the owner of the property gives a buyer an option to purchase the property. While the option is in effect, the option is considered?
    a. Void
    b. A unilateral contract
    c. Executed
    d. Illegal

7. What is the duty of a listing agent upon receiving several offers on a property they have listed?
    a. Deliver each offer to the seller immediately upon receipt.
    b. Accept the highest and best offer on behalf of the seller.
    c. Wait 48 hours to ensure all offers are received.

       d.   Suggest that the seller counter each offer at the same time.

8. You order dinner at a fine dining restaurant. What type of 'contract' do you have in reference to your actions?
   a. Bilateral
   b. Void
   c. Express
   d. Implied

e

9. A seller and an agent have an open listing, what type of agreement is this?
   a. Unilateral
   b. Bilateral
   c. Implied
   d. Purchase and lease back

10. Of the following, what constitutes an open listing?
    a. The seller can employ any number of brokers.
    b. It's an open-ended listing without an expiration date.
    c. The first listing broker is guaranteed a commission.
    d. No counter offers will be considered.

11. A contract that has no legal object is considered?
    a. Voidable
    b. Valid
    c. Void
    d. Unilateral

12. Which of the following would not terminate a listing with a broker?
    a. Bankruptcy of the principal
    b. Death of the broker
    c. Insanity of the broker
    d. A sharp rise in the interest rate

ANSWERS

1. A contract shown by the actions of the parties would be a/an?
   Implied

2. Of the following, what is not necessary for a contract to be valid?
   An earnest money deposit

3. When a person that is 17 years of age signs a lease, it is?
   Voidable

4. Everything in real estate has to be in writing according to the?
   Statute of Frauds

5. A broker presented an offer to her seller. The Seller rejected it. The broker presented a second offer. Prior to the seller accepting or countering the second offer, the buyer calls the agent and rescinds the offer. At this point in time, there is?
   No contract

6. On a For Sale By Owner, the owner of the property gives a buyer an option to purchase the property. While the option is in effect, the option is considered?
   A unilateral contract

7. What is the duty of a listing agent upon receiving several offers on a property they have listed?

Deliver each offer to the seller immediately upon receipt.

8. You order dinner at a fine dining restaurant. What type of 'contract' do you have in reference to your actions?
   Implied

e

9. A seller and an agent have an open listing, what type of agreement is this?
   Unilateral

10. Of the following, what constitutes an open listing?
    The seller can employ any number of brokers.

11. A contract that has no legal object is considered?
    Void

12. Which of the following would not terminate a listing with a broker?
    A sharp rise in the interest rate

Chapter 8

Leasing and Property Management (Salesperson 3%; Broker 5%)

A. Basic concepts/duties of property management

B. Lease Agreements
      1. Types of leases, e.g., percentage, gross, net, ground
      2. Key elements and provisions of lease agreements

C. Landlord and tenant rights and obligations

D. Property manager's fiduciary responsibilities

E. ADA and Fair Housing compliance in property management

F. Setting rents and lease rates (BROKER ONLY)

Basic Concepts/Duties of Property Management

A property manager is a GENERAL AGENT

Owner's interest: Leased Fee
Renter's interest: Lease Hold

Owner: Lessor
Renter: Leasee / Lessee.

The landlord/owner has a reversionary right when there is a lease. (leased fee estate with reversionary rights)

The firm or individual who supervises the operation of another person's or entity's real estate is called a property manager.

The **property manager**, establishes an agency relationship with the property owner by the brokerage engagement commonly known as a management agreement.

As an agent, the property manager has a fiduciary responsibility to the owner of the property and must abide by all the requirements of license law including depositing all funds collected on behalf of the owner or principal into a designated and registered trust account.

Owners pay property managers a fee or a percentage of the rent generated by a property while under a management agreement.

Property managers help owners create budgets, advertise rental properties, qualify tenants, collect rent, comply with local landlord-tenant laws, maintain properties, oversee preventative maintenance, cleaning and construction.

A property manager's primary function is to maximize the financial return that the owner will receive from the property over its economic life so that the owner can obtain the desired rate of return from that property. To obtain the highest return from the property, the property manager undertakes or supervises a variety of activities.

By John A. Yoegel

The duties of a property manager for the purposes of the Real Estate License Exam generally are defined as maximizing income and maintaining or increasing the overall value of the property being managed.

FINANCIAL RESPONSIBILITIES
Some of a property manager's duties include the following responsibilities:
- Creating an annual operating budget: This task includes analyzing the building's income and expenses over time. The manager also examines ways to reduce building expenses.
- Collecting rents: A manager usually creates some system of collecting and accounting for rents.
- Setting rents: The manager examines the rents and vacancy rates for competing buildings in the area and either sets rental rates or recommends rates to the owner.
- Paying bills: A manager is typically responsible for paying bills for operating expenses and repairs and maintenance.
- Preparing periodic financial reports: These reports relate to the building's financial condition and its income and expenses.

PHYSICAL RESPONSIBILITIES
The building manager also is responsible for properly maintaining the property's value, its physical condition, and the physical condition of its buildings. These duties include the following:
- Physical analysis of the building: The property manager analyzes the building with a view toward immediate and long-term repairs and improvements that might be made to enhance the desirability of the building and allow for higher rents.

- Preparation of capital and repairs budgets: Using the property analysis as a basis, the property manager creates a capital budget that includes larger improvements and repairs to the building. Capital budget items typically include the replacement of major fixtures, such as roofs, boilers, and air-conditioning units, while repair budget items deal more with making repairs and maintaining those same fixtures.
- Maintenance: Part of the manager's responsibilities is arranging for routine cleaning and maintenance of the building and grounds, including scheduling janitorial services, preventive maintenance, and needed repairs on equipment like the boiler.

RENTAL RESPONSIBILITIES

A manager usually is responsible for renting the space in a building. However, sometimes an owner takes care of this task directly or hires a real estate agent other than the manager to find tenants and negotiate leases.

- Advertising for tenants is another rental responsibility. "For rent" signs on the building and print ads in appropriate media, such as newspapers for apartments and specialized publications for office or industrial space, can be useful. Billboard, direct mail, and Internet advertising may be used. Radio and TV ads usually are less effective but may prove useful in some markets.
- Recommendations by satisfied tenants can be effective advertising for a building.
- The manager is also responsible for providing necessary services to the tenants as agreed to in the lease, for trying to settle any disputes that may arise with tenants, and for engaging in eviction activities if necessary.

INSURANCE RESPONSIBILITIES

Property managers sometimes analyze the insurance needs of a building they manage or call in insurance experts to do it. Unlike a single-family house, which usually has a single insurance policy that covers a number of things, large complex buildings may require different types of insurance policies to cover specific items. Proper insurance coverage is part of an overall *risk management plan* that a property manager needs to consider.

In general, managing risk, or in some way dealing with potential liability issues, can be handled by a system known as
CART
controlling
avoiding
retaining
transferring risk

Controlling risk means anticipating it and preparing for it.
Avoiding risk means removing the source of danger.
Retaining risk means accepting the liability.
Transferring risk means buying the appropriate type and amount of insurance to cover the payment whenever an insured incident occurs.

The following are types of insurance that are available to cover different types of risks:

Boiler and machinery insurance: Because of the substantial cost of heating units and air-conditioning systems in large buildings, a separate type of insurance is needed to cover the replacement and repair of this type of machinery.

Casualty insurance: This type of insurance covers losses caused by theft, vandalism, and burglary.

Co-insurance: This coverage essentially is for situations in which the owner takes on part of the risk by self-insuring for a portion of the risk. Incorporating a large deductible before the insurance policy starts to pay off is one example.

Errors and omissions insurance: This type of insurance can cover property managers against any errors they make in the performance of their duties. This insurance doesn't cover losses caused by fraud or other dishonest or malfeasant activities.

Fire and hazard insurance: Depending on what it covers, this type of policy sometimes is called an all-risk, all-peril policy. It basically covers loss of the property caused by fire, storms, and other types of damaging conditions. This type of policy usually does not cover flooding and earthquake damage.

Liability insurance: This type of insurance covers losses caused by injuries that are the result of negligence on the part of the landlord. The classic case is the person who falls on an icy sidewalk that the landlord was supposed to have cleaned.

Rent loss insurance: This insurance sometimes is called business interruption insurance or consequential loss insurance. It pays the owner of the building for the loss of rent from tenants if the building is destroyed by fire.

Surety bond: Technically a surety bond provides payment whenever something is not done within an agreed-upon period of time. However, the coverage provided by surety bonds has come to mean making up for losses caused by dishonest acts of an employee.

Lease Agreements

Types of leases, e.g., percentage, gross, net, ground...

Percentage Lease
Percentage lease is a commercial lease in which the rental amount is computed as a certain percentage of the monthly or annual gross sales generated at leased property. In a percentage lease, the tenant pays a base rent plus a percentage of any revenue earned while doing business on the rental premises. This type of lease is more common in commercial real estate markets where there is a charge for rent, operating expenses, maintenance of common areas, and even a share of the gross revenues generated.

Gross Lease
A type of commercial lease where the tenant pays a flat rental amount, and the landlord pays for all property charges regularly incurred by the ownership, including taxes, utilities and water. Most apartment leases resemble gross leases.

Net Lease
A net lease requires the tenant to pay, in addition to rent, some or all of the property expenses that normally would be paid by the property owner.
These include expenses such as property taxes, insurance, maintenance, repair, and operations, utilities, and other items.

- **NNN Lease / Triple Net Lease**

These expenses are often categorized into the "three nets":
1. property taxes
2. insurance
3. maintenance/utilities

NNN Lease, or triple-N for short and sometimes written NNN.

- **Double Net Lease**

A double net lease is a lease agreement in which the tenant is responsible for both:
1. property taxes
2. insurance

- **Single Net Lease**

Only requires the tenant to pay:
1. property taxes

Ground Lease
A ground lease is an agreement in which a tenant is permitted to develop a piece of property during the lease period, after which the land and all improvements are turned over to the property owner. A ground lease indicates that the improvements will be owned by the property owner unless an exception is created and stipulates that all relevant taxes incurred during the lease period will be paid by the tenant.

A ground lease involves leasing land, typically for 50 to 99 years, to a tenant who constructs a building on the property. The ground lease defines who owns the land and who owns the building and improvements on the property.

Ground leases usually require the tenant to pay all property expenses, such as taxes, utilities, and maintenance. In this respect, a ground or land lease is similar to a net lease.

Key elements and provisions of lease agreements

Names and addresses of landlord and tenants.
The tenant may be referred to as the "lessee" and the landlord as the "lessor." They may also be called the "parties" to the agreement, and these are the people who will sign the lease or rental agreement (along with a cosigner, if any).

Rental property address and details.

The property address is often called "the premises." Your lease or rental agreement may also include details on any furnishings, parking space, storage areas, or other extras that come with the rental property.

Term of the tenancy.
The term is the length of the rental. The document should include the beginning date and whether it's a month-to-month tenancy or a lease. If it's a lease, the ending date should also be specified. Leases often have a term of one year.

Rent. Leases and rental agreements usually specify the amount of rent due each month, when and where it's due, acceptable forms of payment, and late fees. Except in areas of rent control, there's no limit on how much rent a landlord can charge. The more popular the area, the more you can expect to pay. However, it's not legal for a landlord to quote a higher rent based on a tenant's race, sex or other group characteristic.

Deposits and fees.
Expect to see details on the dollar amount of a security deposit, cleaning deposit, or last month's rent.

Utilities.
The landlord should state who pays for what utilities. Normally, landlords pay for garbage and sometimes for water, if there is a yard. Tenants usually pay for other services, such as Internet, gas, and electricity.

Condition of the rental unit.
Most leases and rental agreements include a clause in which the tenant agrees that the premises are in habitable (livable) condition and promises to alert the landlord to any defective or dangerous condition.

Tenant's repair and maintenance responsibilities.
A carefully written lease or rental agreement will include a statement that makes the tenant responsible for keeping the rental premises clean and in good condition and obligates you to reimburse the landlord for the cost of repairing damage caused by your abuse or neglect. Some agreements go further and spell out specific tenant responsibilities, such as fixing clogged drains or broken windows. Many leases and rental agreements also tell tenants what they can't do in the way of repairs—such as painting walls or adding built-in bookshelves without the landlord's permission.

When and how landlords may enter the rental unit.
Many state access laws specify when landlords may legally enter rented premises—for example, to deal with an emergency or make repairs—and the amount of notice required. Some landlords include this information in the lease or rental agreement. Others are ignorant of these laws and write entry provisions that are illegal.

Extended absences.
Some leases and rental agreements require a tenant to notify the landlord in advance if you will be away from the premises for a certain number of consecutive days (often seven or more). Such clauses may give the landlord the right to enter the rental unit during your absence to maintain the property as necessary and to inspect for damage and needed repairs. You'll most often see this type of clause if you live in a cold-weather place where, in case of extremely cold temperatures, landlords want to drain the pipes to guard against breakage.

Limits on tenant behavior.
Most form leases and rental agreements contain a clause forbidding tenants from using the premises or adjacent areas, such as the sidewalk in front of the building, in such a way as to violate any law or ordinance, including laws prohibiting the use, possession, or sale of illegal drugs. These clauses also prohibit tenants from intentionally damaging the property or creating a nuisance by annoying or disturbing other tenants or nearby residents—for example, by continuously making loud noise. Leases and rental agreements may prohibit smoking, in individual units as well as in common areas.

Restrictions on number of occupants.

Most landlords will set a limit to the number of people who can live in each rental unit. Landlords are not free to set unreasonably low figures (for example, two people for a two-bedroom flat) in order to maintain a "quiet atmosphere" or to reduce wear and tear. Federal law requires landlords to allow two persons per bedroom unless the landlord can point to legitimate business reasons that justify a lower number (this is difficult to do).

Restrictions on use of the property.
Landlords may throw in all kinds of language limiting tenant use of the rental property and who may stay there. These may be minor (for example, no waterbeds, plants on wood floors, or bikes in the hallway) or quite annoying. These may be in a separate set of rules and regulations or individual clauses. Basically, landlords can set any kind of restriction they want—as long as it's not discriminatory or retaliatory or otherwise violates your state law.

No pets.
Landlords have the right to prohibit all pets, or to restrict the types allowed—for example, forbidding dogs or cats, but allowing birds. However, landlords may not prohibit "service" or "comfort" animals used by physically or mentally disabled people, as provided by the fair housing laws. Many landlords spell out pet rules—for example, that the tenants will keep the yard free of all animal waste or that dogs will always be on leash.

No home businesses.
Landlords may prohibit tenants from running a business from your home, by including a clause specifying that the premises are "for residential purposes only." The concern here is generally about increased traffic and liability exposure if one of your customers or business associates is hurt on the premises. Obviously, working at home on your computer is not likely to bother your landlord, and may not even be noticed

No assignments or sublets without landlord permission.
Most careful landlords will not let tenants turn their rental over to another tenant (called "assignment"), let someone live there for a limited time while you're away (called a "sublet"), or let you rent an extra bedroom to another occupant, with you as the "landlord" (also called a sublet), without their written consent. Lease clauses often specifically prohibit tenants from renting rooms on Airbnb or similar short-term rental services.

Limits on guest stays.
It's common for landlords to limit overnight guests, such as allowing a guest for no more than ten days in any six-month period, with written approval required for longer stays. Landlords do this to keep long-term guests from gaining the status of full-fledged tenants who have not been screened or approved and who have not signed the lease or rental agreement.

Attorney fees and court costs in a lawsuit.
Many leases and rental agreements specify who will pay the costs of a lawsuit if you go to court over the meaning or implementation of a part of your rental agreement or lease—for example, a dispute about rent or security deposits. These clauses do not apply to legal disputes that arise independently of the lease or rental agreement—for example, lawsuits over alleged discrimination.

Grounds for termination of tenancy.
You'll often see a general clause stating that any violation of the lease or rental agreement by you, or by your guests, is grounds for terminating the tenancy according to the procedures established by state or local laws. Rules for terminating a tenancy differ depending on whether or not you sign a lease or rental agreement, and vary by state (and, in some cases, by city, if the property is under some form of rent control).

Forcible entry and detainer
A summary proceeding for restoring to possession of land one who is wrongfully kept out or has been wrongfully deprived of the possession.

Subletting

The leasing of premises by a lessee to a third party for part of the lessee's remaining TIME

Tenement
Everything that may be occupied under a lease by a tenant.

Termination (lease)
The cancellation of a lease by the action of either party. A lease may be terminated by expiration of the term, surrender and acceptance, constructive eviction by lessor, or option, when provided in the lease for breach of covenants.

*open sourced

Landlord and Tenant Rights and Obligations

The Uniform Residential Landlord and Tenant Act, also known as URLTA, is a law governing residential landlord and tenant interactions

Many states have adopted all or part of this Act.

he Uniform Residential Landlord and Tenant Act (URLTA) is a federal law enacted in 1972 to govern residential landlord and tenant interactions.

The Act is not designed for commercial, industrial or agricultural rental agreements.
T
he Act accords the tenants previously unrecognized rights by recognizing the contractual nature of the landlord-tenant relationship. The Uniform Residential Landlord and Tenant makes the communications and business between the landlord and the tenant fair to all parties involved.

The URLTA does not favor any party.
The URLTA comprises of six articles. Each article discusses a separate issue in regards to the relationship between a landlord and tenant.

General Provisions and Definitions
Article II: Landlord Obligations
Article III: Tenant Obligations
Article IV: Remedies
Article V: Retaliatory Conduct
Article VI: Effective Date and Repealer

The purposes of the URLTA are:
(1) to simplify, clarify, modernize, and revise the law governing the rental of dwelling units and the rights and obligations of landlords and tenants;
(2) to encourage landlords and tenants to maintain and improve the quality of housing; and
(3) to make uniform the law among those states which adopt the Act.

Many state have adopted the National Law
For an example. Here is the
Mississippi Residential Landlord and Tenant Act

The "Residential Landlord and Tenant Act" outlines the rights, obligations, and remedies in Mississippi under any rental agreement.

The provisions of this Act apply only to traditional residential "lease" situations—not to condominiums, cooperatives, or land leased for agricultural purposes.

The exercise of any right or remedy under this Act is obligated to be done with good faith, honest belief, and fair dealing.

A landlord may at times adopt rules concerning tenant's use and occupancy of the premises.

They are enforceable against the tenant only if:
Their purpose is to promote the convenience, safety, or welfare of the tenants in the premises, preserve the landlord's property from abuse, or make a fair distribution of services and facilities provided for the tenants. Generally, they are reasonably related to the purpose for which they are adopted; they apply to all tenants in the premises in a fair manner; they are sufficiently explicit in their prohibition, direction, or limitation of the tenant's conduct to fairly inform him of what he must or must not do to comply; and they are not for the purpose of evading the obligations of the landlord. A regulation adopted or amended after the tenant enters into the rental agreement is enforceable against the tenant if reasonable notice of its adoption or amendment is given to the tenant and it does not work a substantial

modification of the rental agreement. Unless otherwise agreed, the tenant shall occupy his dwelling unit only as a dwelling unit.

If a party (whether landlord or tenant) makes a material breach of the lease (or fails to fulfill his duties as a landlord or tenant as outlined by law), the non-breaching party may end the tenancy or resort to any other legal remedy.

FOR THE LEASEHOLDER

You may deliver a written notice to the landlord specifying the acts and omissions constituting the breach and that the rental agreement will terminate upon a date not less than 30 days after receipt of the notice *if the breach is not remedied within a reasonable time* not in excess of 30 days.

*If the tenant's material breach is nonpayment of rent pursuant to the lease, the landlord is not required to deliver 30 days written notice.

The lease shall terminate and the tenant shall surrender possession as provided in the notice.

If the breach is remediable by repairs or the payment of damages and the breaching party adequately remedies the breach prior to the date specified in the notice, the rental agreement shall not terminate.

If the same breach (of which written notice was given) occurs within 6 months of that initial notice, the no breaching party may terminate the lease upon at least 14 days written notice specifying the breach and the date of termination of the lease.

Neither party may end the tenancy for a condition caused by his own deliberate or negligent breach.

If the lease is terminated, the landlord shall return all prepaid and unearned rent and security deposit by the tenant.

If, after 30 days of receipt of written notice, the landlord fails to repair a defect constituting a material breach of lease or duty, you may repair such defect yourself, and shall be entitled to reimbursement of the repair costs within 45 days after submission to the landlord of receipted bills for such work, *provided you have fulfilled your duties as a tenant.*

The repair costs cannot exceed an amount equal to one month's rent; you cannot have exercised this remedy within the preceding six (6) months; and you must be current in your rental payments.

You are not entitled to reimbursement for repair costs higher than the customary charge for such repairs. A tenant's repair costs may be offset against future rent.

At any time after expiration of the lease, a landlord may:
1) recover possession of the dwelling unit;
2) make the tenant involuntarily leave;
3) demand an increase in rent; or
4) decrease services to tenant (if not done in retaliation to tenant's prior written notice of material breach).

Unless the lease fixes a definite term, the length of tenancy shall be week to week (if a tenant pays weekly rent) and in all other cases, month to month.

A month-to-month tenancy requires written notice from either the landlord or tenant given at least 30 days prior to the termination date.

Notice to terminate tenancy is not required when either party commits a substantial breach of lease or duty that materially affects health and safety.

Any payment or deposit of money, the primary function of which is to secure the performance of a rental agreement or any part of such an agreement, other than a payment or deposit, including an advance payment of rent, made to secure the execution of a rental agreement.

The landlord for the tenant who is a party to such agreement shall hold any such payment or deposit of money. The claim of a tenant to such payment or deposit shall be prior to the claim of any creditor of the landlord.

The landlord, by written notice delivered to the tenant, may claim of such payment or deposit only such amounts as are *reasonably necessary to remedy the tenant's defaults* in the:

- payment of rent,
- to repair damages to the premises caused by the tenant,
- exclusive of ordinary wear and tear,
- to clean such premises upon termination of the tenancy, or
- for other reasonable and necessary expenses incurred as the result of the tenant's default,
- if the payment or deposit is made for any or all of those specific purposes.

The written notice by which the landlord claims all or any portion of such payment or deposit shall itemize the amounts claimed by such landlord.

Any remaining portion of such payment or deposit shall be returned to the tenant no later than forty-five (45) days after the termination of his tenancy, the delivery of possession and demand by the tenant.

The retention by a landlord or transferee of a payment or deposit or any portion thereof, in violation of this section and with absence of good faith, may subject the landlord or his transferee to damages not to exceed Two Hundred Dollars ($200.00) in addition to any actual damages.

A landlord shall at all times during the tenancy comply with the requirements of applicable building and housing codes materially affecting health and safety.

They shall also maintain the dwelling unit, its plumbing, heating and/or cooling system, in substantially the same condition as at the inception of the lease, reasonable wear and tear excluded, *unless the dwelling unit, its plumbing, heating and/or cooling system is damaged or impaired as a result of the deliberate or negligent actions of the tenant.*

The landlord and tenant may agree in writing that the tenant perform some or all of the landlord's duties under this section, but only if the transaction is entered into in good faith.

No duty on the part of the landlord shall arise in connection with a defect, which is caused, by the tenant's affirmative act or failure to comply with his obligations.

A tenant shall keep that part of the premises that he occupies and uses as clean and as safe as the condition of the premises permits;

Dispose from his dwelling unit all ashes, rubbish, garbage and other waste in a clean and safe manner in compliance with community standards;

Keep all plumbing fixtures in the dwelling unit used by the tenant as clean as their condition permits;

Use in a reasonable manner all electrical, plumbing, sanitary, heating, ventilating, air conditioning and other facilities and appliances, including elevators, in the premises;

Not deliberately or negligently destroy, deface, damage, impair or remove any part of the premises or knowingly permit any other person to do so;

Conduct himself and require other persons on the premises with his consent to conduct themselves in a manner that will not disturb his neighbors' peaceful enjoyment of their premises;

Inform the landlord of any condition of which he has actual knowledge which may cause damage to the premises;

To the extent of his legal obligation, maintain the dwelling unit in substantially the same condition, reasonable wear and tear excepted, and comply with the requirements of applicable building and housing codes materially affecting health and safety; and

Not engage in any illegal activity upon the leased premises as documented by a law enforcement agency.

Every duty and every act which must be performed as a condition precedent to the exercise of a right or remedy under this chapter, including the landlord's termination of a tenancy or nonrenewable of a lease, imposes an obligation of *good faith* in its performance or enforcement.

Actual eviction is the physical expulsion of a person from land or rental property. It is the physical ouster of a tenant from the leased premises. After actual eviction, the tenant is relieved of any further duty to pay rent. Actual eviction is the physical dispossession of a tenant.

Constructive eviction is a term used in the law of real property to describe a circumstance in which a landlord either does something or fails to do something that he or she has a legal duty to provide, rendering the property uninhabitable.

To maintain an action for damages, the tenant must show that:
the uninhabitable conditions (substantial interferences) were a result of the landlord's actions (not the actions of some third party) and
that the tenant vacated the premises in a reasonable time.

A tenant who suffers from a constructive eviction can claim all of the legal remedies available to a tenant who was actually told to leave.

A tenant who is constructively evicted may terminate the lease and seek damages.

Property Manager's Fiduciary Responsibilities

Common Fiduciary Duties Owed by Property Managers

Since a property manager is a fiduciary they must act with the highest good-faith and fair dealing with respect to the owner's asset and disclose all material information that may affect the owner's decision-making with respect to that asset.

The owner is due:
- Confidentiality
- Obedience
- Loyalty
- Disclosure
- Accountability
- Care

Common sense duties when a fiduciary relationship exists between a manager and an owner.
A property manager is required to disclose any and all rental offers received along with documentation of those offers such that the property owner is well informed about all potential tenants.

A property manager is statutorily required to act for the sole benefit of the asset owner in matters that evolve from the relationship, whether or not those matters are seemingly insignificant or they are significantly material.

Information about a tenant whom falls behind on their rent must be immediately communicated to the asset owner.

If a manager receives information that a tenant has caused damage to a property the owner should be notified as soon as feasibly possible.

THE PROPERTY MANAGEMENT CONTRACT

The property management agreement is a formal, legal contract defining the relationship between the owner and the manager for a specific property. The contract creates the manager's legal authority for the operation of that property and relies on the basic principles of contract law. In summary, the management contract must have an offer and acceptance, consideration, reality of consent, legality of object, and competent parties.

NATIONAL ASSOCIATION OF RESIDENTIAL PROPERTY MANAGERS
CODE OF ETHICS

The National Association of Residential Property Managers (NARPM) promotes a high standard of business ethics, professionalism, and fair housing practices. NARPM's members subscribe to the following Code of Ethics for property managers of single family and other small residential properties.

Article 1. DUTY TO PROTECT THE PUBLIC – It is the duty of the Property Manager to protect the public against fraud, misrepresentation, and unethical practices in property management.

Article 2. DISCRIMINATION – The Property Manager shall not discriminate in the rental, lease, or negotiation for real property based on race, color, religion, sex, national origin, familial status, or handicap and shall comply with all federal, state, and local laws concerning discrimination.

Article 3. DUTY TO THE CLIENT – The Property Manager has a fiduciary responsibility to the Client and shall at all times act in the best interests of the Client.

Article 4. DUTY TO TENANTS – The Property Manager shall treat all Tenants professionally when applying for, living in, and vacating a managed residence. The Property Manager shall hold in high regard the safety and health of those lawfully at a managed property.

Article 5. PROPERTY CONDITION – The Property Manager shall manage all properties in accordance with safety and habitability requirements of the local jurisdiction.

Article 6. PROTECTION OF FUNDS – The Property Manager shall hold all funds received on behalf of others in compliance with state law with full disclosure to the Client and must never commingle the firm's or personal funds with those of the Client.

Article 7. DUTY TO DISCLOSE EXPERTISE – The Property Manager must provide accurate information within his area of expertise, but refrain from the unauthorized practice of other professions including but not limited to the law, accounting, financial planning, construction, and contracting.

Article 8. DUTY TO FIRM – The Property Manager shall act in the best interests of their Employer.

Article 9. RELATIONS WITH COMPETITORS – The Property Manager shall refrain from criticizing competitors or their business practices. In the event of a controversy between Property

Managers with different firms, the Property Managers shall submit the dispute to arbitration rather than litigate the matter.

Article 10. PRICE FIXING – The Property Manager shall not engage in the improper acts of price fixing, antitrust, or anti competition with other Property Managers.

Article 11. DUTY TO REMAIN EDUCATED – The Property Manager shall strive to be informed about relevant matters affecting the property management field on a local, state, and national level.

Article 12. IMPROVING THE PROFESSION – The Property Manager shall strive to improve the property management profession by sharing with others their lessons or experience for the benefit of all.

NATIONAL ASSOCIATION OF RESIDENTIAL PROPERTY MANAGERS
STANDARDS OF PROFESSIONALISM

The National Association of Residential Property Managers (NARPM) promotes a high standard of business ethics, professionalism, and fair housing practices. NARPM's members subscribe to the following Standards of Professionalism for property managers of single family and other small residential properties.

DUTY TO THE PUBLIC
The Property Manager shall endeavor to eliminate in the community, through the normal course of business, any practices which could be damaging to the public or bring discredit to the profession. The Property Manager shall assist the governmental agency charged with regulating the practices of property managers.
The Property Manager shall comply with all local and state ordinances regarding real estate law, licensing, insurance, and banking.

DISCRIMINATION
It is the duty of the Property Manager to educate those with whom the Property Manager is affiliated to comply with all fair housing laws.

DUTY TO THE CLIENT
The Property Manager shall use a written management agreement outlining all responsibilities and fees. The Client will be provided a copy and the
Property Manager will maintain a copy. The Property Manager shall communicate regularly with the Client and provide written reports of receipts and disbursements on a regular, agreed upon basis. In the event of any dispute, the Property Manager shall provide a written accounting as soon as practical. Tenant applications shall be reviewed and verified in order to determine the Applicant's ability to pay and to determine the likelihood that the Applicant will comply with all provisions of the rental

agreement.

The Property Manager shall accept no commissions, rebates, profits, discounts, or any other benefit which has not been fully disclosed to and approved by the Client.

DUTY TO TENANTS

The Property Manager shall offer all Applicants a written Application. The Property Manager shall provide all Tenants with a copy of the signed rental agreement with all addenda.

The Property Manager shall make all disclosures as required by state and local laws and provide the Tenant an opportunity to complete a written condition report at the time of moving in.

The Property Manager shall respond promptly to requests for repairs. Within the time prescribed by law, a written deposit refund determination shall be provided to the Tenant after they have vacated the property. No undue delay in refunding or accounting for the security deposit shall take place.

The Property Manager shall avoid exaggeration, misrepresentation, misinformation, or concealment of pertinent facts relating to the advertising, leasing, and management of a property.

PROPERTY CONDITION

The Property Manager shall not manage properties for Clients who refuse or are unable to maintain their property in accordance with safety and habitability requirements of the local jurisdiction.

PROTECTION OF FUNDS

The Property Manager shall hold all funds received on behalf of others in compliance with state law with full disclosure to the Client and must never commingle the firm's or personal funds with those of the Client.

DUTY TO DISCLOSE EXPERTISE

If a client engages a Property Manager's services in a field where the Property Manager lacks experience and competency, the Property Manager shall fully disclose this fact to the Client.

DUTY TO FIRM

The Property Manager shall have no undisclosed conflict of interest with their Employers and shall notify their Employers immediately if a conflict should arise. The Property Manager shall receive no kickbacks, rebates, or any other benefit without full disclosure to Employers.

RELATIONS WITH COMPETITORS

The Property Manager shall refrain from criticizing competitors or their business practices. In the event of a controversy between Property Managers with different firms, the Property Managers shall submit the dispute to arbitration rather than litigate the matter.

PRICE FIXING

Unless the Property Manager is purchasing another management company, fees, commissions, and compensations shall not be discussed with other Property Managers. The Property Managers shall always seek to avoid the appearance of impropriety in these matters.

The Property Manager's fees, commissions, and compensations shall be determined by the manager or the Property Manager's Broker based upon, but not limited to, expertise, experience, and the cost of service and expense.

DUTY TO REMAIN EDUCATED

The Property Manager shall maintain their real estate licenses by meeting continuing education requirements as set out by the state in which they work.

IMPROVING THE PROFESSION

The Property Manager shall strive to improve the property management profession by sharing with others their lessons or experience for the benefit of all.

ADA and Fair Housing Compliance in Property Management

Accessibility Requirements of the Fair Housing Act

The Act requires that covered multifamily dwellings be designed and constructed with the following accessible features:

The public and common use areas must be readily accessible to and usable by persons with disabilities;

All doors designed to allow passage into and within all premises of covered dwellings must be sufficiently wide to allow passage by persons with disabilities, `including persons who use wheelchairs;

All premises within covered dwellings must contain the following features:
- An accessible route into and through the dwelling unit;
- Light switches, electrical outlets, thermostats, and other environmental controls in accessible locations;
- Reinforcements in bathroom walls to allow the later installation of grab bars;
- Usable kitchens and bathrooms such that an individual using a wheelchair can maneuver about and use the space.

Types of Dwellings Covered by the Act

The Fair Housing Act requires all "covered multifamily dwellings" designed and constructed for first occupancy after March 13, 1991, to be readily accessible to and usable by persons with disabilities.

In buildings with four or more dwelling units and at least one elevator, all dwelling units and all public and common use areas are subject to the Act's design and construction requirements.
In buildings with four or more dwelling units and no elevator, all ground floor units and public and common use areas are subject to the Act's design and construction requirements.

Dwellings subject to the Act's design and construction requirements include condominiums, cooperatives, apartment buildings, vacation and time share units, assisted living facilities, continuing care facilities, nursing homes, public housing developments, HOPE VI projects, projects funded with HOME or other federal funds, transitional housing, single room occupancy units (SROs), shelters designed as a residence for homeless persons, dormitories, hospices, extended stay or residential hotels, and more.

Housing or some portion of housing covered by the Act's design and construction requirements may be subject to additional accessibility requirements under other laws.

Factors to be considered in determining whether a facility contains dwellings include, but are not limited to:
(1) the length of time persons will stay in the project;
(2) whether the rental rate for the unit will be calculated on a daily, weekly, monthly or yearly basis;
(3) whether the terms and length of occupancy will be established through a lease or other written agreement;
(4) how the property will be described to the public in marketing materials;
(5) what amenities will be included inside the unit, including kitchen facilities;
(6) whether the resident will possess the right to return to the property; and
(7) whether the resident will have anywhere else to return.

The Fair Housing Act's design and construction requirements apply only to covered multifamily dwellings — that is, buildings having four or more dwelling units built for first occupancy after March 13, 1991.

Disabilities

In essence, a landlord may not:

Refuse to let a disabled person make **reasonable modifications** to the dwelling or common use areas, **at their expense**, if necessary for the disabled person to use the housing. (Where reasonable, the landlord may permit changes only if the disabled person agrees to restore the property to its original condition when they move)

Refuse to make r**easonable accommodations** in rules, policies, practices or services if necessary for the disabled person to use the housing. Example would be a Handicap Parking Spot.

What is the difference between a service animal and an emotional support animal?

Service animals are defined as dogs that are individually trained to do work or perform tasks for people with disabilities. These tasks can include things like pulling a wheelchair, guiding a person who is visually impaired, alerting a person who is having a seizure, or even calming a person who suffers from Post-Traumatic Stress Disorder. The tasks a service dog can perform are not limited to this list. However, the work or task a service dog does must be directly related to the person's disability.

Service dogs may accompany persons with disabilities into places that the public normally goes. This includes state and local government buildings, businesses open to the public, public transportation, and non-profit organizations open to the public. The law that allows a trained service dog to accompany a person with a disability is the Americans with Disabilities Act (ADA).

An **emotional support animal** is an animal (typically a dog or cat though this can include other species) that provides a therapeutic benefit to its owner through companionship. The animal provides emotional support and comfort to individuals with psychiatric disabilities and other mental impairments.

The animal is **not** specifically trained to perform tasks for a person who suffers from emotional disabilities. Unlike a service animal, an emotional support animal is not granted access to places of public accommodation.

Under the federal Fair Housing Act (FHA), an emotional support animal is viewed as a "reasonable accommodation" in a housing unit that has a "no pets" rule for its residents.

HUD defines an emotional support animal as an animal that "provides emotional support that alleviates one or more identified symptoms or effects of a person's disability.

These animals do not need specialized training.

Does the Fair Housing Act (FHA) apply to all housing?

The Fair Housing Act (FHA) does apply to almost all housing types including those for sale or rent.

This includes apartments, condominiums, and single family homes.

There are some major exceptions, *such as buildings with four or fewer units* where the landlord lives in one of the units.

The law also excludes private owners of single-family housing sold or rented without the use of a broker (who do not own more than three single family home) and housing operated by organizations and private clubs that limit occupancy to members.

The FHA would then cover homes in a planned community with a "no pets" restriction, owned or rented condominiums with a "no pets" covenant, and apartments with a "no pets" clause in the lease.

As long as those housing units do not fall within listed exceptions, landlords or housing associations must comply with the FHA.

Landlords have wide discretion when picking new tenants. However, there are certain restrictions. When making a decision, landlords may use criteria such as criminal history, credit rating, and financial stability.

Other factors, such as a potential tenant's race or gender, may not be taken into consideration.

Activities Prohibited Under the Fair Housing Act

The Fair Housing Act prohibits discriminatory practices in housing. Under the Act, landlords may not discriminate against tenants or potential tenants on the basis of
race, gender, religion, familial status, disability, or ethnicity.

The actions covered under the Act include:

- Deciding whether to rent an apartment to a potential tenant,
- Setting particular rules for individual tenants, and
- Advertising that the apartment is only available to certain people.

Landlords are also required to make **reasonable accommodations** for tenants with disabilities. That can include giving lower level units to tenants in wheelchairs and installing ramps on doorways.

However, if the landlord owns an older building and accommodating a tenant with a disability would require a major remodel, the landlord is usually not required to add the accommodations.

Under federal law, disabled tenants and prospective tenants with a disability have the right to apply for and live in a rental unit regardless of their impairment.

When a landlord rejects disabled tenants based on the use of a discriminatory housing practice, they have violated the law.

Who Qualifies as Disabled under the Fair Housing Acts?

The federal Fair Housing Act and the Fair Housing Amendments Act (42 U.S. Code §§ 3601-3619, 3631) forbid discrimination of tenants or prospective tenants because of a disability or the disability of a person associated with them.

The law protects the following people:

- A person with a mental or physical disability that substantially limits a person's ability to perform one or more major life activities; or
- A person that has a record of the disability; or
- A person that is considered by others as having the disability

Types of protected disabilities include mobile, visual, and hearing impairments, mental retardation, alcoholism (if being treated in a recovery program), drug addiction (not caused by the use of an illegal controlled substance), mental illness, and HIV/AIDS.

A Landlord May Not Ask Discriminatory Questions

If there is not an accommodation request, the Fair Housing Acts prohibit the landlord from asking whether the applicant has a disability or about the severity of the impairment.

Landlords must treat disabled applicants and tenants in the same way as those without a disability:

They cannot request medical records, nor guide a tenant to a specific unit.

However, a landlord may ask all prospective tenants, including disabled applicants, about whether:

- The applicant can meet tenancy requirements;
- The applicant abuses or is addicted to an illegal controlled substance;
- The applicant qualifies for a rental unit available only to people with a disability or a certain type of disability; or
- The applicant qualifies for a rental unit that is offered on a priority basis to people with a disability or with a certain type of disability.

Mental Illness and the Possibility of Direct Threats

A landlord may not exclude an applicant because of fear or speculation that the mentally ill person poses a danger.

The landlord can assess, however, whether the individual is a direct threat by relying on trustworthy and objective information regarding current conduct or specific acts, such as threats or an assault on another tenant.

The landlord must consider several factors, including:
- The nature and severity of the risk of injury
- The likelihood of injury
- Whether a reasonable accommodation can eliminate the direct threat
- The landlord must also consider whether the tenant's medication or treatment has eliminated the direct threat.

If after evaluating reliable and objective evidence the landlord can ascertain that the individual poses a direct threat, then the landlord may reject the individual.

The Right to an Accommodation
Disabled tenants may request the landlord make reasonable accommodations to rules, policies, practices, or services when it will afford the person equal opportunity to use/enjoy the rental unit and the common areas.

There must be a relationship between the modification and the disability.

Reasonable requests include the permission to use a service animal, permission to mail a rent payment, or a request to have a parking space large enough for wheelchair access.

A landlord does not have to make accommodations for a reasonable request that is unrelated to a tenant's disability or for a request that is not reasonable because it will cause an undue financial and administrative burden on the landlord. However, when a request is unreasonable, HUD requires the landlord and the tenant to proceed in an "interactive process" to reach a reasonable compromise.

The Right to Make a Modification
If reasonable, disabled tenants may modify a rental unit to make it safe and comfortable to live in. If the modification will create an inappropriate living condition for the next tenant, the landlord may agree to the modification upon the condition that the tenant restore the unit to its original condition prior to leaving. In this circumstance, the landlord may require the tenant to put money in an interest-bearing escrow account.

All modifications are subject to approval with the landlord. The landlord may ask for a description of the proposed modification and any necessary building permits.

Common modifications include wheelchair ramps, lowered countertops, and special door handles.

Offering Proof of a Disability and the Need for Accommodation or Modification
In some cases, a disabled tenant will need to provide proof of their disability or proof of the relationship between the disability and the requested accommodation or modification.

If the disability is obvious and the need for the requested accommodation or modification is apparent, then the landlord may not ask for further verification.

If the disability is obvious but the need for the accommodation or modification is not, the landlord may only ask for necessary disability-related information.

When a disability is less apparent, a landlord may request information that verifies the disability, describes the requested accommodation, and establishes the connection between the disability and the accommodation or modification.

Disabled tenants may offer verification of their impairment by:
- Giving a credible statement;
- Offering proof of receiving Supplemental Security Income or Social Security Disability Insurance when the individual is under age 65;
- Requesting a doctor, a medical provider, a peer support group, a nonmedical service agency, or a reliable third party provide information about their disability.

Under federal law, disabled tenants and prospective tenants with a disability have the right to apply for and live in a rental unit regardless of their impairment.

When a landlord rejects disabled tenants based on the use of a discriminatory housing practice, they have violated the law.

What to Do if You See a Fair Housing Violation

If you believe you or a loved one has been the victim of a Fair Housing Act violation, you can file a complaint with the Department of Housing and Urban Development (HUD) online or by phone.

Someone within HUD will investigate your complaint and determine whether the facts listed are indeed a violation of the Fair Housing Act. If so, the case will be scheduled for a hearing in front of a HUD administrative judge.

A housing specialist will argue against the landlord on your behalf, so you do not need to hire an attorney for this procedure, unless you want one.

HUD will assess fines against landlords who violate the Fair Housing Act in the following amounts:
- $16,000 for first time violators,
- $37,500 if the landlord has violated the Fair Housing Act before the current complaint, and
- $65,000 if the landlord has violated the Fair Housing Act two or more time before the current complaint.

Types of Complaints Investigated by FHEO

FHEO investigates complaints, which may be one or both of the following types:
- Discrimination under the Fair Housing Act (including housing that is privately owned and operated)
- Discrimination and other civil rights violations in housing and community development programs, including those funded by HUD

Retaliation Is Illegal

It is illegal to retaliate against any person for making a complaint, testifying, assisting, or participating in any manner in a proceeding under HUD's complaint process at any time, even after the investigation has been completed.

The Fair Housing Act also makes it illegal to retaliate against any person because that person reported a discriminatory practice to a housing provider or other authority. If you believe you have experienced retaliation, you can file a complaint.

Setting Rents and Lease Rates (BROKER ONLY)

The amount of rent you charge your tenants should be a percentage of your home's market value. Typically, the rents that landlords charge fall between 0.8% and 1.1% of the home's value.

For example, for a home valued at $250,000, a landlord could charge between $2,000 and $2,750 each month

How to Determine the Rental Cost of a Property
Co-authored by Carla Toebe

Setting the right rent for your investment property involves more than simply trying to make a profit. Tenants have so many choices when it comes to rental properties, so you have to make yours stand out. This means setting the right rental price that attracts high-quality tenants and reflects the positive attributes of your property. With a little research, math and market know-how, you can determine the appropriate rental price for your investment property.

Method 1
Using Your Home's Value

Calculate 1.1 percent of the value of your property. This will result in the monthly amount you should charge renters. Professional investors use this percentage as a rule of thumb for determining the rental price of a unit.

For example, if you are renting out an apartment in your home and your home is worth $90,000, use the equation $90,000 x .011 = $990. This would be the monthly amount you could charge renters for the unit.

Understand the limitations of using this calculation. While it might be a good place to start, this flat calculation fails to take into account other factors that add to or detract from the rental value of a property. Also, if the home is in a high-income neighborhood, the percentage calculation might result in a rental price that is too high.

Other considerations, such as location, nearby amenities, design features and layout, also affect how much rent you can charge.

Try the same calculation using a range between 1.0% to 1.3%, based upon rent rates and availability of similar rental properties in the area.

Consider the market. If the property is located in a hot market with fierce competition from other rental properties, this formula may make the rent too high to compete with other properties. In this case, you should survey the current market by comparing your unit to other comparable rental properties to find the ideal cost.

Method 2
Researching Comparable Units

Research rental prices for units similar to yours. Find out how much rent others are charging for comparable units. Look on sites like Craigslist, Zillow and Trulia. Drive around the neighborhood to find rental properties that are not listed on these sites.

Look for units that match yours in square footage, number of bedrooms and bathrooms, age, amenities and location.

Make a list of properties that are similar to yours and write down how much rent the owners are charging and the occupancy rate. Assess whether you can ask the same, more or less rent than these properties based on the location, amenities and size of yours.

Keep in mind that the advertised rental price of a property might be too high. If, for example, you find a property similar to yours that has been vacant for a long time, the rental price the owners are asking might be too high. Take this into consideration when setting the rental price for your unit.

Contact property managers to determine a rental price. If you plan to hire a property management company to oversee your property, they should have a good idea of what rent you can charge. Otherwise, you can contact local property managers and ask them about rental prices in your area to get a sense of what you should be charging.

Setting the right rent is part of a property manager's responsibilities. Property managers understand the local market and know the rental values of comparable properties in the area.

Work with an agent. Rental agents, property managers, and some real estate agents who deal with rentals have a keen understanding of the local rental market. They are familiar with all of the other rental properties in the area. This makes them qualified to assess the positives and negatives of your rental property and set the appropriate rental price. Since they do showings, they also know what tenants like and don't like. An agent will know what tenants will be willing to pay for the location, size and amenities of your property.

Most real estate agents do not deal with rentals, although some might. For this reason, you might want to contact a property management company or rental agent in your area, as these tend to specialize in rental units exclusively.

Calculate rental price per square foot. If you cannot find other similarly-sized rental units in your area, determine the rental price per square foot of unit that is similar in other ways. Apply the rental price per square foot to your unit to set the rental price.

To calculate the rental price per square foot, divide the rental price by the total square footage of the unit.

For example, suppose you have a three-bedroom, 1,500 square-foot unit available. A nearby two-bedroom, 1,000 square-foot unit is renting for $1,250 per month. Calculate the rental price per square foot of the nearby unit with the equation $1,250 / 1,000 square feet = $1.25 per square foot.

Apply the rental price per square foot to set the rental price for your unit. Multiply 1,500 square feet x $1.25 = $1,875. Based on the rental price per square foot, you can ask $1,875 for your unit.

Note that smaller properties generally rent for more per foot than larger properties.

Method 3
Understanding Factors that Impact Rental Value

Consider the location. Location is the key factor that commands higher rent. People are generally willing to do without certain amenities if the property is in a convenient and popular location.

If the property is near schools, it may be more valuable to families with children.
Students may be willing to pay more for rental units within walking distance to local colleges.
Renters also tend to be willing to pay more for units near public transportation.

Consider available amenities. Renters are willing to pay more for certain conveniences and comforts. For example, rental properties go for higher rent in planned developments with attractive facilities. Desirable features can make one property command a higher rent than a comparable property without them.

Pools and tennis courts make rental units more attractive and can increase their rental value. In fact, any outdoor space, such as a balcony or deck, makes a unit more attractive to renters.

Renters also are willing to pay for readily available or covered parking, especially in urban areas. Renters prefer off-street parking, but nearby on-street parking can also appeal to renters.

Renters want convenient laundry facilities. If laundry facilities are in the building, or preferably in the unit, the renters will be willing to pay more.

Consider the desirability of your unit. The size and layout of the unit affects the rental value. Also, quality tenants are willing to pay top dollar for contemporary design elements. In addition, high-end finishes and appliances command higher rents.

The square footage affects the rental value. If a renter sees a 700 square foot one-bedroom apartment and a 1,000 square foot one-bedroom apartment, she will likely be more attracted to the larger one and be willing to pay more.

The floor level is important to renters. You can charge more for units on higher floors than for ground-level units, especially if there is an elevator. However, if the property is a walk-up, you may need to charge less rent for the higher floors because tenants will be less willing to climb the stairs.

A washer and dryer in the unit appeals to most renters. Tenants will be willing to pay for the convenience and privacy of having their own washer and dryer that they don't have to share with their neighbors. If you don't want to purchase a washer and dryer, at least think about installing washer dryer hookups so tenants can bring their own appliances.

Most tenants expect air conditioning, especially in areas with hot and humid weather conditions. Renters will be willing to pay more for central air conditioning than a property with window units.

Offer free wireless internet. Renters expect the convenience of wireless internet, and quality tenants will be attracted to properties that offer this service.

The layout of the unit affects the rental value. Renters love an open floor plan. A unit with an open floor plan looks bigger and will command a higher rent than one without it.

Renters are willing to pay for hardwood floors. If you can boast that your property has hardwood floors, you will be ahead of the competition.

Tenants need lots of storage space. They will be willing to pay higher rent for a property with extra closets, especially walk-in closets.

Adjust rental prices based on the market. For example, when the economy is bad, the demand for rental properties increases because people don't want to purchase homes. This means that you can charge more for your rental properties. Conversely, when demand for rental properties declines, you must charge less to continue to attract tenants.

Also, if you rent seasonally, the rental price you can charge will increase during the peak season. It will decrease during the off season.

Think about the type of lease you can offer (month-to-month, a fixed end date, fixed number of months, option to purchase, etc.) and what type of impact this might have on who is willing to rent.

You can charge more for short term leases than long term leases. For example, you can charge $1000 month to month or $900 a month if the tenant signs a lease for a year. Generally, it is acceptable to change the lease based on the terms of the contract, so long as all applicants are quoted the same terms and prices.

There is a limit on how much you can charge for a deposit. If your deposit is too high, you may have trouble attracting renters.

When determining the deposit, consider the risk factor of the applicant. Factors to consider include credit score, former rental history, income, and any criminal history. For example, an applicant with a good credit score should receive a lower deposit than one with a poor credit score.

Method 4
Deciding to Raise the Rent

Decide if you should raise the rent for occupied units. Raising the rent for occupied units requires similar considerations as setting the rent for vacant units. Consider the current rental market in your area. Also, think about whether or not you want to risk losing valuable tenants.
Compare your rental rates with others for similar properties in the area. If your rent is lower than others, judge whether you offer enough amenities to justify raising the rent. Decide whether you want to raise rent across the board or just for specific units.

Think about your long-term, valuable tenants. It's hard to put a price on reliable tenants who treat your property like their own. Decide if you would be willing to lose those tenants if they don't want to pay the increased rent, and if so, whether you'd be willing to exclude any of them from a rental increase.

If you have multiple units, you may want to only increase the rent on certain units at any one time. Stagger the rent increases over time, so that you do not risk losing all of your tenants at the same time.

Check your state laws. In the US, states have laws regarding how rent increases are to be determined and communicated to the tenant. These laws may state how many day's notice is needed before you can increase the rent. You should also be aware if rent control is instituted in your area. You should read the Landlord Tenant Act for your state.

Commercial leases often have different regulations than residential ones do.
If you're uncertain about the laws in your state, check with an attorney, preferably one who specializes in real estate or in landlord-tenant law.

Justify your reasons for raising the rent. Explain to tenants the reasoning behind the higher rent. If higher property taxes or operating costs warrant the increase, make sure tenants understand this. Make them aware of any added value they can expect because of the increase. For example, perhaps you are hiring a better janitorial service. Or, maybe you are planning

Communicate with tenants about the rent. Build a plan for increasing rents into your leases so tenants know when to expect them. Provide tenants with written notification of planned increases in the rent. Adhere to the notification guidelines specified in the lease so tenants receive sufficient advance notice. Use clear and concise language, and be professional by sending a typed letter on company letterhead.

Chapter 9

Transfer of Title (Salesperson 8%; Broker 7%)

A. Title Insurance
1. What is insured against
2. Title searches, title abstracts, chain of title
3. Marketable vs insurable title
4. Potential title problems and resolution
5. Cloud on title, suit to quiet title (BROKER ONLY)

B. Deeds
1. Purpose of deed, when title passes
2. Types of deeds and when used
3. Essential elements of deeds
4. Importance of recording

C. Escrow or closing; tax aspects of transferring
title to real property
1. Responsibilities of escrow agent
2. Prorated items
3. Closing statements/TRID disclosures
4. Estimating closing costs
5. Property and income taxes

D. Special processes
1. Foreclosure
2. Short sale

E. Warranties
1. Purpose of home or construction warranty programs
2. Scope of home or construction warranty programs

TRANSFER BY OPERATION OF LAW
Eminent domain (through condemnation)
Escheat
Any type of foreclosure; for example, delinquent real estate
taxes or special assessments, mortgage or deed of trust laws, mechanic's liens, judgment liens.

TRANSFER BY NATURAL FORCES
- **Accretion**
  The slow accumulation of soil, rock, or other matter deposited on one's property by the movement of water. The opposite of erosion.
- **Erosion**
  The gradual wearing away of the land.
- **Avulsion**
  The sudden and violent tearing away of the land.
  Other acts of nature such as earthquakes, hurricanes, etc.
- **Alluvium**
  The deposit of soil, rock, or other matter on one's property

Accession
The acquiring of property that is abandoned when a commercial tenant leaves trade fixtures behind and moves.

TRANSFER BY ADVERSE POSSESSION
- Possession by the trespasser **must be open, notorious, continuous for a statutory number of years, hostile, and adverse** to the true owner.
- Each jurisdiction has its own minimum requirements before an adverse possession claim can be filed.

TRANSFER OF A DECEASED PERSON'S PROPERTY

1. TESTATE
Transfer of title by will. Property passes by Devise

Divisor – The one who dies
Divisee – The survivor

A will is a testamentary instrument that becomes effective only after the death of its maker.

Codicil
A modification of or an amendment to a will.

Holographic Will
A will is in its maker's own
handwriting.

A **nuncupative** will is given verbally by its maker. Some states do not permit property to be conveyed by oral or handwritten wills.

2. INTESTATE
Transfer of title by descent
- The laws of the state determine to whom ownership passes when a person dies intestate.

- The laws of intestate succession vary from state to state.
- Generally, there are primary heirs (spouse, children).
- The closeness of one's relationship to the deceased determines the amount of the estate that will be received.

ESCHEAT – Property becomes owned by the state. Land cannot be ownerless

PROBATE
- It is a legal process that proves or confirms the validity of the will. Determines the precise assets of the deceased person.
- Identifies the persons to whom the assets are to pass. Takes place in the county where the decedent resided.
- An **administrator/administratrix** (male/female) is appointed if there is no will designating an executor/executrix.
- Legal procedures vary considerably from state to state
- Decedent's debts must be satisfied before any property can be disbursed to the devisees or heirs.
- Taxes are paid first.

Alienation

Foreclosure vs. forfeiture:
Foreclosure is the loss of property to pay off a debt.
Forfeiture is losing the property because of disobeying a condition in the deed.

Garn Act (Garn-St. Germain Depository Institutions Act)
Federal statute enabling federally chartered banks to enforce their due-on-sale (alienation) clauses even if state laws prohibit such clauses.

Voluntary Alienation
Normal transfer of title, as opposed to

Involuntary alienation when a property is sold in foreclosure or at a tax sale.
Delivery and acceptance:

- **Judicial Foreclosure** Legal event whereas the lender receives a court order. The sale of the property is approved by the court. Property is usually sold to the highest bidder.

- **Non-judicial Foreclosure** Standard in a Deed of Trust. Allows the Trustee to sell the property to the highest bidder for the lender. Seller financing often has a Deed of Trust because it's easier to foreclose on the property.

- **Strict Foreclosure**
A decree orders the debt to be paid within a set time limit. If the payment is not met, the mortgagor's right of equitable redemption is forever lost.
The lien holder takes possession when the court awards title to him.

- **Deed in Lieu of Foreclosure**
A friendly foreclosure. The property usually reverts back to the lender in a better condition than other foreclosures. The borrower will attempt to surrender the deed. The lien holder is not forced into accepting it.
Banks sometimes will not take a Deed in Lieu of Foreclosure because they may have to pay off a second loan.

- **Short Sale** – The lien holder negotiates to avoid foreclosure. The lien holder accepts less than the loan amount.

REDEMPTION – The action of saving your ownership of a property
- **Equitable Redemption**

Occurs prior to the sales. The borrower pays the stated amount and the mortgage is reinstated.
- **Statutory Redemption** After the public sale the borrower has a certain amount of time to redeem his property.

DEFICIENCY JUDGMENT – If the lender is unable to recover the amount due on a defaulted loan, the lender may sue the borrower for the outstanding balance.

Non-recourse Loan

One for which the borrower is not personally liable (i.e., no deficiency judgment is possible). The lender is satisfied by the value of the property alone as security for the loan.

REO – Real Estate Owned. Bank ownership. The property has been foreclosed and is now owned by the bank.

Title Insurance

Protection for the buyer against previous title defects that may become known in the future. Owner's policy purchased by seller insures up to contract price; Lender's policy purchased by buyer insures lender up to balance of loan.

Title insurance can be purchased on its own or as a supplement to an attorney's opinion of title or a certificate of title.

Title insurance provides protection for the buyer, defending the new owner if any future claim is made against title to the property.

Preliminary
1. Name of insured party
2. Legal description of property
3. Estate or interest covered
4. Conditions and stipulations
5. Schedule of exceptions

The title insurance premium is paid once, at the closing.
The insurer's liability cannot exceed the face amount of the policy unless an inflation rider is included.

Standard Coverage Policy

insures against:
- Defects found in public records.
- Forged documents.
- Incompetent grantors. Incorrect marital statements. Improperly delivered deeds.

Extended Coverage Policy

insures against:
- All perils insured against by the standard coverage policy.
- Property inspection, including unrecorded rights of persons in possession.
- Examination of survey.
- Unrecorded liens not known by the policyholder.
- Coverage beyond a standard A.L.T.A. title policy insuring most of the standard exceptions such as
- facts which a survey would show,
- parties in possession and
- unrecorded mechanic's liens.

TYPICAL EXCLUSIONS
- Defects and liens listed in the policy. Defects known to the buyer.
- Changes in land use brought about by changes in zoning ordinances.

TYPES OF POLICIES
- **Owner's policy**

Issued for the benefit of the owner.
- **Lender's Policy**

In many cases where a mortgage loan is involved, the lender requires a title policy that at least covers the lender's portion of the purchase price.

Marketable Title vs. Insurable Title

Marketable Title
- The chain of ownership (title) to a particular piece of property is clear and free from defects.
- It can be marketed for sale without additional effort by the seller or potential buyer.

Insurable Title
- The property may have a known defect or defects in the chain of title.
- However, with an insurable title, a title insurance company has agreed in advance to provide insurance against the defects ever affecting the ownership or value of the property.
- **UNMARKETABLE TITLE** can still be transferred, but its defects may limit or restrict its ownership.

Transferability
A characteristic of value indicating that a property has good title and marketable title.

Title searches, title abstracts, chain of title

Title Search
- Title search is an examination of all the public records to determine whether any defects exist in **the chain of title**.
- Title searches also make note of any other encumbrances on the property.

Abstract of title
- An abstract of title is a report of what was found in a title search, which is a search of essentially all public records related to the property's title, such as previous deeds and liens. These records are usually found in the county recorder's office or land records office of the county in which the property is located.

Chain of Title
- A historical "chain" linked from the first recorded title of a property down through each subsequent conveyance.

Title commitment
- The preliminary promise by a title company to insure the title to a property if stated requirements are met (e.g. payoff of existing trust deed).
- It reveals the results of a title search and specifies any exceptions to coverage.

Certificate of Title
- A statement of opinion prepared by a title company, licensed abstractor or attorney on the status of title to a parcel of real property, based on an examination of public records.

- **Abstract and Attorney's Opinion**
  Attorney's opinion issued on basis of the abstract

TRANSFER TAX STAMPS
Usually payable when the deed is recorded; also, called "documentary stamps."

Potential title problems and resolution
Cloud on title, suit to quiet title

A cloud is something that casts doubts on the grantor's ownership of the property.
A defect that may adversely affect the marketability of a title, such as an unreleased lien. Clouds may often be cleared up by a quitclaim deed or a quiet title suit.

Suit to quiet title
A court action to establish property ownership when title is clouded.
A court action to remove a cloud on title and determine one's right to an ownership interest.

Clear title has been expanded to mean no problems such as illegal structures or unpermitted improvements to the property. In general, though, proof of good title can be accomplished in several different ways

Deeds

Purpose of deed, when title passes

Evidence of title ownership. Alienation of the seller. To show ownership from one person to another person.

TYPES OF DEEDS
Deeds show the covenants by which a grantor is bound to the buyer in the transaction

Condition Precedent
A condition that must be met prior to the transfer of title.

EXECUTION OF CORPORATE DEEDS
The deed must be signed by an authorized corporate officer.

General Warranty Deed
The deed that gives the most protection to the buyer.

It has 5 covenants.
1. Covenant of **Seisen**
2. Covenant of quiet enjoyment: Quiet enjoyment means that the grantor guarantees that no one else can come along and claim ownership of the property. It also means that if a later party's title claim is found to be better than the owner's title, the grantor is liable for any losses.
3. **Covenant against encumbrances:** The grantor guarantees that the title to the property has no encumbrances like an easement or lien. Easements are rights that enable someone else to use some of the property, and liens are financial claims against the property. The only exceptions to this warranty are encumbrances that are specifically stated in the deed.
4. **Covenant of further assurance:** In this covenant, the grantor promises to obtain and provide documents necessary to clear up any problem that comes up with the title.
5. **Covenant of warranty forever:** The grantor guarantees to pay all costs to clear up any title problems at any time in the future.

A particular feature of a general warranty deed is that warranties cover any title problems that may have occurred during the ownerships of all past owners.

Special Warranty Deeds
Has two warranties
1. The first is that the grantor has title to the property.
2. The second is a guarantee that nothing was done to affect the title during the grantor's ownership, and if a problem did exist, the grantor will correct it.

Because of the limited warranties, people acting as third parties sometimes use special warranty deeds. **The executor of an estate uses a special warranty deed to convey property belonging to an estate or trust.**

GRANT DEED
Grant deeds are used in a few states and provide limited warranties. The grantor guarantees that the property hasn't been conveyed to anyone else, that no encumbrances limit the use of the property except the ones specifically listed in the deed, and that if the grantor later obtains any other title to the property, it will be conveyed to the grantee.
These guarantees are limited to the period of time the grantor owned the property. The grant deed is used in only a few states, but if yours is one, you need to remember this information.

Bargain and Sale Deed
1. Contains no warranties against encumbrances unless stated.
2. Only implies that the grantor holds title and is in possession
3. That the grantor has full title to the property is implied.

4. Essentially it gives no protection to the grantee. This type of deed sometimes is used in foreclosure and tax sales.

Quitclaim Deed
1. Contains no warranties and gives no implication of how much or how good the grantor's title to the property is
2. Usually transferred between people who know each other.
3. Used to clear up clouds/defects on title or relinquish an inchoate interest.
4. Least protection.
5. Carries no covenants or warranties whatsoever.
6. May be used to transfer an easement.
7. Quitclaim deeds sometimes are used for uncomplicated transfers

Reconveyance Deed
1. Executed by the trustee to return (reconvey) title to property held in trust.
2. *A trust deed is used to convey ownership by a trustor to a trustee for the benefit of a beneficiary as security for a debt.*
3. a reconveyance deed is used to reconvey title to property from a trustee back to a trustor after a debt for which the property is security has been paid off.

Trustee's Deed
1. Used to convey property out of a trust to anyone other than the trustor.
2. Executed by the authority granted to the trustee.

Trust Deed
A 3-party security instrument for a promissory note that transfers title from the trustor (borrower) to a trustee (third party) to be held for the benefit of the beneficiary (lender). Must be released when the loan is paid

Executor's Deeds, Administrator's Deeds, Sheriff's Deeds
1. A deed executed pursuant to a court order.
2. Used to convey title to property transferred by court order or by will.
3. An executor's deed in the case of a deceased person's estate and a sheriff's deed in the case of a sale of property seized by a local unit of government town or the bank are two examples of such court-ordered deeds. State law establishes these deeds, and state law governs their form.

WHEN TITLE PASSES
Ownership passes when the buyer accepts the delivered and signed deed.

Essential elements of deeds

- It must be in writing,
- competent grantor,
- named grantee,
- recital of consideration,
- words of conveyance, habendum (type of ownership),
- **legal description**,
- signature of the grantor
- delivery and acceptance.

The tax assessor's parcel number: use of a system of identifying properties that looks similar to the recorded plat map.

Importance of recording

Recording

Entering documents into the public record. Any written document that affects any state, right, title, or interest in land must be recorded in the county where the land is located to serve as constructive notice.

Constructive Notice to the World
That legal notice presumed by entering a document into the public record, meaning any interested person (e.g., buyer) could have investigated the record or the property. Possession of the property is also considered to be constructive notice.

Torrens system: The Torrens system is based on proper registration of the title
The Torrens system gradually is falling out of use in the United States, but some states or areas within states may still use it.

Race Notice
Term referring to the fact that the date and time of recording determine priority of recorded documents, liens, etc. Comes from a "race" to the courthouse.

Et a
Latin, meaning "and others".

Et ux / Et uxor
Latin, meaning "and wife".

Et vir
Latin, meaning "and husband".

Escrow or Closing; Tax Aspects of Transferring Title to Real Property

Title Company Closing

Closing performed by a title company closer as agent for the broker. The practice is usually completed in two parts:
the loan closing (buyer and lender), and
the real estate transaction closing (buyer and seller).

Escrow Closing

An escrow is a method of closing a real estate transaction.
A closing in which the funds, title, releases, recordings are placed into escrow for processing by the escrow agent, with the actual title transfer taking place after all these items are completely processed.

Responsibilities of escrow agent
The escrow agent is given the responsibility to oversee and coordinate the closing activities, acting as a neutral third party between the buyers and sellers. The escrow agent may be an attorney, a title company, a trust company, an escrow company or the escrow department of a lending institution. Your escrow officer must follow the instructions of both parties (buyers and sellers) involved in the transaction.
They are a neutral third party. Also, called the Transactional Agent.

Prorated items

Prorating

The fair-share buyer-seller splitting of expenses that extend over closing.

Real Estate Settlement Procedures Act

RESPA is a federal law designed to protect consumers who borrow money through a federally related mortgage loan
RESPA prohibits kickbacks or undisclosed fees usually secretly paid for referring business to someone.

Closing statements/TRID disclosures

Closing Disclosure Statement (closing/settlement statement):

Although the Closing Disclosure Statement would have already been delivered to the buyer/borrower, until the closing is complete and final costs are allocated, the final settlement statement can't be prepared.
Yoegel, John A.. Real Estate License Exams For Dummies (pp. 141-142). Wiley. Kindle Edition.

The most common form of closing statement for residential properties is the **Closing Disclosure Statement,** required under the Combined TILA-RESPA Disclosure Rule, which is prepared at or just after closing.

Copies of the statement are sent to the buyer and seller along with many other necessary documents.

It's primarily a financial document stating who owes what to whom and who has already given over money that will be distributed.

At least three days before the mortgage closing, a settlement statement or closing statement of costs must be prepared and given to the borrower.

Estimated costs: The lender must give the borrower a loan estimate of all costs associated with the mortgage loan no more than three days after receiving the application.

Estimating closing costs

A **credit** is an amount owed to the buyer or seller or something for which they've already paid.

A debit is something that the buyer or seller owes.

Purchase Price
a debit to the buyer,

Mortgage Payoff
credit to the seller - debit to the buyer

Down Payment
a credit to the buyer

Two types of payments and costs that are allocated between the buyer and seller at closing
are **accrued** items and **prepaid items**:
1. An *accrued* **expense** is an accounting expense recognized in the books **before** it is paid for.
2. A **prepaid item** is an accounting expense recognized in the books **after** it is paid for.

Property and income taxes

Transfer Tax
A tax charged by the state to transfer an interest in real estate which helps establish an accurate value
for tax assessment purposes.

Property Tax
A tax based on the assessed value of real property; 100% deductible on income tax.

The Taxpayer Relief Act of 1997
Passed by Congress to greatly reduce the tax on the gain to be realized on the sale of real estate,
especially for residential real estate. With the passage of the Act, individuals can exclude up to $250,000
of capital gains from taxation, while married couples can exclude up to $500,000. (personal residence)

Capital Gains
Capital gains are profits that an individual receives from an appreciation in the value of an investment.
Capital gains are the difference between the sale price of an investment and the original purchase price
of that investment.

Capital Gains Tax Exclusions
single – $250,000
married – $500, 0o0
Must have lived in the property 2 of the last 5 years. (The time does not have to be continuous.) Capital
Gains Exclusion can be taken every 2 years.

Nursing Home Exception: While normally you are required to own, and live in the house for two of the
last five years, people who end up living in a nursing home can have this requirement lessened to only
one out of five years. In addition, time spent in the nursing home counts towards the use test as if it
were the original home.

Home Office Exception: Be aware that if you are taking depreciation deductions for a home office, that
amount will be subtracted from your capital gains exclusion. For example, if you were normally entitled
to $250,000, but had taken $50,000 in depreciation deductions for a home office, you would only be
entitled to a $200,000 exclusion from your capital gains.

1031 Tax Deferred Exchange
Thanks to IRC Section 1031, a properly structured 1031 exchange allows an investor to sell a property, to
reinvest the proceeds in a new property and to defer all capital gain taxes. IRC Section 1031 (a)(1) states:

"No gain or loss shall be recognized on the exchange of real property held for productive use in a trade or business or for investment, if such real property is exchanged solely for real property of like-kind which is to be held either for productive use in a trade or business or for investment."

An exchange of like-kind property under IRS Code 1031 in which parties may defer any capital gains tax due.

Identification Period
A maximum of 45 calendar days from the relinquished property closing to properly identify potential replacement property or properties.

Exchange Period
Maximum of 180 calendar days after the relinquished property closing.

BASIC 1031 exchange terminology:

BOOT: "Non like-kind" property received; "Boot" is taxable to the extent there is a capital gain.

CASH BOOT: Any proceeds actually or constructively received by the taxpayer.

LIKE-KIND PROPERTY: Any real property held for productive use in trade or business or held for investment; both the relinquished and replacement properties must be considered like-kind to qualify for tax deferral.

QUALIFIED INTERMEDIARY: The entity who facilitates the exchange; defined as follows: (1) Not a related party (i.e. agent, attorney, broker, etc.) (2) Receives a fee (3) Receives the relinquished property from the taxpayer and sells to the buyer (4) Purchases the replacement property from the seller and transfers it to the taxpayer; Asset Preservation, Inc. (API) is a qualified intermediary.

RELINQUISHED PROPERTY: Property given up by the taxpayer; also, referred to as the sale, exchange, down leg or Phase I property.

REPLACEMENT PROPERTY: Property received by the taxpayer; also, referred to as the purchase, target, up leg or Phase II property.

Depreciation – Straight-Line Method
Determines the equal annual depreciation allowed in a straight line from the adjusted basis to zero, and computed by dividing the adjusted basis by the estimated years remaining of economic life.

Recovery of an investor's cost of a property down to zero over 27.5 years (residential) or 39 years (non-residential). Divide the value of an income property by 27.5 (or 39), then deduct that amount on income tax each year. Depreciation also reduces the adjusted basis of the building.

Interest Deduction
Interest paid on a 1st mortgage is 100% deductible on income tax.

Basis
Original cost of a property.

Capital Gain
The difference between the adjusted basis of property and selling price

Tax Shelter
Any legal tax advantage that defers or eliminates tax liability, such as property tax and mortgage interest deductibility, depreciation, etc.

County Assessor

A county official (or sometimes the county treasurer in small counties) who determines the assessed valuation of real property.

County Board of Equalization
The county commissioners, when meeting to review the assessment of all taxable property in the county, and hear appeals from protests filed with the county assessor. The state board of equalization meets each year to determine if each county has assessed at the percentage of actual value prescribed by law.

County Treasurer
A county official who collects the taxes and determines the budget for schools, road maintenance, etc.

Commercial Assessed Valuation
A percentage of actual value for non-residential property used to compute property tax.

Warranties
Purpose of home or construction warranty programs

For many people, a home is the most expensive purchase they ever make. It's no wonder, then, that buyers of newly built homes are interested in warranties, which promise to repair or replace certain elements of the home, if necessary, within a certain time. According to the Federal Trade Commission, the nation's consumer protection agency, if you're considering a home warranty it's important to understand what it covers, how to make a claim, and the process for resolving disputes that may arise between you and the builder or warranty company.

Many home warranties are backed by the builder; others are purchased by the builder from an independent company that assumes responsibility for certain claims. Some home owners purchase additional coverage on their own from third-party warranty companies to supplement the coverage their builder provides. These add-on service contracts are commonly called warranties. The Federal Housing Authority (FHA) and the Department of Veterans' Affairs (VA) require builders to purchase a third-party warranty as a way to protect buyers of newly built homes with FHA or VA loans.

Scope of home or construction warranty programs

Coverage
Warranties for newly built homes generally offer limited coverage on workmanship and materials relating to various components of the home, such as windows, heating, ventilation and air conditioning (HVAC), plumbing, and electrical systems for specific periods.

Warranties also typically define how repairs will be made.

The duration of coverage varies depending on the component of the house.

Coverage is provided for workmanship and materials on most components during the first year. For example, most warranties on new construction cover siding and stucco, doors and trim, and drywall and paint during the first year.

Coverage for HVAC, plumbing, and electrical systems is generally two years. Some builders provide coverage for up to 10 years for "major structural defects," sometimes defined as problems that make a home unsafe and put the owner in danger. For example, a roof that could collapse is a "major structural defect."

Most warranties for newly built homes, however, do not cover expenses an owner may incur as a consequence of a major construction defect or warranty repair, like the cost of having to move out of one's home while repairs are being made. Nor do they typically cover:
- household appliances
- small cracks in brick, tile, cement or drywall
- components covered under a manufacturer's warranty

Homeowners Insurance

(Separate Policy) Renters Insurance

Renters get their own insurance

Homeowners insurance protects your home and personal property against damage or loss. It insures you in case someone gets hurt while on your property. You may already have insurance on your home if you have a mortgage on the property.

Renters insurance offers rente'rs coverage similar to homeowners insurance.

What Can Homeowners or Renters Insurance Cover?

Homeowners or renter's insurance may pay claims for:

- Damage to your home, garage, and other outbuildings

- Loss of furniture and other personal property due to damage or theft, both at home and away

- Extra living expenses if you live in temporary housing until your house is being repaired

Homeowners or renter's insurance may also pay for:

- Physical injury and property damage that you cause to others through negligence

- Accidents happening in and around your home, as well as away from home, for which you are responsible

- Injuries occurring in and around your home to anyone other than you or your family

- Limited coverage for money, gold, jewelry, and stamp and coin collections

- Personal property in storage

Chapter 10

Practice of real estate (Salesperson 13%; Broker 14%)
A. Trust/escrow accounts
1. Purpose and definition of trust accounts,
including monies held in trust accounts
2. Responsibility for trust monies, including
commingling/conversion
B. Federal fair housing laws and the ADA
1. Protected classes
2. Prohibited conduct (red-lining,
blockbusting, steering)
3. Americans with Disabilities (ADA)
4. Exemptions
C. Advertising and technology
1. Advertising practices
a) Truth in advertising
b) Fair housing issues in advertising
2. Use of technology
a) Requirements for confidential
information
b) Do-Not-Call List
D. Licensee and responsibilities
Employee
Independent Contractor
Due diligence for real estate transactions
Supervisory responsibilities (BROKER ONLY)
a) Licensees
b) Unlicensed personnel
E. Antitrust laws
1. Antitrust laws and purpose
2. Antitrust violations in real estate

Trust/Escrow Accounts

Purpose and definition of trust accounts, including monies held in trust accounts

Trust Accounts

Bank accounts to maintain funds that belong to the public -i.e., buyers' earnest money, tenants' security deposits, owners' rental income.

Real estate trust fund accounts, also called earnest money or escrow accounts, are accounts that a brokerage company will set up at a bank or some other recognized depository. They are money or other things of value that are received by a broker or salesperson on behalf of an individual (usually the buyer) that is held for the benefit of others in the performance of any acts for which a real estate license is required.

Any and all money that a client gives the company or the company receives on the client's behalf goes into a trust fund account.

When a brokerage company sets up a trust fund account for the benefit of its clients, the broker is the **trustee** for the account. This means that the broker is primarily responsible for the money that is in the account.

The trust fund account keeps the client's money segregated from the broker's money. This ensures that any money the client wishes to use for a real estate transaction remains in a secure account only accessible to the client or the broker. Another benefit is insurance.

As long as the money is deposited in a federally insured bank by the FDIC (Federal Deposit Insurance Corporation), each client's funds are insured up to $100,000

Responsibility for trust monies, including commingling/conversion

Commingling

Commingling is the act of mixing or mingling client's funds with the broker's own money.

Generally, a licensee or broker found guilty of mixing or commingling his client's funds with his own personal account can have his license suspended or revoked.

Mixing or depositing client's funds with broker's personal funds or business operating account.

Commingling is illegal.

A broker runs the risk of losing his license if he uses any money out of the trust fund account for his own personal use. A broker is not only responsible for his own actions, but also for the actions of his salespeople. Thus, he may also be held liable for any commingling, diversion and/or conversion of his client's money done by his salespeople.

Diversion

The criminal use of trust account funds for the benefit of other than the owner of those funds.

Conversion

Converting trust account funds to personal use.

Federal Fair Housing Laws and the ADA

The Fair Housing Act

The Fair Housing Act protects people from discrimination when they are renting or buying a home, getting a mortgage, seeking housing assistance, or engaging in other housing-related activities.

Who Is Protected?
The Fair Housing Act prohibits discrimination in housing because of:
- Race
- Color
- National Origin
- Religion
- Sex
- Familial Status
- Disability

What Types of Housing Are Covered?
The Fair Housing Act covers most housing. In very limited circumstances, the Act exempts owner-occupied buildings with no more than four units, single-family houses sold or rented by the owner without the use of an agent, and housing operated by religious organizations and private clubs that limit occupancy to members.

What Is Prohibited?

In the Sale and Rental of Housing:
- It is illegal discrimination to take any of the following actions because of race, color, religion, sex, disability, familial status, or national origin:
- Refuse to rent or sell housing
- Refuse to negotiate for housing
- Otherwise make housing unavailable
- Set different terms, conditions or privileges for sale or rental of a dwelling
- Provide a person different housing services or facilities
- Falsely deny that housing is available for inspection, sale or rental
- Make, print or publish any notice, statement or advertisement with respect to the sale or rental of a dwelling that indicates any preference, limitation or discrimination
- Impose different sales prices or rental charges for the sale or rental of a dwelling
- Use different qualification criteria or applications, or sale or rental standards or procedures, such as income standards, application requirements, application fees, credit analyses, sale or rental approval procedures or other requirements
- Evict a tenant or a tenant's guest
- Harass a person
- Fail or delay performance of maintenance or repairs
- Limit privileges, services or facilities of a dwelling
- Discourage the purchase or rental of a dwelling
- Assign a person to a particular building or neighborhood or section of a building or neighborhood
- For profit, persuade, or try to persuade, homeowners to sell their homes by suggesting that people of a particular protected characteristic are about to move into the neighborhood (blockbusting)
- Refuse to provide or discriminate in the terms or conditions of homeowner's insurance because of the race, color, religion, sex, disability, familial status, or national origin of the owner and/or occupants of a dwelling
- Deny access to or membership in any multiple listing service or real estate brokers' organization

In Mortgage Lending:

It is illegal discrimination to take any of the following actions based on race, color, religion, sex, disability, familial status, or national origin:

- Refuse to make a mortgage loan or provide other financial assistance for a dwelling
- Refuse to provide information regarding loans
- Impose different terms or conditions on a loan, such as different interest rates, points, or fees
- Discriminate in appraising a dwelling
- Condition the availability of a loan on a person's response to harassment
- Refuse to purchase a loan

Harassment:
The Fair Housing Act makes it illegal to harass persons because of race, color, religion, sex, disability, familial status, or national origin. Among other things, this forbids sexual harassment.

Other Prohibitions:
In addition, it is illegal discrimination to:

- Threaten, coerce, intimidate or interfere with anyone exercising a fair housing right or assisting others who exercise the right
- Retaliate against a person who has filed a fair housing complaint or assisted in a fair housing investigation

Advertising:

What Is Prohibited?
In nearly all housing, including private housing, public housing, and housing that receives federal funding, the Fair Housing Act prohibits the making, printing and publishing of advertisements that indicate a preference, limitation or discrimination because of race, color, religion, sex, disability, familial status, or national origin.

The prohibition applies to publishers, such as newspapers and directories, as well as to persons and entities who place real estate advertisements in newspapers and on websites. It also applies where the advertisement itself violates the Act, even if the property being advertised may be exempt from the provisions of the Act.

Other federal civil rights laws may also prohibit discriminatory advertising practices.

Examples of advertising that may violate the Act include phrases such as "no children," which indicates discrimination on the basis of familial status, or "no wheelchairs," which indicates disability discrimination.

Additional Protections For Persons With Disabilities:

Housing providers must make reasonable accommodations and allow reasonable modifications that may be necessary to allow persons with disabilities to enjoy their housing.

Civil Rights Act of 1866
Gave all citizens the same rights as those previously only enjoyed by whites to inherit, purchase and sell real and personal property.

Civil Rights Act of 1964
Title VI prohibits discrimination in any programs receiving federal funds, such as FHA and VA loans or urban renewal projects.

Civil Rights Act of 1968
Title VIII a/k/a the Federal Fair Housing Act prohibits discrimination in housing based on national origin, color, religion and race. Enforced by HUD (Department of Housing and Urban Development).

Fair Housing Amendments Act of 1988

Added protection for people with physical or mental handicaps plus familial status. Also, gave H.U.D. increased enforcement power, removed the cap on punitive damages, et

Fair Housing Act of 1974
Added sex (gender) as a protected class.

Protected Classes
A category protected in law from housing discrimination. Federal law includes
1. race
2. color
3. religion
4. national origin
5. sex
6. familial status
7. handicap

States and even local governments may have additional protected classes

Familial Status
A fair housing protected class prohibiting discrimination against individuals under the age of 18 living with a parent or legal guardian, including pregnant women or a person waiting to be claimed by a legal guardian.

Prohibited conduct (red-lining, blockbusting, steering)

Blockbusting
The illegal act of inducing owners to sell now because property value will decrease due to real or rumored moving into the neighborhood by persons of any protected class.

Redlining
Illegal restriction on the number of loans or the loan-to-value ratio in specific areas based on grounds that exclude any protected class.

Steering
The discriminatory practice of directing homebuyers to (or away from) specific areas based on a protected class to maintain homogeneity

Americans with Disabilities (ADA)

Americans with Disabilities Act (ADA)
A federal law (1992) intended to prevent discrimination against disabled persons in 4 areas: public transportation, public accommodations, government services and telecommunications.

Handicap
A mental or physical impairment that substantially limits activity such as hearing, seeing, walking, learning, etc.

Exemptions

Real estate agents are held to a higher standard in fair housing matters. It may be legal to discriminate but it is not ethical or acceptable.

The 1968 Federal Fair Housing Act was written with certain exceptions, or cases in which people, in a sense, can discriminate in housing issues. In addition to remembering the exceptions themselves for test purposes, you need to remember these two important factors with respect to these exceptions:

Even if an exception is legal for an individual (such as the owner of a single-family home selling her house), a real estate agent is not permitted to participate in the exception. Real estate agents are held to a higher standard in fair housing matters.

Discriminatory advertising may not be used; again, even when the exception itself is legal. The owner of a single-family home can't use discriminatory advertising in selling her house, even though she could discriminate in the ultimate sale itself.

Don't forget that regardless of exemptions permitted by the 1968 Federal Fair Housing Act, the 1866 Civil Rights Act permits no exceptions with respect to race.

The exceptions in the 1988 Law are as follows.

Age: An exemption is provided to housing protections afforded to age and familial classes intended for older people. Housing may be restricted to people 62 or older or 55 or older in cases where at least one occupant per unit is 55 and at least 80 percent of the units are occupied by people ages 55 or older. In these cases, children may be excluded.

Owner-occupied housing: Multifamily housing of two to four units, where one of the units is owner-occupied, is exempt from fair housing laws.

Private clubs: An organization that restricts its membership may provide restricted housing to its members, as long as it doesn't offer housing to the general public.

Public-law occupancy standards: Local maximum occupancy standards aren't superseded in their application by the Fair Housing Act. For example, if a local law provides a maximum occupancy of two people per bedroom and you rent out a studio apartment in a building you own, you can't be forced to rent the apartment to a couple with a child.

Religious organizations: Housing sponsored by a religious organization may be restricted to members of that particular religious organization, provided the religion doesn't discriminate in its membership policies.

Single-family housing: The sale or rental of a single-family house is exempted from the rules of the Fair Housing Act if the owner doesn't own more than three units at one time, and neither a broker nor discriminatory advertising is used. If such a property is sold, no more than one house can be sold during every two-year period.

Advertising and Technology

Advertising practices

Blind Ad
An advertisement that disguises the identity of the advertiser, i.e. contains a phone number with no other identifying data. Licensed brokers should not use blind ads and must disclose agency.

Puffery
An exaggerated opinion, not necessarily based in fact, intended to portray a property in a more favorable light. Example: "This property is one of the best buys in the neighborhood. It is sure to go up in value".

Fraud
Intentional deception or misrepresentation – a material misstatement of fact.

Truth in advertising
When consumers see, or hear an advertisement, whether it's on the Internet, radio or television, or anywhere else, federal law says that ad must be truthful, not misleading, and, when appropriate, backed by scientific evidence.

The Federal Trade Commission enforces these truth-in-advertising laws, and it applies the same standards no matter where an ad appears – in newspapers and magazines, online, in the mail, or on billboards or buses.

The FTC looks especially closely at advertising claims that can affect consumers' health or their pocketbooks – claims about food, over-the-counter drugs, dietary supplements, alcohol, and tobacco and on conduct related to high-tech products and the Internet. The FTC also monitors and writes reports about ad industry practices regarding the marketing of alcohol and tobacco.
When the FTC finds a case of fraud perpetrated on consumers, the agency files actions in federal district court for immediate and permanent orders to stop scams; prevent fraudsters from perpetrating scams in the future; freeze their assets; and get compensation for victims.

Use of technology

Traditional forms of advertising, including billboards, newspapers, magazines and radio, are progressively becoming replaced by online advertisements.

Targeted advertising
is a form of advertising where online advertisers can use sophisticated methods to target the most receptive audiences with certain traits, based on the product or person the advertiser is promoting.

These traits can be demographic which are focused
- on race
- economic status
- sex
- age
- the level of education
- income level
- employment
- psychographic (a qualitative methodology used to describe consumers on psychological attributes)

Attributes focused based on the consumer's values, personality, attitudes, opinions, lifestyles and interests.

They can also be behavioral variables, such as browser history, purchase history, and other recent activity.

Targeted advertising is focused on certain traits and the consumers who are likely to have a strong preference will receive the message instead of those who have no interest and whose preferences do not match a product's attribute.
This eliminates wastage.

Information and communication technology (ICT) space has transformed over recent years, resulting in targeted advertising.

Through the emergence of new online channels, the need for targeted advertising is increasing because companies aim to minimize wasted advertising by means of information technology.

Some Platforms
- Email
Despite the prevailing acceptable use policies, electronic mail marketing rapidly expanded and eventually became known as "spam."
- Display ads
- Search ads
- Twitter
- Facebook
- More Platforms developed everyday

IDX Technology
The technology used by real estate professionals to put the MLS on their website.

Requirements for confidential information

Confidentiality
A duty of an agent to maintain the trusted confidence and secrets of a principal. Neither agent nor non-agent transaction brokers may reveal anything that would weaken the principal's or client's position.

Confidentiality is best addressed in the Realtors® Code of Ethics:
Standard of Practice 1-9
The obligation of REALTORS® to preserve confidential information (as defined by state law) provided by their clients in the course of any agency relationship or non-agency relationship recognized by law continues after termination of agency relationships or any non-agency relationships recognized by law. REALTORS® shall not knowingly, during or following the termination of professional relationships with their clients:
reveal confidential information of clients; or
use confidential information of clients to the disadvantage of clients; or
use confidential information of clients for the REALTOR®'s advantage or the advantage of third parties unless:
a) clients consent after full disclosure; or
b) REALTORS® are required by court order; or
c) it is the intention of a client to commit a crime and the information is necessary to prevent the crime; or
d) it is necessary to defend a REALTOR® or the REALTOR®'s employees or associates against an accusation of wrongful conduct.

THE TELEPHONE CONSUMER PROTECTION ACT

The Do Not Call Registry
Congress directed the FTC (Federal Trade Commission) to prescribe rules prohibiting abusive and deceptive telemarketing acts or practices.
Since 2003, Americans have been able to opt out of receiving most telemarketing calls by putting their phone numbers on the National Do Not Call Registry, and millions of them have done so.

The Registry now has more than 221 million telephone numbers on it, giving these consumers a little more peace and quiet during their dinner hour.

Not only is the Do Not Call program wildly popular with consumers, but it also helps telemarketers operate more efficiently by screening out consumers who do not want to be contacted.

The Registry only contains phone numbers, no other personally identifiable information, and we do not keep a record of whether the numbers are land line or cell phones.

There are some exemptions to the Do Not Call rules.

Because of the limits to FTC's authority, the Registry does not apply to political calls or calls from non-profits and charities (but the Registry does cover telemarketers calling on behalf of charities). Also, calls from legitimate "survey" organizations are not covered because they are not offering to sell anything to consumers.

Finally, calls are permitted from companies with which you have done or sought to do business. Specifically, a company can call you up to **18 months after you last did business with it.**

ENFORCEMENT OF THE DO NOT CALL REGISTRY
The FTC takes aggressive legal action to make sure telemarketers abide by the Do Not Call Registry.

ROBOCALLS AND THE DO NOT CALL REGISTRY
The use of pre-recorded message telemarketing, where a sales pitch to a live consumer begins with or is made entirely by a pre-recorded message, violates the Amended TSR because the telemarketer is not connecting the call to a sales representative within two (2) seconds of the people completed greeting.

On September 1, 2009, new FTC rules went into effect prohibiting most prerecorded telemarketing calls, commonly known as robocalls, unless the telemarketer has the consumer's prior written authorization to transmit such calls.

THE ACT

FAIR HOUSING ADVERTISING

Policy.

It is the policy of the United States to provide, within constitutional limitations, for fair housing throughout the United States. The provisions of the Fair Housing Act make it unlawful to discriminate in the sale, rental, and financing of housing, and in the provision of brokerage and appraisal services, because of race, color, religion, sex, handicap, familial status, or national origin. The Fair Housing Act, makes it unlawful to make, print, or publish, or cause to be made, printed, or published, any notice, statement, or advertisement, with respect to the sale or rental of a dwelling, that indicates any preference, limitation, or discrimination because of race, color, religion, sex, handicap, familial status, or national origin, or an intention to make any such preference, limitation, or discrimination.
However, the prohibitions of the act regarding familial status do not apply with respect to housing for older persons.

Purpose.

The purpose of this part is to assist all advertising media, advertising agencies and all other persons who use advertising to make, print, or publish, or cause to be made, printed, or published, advertisements with respect to the sale, rental, or financing of dwellings which are in compliance with the requirements of the Fair Housing Act.

These regulations also describe the matters this Department will review in evaluating compliance with the Fair Housing Act in connection with investigations of complaints alleging discriminatory housing practices involving advertising.

Definitions.

(a) Assistant Secretary means the Assistant Secretary for Fair Housing and Equal Opportunity.
(b) General Counsel means the General Counsel of the Department of Housing and Urban Development.
(c) Dwelling means any building, structure, or portion thereof which is occupied as, or designed or intended for occupancy as, a residence by one or more families, and any vacant land which is offered for sale or lease for the construction or location thereon of any such building, structure, or portion thereof.
(d) Family includes a single individual.
(e) Person includes one or more individuals, corporations, partnerships, associations, labor organizations, legal representatives, mutual companies, joint-stock companies, trusts, unincorporated organizations, trustees, trustees in cases under Title 11 of the United States Code, receivers, and fiduciaries.
(f) To rent includes to lease, to sublease, to let and otherwise to grant for a consideration the right to occupy premises not owned by the occupant.
(g) Discriminatory housing practice means an act that is unlawful under section 804, 805, 806, or 818 of the Fair Housing Act.
(h) Handicap means, with respect to a person—
(1) A physical or mental impairment which substantially limits one or more of such person's major life activities,
(2) A record of having such an impairment, or
(3) Being regarded as having such an impairment.
This term does not include current, illegal use of or addiction to a controlled substance.
For purposes of this part, an individual shall not be considered to have a handicap solely because that individual is a transvestite.
(i) Familial status means one or more individuals (*who have not attained the age of 18 years*) being domiciled with—
(1) A parent or another person having legal custody of such individual or individuals; or
(2) The designee of such parent or other person having such custody, with the written permission of such parent or other person.
The protections afforded against discrimination on the basis of familial status shall apply to any person who is *pregnant* or is in the process of securing legal custody of any individual who has not attained the age of 18 years.

Scope.
(a) General.

This part describes the matters the Department will review in evaluating compliance with the Fair Housing Act in connection with investigations of complaints alleging discriminatory housing practices involving advertising. Use of these criteria will be considered by the General Counsel in making determinations as to whether there is reasonable cause, and by the Assistant Secretary in making determinations that there is no reasonable cause, to believe that a discriminatory housing practice has occurred or is about to occur.

(1) Advertising media.
This part provides criteria for use by advertising media in determining whether to accept and publish advertising regarding sales or rental transactions. Use of these criteria will be considered by the General Counsel in making determinations as to whether there is reasonable cause, and by the Assistant Secretary in making determinations that there is no reasonable cause, to believe that a discriminatory housing practice has occurred or is about to occur.

(2) Persons placing advertisements.
A failure by persons placing advertisements to use the criteria contained in this part, when found in connection with the investigation of a complaint alleging the making or use of discriminatory advertisements, will be considered by the General Counsel in making a determination of reasonable cause, and by the Assistant Secretary in making determinations that there is no reasonable cause, to believe that a discriminatory housing practice has occurred or is about to occur.

(b) Affirmative advertising efforts.
Nothing in this part shall be construed to restrict advertising efforts designed to attract persons to dwellings who would not ordinarily be expected to apply, when such efforts are pursuant to an affirmative marketing program or undertaken to remedy the effects of prior discrimination in connection with the advertising or marketing of dwellings.

Use of words, phrases, symbols, and visual aids.
The following words, phrases, symbols, and forms typify those most often used in residential real estate advertising to convey either overt or tacit discriminatory preferences or limitations. In considering a complaint under the Fair Housing Act, the Department will normally consider the use of these and comparable words, phrases, symbols, and forms to indicate a possible violation of the act and to establish a need for further proceedings on the complaint, if it is apparent from the context of the usage that discrimination within the meaning of the act is likely to result.

(a) Words descriptive of dwelling, landlord, and tenants.
White private home, Colored home, Jewish home, Hispanic residence, adult building.

(b) Words indicative of race, color, religion, sex, handicap, familial status, or national origin–
(1) **Race**–Negro, Black, Caucasian, Oriental, American Indian.
(2) **Color**–White, Black, Colored.
(3) **Religion**–Protestant, Christian, Catholic, Jew.
(4) **National origin**–Mexican American, Puerto Rican, Philippine, Polish, Hungarian, Irish, Italian, Chicano, African, Hispanic, Chinese, Indian, Latino.
(5) **Sex**–the exclusive use of words in advertisements, including those involving the rental of separate units in a single or multi-family dwelling, stating or tending to imply that the housing being advertised is available to persons of only one sex and not the other, except where the sharing of living areas is involved. Nothing in this part restricts advertisements of dwellings used exclusively for dormitory facilities by educational institutions.
(6) **Handicap**–crippled, blind, deaf, mentally ill, retarded, impaired, handicapped, physically fit. Nothing in this part restricts the inclusion of information about the availability of accessible housing in advertising of dwellings.
(7) **Familial status**–adults, children, singles, mature persons. Nothing in this part restricts advertisements of dwellings which are intended and operated for occupancy by older persons and which constitute housing for older persons as defined in Part 100 of this title.
(8) **Catch words**–Words and phrases used in a discriminatory context should be avoided, e.g., restricted, exclusive, private, integrated, traditional, board approval or membership approval.

(c) Symbols or logotypes.
Symbols or logotypes which imply or suggest race, color, religion, sex, handicap, familial status, or national origin.

(d) Colloquialisms.
Words or phrases used regionally or locally which imply or suggest race, color, religion, sex, handicap, familial status, or national origin.

(e) Directions to real estate for sale or rent (use of maps or written instructions).

Directions can imply a discriminatory preference, limitation, or exclusion.

For example, references to real estate location made in terms of racial or national origin significant landmarks, such as an existing black development (signal to blacks) or an existing development known for its exclusion of minorities (signal to whites).

Specific directions which make reference to a racial or national origin significant area may indicate a preference. References to a synagogue, congregation or parish may also indicate a religious preference.

(f) Area (location) description.

Names of facilities which cater to a particular racial, national origin or religious group, such as country club or private school designations, or names of facilities which are used exclusively by one sex may indicate a preference.

Selective use of advertising media or content.

The selective use of advertising media or content when particular combinations thereof are used exclusively with respect to various housing developments or sites can lead to discriminatory results and may indicate a violation of the Fair Housing Act.

For example, the use of English language media alone or the exclusive use of media catering to the majority population in an area, when, in such area, there are also available non-English language or other minority media, may have discriminatory impact.

Similarly, the *selective use of human models* in advertisements may have discriminatory impact. The following are examples of the selective use of advertisements which may be discriminatory:

(a) Selective geographic advertisements.

Such selective use may involve the strategic placement of billboards; brochure advertisements distributed within a limited geographic area by hand or in the mail; advertising in particular geographic coverage editions of major metropolitan newspapers or in newspapers of limited circulation which are mainly advertising vehicles for reaching a particular segment of the community; or displays or announcements available only in selected sales offices.

(b) Selective use of equal opportunity slogan or logo.

When placing advertisements, such selective use may involve placing the equal housing opportunity slogan or logo in advertising reaching some geographic areas, but not others, or with respect to some properties but not others.

(c) Selective use of human models when conducting an advertising campaign.

Selective advertising may involve an advertising campaign using human models primarily in media that cater to one racial or national origin segment of the population without a complementary advertising campaign that is directed at other groups.

Another example may involve use of racially mixed models by a developer to advertise one development and not others.

Similar care must be exercised in advertising in publications or other media directed at one particular sex, or at persons without children.

Such selective advertising may involve the use of human models of members of only one sex, or of adults only, in displays, photographs or drawings to indicate preferences for one sex or the other, or for adults to the exclusion of children.

Fair housing policy and practices.

In the investigation of complaints, the Assistant Secretary will consider the implementation of fair housing policies and practices provided in this section as evidence of compliance with the prohibitions against discrimination in advertising under the Fair Housing Act.

(a) Use of Equal Housing Opportunity logotype, statement, or slogan.

All advertising of residential real estate for sale, rent, or financing should contain an equal housing opportunity logotype, statement, or slogan as a means of educating the home seeking public that the property is available to all persons regardless of race, color, religion, sex, handicap, familial status, or national origin.

The choice of logotype, statement or slogan will depend on the type of media used (visual or auditory) and, in space advertising, on the size of the advertisement.

Table I (see Appendix I) indicates suggested use of the logotype, statement, or slogan and size of logotype. Table II (see Appendix I) contains copies of the suggested Equal Housing Opportunity logotype, statement and slogan.

(b) Use of human models.

Human models in photographs, drawings, or other graphic techniques may not be used to indicate exclusiveness because of race, color, religion, sex, handicap, familial status, or national origin. If models are used in display advertising campaigns, the models should be clearly definable as reasonably representing majority and minority groups in the metropolitan area, both sexes, and, when appropriate, families with children. Models, if used, should portray persons in an equal social setting and indicate to the general public that the housing is open to all without regard to race, color, religion, sex, handicap, familial status, or national origin, and is not for the exclusive use of one such group.

(c) Coverage of local laws.

Where the Equal Housing Opportunity statement is used, the advertisement may also include a statement regarding the coverage of any local fair housing or human rights ordinance prohibiting discrimination in the sale, rental or financing of dwellings.

(d) Notification of fair housing policy–

(1) Employees. All publishers of advertisements, advertising agencies, and firms engaged in the sale, rental or financing of real estate should provide a printed copy of their nondiscrimination policy to each employee and officer.

(2) Clients. All publishers or advertisements and advertising agencies should post a copy of their nondiscrimination policy in a conspicuous location wherever persons place advertising and should have copies available for all firms and persons using their advertising services.

(3) Publishers' notice. All publishers should publish at the beginning of the real estate advertising section a notice such as that appearing in Table III. The notice may include a statement regarding the coverage of any local fair housing or human rights ordinance prohibiting discrimination in the sale, rental or financing of dwellings.

APPENDIX I TO PART 109–FAIR HOUSING ADVERTISING

The following three tables may serve as a guide for the use of the Equal Housing Opportunity logotype, statement, slogan, and publisher's notice for advertising:

Table I

A simple formula can guide the real estate advertiser in using the Equal Housing Opportunity logotype, statement, or slogan. In all space advertising (in regularly printed media such as newspapers or magazines) the following standards should be used:

Size of Advertisement

1/2 page or larger

Size of Logo-type in Inches

2x2

1/8th page up to 1/2 page

1x1

4 column inches to 1/8 page

1/2 by 1/2

less than 4 column inches

Equal Housing Opportunity slogan should be used.

In any other advertisements, if other logotypes are used in the advertisement, then the Equal Housing Opportunity logo should be of a size at least equal to the largest of the other logotypes; if no other logotypes are used, then the type should be bold display face which is clearly visible.

Alternatively, when no other logotypes are used, 3 to 5 percent of an advertisement may be devoted to a statement of the equal housing opportunity policy.

In space advertising which is less than 4 column inches (one column 4 inches long or two columns 2 inches long) of a page in size, the Equal Housing Opportunity slogan should be used.

Such advertisements may be grouped with other advertisements under a caption which states that the housing is available to all without regard to race, color, religion, sex, handicap, familial status, or national origin.

Table II

Illustrations of Logotype, Statement, and Slogan. Equal Housing Opportunity Logotype: Equal Housing Opportunity Statement:

We are pledged to the letter and spirit of U.S. policy for the achievement of equal housing opportunity throughout the Nation. We encourage and support an affirmative advertising and marketing program in which there are no barriers to obtaining housing because of race, color, religion, sex, handicap, familial status, or national origin. Equal Housing Opportunity Slogan: "Equal Housing Opportunity."

Table III
Illustration of Media Notice–Publisher's notice:

All real estate advertised herein is subject to the Federal Fair Housing Act, which makes it illegal to advertise "any preference, limitation, or discrimination because of race, color, religion, sex, handicap, familial status, or national origin, or intention to make any such preference, limitation, or discrimination."

We will not knowingly accept any advertising for real estate which is in violation of the law. All persons are hereby informed that all dwellings advertised are available on an equal opportunity basis.

END

Licensee and Responsibilities
It is critical that business owners correctly determine whether the individuals providing services are employees or independent contractors.

Generally, you must withhold income taxes, withhold and pay Social Security and Medicare taxes, and pay unemployment tax on wages paid to an **employee.**
You do not generally have to withhold or pay any taxes on payments to independent **contractors.**

Employee

If you perform services that can be controlled by an employer (what will be done and how it will be done), you are an employee.

90% of income comes from salary or wages.

This applies even if you are given freedom of action.

What matters is that the employer has the legal right to control the details of how the services are performed.

Your earnings as an employee may be subject to FICA (Social Security tax and Medicare) and income tax withholding.

Independent Contractor

The general rule is that an individual is an independent contractor if the payer has the right to control or direct *only the result of the work* and not what will be done and how it will be done.

The earnings of a person who is working as an independent contractor are subject to Self-Employment Tax.

Most real estate professionals operate their business as a sole proprietorship. This means that you are not someone's employee, you haven't formed a partnership with anyone, and you have not incorporated your business.

IRS Mandatory Terms for an Independent Contractor

The individual must be a licensed real estate professional;
90% of all of their payments must be directly related to sales or other output, rather than the number of hours worked; and

Their services must be performed under a written contract providing that they will not be treated as employees for federal tax purposes.

Statutory Nonemployees

Licensed real estate agents are statutory nonemployees and are treated as self-employed for all Federal tax purposes, including income and employment taxes, if:

This category includes individuals engaged in appraisal activities for real estate sales if they earn income based on sales or other output.

Due diligence for real estate transactions

Due diligence means taking caution, performing calculations, reviewing documents, procuring insurance, walking the property, etc. — essentially doing your homework for the property

BEFORE you actually make the purchase.

Due diligence is the time a buyer has after signing a contract to assure themselves they are getting the asset they are paying for.

Laws involving real estate due diligence vary from state to state. Your real estate agent should be able to provide specific information about which legal issues pertain to you, and what your options are if problems arise.

Common Due Diligence Items
1. Study the Marketplace
2. Visit the Property
3. Hire a Building Inspector
4. Check Zoning Laws
5. Research the Title
6. Access the Most Recent Land Survey
7. Get an Appraisal
8. Schedule an Environmental Assessment
9. Figure Out Financing
10. Investigate Title Insurance

Supervisory Responsibilities (BROKER ONLY)
A licensed individual Broker has daily duties that include writing contracts and overseeing transactions for sales and purchasing activities on homes, land, and commercial properties.

A broker has attained a higher-level license than a real estate agent and has the ability to hire real estate agents to work as a team under their supervision.

Licensees

It shall be the duty of the responsible broker to instruct the licensees licensed under that broker in the:
- fundamentals of real estate practice
- ethics of the profession and the Mississippi Real Estate License Law
- exercise supervision of their real estate activities for which a license is required

A real estate broker who operates under the supervision of a responsible broker must not at any time act independently as a broker.

A responsible broker must maintain an office and display the license therein. If the broker has more than one office, the broker shall display a branch office license in each branch office.

The broker is responsible for the real estate practices of those licensees.

Typically, unlicensed assistants MAY:
1. Provide "general" information about listed properties such as location, availability, and address (without any solicitation on behalf of the assistant).
2. Perform clerical duties, which may include answering the telephone and forwarding calls.
3. Complete and submit listings and changes to a multiple listing service, type contract forms for approval by the licensee and the principal broker, pick-up and deliver paperwork to other brokers and salespersons, obtain status reports on a loan's progress, assemble closing documents and obtain required public information from governmental entities.

Antitrust Laws

Antitrust laws and purpose
U.S. Department of Justice
Washington, DC 20530

Many consumers have never heard of antitrust laws, but when these laws are effectively and responsibly enforced, they can save consumers millions and even billions of dollars a year in illegal overcharges. Most States have antitrust laws, and so does the Federal Government. Essentially, these laws prohibit business practices that unreasonably deprive consumers of the benefits of competition, resulting in higher prices for inferior products and services.

This information was prepared to alert consumers to the existence and importance of antitrust laws and to explain what you can do for antitrust enforcement and for yourself.

Antitrust Enforcement *and the* Consumer

Many consumers have never heard of antitrust laws, but when these laws are effectively and responsibly enforced, they can save consumers millions and even billions of dollars a year in illegal overcharges. Most States have antitrust laws, and so does the Federal Government. Essentially, these laws prohibit business practices that unreasonably deprive consumers of the benefits of competition, resulting in higher prices for inferior products and services.

1. What Do the Antitrust Laws Do for the Consumer?
Antitrust laws protect competition. Free and open competition benefits consumers by ensuring lower prices and new and better products. In a freely competitive market, each competing business generally will try to attract consumers by cutting its prices and increasing the quality of its products or services. Competition and the profit opportunities it brings also stimulate businesses to find new, innovative, and more efficient methods of production.

Consumers benefit from competition through lower prices and better products and services. Companies that fail to understand or react to consumer needs may soon find themselves losing out in the competitive battle.

When competitors agree to fix prices, rig bids, or allocate (divide up) customers, consumers lose the benefits of competition. The prices that result when competitors agree in these ways are artificially high; such prices do not accurately reflect cost and therefore distort the allocation of society's resources. The result is a loss not only to U.S. consumers and taxpayers, but also the U.S. economy.

When the competitive system is operating effectively, there is no need for government intrusion. The law recognizes that certain arrangements between firms—such as competitors cooperating to perform joint research and development projects—may benefit consumers by allowing the firms that have reached the agreement to compete more effectively against other firms. The law does not condemn all agreements between companies, only those that threaten to raise prices to consumers or to deprive them of new and better products.

But when competing firms get together to fix prices, to rig bids, to divide business between them, or to make other anticompetitive arrangements that provide no benefits to consumers, the Government will act promptly to protect the interests of American consumers.

2. What Are the Federal Antitrust Laws, and What Do They Prohibit?
There are three major Federal antitrust laws:
The Sherman Antitrust Act
The Clayton Act
The Federal Trade Commission Act

The Sherman Antitrust Act
The Sherman Antitrust Act has stood since 1890 as the principal law expressing our national commitment to a free market economy in which competition free from private and governmental restraints leads to the best results for consumers. Congress felt so strongly about this commitment that there was only one vote against the Act.

The Sherman Act outlaws all contracts, combinations, and conspiracies that unreasonably restrain interstate and foreign trade. This includes agreements among competitors to fix prices, rig bids, and allocate customers. The Sherman Act also makes it a crime to monopolize any part of interstate commerce. An unlawful monopoly exists when only one firm controls the market for a product or service, and it has obtained that market power, not because its product or service is superior to others, but by suppressing competition with anticompetitive conduct. The Act is not violated simply when one firm's vigorous competition and lower prices take sales from its less efficient competitors—that is competition working properly.

Sherman Act violations involving agreements between competitors usually are punished as criminal felonies. The Department of Justice alone is empowered to bring criminal prosecutions under the Sherman Act. Individual violators can be fined up to $1 million and sentenced to up to 10 years in Federal prison for each offense, and corporations can be fined up to $100 million for each offense. Under some circumstances, the maximum fines can go even higher than the Sherman Act maximums to twice the gain or loss involved.

The Clayton Act
The Clayton Act is a civil statute (carrying no criminal penalties) that was passed in 1914 and significantly amended in 1950. The Clayton Act prohibits mergers or acquisitions that are likely to lessen competition. Under the Act, the Government challenges those mergers that a careful economic analysis shows are likely to increase prices to consumers. All persons considering a merger or acquisition above a certain size must notify both the Antitrust Division and the Federal Trade Commission.

The Act also prohibits other business practices that under certain circumstances may harm competition.

The Federal Trade Commission Act
The Federal Trade Commission Act prohibits unfair methods of competition in interstate commerce, but carries no criminal penalties. It also created the Federal Trade Commission to police violations of the Act.

The Department of Justice also often uses other laws to fight illegal activities, including laws that prohibit false statements to Federal agencies, perjury, obstruction of justice, conspiracies to defraud the United States, and mail and wire fraud. Each of these crimes carries its own fines and imprisonment terms which may be added to the fines and imprisonment terms for antitrust law violations.

3. How Are Antitrust Laws Enforced?
There are three main ways in which the Federal antitrust laws are enforced:
1. Criminal and civil enforcement actions brought by the Antitrust Division of the Department of
2. Civil enforcement actions brought by the Federal Trade
3. Lawsuits brought by private parties asserting damage

The Department of Justice uses a number of tools in investigating and prosecuting criminal antitrust violations. Department of Justice attorneys often work with agents of the Federal Bureau of Investigation (FBI) or other investigative agencies to obtain evidence. In some cases, the Department may use court authorized searches of businesses and secret recordings by informants of telephone calls and meetings. The Department may grant immunity from prosecution to individuals or corporations who provide timely information that is needed to prosecute others for antitrust violations, such as bid rigging or price fixing.

A provision in the Clayton Act also permits private parties injured by an antitrust violation to sue in Federal court for three times their actual damages plus court costs and attorneys' fees. State attorneys general may bring civil suits under the Clayton Act on behalf of injured consumers in their States, and groups of consumers often bring suits on their own. Such civil suits following criminal enforcement actions can be a very effective additional deterrent to criminal activity.

Most States also have antitrust laws closely paralleling the Federal antitrust laws. The State laws generally apply to violations that occur wholly in one State. These laws typically are enforced through the offices of State attorneys general.

4. How Do Antitrust Violators Cheat the Consumer?

The worst antitrust offenses are cartel violations, such as:

1. **Price fixing:** Price fixing occurs when two or more competing sellers agree on what prices to charge, such as by agreeing that they will increase prices a certain amount or that they won't sell below a certain
2. **Bid rigging:** Bid rigging most commonly occurs when two or more firms agree to bid in such a way that a designated firm submits the winning bid, typically for local, State, or Federal Government contracts.
3. **Customer allocation:** Customer- allocation agreements involve some arrangement between competitors to split up customers, such as by geographic area, to reduce or eliminate competition.

Such price-fixing, bid-rigging, and customer- allocation agreements, unlike joint research agreements for example, provide no plausible offsetting benefits to consumers. Also, these agreements are generally secret, and the participants mislead and defraud customers by continuing to hold themselves out as competitors despite their agreement not to compete.

There can be no doubt that price fixing, bid rigging, and customer allocation harm consumers and taxpayers by causing them to pay more for products and services and by depriving them of other byproducts of true competition. Nor is there usually any question in the minds of violators that their conduct is unlawful. It has been estimated that such practices can raise the price of a product or service by more than 10 percent, sometimes much more, and that American consumers and taxpayers pour billions of dollars each year into the pockets of cartel members. People who take consumer and taxpayer money this way are thieves.

5. What Kinds of Cases Has the Justice Department Brought?

Because of the harm that cartel violations cause, the Justice Department's number one antitrust priority is criminal prosecution of those activities. The Department has obtained price-fixing, bid-rigging, or customer-allocation convictions in the soft drink, vitamins, trash hauling, road building, and electrical contracting industries, among others, involving billions of dollars in commerce. And in recent years, grand juries throughout the country have investigated possible violations with respect to fax paper, display materials, explosives, plumbing supplies, doors, aluminum extrusions, carpet, bread, and many more products and services. The Department also investigates and prosecutes bid rigging in connection with government procurement.

The imposition of unprecedented fines against foreign firms and jail sentences against foreign nationals residing outside of this country sends a powerful deterrent message that the United States is committed to vigorous antitrust enforcement against cartels that impact U.S. commerce, no matter where the participants may be found.

6. What Can You Do for Antitrust Enforcement and for Yourself?

Because they are by their nature secret, price-fixing, bid-rigging, and customer- allocation conspiracies are difficult to detect and prove. For that reason, law enforcement officials rely on complaints and information from consumers and competitors. A large percentage of all Federal antitrust investigations results from complaints received from consumers or people in business by phone or mail or in person.

7. How Can You Know If the Antitrust Laws Are Being Violated?

If any person knows or suspects that competitors, suppliers, or even an employer are violating the antitrust laws, that person should alert the antitrust authorities so that they can determine whether to investigate.

Price-fixing, bid-rigging, and customer- allocation conspiracies are most likely to occur where there are relatively few sellers who have to get together to agree. The larger the group of sellers, the more difficult it is to come to an agreement and enforce it.

Keep an eye out for telltale signs, including, for example:

Any evidence that two or more competing sellers of similar products have agreed to price their products a certain way, to sell only a certain amount of their product or to sell only in certain areas or to certain Large price changes involving more than one seller of very similar products of different brands, particularly if the price changes are of an equal amount and occur at about the same

Suspicious statements from a seller suggesting that only one firm can sell to a particular customer or type of customer.

Fewer competitors than normal submit bids

Competitors submit identical

The same company repeatedly has been the low bidder on contracts for a certain product or service or in a particular

Bidders seem to win bids on a fixed rotation.

There is an unusual and unexplainable large dollar difference between the winning bid and all other

The same bidder bids substantially higher on some bids than on others, and there is no logical cost reason to explain the

These signs are by no means conclusive evidence of antitrust violations. More investigation by trained lawyers and investigators would be required to determine that. But they may be an indication of collusion, and the people who enforce the antitrust laws want to hear about them.

8. What Is the Public's Role in Antitrust Enforcement?

Effective antitrust enforcement requires public support. Public ignorance and apathy can weaken antitrust enforcement more than anything else. Whether you are a businessperson or a consumer, if you encounter business behavior that appears to violate the antitrust laws, do not hesitate to inform the enforcement authorities of your suspicions. That is often the only way violations can be uncovered, and failing to uncover and punish antitrust violations not only penalizes consumers and taxpayers but also the vast majority of honest Business people who scrupulously observe the antitrust laws.

Antitrust violations in real estate

The most common violations in real estate are:

1. **Price fixing:** Price fixing occurs when two or more competing sellers agree on what prices to charge, such as by agreeing that they will increase prices a certain amount or that they won't sell below a certain

2. **Bid rigging:** Bid rigging most commonly occurs when two or more firms agree to bid in such a way that a designated firm submits the winning bid, typically for local, State, or Federal Government contracts.

3. **Customer allocation:** Customer- allocation agreements involve some arrangement between competitors to split up customers, such as by geographic area, to reduce or eliminate competition.

4. **Group Boycotting:** People, real estate boards or companies getting together to boycott a competitor.

You, as an individual or single company can set commission rates.

You as an individual can boycott certain people.

Chapter 11
Real Estate Math

Calculating taxes due

You can calculate taxes due using one of the following three methods, depending on how the municipality calculates taxes or how the exam question is asked.

1. **Mills:** This method bases the tax rate on so many tenths of a penny (or mills) in taxes for each dollar of assessed value.
2. **Dollars per hundred:** This method bases the tax rate on so many dollars of tax for each $100 of assessed value.
3. **Dollars per thousand:** This method bases the tax rate on so many dollars of tax per $1,000 of assessed value. You need to be familiar with all three methods for exam purposes.

An amortization schedule is a table detailing each periodic payment on an amortizing loan

Rate Per Year	5 years	10 years	15 years	20 years	25 years	30 years	35 years	40 years
5	18.88	10.61	7.91	6.6	5.85	5.37	5.05	4.83
5 1/2	19.11	10.86	8.18	6.88	6.15	5.68	5.38	5.16
6	19.34	11.11	8.44	7.17	6.45	6	5.71	5.51
6 1/2	19.57	11.36	8.72	7.46	6.76	6.32	6.05	5.86
7	19.81	11.62	8.99	7.76	7.07	6.66	6.39	6.22
7 1/2	20.04	11.88	9.28	8.06	7.39	7	6.75	6.59
8	20.28	12.14	9.56	8.37	7.72	7.34	7.11	6.96
8 1/2	20.52	12.4	9.85	8.68	8.06	7.69	7.47	7.72
9	20.76	12.67	10.15	9	8.4	8.05	7.84	7.72
9 1/2	21.01	12.94	10.45	9.33	8.74	8.41	8.22	8.11
10	21.25	13.22	10.75	9.66	9.09	8.78	8.6	8.5
10 1/2	21.5	13.5	11.06	9.99	9.45	9.15	8.99	8.89
11	21.75	13.78	11.37	10.33	9.81	9.53	9.37	9.29
11 1/2	22	14.06	11.69	10.67	10.17	9.91	9.77	9.69
12	22.25	14.35	12.01	11.02	10.54	10.29	10.16	10.09
12 1/2	22.5	14.64	12.33	11.37	10.91	10.68	10.56	10.49
13	22.76	14.94	12.66	11.72	11.28	11.07	10.96	10.9
13 1/2	23.01	15.23	12.99	12.08	11.68	11.46	11.36	11.31
14	23.27	15.53	13.32	12.44	12.04	11.85	11.76	11.72
14 1/2	23.53	15.83	13.66	12.8	12.43	12.25	12.17	12.13
15	23.79	16.14	14	13.17	12.81	12.65	12.57	12.54
15.5	24.06	16.45	14.34	13.54	13.20	13.05	12.98	12.95

Go to the top to find the years of the loan.
Go to the left-hand side to find the interest amount quoted
YEARS

Interest Rate

Where do they meet?
That is the number to use.

Towana was offered a loan of $150,000 with a 7% interest rate for 15 years. What is her monthly payment?

Step One: Loan of $150,000 divided by 1000 = **150**
Step Two: Find 15 years at the top
Step Three: Find 7% on the left side

Where does 15 years and 7% meet?

8.99

8.99 X 150 = **$1,348 is her payment.**

Carl and Sandy are attempting to purchase their first home together. They have been told by the lender that they can afford $1,000 a month. They found a property that they would like to buy. After their down payment of $2,500, the loan amount is $150,000.

Should they get a 15-year loan at 6%
Or a 30-year loan at 7%?

15-year loan at 6% = 8.44

Amortization Table - Monthly Payment per $1000 of loan

Rate Per Year	5 years	10 years	15 years	20 years	25 years	30 years	35 years	40 years
5	18.88	10.61	[redacted]	6.6	5.85	5.37	5.05	4.83
5 1/2	19.11	10.86	[redacted]	6.88	6.15	5.68	5.38	5.16
6	[redacted]	[redacted]	[redacted]	7.17	6.45	6	5.71	5.51
6 1/2	19.57	11.36	8.72	7.46	6.76	6.32	6.05	5.86
7	19.81	11.62	8.99	7.76	7.07	6.66	6.39	6.22
7 1/2	20.04	11.88	9.28	8.06	7.39	7	6.75	6.59
8	20.28	12.14	9.56	8.37	7.72	7.34	7.11	6.96
8 1/2	20.52	12.4	9.85	8.68	8.06	7.69	7.47	7.72
9	20.76	12.67	10.15	9	8.4	8.05	7.84	7.72
9 1/2	21.01	12.94	10.45	9.33	8.74	8.41	8.22	8.11
10	21.25	13.22	10.75	9.66	9.09	8.78	8.6	8.5
10 1/2	21.5	13.5	11.06	9.99	9.45	9.15	8.99	8.89
11	21.75	13.78	11.37	10.33	9.81	9.53	9.37	9.29
11 1/2	22	14.06	11.69	10.67	10.17	9.91	9.77	9.69
12	22.25	14.35	12.01	11.02	10.54	10.29	10.16	10.09
12 1/2	22.5	14.64	12.33	11.37	10.91	10.68	10.56	10.49
13	22.76	14.94	12.66	11.72	11.28	11.07	10.96	10.9
13 1/2	23.01	15.23	12.99	12.08	11.68	11.46	11.36	11.31
14	23.27	15.53	13.32	12.44	12.04	11.85	11.76	11.72
14 1/2	23.53	15.83	13.66	12.8	12.43	12.25	12.17	12.13
15	23.79	16.14	14	13.17	12.81	12.65	12.57	12.54
15.5	24.06	16.45	14.34	13.54	13,20	13.05	12.98	12.95

30-year loan at 7% = 6.66

Amortization Table - Monthly Payment per $1000 of loan

Rate Per Year	5 years	10 years	15 years	20 years	25 years	30 years	35 years	40 years
5	18.88	10.61	7.91	6.6	5.85		5.05	4.83
5 1/2	19.11	10.86	8.18	6.88	6.15		5.38	5.16
6	19.34	11.11	8.44	7.17	6.45		5.71	5.51
6 1/2	19.57	11.36	8.72	7.46	6.76		6.05	5.86
7							6.39	6.22
7 1/2	20.04	11.88	9.28	8.06	7.39	7	6.75	6.59
8	20.28	12.14	9.56	8.37	7.72	7.34	7.11	6.96
8 1/2	20.52	12.4	9.85	8.68	8.06	7.69	7.47	7.72
9	20.76	12.67	10.15	9	8.4	8.05	7.84	7.72
9 1/2	21.01	12.94	10.45	9.33	8.74	8.41	8.22	8.11
10	21.25	13.22	10.75	9.66	9.09	8.78	8.6	8.5
10 1/2	21.5	13.5	11.06	9.99	9.45	9.15	8.99	8.89
11	21.75	13.78	11.37	10.33	9.81	9.53	9.37	9.29
11 1/2	22	14.06	11.69	10.67	10.17	9.91	9.77	9.69
12	22.25	14.35	12.01	11.02	10.54	10.29	10.16	10.09
12 1/2	22.5	14.64	12.33	11.37	10.91	10.68	10.56	10.49
13	22.76	14.94	12.66	11.72	11.28	11.07	10.96	10.9
13 1/2	23.01	15.23	12.99	12.08	11.68	11.46	11.36	11.31
14	23.27	15.53	13.32	12.44	12.04	11.85	11.76	11.72
14 1/2	23.53	15.83	13.66	12.8	12.43	12.25	12.17	12.13
15	23.79	16.14	14	13.17	12.81	12.65	12.57	12.54
15.5	24.06	16.45	14.34	13.54	13.20	13.05	12.98	12.95

Loan: $150,000 divided by 1000 - 150

15-year loan at 6% = 8.44 X 150 = 1266

30-year loan at 7% = 6.66 X 150 = 999

Which loan should Carl and Sandy take?
*They can only afford $1,000 a month

Pre-Qualification Letter
ABC Bank of Mississippi
Gopher Toes, Mississippi

1. **Sale Price: $300,000.00**
2. **Down Payment: 20%**
3. **Interest Rate: 6.5%**
4. **Terms: 30 years**
5. **Homeowner's Insurance: $1850.00 per year**
6. **Property Tax: Assessed at 70% of its purchase price and $2.84 per $100.00. (mill rate)**
7. **What is the monthly payment?**

$300,000 x .8 = $240,000 * Loan Amount
(Use Amortization Table) 6.5 at 30 years = 6.32
$240,000 divided by 1000 = 240
240 x 6.32 = **$1516.80** * monthly loan payment
1850 divided by 12 months = **154.16** * insurance per month
300,000 x.70 = 210,000
210,000 divided by 100.00 = 2100
2100 x 2.84 = 5964 divided by 12 months = **497**
Add: $1516.80 + 154.16 + 497 = 2167.96

Straight Line Method of Depreciation
Depreciation is a method of reallocating the cost of a tangible asset over its useful life span.
Land value is deducted.
Land does not depreciate.

EXAMPLE:

Purchase price of investment property: $800,000
Subtract the land value: -200,000
amount you can depreciate:-------------------------
                           $600,000

The IRS uses 27.5 years for investment property.

600,000 divided by 27.5 = 21,818.18

$21,818.18 is what an investor can depreciate on taxes.

The Most Important Chapter in This BOOK
Student Gifts to Students

Part One

1. **Avulsion**- a tearing away of land due to an earthly violent event. It's sudden.

> Example; a sweeping swollen river swept away an outcropping of land or an earthquake tore away some land. The exam may say that the two ends of a barrier island got washed away during a hurricane.

2. **A Specific lien** is specifically attached to the property. A **voluntary specific lien** would be financing a swimming pool. An **involuntary specific lien** would be taxes or a mechanics lien.

3. An example of a right, improvement or privilege that belongs to and conveys with a property is an **appurtenance**.

> **"In addition to"**. (Example an **easement appurtenant** is ownership of a property with a **right of way** over someone else's property. Example: Tom owns his homestaed in addition to a right away over Bob's property. Appurtenant may also be the percentage ownership of a parking structure owned by a condominium owner. You own the condo "in addition to" a portion of the parking structure

4. The last entities to receive money after **probate** are the **heirs**. The first **liens** to be paid are taxes. (Taxes include **Ad Valorem** and **Special Assessments**.)

5. **Private Restriction**: vs. **Public Restriction**

Private Restrictions
A Deed Restriction
A Limitation on Use
An example would be purchasing a home in a town that doesn't allow the owner to cut down any oak trees on his property. Even though the owner holds the title to the property, he is limited or restricted on his own land.

Public Restrictions
Zoning
Home Owners Association Rules
Environmental Hazards (what materials can be stored on the real property)
Public Easements and

6. **General lien vs. specific lien.** – need to know the difference

Specific Liens
Specific liens are liens specifically on a single property.
Mortgage liens and Trust Deeds
Property taxes are also liens
Ad Valorem taxes, meaning according to value.
Special Assessments: A special assessment is an added tax that is paid for by the people who benefit from an improvement.
Taxes take priority.
Mechanics liens

General Liens
General liens are liens on everything you own.
A judgment
Inheritance taxes
Income tax
Debts due of a deceased person
A General lien could be a lien on several properties one person owns.

7. **Testate vs. Intestate**

> **Testate**
> with will – two syllables
> His will passes by **devise**.
> Executor's deed

> **Intestate**
> with out will –
> three syllables
> His property
> passes by descent
> and distribution.

8. If a person dies intestate and the state cannot find any living heirs, his property will escheat to the state. Land cannot be ownerless.

9. **Divisor** is the giver of the property when he testate. Devisee is the one inheriting the property. (OR OR is the GIVOR......EE EE is the Gimmee the Propertee.)

10. **Land**- Real Estate,. Land does not depreciate.

11. When **title** is granted in a **life estate** the person will own the property until he dies.

12. **Adverse Possession** - open, notorious, hostile and continuous possession. It's a taking of legal title from another person by meeting the statutory amount of time of open, notorious, hostile and continuous possession.

13. When the seller can furnish title insurance, the buyer can be assured he is getting fee simple title. (highest form of ownership)

14. If a homeowner is concerned that the construction project next door is encroaching on her property, she should hire a surveyor.

15. Paintings and furniture are personal property and are transferred by Bill of Sale.

16. The four unities of joint tenancy are time, title, interest and possession. The only unity for **Tenancy In Common** is possession.

17. The last surviving person owning as joint tenants owns the property themselves. JTWROS – Joint Tenancy with Rights of Survivorship.

18. When a husband and wife own property as **Tenant by the Entirety**, they both need to sign the listing agreement even if one spouse has a large amount of unpaid debt. With **Tenancy by the Entirety** the husband is a ½ person and the wife is a ½ person. The listing agreement needs at least one full person to sign.

19. If a tenant wants to sell his interest in the property and his partners do not, he can get a **suit to partition** and sell his interest only.

20. If a joint tenant is granted a **suit to partition**, the owners are now tenants in common.

21. A Tenancy by the Entirety cannot be partitioned.

22. A limited partner's liability is limited to his investment. General partners run the business.

23. Timeshare owners hold title as Tenants in Common. Several people own one unit.

24. You can will your interest in real estate if you own as **Tenancy in Common**.

25. Ownership in a resort condominium which allows the owner a specific amount of occupancy each year is a timeshare.

26. If your buyer wants to get a divorce before her and her husband complete a transaction to purchase a home, you should tell her to go see an attorney.

27. Common elements in a condominium do not include the owner's assigned parking spot.

28. In a Cooperative (Co-op) or (stock cooperative) a person owns stock in a corporation that owns the building in which he lives. The amount of stock could identify the square footage of his unit. They look very similar to a condo. A Cooperative is considered personal property because the residents own the stock and not the building. Stock is chattel. If a stockholder doesn't pay his mortgage, the other stock holders will have to pay his shares in order for the corporation to avoid loan default.

29. A condominium cannot eminent domain the three homes adjacent to their parking lot in order to expand the condo's parking lot.

30. A water company may lay pipes upon private property through an **easement in gross**. Easement in gross is for utility companies. An easement in gross does not have a dominant tenement.

31. Bob allowed Tom to hunt on his farm during hunting season. This is a **license**. A license is a revocable right that is temporary.

32. A judgment is not necessarily an **encumbrance**.

33. All property liens are encumbrances.

34. An **easement by necessity** is important to a land locked property.

35. **Condominium- Fee-simple** (the highest form of ownership) Ownership includes a share in the common elements. It's a condo. You own your unit and what's in it. You also own a portion of the common areas like the pool, elevators, hallways, and entryway. The ownership interest in the common area are appurtenances.

36. A corporation pays double taxation. An "S Corporation" is considered a pass thru company.

37. File Form IRS 8300 for cash transfers of $10,000 or over

38. Caveat Emptor vs. Caveat Venditor

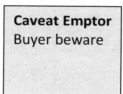

Caveat Emptor
Buyer beware

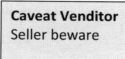

Caveat Venditor
Seller beware

39. **Home Owners Association– CC and R's.** At the close the buyer will receive additional paperwork.

40. The homeowners enforce the CC and Rs in a Neighborhood Association.

41. The wall on the outside patio between two townhomes (garden homes) is called a **party wall.**

42. A husband and wife took ownership of their real estate in Joint tenants to avoid probate.

43. A landowner who sells his farm must specifically reserve the mineral rights or they will automatically pass to the buyer.

44. **Emblements** - Crops that require annual planting and harvesting. Examples are corn, peas, beans, tomatoes, cucumbers, and squash. They are personal property. If a tenant farmer has planted his yearly crops and then gets evicted before the crops are ready for harvest, the landlord cannot touch the crops. The crops of the evicted farmer tenant are his personal property. The farmer is allowed to maintain the crops and harvest them. A farmer is entitled to the fruits of his labor

45. The furniture in your house is **personal property.**

46. **Real property** is land and the area below and above the surface to infinity and all of the improvements thereon. **Service, Subsurface and air rights**.

47. The intention of the party who annexed a **fixture** to real property is the most important factor in determining if something is real or personal. (Example: Was the freestanding refrigerator enclosed into the cabinets meant to be a permanent fixture? The intention of the owners who moved it into place and installed it will determine the answer.

48. The price of a fixture does not determine if it is real or personal.

49. Standing timber is **real property**. A vineyard is **real property**.

50. When lumber or bricks are left on a driveway in order for the homeowner to build a new fence, they are considered **personal property.** They are still movable. Once the lumber or bricks are built into a wall, it is now annexed and become real property. They are fixtures.

51. Once planted oranges and apple trees are real estate. If an orange or apple falls from the tree, it becomes personal property.

52. Crops planted yearly are personal property called **emblements**. (chattel)

53. A **lease** is personal property. (**Leasehold**) It's a piece of paper that gives a lessee the right to live in a landlord's real property. You can pick up a piece of paper and move it. **Real property** is immovable. Stock is also personal. Stock is the piece of paper that gives you an interest in a corporation. Personal property is movable, real property can't be moved.

54. Fructus Industrials: crops (as wheat, corn) produced by labor on the part of man for industry.

55. A personal property loan document is called a Chattel Mortgage. (Chattel is the French word for cattle. Cattle are movable.

56. Inventory and equipment are personal property. **Personal Property** is transferred by a **"Bill of Sale**.

57. The renter is responsible for insuring his personal property. Renter's Insurance. It's personal property.

58. **Land** is not a fixture. **Land** is **real property**. **Fixtures** are attached to the land or the building attached to the land. (Trees, fences, shrubs or an attached door, doorknob, window, awning, faucet, sink.)

59. **Trade fixtures** are personal property. Trade Fixtures are a commercial tenant's personal property. A trade fixture is a renter's personal property attached to the landlord's real property. At the end of the lease, the tenant removes the trade fixture and takes it with him.

60. The most **Trade Fixture** used in a course of business is a bowling alley.

61. **Immobility** is the physical characteristic in which a city, county or state would depend upon in order to predict future tax income from property owners.

62. When the developer built two identical homes with the same material, the one that was located on the sand beach was more expensive than the one located 10 blocks inland because of situs. (area preference or location)

63. Supply and demand deals with scarcity.

64. Section 16 is set aside for schools.

65. A metes and bounds description is a story. H surveyor walks the boundaries of the property and returns to the Point of Beginning.

66. The purpose of a correction line is to offset the earth. The earth is not flat. (Rectangular survey system.)

67. 640 acres is one square mile. 640 acres is usually in a question asking which area size is smallest. One square mile or 640 acres is usually the answer.

68. The area of the country that uses metes and bounds are the original 13 colonies and the older parts of the United States and Texas. It might say the original 13 states.

69. The north south lines in a government survey are called **meridians**. **Range lines** run parallel.

70. The east west lines are **baselines**. **Township lines** run parallel.

71. A **township** contains 36 sections. Each section is one square mile.

72. An Oak Tree, rock or a man-made monument can be a landmark used in the measurement of land when using the "**metes and bounds**" approach. **Point of Beginning or POB.** The surveyor will always return to the POB. The **Metes and Bounds** question. = **"Point of Beginning".** There's a question that will just say either "a very large oak tree" or "A large boulder. If you get that question, your answer is "metes and bounds".

73. **Easement by Necessity**– A property cannot be land locked.

74. Squatters Rights deal with adverse possession.

75. A truck driver has an **easement** over his neighbor's property in order to store his large truck when he is not working. The **easement** may be terminated if the man sells his truck and retires. **(**Or the merging of titles.)

76. Sharing a driveway is an **encumbrance**.

77. The best way to find an **encroachment** is to hire a surveyor.

78. An **easement** terminates with the **merger of titles**. (Merger of title means that one entity bought both properties.)

79. When a gas company would like to bury its pipes over the property of several homes, they will apply for an **easement in gross**. There is no dominant tenement in an Easement in Gross.

80. An **easement by necessity** is important to a land locked property.

81. Bob allowed Tom to hunt on his farm during hunting season. This is a **license**. A license is a revocable right that is temporary.

82. A **Less Than Freehold Estate** is a Leasehold. Not a life estate. **Freehold** estates involve ownership, Non-freehold estates involve tenants.

83. Mary was granted a life estate for her life. Upon her passing the property will pass to her child. The type of ownership the child has is remainder. (Remainder man)

84. **Fee simple absolute** is the highest form of ownership. (They may just call it Fee Simple or Fee Simple Estate.)

85. **Fee simple defeasible** means the highest form of ownership with a condition. An example would be a hospital that is given property to keep as long as they remain a nonprofit or a zoo that receives property by deed and is allowed to keep it as long as they don't charge an admission fee.

86. When a hospital receives a gift of ownership from an older couple which states that the hospital will get the property when the old couple dies, the hospital is the remainder man.

87. **Remainder- remainder man**- in a life estate. The person who gets the property after the life estate holder dies.

88. **Reversion** in a life estate. An example would be, "Bob gave a life estate to Sal. When Sal dies, the property will revert back to Bob."

89. **Pur Autre Vie** means "for the life of another". It's a life estate based on another's life

90. Carol had a life estate. She rented the property to Tom for five years. In year three Carol died. The lease is now void. It was only valid during the term of the life.

91. A special assessment can be charged a neighborhood to help pay for new street improvements, sewer lines or road repairs.

92. When a city builds a new cement walkway down a dirt road, the people whose homes are benefiting from the new walkway pays the special assessment.

93. A special assessment and ad valorem taxes are encumbrances.

94. Property taxes are specific liens.

95. When one co-owner wants to sell his interest in real estate and the other co-owners don't, he may bring a legal action to the courts to sell his interest. It's called a **Suit for Partition** or **Partition the Property**. His interests will be sectioned off (partitioned from the rest of the property) and can be sold.

96. **Severalty** – to own to the exclusion of anyone else. Own it by yourself.

97. When there is a **Tenants by the Entirety** ownership, a broker should get both husband and wife to sign the listing. With **Joint Tenancy** and **Tenancy in Common**, you only need one person to list a property. All owners must sign to actually sell it.

98. **JTWROS**- Joint tenancy with the right of survivorship.

PART TWO

1. The least obvious lead product to be found on a property is a lead pipe. It's a **latent defect**. (Latent Defect is an unseen defect.)

2. **Zoning** changes require a public hearing first.

3. **UFF (UFFI) or Urea Formaldehyde Foam** is **pumped** between the walls and banned in the 70's. When you see the word "pumped" in a question, UFF is the only could be answer.

4. **PUD: Planned Unit Development**, A project or subdivision that has individually owned parcels and homes, together with stores, schools, churches, recreational or landscaping elements owned by a home-owner's association and managed for the mutual benefit of all homeowners.

5. When the developer of an apartment complex is forced into having two parking spaces for each unit, it is a building code. It is **police power**.

6. A government entity can take your property by **eminent domain**. The only person who can do **Reverse Condemnation** is the property owner.

7. **Joint and Several Liability** is when a single person and a group is held liable for damages.

8. **Retroactive Liability** is liability extending back to the previous owners of a parcel of land.

9. **Lead Poisoning** is a potential cause of mental retardation in children.

10. **Lead Based Paint Disclosure Act** is a federal law that gives the buyer 10 days after an accepted offer to inspect a home built **before 1978**.

11. **CERCLA** is associated with **Superfund** and holds the responsible polluting party for the clean-up or liability **without excuse.**

12. **SARA** expanded the innocent landowner fund.

13. **Brownfields Legislation** helps revitalize deserted, defunct and polluted areas of contamination.

14. **Strict Liability** is when the owner of a polluted property is responsible for the cleanup **Without Excuse. CERCLA**

15. **Zoning Ordinance**- Defines how property in specific geographic zones can be used. It regulates lot sizes, density, height structures and purpose. Government Law. **Police Power**.

16. **Amenities**- They enhance value by a home's proximity to amenities off the property. Examples are a bike trail, a community pool or a beautifully shaded park.

17. What should an agent tell a buyer if the buyer would like to have a test for radon done? Hire a professional because you can't smell or see radon and it causes lung cancer.

18. **Radon Gas** can be Easily Mitigated. It enters the house through the basement. It costs about $3000.

19. **Zoning** is local government police power. States allow the cities to do their own zoning through State Enabling Acts. "**State Enabling rights**".

20. Flood insurance is required when a property is in a **SFHA. Special Flood Hazard Area. (FEMA flood area)**

21. When you want to extend your patio, check **setback limits** first.

22. When a commercial property is in a neighborhood that gets downzoned, the property gets **grandfathered in** and is of **non-conforming use**. If the property burns down or gets destroyed, it cannot be built back without getting a **conditional use permit**.

23. A public limitation on use would be caused by **police power**. **(Eminent domain – zoning)**

24. A private limitation would be a deed restriction. (I can't cut down my oak trees.)

25. An easement created by adverse use is a **Prescriptive Easement**. (Prescription)

26. Restrictive covenants and shared driveways are encumbrances on the property. (An **encumbrance** is something that bothers the property.)

27. A current lawsuit on real property is called a **Lis pendens**. (Litigation Pending)

28. Police power allows the government to place restrictions on the use of private property.

29. An owner wants to construct a fence beyond the **setback limits**. In order to do this, she must obtain a **variance**.

30. After an owner built a factory on his property, the city downzoned the neighborhood to residential. In this case, the factory will be **grand fathered in**.

31. **Compensation** usually follows the court action of **condemnation**. **(eminent domain)**

32. **Set back limits** are the difference between the lot line and the improvements.

33. The homeowners enforce the CC and Rs in a Neighborhood Association.

34. Eminent Domain, Condemnation and Just Compensation are words that go together. One will be in the question and one of the others will be in the answer.

35. A county airport took several streets of homes in order to expand its runway through the government power of eminent domain.

36. When the county took several streets through eminent domain to extend an airport runway, they left one house which is now experiencing extreme noise and shaking due to the expansion. The homeowner may be able to get the county to take the property through the use **of reverse condemnation**. Only a homeowner can apply for reverse condemnation. It's forcing the government (reverse eminent domain) entity to take your property.

37. A condominium complex cannot eminent domain the three houses adjacent to their parking lot to extend their parking.

38. **Bulk Zoning -** regulations restrict the density in a given area. Bulk Zoning include, open space requirements, floor area ratios and setback requirements.

Student Gifts to Students

Part Three

1. **Diminishing Returns**- The point in time when improvements can't add value to a property anymore. The property is over built or over improved for the neighborhood.

2. **Progression** - the least expensive or smallest home in the neighborhood made up of larger and more expensive homes.

3. **Regression**. The doctor suffered from regression when he built a very large home in a neighborhood of very small homes.

4. **Physical Deterioration**- a leaky roof, a cracked foundation wall, worn out window tracks. Fixable.

5. **Functional Obsolescence**- a four bedrooms two story home with one bathroom. A home with three bedrooms on the second floor and one bathroom on the first floor. Loss in value. Something on the property. Usually Fixable

6. **External Obsolescence**- Loss in value due to an airport expanding its runway and now planes fly over a neighborhood at a low altitude. A deteriorating neighborhood with buildings not being maintained. External is something outside the property. Could be a tainted water well. Could be a public dump or railroad tracks.

7. **External obsolescence** could result from a gas storage tank located near the property.

8. A single car garage could cause **functional obsolescence**.

9. A poor floor plan can cause functional obsolescence.

10. When finding the "**Highest and best use**" of a property is not concerned with the loans on the property. (Concerned with net yield, utility of neighborhood and relationship to development.)

11. The final analysis an appraiser uses for the different approaches to value is **reconciliation**. **Reconciliation** is the last step an appraiser takes. **Stating the problem** is the first step an appraiser takes.

12. Dry rot and termite damage are **physical deterioration**.

13. The "highest and best use property" is the one that delivers the highest net return.

14. Normal wear and tear on a building is neither external nor functional (internal) obsolescence.

15. When an appraiser is doing an appraisal, he does not use 'land depreciation'.

16. When an agent wants to do a **CMA** in a neighborhood of mostly foreclosures, he will take the actual arm's length (or more) **sales comparisons** from the bank instead of the foreclosed price

17. **Substitution** - what an appraiser uses to determine value by comparing equally desirable substitutes nearby.

18. **CMA- Comparative Market Analysis**- Benefits the Seller. It helps agents determine a price range for a property to list. It doesn't determine value. Only an appraisal can determine value.

19. The economic life of a building has come to an end when the value of the land and the building equals the value of the land only. It's a tear down.

20. The best reason for buying real estate is appreciation.

21. In a **sales comparison approach** to appraisal, you subtract or add from the comparable, not the subject property.

22. GRM - Gross Rent Multiplier. Residential homes.

23. **Comparable** - a name for sold homes used in an appraisal or a CMA. The comparable gets adjusted when comparing it to the subject property.

24. A capitalization rate incorporates return on land and building and recapture of the building.

25. **USPAP** relates to the appraisal specialty of real estate.

26. The replacement cost approach is appropriate to appraise a new home as opposed to an old home, condominium or tract home. (Imagine the home was built on a ranch or farm where there are no comparable properties.)

27. Comparison, income and replacement costs are the three best ways to determine value.

28. A post office or city hall is best appraised using the cost approach. (Special purpose buildings use the cost approach / replacement cost.)

29. When the appraiser uses the monthly rental income or total monthly income to find value, he is using the GRM (Gross Rent Multiplier)

30. When an appraiser is using the income approach to a building, he is not concerned about the price of the building next door.

31. **Capitalization** is an investor's rate of return.

Student Gifts to Students

Part Four

1. **Home Affordable Modification Program**: Helps homeowners avoid foreclosure by lowering their monthly payment. (Making monthly payments affordable)

2. **FHA loan** = 3.5% down. FHA is an insurance company. It insures the bank will get its money.

3. Definition of **Points**. One point equals one percent of the loan.

4. Banks sometimes will not take a **Deed in Lieu of Foreclosure** because junior liens may need to be paid off.

5. Lender can decline a loan based on the applicant's income. It would not be a violation of **Fair Lending Laws.**

6. **Usury Laws** protect the consumer.

7. A **"Purchase Money Mortgage"** is a form of Seller Financing.

8. **Equal Credit Opportunity Act** - Age is a protected class. A 93-year-old person can get a 30-year loan.

9. Equal Credit Opportunity Act does not address interest rates. Banks set their own rates.

10. **Public assistance** is considered income when deciding to rent or sell to someone.

11. Commission is not considered income when renting or applying for a loan.

12. There can be discount points on a VA and a FHA loan.

13. **ECOA – Equal Credit Opportunity Act**. Legislation preventing discrimination in lending.

14. **Trigger Terms**- The amount or percentage of any down payment, the number of payments or period of repayment, the amount of any payment and the amount of any finance charge.

15. **Annual Percentage Rate**- a Trigger term, which must be clearly stated for comparative purposes for the true the cost of loans.

16. **Regulation Z/ Truth in Lending** - Disclosure of the true cost of credit. Includes Trigger Terms and a Three-Day Right of Rescission if the home loan is based on the home you live in.

17. Federal Trade Commission- FTC the agency that enforces Regulation Z and Truth in Lending.

18. **RESPA- Real Estate Settlement Procedures Act**. Settlement of cost legislation. Prohibits undisclosed kickbacks.

19. **Private Mortgage Insurance (PMI)** is not needed when you put 20% down.

20. A bank that substitutes its judgment on behalf of another bank is a **bank intermediary**.

21. Mortgage brokers do not lend their own money.

22. Mortgage brokers have more loan products than do mortgage bankers.

23. **Regulation Z** requires that the buyer have a three day right of rescission if the loan is on his personal residence.

24. A **CMA and BPO** differ from an appraisal in that the appraisal "can determine more". An appraisal can determine value while a BPO and CMA estimates a selling range.

25. A loan that only interest is paid and at the end has a **balloon payment** is a straight loan. (term loan)

26. A loan with a partial payment is a **partially amortized loan**. There is a balloon payment.

27. The mother or father of an active military person cannot get a **DVA-VA loan**.

28. **The Truth in Lending Act (Regulation Z)** is designed to disclose the true cost of lending and advertising.

29. When a FHA or DVA-VA buyer wants to take out a loan, he must go to a qualified lender. FHA and DVA does not lend money. FHA is an insurance company and DVA-VA is a guarantee company.

30. A mortgage broker cannot take a kick back for an appraisal.

31. A **subordination agreement** is a release for a lender to take a second position. The second loan on your house is a subordinated loan to the first lien holder (loan, lender).

32. A Reverse Amortization Loan is a **reverse mortgage**. It is for older people who would like to have tax-free income. (Seniors, retired couple)

33. Each **discount point** equals 1% of the loan not the sales price.

34. The disadvantage in investing in real estate is that the money is not easily accessible. It is not easily liquid.

35. The Real Estate Settlement Procedures Act (RESPA) is designed to regulate disclosure of closing information.

36. **Leverage**- using other people's money. Financing by using borrowed funds.

37. You can have points on both FHA and VA. Both are assumable. A non-veteran can assume a VA loan.

38. A **Fully Amortized Mortgage** has the same payment each month with the amount going to interest decreasing monthly and the amount going toward principal increasing each month. No balloon payment. It reverses over time.

39. **Pre-payment penalties** or the total amount of interest paid does not have to be disclosed with Regulation Z.

40. **Novation** is the substitution of one party on a loan for another. It would be used when someone is assuming a loan regardless of the type of loan. Novation would release the seller from responsibility if the new person defaults.

41. Qualified lenders supply the funds for **FHA and VA loans**.

42. Amortization is the liquidation of a debt thru periodic payments.

43. The seller becomes the lender in a **"land contract"**, "seller carryback", **"purchase money mortgage"** and "contract for deed".

44. The buyer holds **equitable title**. The seller holds **legal title**. You can devise both titles.

45. A **sale-leaseback** is a transaction where the seller leases back the property from the new owner.

46. **Discount points** charged on a loan yield a higher return for the lender.

47. A **graduated payment mortgage** causes the payment to go up gradually.

48. A **sale-leaseback** is usually done so that the seller can write off the rental amounts paid.

49. A **mortgage broker** arranges loans between borrowers and lenders. A **mortgage banker** works for a bank.

50. The holder of a second mortgage most likely signed a **subordination agreement**.

51. A **"Mortgage Satisfaction"** document is a bank releasing a lien.

52. The borrower / mortgagor signs the mortgage.

53. A wraparound mortgage is a **junior mortgage**. It encompasses the difference between the existing mortgage and the total loan. The interest is usually lower than the prevailing rate.

54. The first mortgage recorded takes precedence unless there is a **subordination agreement**.

55. A developer would get a **blanket mortgage** on his property. He subdivides the lots and records the new legal description. A **partial release clause** allows for the payment and then release of certain parcels.

56. A **balloon payment** is the last payment that pays the unpaid balance on a mortgage at a predetermined time. It is the largest payment.

57. **Loan Originator** – meets with the borrower who fills out the loan application. He obtains all the needed documents.

58. **Loan Processor** – Orders the reports such as appraisals, title report, termite inspection and other inspections.

59. **Underwriter** – reviews and evaluates the information.

60. If the foreclosure sale proceeds are less than the amount owned, the mortgagee may obtain a **deficiency judgment** against the mortgagor for the unpaid balance.

61. Payment under an **adjustable rate mortgage** may go up and down.

62. Personal property is transferred by **Bill of Sale**.

63. Banks set their own interest rates.

64. In some cases, a seller financing a property will use a deed of trust because it's easier to foreclose on than a regular mortgage.

FDIC – Federal Deposit Insurance Corporation Deposits in banks are insured up to **$250,000** per depositor.

Student Gifts to Students

Part Five

1. You are not a **REALTOR (Trademarked)** until you join the National Association of Realtors. It's trademarked. The National Association of Realtors subscribes to a Code of Ethics. (**Realtists** are a parallel organization who also subscribes to a code of ethic.)

2. Know at what point a broker earns his commission. When he brings **a ready willing and able buyer who can meet the terms of the listing agreement**. (They may call the listing agreement "the contract".)

3. A salesperson's death does NOT kill the deal.

4. A seller does not have to accept an offer lower than the asking price.

5. A **trust account** is a checking account. A demand Account.

6. A broker and her **unlicensed assistant** were travelling to deliver a signed counter offer to their client. On their way, they got into a terrible car crash and the broker was rushed to the hospital. What should the unlicensed assistant do? Carry the counter offer to the client before going to the hospital. Offers and counter offers need to be delivered ASAP. As long as the Broker is alive, the deal is alive. Also, an unlicensed personal assistant can "carry paper". An unlicensed personal assistant can refer buyers and sellers to the broker.

7. **Protection clause**- extends the period of time that a seller agrees to pay a commission.

8. **Commingling**- Unlawful mixing of the broker's money and his client's funds.

9. A couple made an offer on a home and before it was accepted they made another offer on another home. They can either back out of the first offer if it is not accepted or buy both. If both offers get accepted before they back out, the buyers are responsible to both contracts. Be careful on this question because one version talks about a couple that maybe they wanted to buy both houses.

10. What can cancel all contracts? Mutual consent of all parties. (Or death, insanity or bankruptcy.)

> **Delegated authority and consent to act create agency.**

11. **Delegated authority**- the principal's act that creates agency.

12. **Consent to act**- to create agency the principal delegates authority, and the broker must do this.

13. **Principal**- The person or entity that delegates authority in order to create an agency relationship. It's the **Client**.

14. Do not **comingle**.

15. A Buyer made an offer on Bob's house that included a contingency that he would buy Bob's home if he can sell his home first. Bob accepted. In order for Bob to protect himself, he added an escape clause so he wouldn't be caught up in a lengthy transaction. He included in the acceptance that if another ready, willing and able buyer made a genuine offer to purchase Bob's house, he would give the first purchaser a 48 hour **first right of refusal**.

16. An owner's death kills the listing. A fire to the property does not necessarily kill a listing.

17. When a seller accepts an offer from a buyer who needs to sell his or her own home first, to keep from being caught in a lengthy transaction the seller can add an escape clause to the contract.

18. A **Customer** is someone you work with. A customer is not represented.

19. A **Client** is someone you work for.

20. **Commingling** is the mixing of the broker's funds with the client trust account funds. It's illegal.

21. **Unlicensed Personal Assistant's** duties must be defined in the **broker's policy and procedures manual**. They can carry paper.

22. A good training program creates a high morale in the brokerage.

23. A Broker is responsible for the direct supervision of a brokerage firm. A broker is responsible for the real estate activities of his salespeople. A broker is not responsible for everything his salespeople do in their day-to-day lives.

24. Only one owner of the property needs to sign the listing agreement. If the agent brings a ready, able and willing buyer that can meet the terms of the listing agreement and the other property owners refuse to sell the property, the agent is entitled to her commission from the person who signed the listing.

25. When a salesperson had a listing with Bob but Bob died in a car accident before the salesperson could procure a buyer, the listing terminates immediately.

26. A broker can take money out of the client trust account only if the buyer and seller have given written approval.

27. The person named in a corporate resolution is the person authorized to sign a listing agreement for a corporation.

28. The type of listing in which the listing agent is least likely to know what his commission will be is a net listing.

29. The listing broker is responsible to pay the selling broker as per written agreement.

30. A listing broker has earned her commission on the sale of a property even if it's a land contract to be completed in four years and agreed upon by both buyer and seller.

31. When a seller is refusing to pay the listing broker after the transaction has closed, the listing agent still needs to turn the earnest money back to the buyer. The listing broker can then sue the seller in court for her earned commission.

32. Bob secured a six-month Exclusive Right Listing Agreement with Sam. Two months into the contract, Sam gave written notice to Bob that he no longer wanted to sell. The contract will be cancelled but Sam will be liable for any expenses incurred by agent Bob.

33. On a contingent offer from a buyer, the agent has not earned his commission until the contingency is removed. An example would be a buyer making an offer based on him securing financing.

34. The broker is not entitled to a commission if the seller sells the property one day after the expiration of the listing unless there is a protection clause in the listing and the agent was the procuring cause of the transaction.

35. A **General Agent** is a property manager. A property manager's primary responsibility is to get the highest net return for the property owner. A General Agent is hired to do general duties.

36. All money collected by sub agents must be given to the broker...

37. **Special Agent** is a listing / Seller's Agent or a Selling / Buyer's Agent. They are hired to do one specific act.

Seller = Client = Principle = Fiduciary

Seller's Agent = Listing Agent

Buyer

Selling Agent = Buyer's Agent

If a **Buyer's Agent / Selling Agent** gets a written buyer's agreement for representation, then the buyer becomes a client.

---

38. **Independent Contractor- vs. Employee**

39.

INDEPENDENT CONTRACTOR
90% of income comes from Commission or sales.

EMPLOYEE
90% of income comes from salary and wages.

Independent Contractor
Broker can't tell you how to do your job.

40.

Employee
Broker can tell you exactly how to do your job.

41.

42. **Covenant of Seisin**- the grantor's expression that he or she has possession and the right to convey the property. Example: When there are three partners who own an apartment complex and one of the partners is trying to sell 100% ownership of the property without the other two partners knowing it, he has violated the **Covenant of Seisen.** In this case, the deal will fail because of **Impossibility of Performance**.

43. For an acceptance to be valid it must be **Delivered and Accepted**.

44. An Offer becomes the **Purchase Agreement/Contract** once it's accepted. It is the same document. The Purchase Agreement defines the legal rights of the seller and buyer. It is a legal document between the seller and buyer.

45. **Equitable Title** is also known as an insurable interest of real estate. It's the Buyer's interest. It can be willed.

46. **Net Listings** are prohibited in most states because of the uncertainty of the selling price. An example would be your Client says to you that he needs $500,000 from the sale and you can keep anything you above that.

47. **Exclusive Right to Sell** is a listing stating the listing agent will get paid regardless of who procures the buyer. (Procuring Cause) A broker will spend more money on advertising on this listing.

48. **An Open Listing** is hiring multiple agents. Only the real estate firm who procures the buyer gets paid by the seller. A unilateral contract.

49. **An Exclusive listing** is when the seller wants an exclusive agent but reserves the right to sell the property himself without paying a commission.

50. **Earnest Money** can be used as **liquidated damages** if it is stated in the contract. **Earnest money** is given by the buyer when he makes an offer in order to show his true intention to move forward with the transaction. Money Talks.

51. **Consideration** is not a legal requirement of agency. (cash or equivalent) You may do representation for free.

52. Undisclosed **dual agency** is an illegal form of real estate representation.

53. Delivery of the Deed gives **Legal Title** to the Buyer.

54. **Agency Disclosure** is informing clients/fiduciaries and customers of your relationships which each person.

55. The **primary duty of a property manager** is to get the highest net return for the owner.

56. Giving a seller an Estimation of Proceeds from an income property to determine their net profit before listing the building for sale in an example of **Care**.

57. **Obedience** is the type of duty required of an agent when asked by an owner not to place a "Seller Financing" sign in the yard. (Or any sign)

58. A **Subagent** is an agent's agent. The agents of the responsible broker are sub agents.

59. **The Protection Clause** in the listing extends the period of time that a seller agrees to pay a commission.

60. Representing both sides of the same transaction with written permission explaining what is due each party is **Dual Agency**.

61. A duty to a **principal** that includes **confidentiality is loyalty**.

62. To create agency the principal **Delegates Authority**, and the broker must **Consent to Act**.

63. A **Principal-Client** is the person or entity that delegates authority in order to create an agency relationship.

64. The buyer and attorney can decide and determine the method of ownership. The attorney is the **Conveyancer**. A **Conveyancer** is an attorney. Brokers and agents cannot practice law. If a Client or customer asks an agent how they should take title to a property, you tell then to ask an attorney.

65. **Caveat Emptor** means Buyer Beware. Caveat Venditor means Seller Beware.

66. When a salesperson doesn't know something, but should have, he did not practice care. **Negligent Misrepresentation**. (If an agent tells a client that her fireplace will add ambiance in winter and the client buys the property and then finds out the fireplace is actually just a fake fireplace front, it is **Negligent Misrepresentation**.) OR (A buyer tells her agent she wants to purchase a home in order to have a beauty salon in her garage. She would like to have a home-based business. The agent shows the buyer a home with the garage big enough for the home-based salon. The buyer purchases the property. When the new homeowner is moving in her salon equipment, the city code enforcer pulls up and tells her the neighborhood is not zoned for home based business). The agent did not practice care.

67. **(Negligent Misrepresentation)** The agent is responsible for actual damages. Her **E and O insurance** will help her pay for her mistake. E and O insurance will not help an agent when the agent commits fraud.

68. The agent will be responsible for **Actual Damages**. Her **E and O insurance** should help cover it.

69. The death of an associated broker does not cancel a contract. Associated brokers are broker agents (subagents). The death of the Responsible Broker kills the deal. Agents can die and the deal stills lives.

70. An agent gets to keep his commission if the seller lied about a **material fact** and the buyer finds out after the close. **The Purchase Agreement** is between the Seller and Buyer. Neither agent is a party to the Purchase Agreement.

71. An **open agreement** is when the seller hires multiple agents. The agent that gets paid is the one that procures the buyer. (The **procuring cause**)

72. A **counter offer** voids an offer.

73. A broker or agent should caution the seller not to respond to all multiple offers at the same time.

74. The phrase **"procuring cause"** is most important to the broker and seller in an open listing contract. "Procure the Buyer"

75. It is unethical for a broker representing the seller to tell the buyer the lowest price a seller will accept.

76. Offers and Counteroffers must be delivered ASAP.

77. Monies in a **trust account (escrow account)** are not assets of the broker. It is the client's funds and **accurate records** must be kept.

78. A broker's **trust account (escrow account)** is a non-interest bearing checking account.

79. If a broker would like to buy his seller's property, he should make his true intentions known.

80. A broker should tell his seller the ramifications and effects of an offer and to present all offers to the seller as soon as possible. A broker may not hold back any offers from the seller even if he believes the seller will reject them.

81. An agent may never give law advice or accounting advice.

82. When a **For Sale by Owner** sign contains the term "principals only", it is telling licensees not to bother the seller.

83. The relationship with the principal/client is one of **fiduciary**.

84. If a seller tells you that the roof was replaced 5 years ago and the patio was added without a permit, you should tell the seller to **disclose it**.

85. It is unethical for the Seller's Agent to tell the buyer the lowest price the seller will accept.

86. When selling a property with an illegal addition of 600 feet, the seller's agent should **disclose** that the buyer might be forced to remove the addition.

87. Present all offers as soon as possible. If you have more than one offer, submit them at the same time.

88. Disclose that a property has a shared driveway because a shared driveway is an encumbrance and a **material fact** that must be disclosed

89. **Fiduciary**- a type of relationship based on trust and confidence. The Listing Broker owes the Seller Fiduciary Duties.

Student Gifts to Students

Part Six

1. **Commission** is negotiable.

Antitrust Act (Sherman Antitrust Act)
Everything is negotiable.
The Board of Realty or similar organization cannot set commissions.
Brokers from separate companies cannot get together to stamp out competition of other brokers. They cannot get together and boycott other brokers.
Brokers from separate companies cannot price fix.
Fines for individuals: Up to one million dollars and 10 years in jail.

2. **Constructive Notice**- By recording a **deed** a person has given **Constructive Notice to the world**. Once the deed is recorded everyone has been given notice whether they know about it or not. An unrecorded deed is valid only to those parties involved and to those who actually know about it.

3. **Covenant of Seisin**- the grantor's expression that he or she has possession and the right to convey the property. Example: When there are three partners who own an apartment complex and one of the partners is trying to sell 100% ownership of the property without the other two **partners knowing it, he has violated the Covenant of Seisen. In this case, the deal will fail because of Impossibility of Performance**.

4. A prospective buyer has the right to demand his deposit money back before the offer is accepted. If a buyer makes an offer and on her way home she finds a property she likes better and wanted to make an offer, she can withdraw the first offer before it's accepted and purchase the other property.

5. **Liquidated Damages- Earnest Money** can become **Liquidated Damages** if the buyer **breaches** the **Purchase Contract**

6. The first person to record the deed is the owner. An **unrecorded deed** is valid only between the parties involved and to those who have been given notice.

7. A **Power of Attorney** allows someone to act for someone else. If an **unmarried minor** was given a power of attorney by his brother to sign on his behalf, only the **unmarried minor** needs to sign. The contract is also a voidable contract.

8. **Devise** is the transfer of real property by a will. (A **Codicil** is used to change a will.)

9. **Dower** is woman and **Curtsey** is man.

10. Executor is a man and executrix is a woman.

11. When an investor would like to purchase a property to build a casino in a non-casino state, the contract will fail because of **Impossibility of Performance**. When a person would like to purchase an unlicensed whiskey store in order to run a whiskey store, the contract will fail for Impossibility of Performance.

12. **A Tie In - Tying Arrangement (tie-in)**: Requiring a buyer to list his or her current home with the same agent in order to purchase the desired new home the buyer wants.

Student Gifts to Students

Part Seven

1. The agent's obligation to the seller in regards to disclosure is to have him disclose all **material defects**.

2. **Seller's Property Disclosure Act** is legislation requiring the seller to reveal the honest condition of the property whether a defect is seen or a **Latent Defect**.

3. When a town installs sidewalks, gutters and lighting down a dirt road. The added tax increase levied on the property owners in that city is called a **special assessment**.

4. A Listing agent noticed shingles that were broken on the roof. He should **disclose** that defect.

5. A **Buyer's Agent** was told a property had no defects. Upon his inspection, he found several problems. The agent should **disclose the defects** to his buyer.

6. Who keeps the **Purchase Agreement**? Both Seller and Buyer and Both Agents.

7. When an inspector asks if he can remove a piece of drywall from the basement wall, he is looking for a **latent defect**.

Student Gifts to Students

Part Eight

1. Title to property transfers only when the **deed** is **delivered and accepted**.

2. The "**Procuring Cause**" is the person who will get paid in an "**Open Listing**".

3. How does an owner of an apartment complex and a real estate broker enter into an agreement for the broker to manage the property? Through the use of a **Property Management Agreement**.

4. Who does the listing agent owe **fiduciary duties** to? **The Client**

5. When a tenant vacates their lease because the landlord will not fix the heat, it called **constructive eviction.**

6. Leases and agreements must be in writing to bring action. Everything in real estate has to be in writing to be enforceable in court according to the **Statue of Frauds**.

7. **Habendum clause**- "To have and to Hold" A granting clause in the deed.

8. **Percentage Lease**- Used for shopping centers or stores, sometimes restaurants. The rent includes a percentage of the tenant's sales receipts. An example would be "$2000 a month plus 2 percent of the store's sales total".

9. **Stature of Frauds** requires all real estate contracts regardless of what type to be in writing.

10. Violation of **Specific Performance** is when the seller took the drapes and water softener which were fixtures attached to the property. A court order requiring a promise to be carried out is a suit for **Specific Performance**.

11. An **Exclusive Agreement** does not guarantee you a commission but an **Exclusive RIGHT Agreement** does. A broker will spend more money on advertising with an **Exclusive RIGHT Agreement**. The **Exclusive Agreement** allows the seller to sell it him or herself without paying a commission. (If it doesn't RIGHT, then it's wrong for you.)

12. When a broker receives an **earnest money deposit check**, he must deliver it to the **trust account – escrow account** by the end of the next business or banking day or in a timely manner according to state laws.

13. A property manager's duties do not include investing the property owner's funds.

14. **Novation**: an agreement to replace an old debtor with another one. (Used when assuming a loan.)

15. **Subletting** is when a tenant rents his place to another tenant.

16. When an agent collects money from a tenant, the agent gives it to her broker, not the owner.

17. The term that best describes a tenant's interest in property is **Lease Hold Estate**. It is **personal property**. It's a reversionary estate since it reverts back to the owner.

18. An option contract is a **unilateral contracted**. In a "rent to own", the renter need not buy but if he chooses to buy, the seller must sell.

19. An **Option** and a **Listing** are both **Unilateral Contracts**. ("I will do something if you do something first.") Only one person is forced into doing something.

20. A contract with an **unmarried minor** is a **Voidable Contract**. At any time the minor can change his mind. An adult cannot force a minor to complete a transaction.

21. **Net lease**- when a tenant pays all or some of the landlord's operating expenses.

22. An agent does not have to disclose if a felony was committed on a property.

23. Acknowledgement is needed when parties want to record a sales contract.

24. A court order to carry out a promise is a suit for **Specific Performance.**

25. If Carol and Tom had a verbal agreement to sell property to each other and Carol backed out, Tom could not take Carol to court because there was no written contract.

26. In an option contract the seller must sell but the buyer is not forced into buying. It's a **unilateral contract**.

27. Sales contracts generally may be assigned to other people if both buyer and seller give written permission.

28. When Tom threatened to beat up Bill if Bill didn't sign a contract, Bill was under duress. The contract may be voided even if both parties sign.

29. If a buyer withdraws his offer before the seller accepts it, the buyer is entitled to his earnest money deposit.

30. When a seller rejects an offer, it should be noted on the offer and a copy sent to the offeror.

31. Earnest money deposits may serve as liquidated damages.

32. The rescission of a contract is a return to status quo.

33. The buyer takes possession at the transfer of title.

34. Liquidate damages are negotiated.

35. An earnest money deposit does not make the contract valid.

36. All grantors are required to sign the deed. Only one owner is required to sign the listing agreement. If only one seller signs and the listing agent brings a ready willing and able buyer who meets the term of the contract, the person who signed is responsible for the commission payment.

Student Gifts to Students

Part Nine

1. An owner's **title insurance** protects the owner from loss to a claimant with superior right of title. Title insurance insures up to the date it's issued.

2. An **abstract of title** is the history of the recorded documents on the property.

3. The attorney reads the abstract of title. **Abstract and Opinion.**

4. The **Grantor** signs the Deed.

5. Real Estate is not easily liquid. If you need money it will take some time to get the money out of real estate. (Example: re-finance or sell it or new loan.)

6. **Novation**: an agreement to replace an old debtor with another one. (Used when assuming a loan.)

7. **Title insurance** extends to unrecorded documents.

8. You are assured you are getting fee simple ownership when the seller can furnish title insurance.

9. **Seisen** is legal ownership. To be seized in property means you own it. The Covenant of Seisen.

10. When an elderly couple gifts a property to a hospital but reserve the right to have a **life estate**, the hospital is said to be the Remainder Man.

11. **General Warranty Deed = Fee Simple Absolute Title.** The deed with the highest form of protection.

12. A deed defines the covenants by which the grantor is bound.

13. Ownership by **Joint Tenancy** has an advantage because a person can avoid the expense and delay of probate. Joint Tenancy with Rights of Survivorship = JTWROS

14. **Title Insurance**- When issued, it insures that the title is free of all encumbrances, defects and liens except for those listed. It protects against loss from title defects. Title Insurance extends to unrecorded documents.

15. **Trust deed**- most often seen in seller financing situations. A way of conveying real estate by the trustor.

16. Covenant of Quiet Enjoyment- the Grantor guarantees that title is good and is insuring against other parties who might claim superior title.

17. **Quitclaim deed**- the deed that gives the least protection. A deed that offers the grantee no warranty as to the status of the property title. Quitclaim deeds are used to remove a cloud on title. (Quiet a Title)

18. **Joint Tenancy**- The last one living owns in severalty. **JTWROS:** Joint Tenancy with Rights of Survivorship

19. Trust Account– Escrow Account- A checking account (demand account), non-interest bearing. The funds deposited belong to the clients and customers. Trust Account Funds are not the assets of the broker.

20. Boot is related to a **1031 tax deferred exchange**.

21. If Al puts a deed in a box conveying his property to Tom at Al's death, the deed was not delivered to Tom. When all died, Tom had no rights to the property and the property goes to Al's heirs. A properly executed deed needs to be delivered and accepted.

22. **Involuntary alienation** is transfer of property without the owner's consent. Involuntary alienation could be a foreclosure.

23. A deed that limits liability of the grantor to the time of his ownership only is a special warranty deed. A general warranty deed extends the liability to all previous owners as well as the current owner.

24. A corporate seal on a deed indicates the property was purchased by a corporation.

25. Recording a deed is not necessary to make the transfer legal. The deed will be legal between the parties and anyone that knows about it. Recording the deed gives constructive notice to the world. The first one to record the deed will create ownership if there is a dispute.

26. A **quitclaim deed** offers the least protection to the buyer. A general warranty deed creates the most protection to the buyer.

27. An acknowledgement is the signing. A notary public will witness an acknowledgement to make sure the signing was voluntary and to witness that the person signing is who he or she say they are.

28. An acknowledgement may be called a declaration.

29. A deed must be signed by the grantor to be recorded.

30. A valid deed is least likely to be conveyed by an **unmarried minor**.

31. The deed that conveys no warranties is the quitclaim deed.

32. Lack of money in a transaction does not affect the validity of the deed. It could be a gift.

33. If Joe, Tom and Al are partners and Joe attempts to sell 100% interest in the property without the knowledge of his two partners. Joe has violated the covenant of **seisin**. The transaction will fail because of Impossibility of Performance.

34. A standard **title insurance** policy insures against forgery of a deed.

35. **An extended title insurance policy i**nsures against hidden risks that an inspection of the physical property could reveal such as easements, encumbrances, property lines, mechanic liens, mining rights, oil rights and rights of parties.

36. An **extended title insurance policy** (may call it an ALTA policy) does not include the disclosure of zoning or changes in zoning.

37. An **abstract of title** is a history of the recorded documents. The recorded documents can include deeds, rental agreements, mortgages, mechanic liens.

38. Tracing the conveyances and encumbrances of real property is a title search. The abstract is the actual history.

39. Both buyer and seller must consent in writing before a broker is allowed to take an advance of money out of an escrow / trust account.

40. If a buyer is purchasing property out of state and has never seen the property, he should obtain an extended coverage title insurance.

41. Title insurance is only paid once at the purchase. It extends up to the date it's issued.

42. **RESPA** is designed to disclose closing data. There cannot be an undisclosed kick back.

43. The person who receives the title by deed is the buyer. (grantee)

44. Grantor- The person who sells the property. The one conveying the property to the Grantee by deed. It's the seller. The Grantor is the only person(s) who signs the deed.

Student Gifts to Students

Part Ten

1. A **convicted drug dealer** is not protected under federal fair housing laws. A convicted drug user may be protected under the **American with Disabilities Act.**

2. If someone discriminates but they don't know they did because they are just basically ignorant or stupid, it is still a violation.

3. **Civil Rights Act of 1968** is also known as the Fair Housing Act.

4. An owner of a property can discriminate if he lives on his 1-4-unit property.

5. A man going door-to-door in an older neighborhood and telling the residents that children or a family from another country will be moving into their quiet neighborhood is guilty of **blockbusting/panic peddling.**

6. **Civil rights act of 1866** prohibits discrimination on race. It was the first act.

7. **ADA- American with Disability Act**- Prohibits discrimination based on disability. An office with 15 or more employees must be accessible to those with disabilities.

8. Religious organizations and private clubs may be allowed to discriminate under certain circumstances.

9. **Steering**- is when an agent shows minority buyers properties only in certain neighborhoods instead of the entire market.

10. **Steering** is when an agent shows a buyer properties only in neighborhoods where the agent believes the buyer should live.

11. **Redlining**- when a lending institution decides NOT to lend money within a specific neighborhood based on a heavy population of a protected class.

12. **Blockbusting**- Trying to induce owners to sell their property because minorities or any protected group is moving into their neighborhood. Also, called **Panic Peddling**.

13. **62 years and older**- Senior Housing exempt from **familial status** discrimination.

14. **Title VIII**- The Federal Fair Housing Act of 1968.

15. **EHO Poster- the Equal Housing Opportunity Poster** must be conspicuously displayed in all real estate, appraising and lender offices. If the poster is not conspicuously displayed, it is considered, **"Prima Facie Discrimination".**

16. **Familial Status**- A protected class that includes women who are pregnant or have children under 18. It's the status of the family. An unmarried woman with kids is protected. Children under 18 are protected.

17. An owner of an apartment complex cannot segregate families with children into certain buildings within a complex. A landlord cannot decide to NOT rent to an unmarried woman with kids or a pregnant woman based on **Familial Status** unless the landlord/owner lives in the 1-4-unit building.

18. Complexes built for a segment of the population who are 55 years of age and older may discriminate based on familiar status. A senior complex can choose not to rent to someone

based on the age of the children. When the senior complex bases the decision not to rent because of familiar status, **Fair Housing Laws** protect the senior complex.

19. AIDS, HIV and a convicted drug user are protected under disability.

20. **HUD**- The enforcement agency who oversees **fair housing laws**.

21. **A Tie In - Tying Arrangement (tie-in):** The agent tied in the sale of a listing client' home if the client also turns around and buys swamp land the agent is selling.

22. **Boycotting** is the illegal action where two or more brokers agree not to cooperate with a third broker.

23. One broker may decide on his own to not pay another agent the same commission split as he offers others. An agent acting on his own can decide to boycott another agent as long as he does not get together with other brokers to do the same.

24. **REALTORS Code of Ethics** is the standard of ethical behavior for Realtors. (*National Association of Realtors Trademark)

25. **Puffing** is an agent's exaggerated opinion. Not illegal. **Puffing** could lead to **misrepresentation**.

26. **HUD** protects people dealing with **Fair Housing** complaints. You have one year to file a complaint. Some people will take their complaint to the courts because the courts do not cap rewards.

27. A handicapped person may make **Reasonable Alterations or Accommodations** to an apartment or rental at his cost but he must return the apartment to its original condition at the end of the lease (also at his cost). The least likely thing to be brought back to its original condition is the handrail screwed into tile in the shower. (They are left because it will do more damage to remove them.)

28. Brokers cannot get together and price fix commissions, fees or boycott other agents. **(Sherman Antitrust Act)**

29. **Laches** is when you waited too long to sue someone. (Laches=locks=locked out of suing) (For instance, if you wait one year and three days to file a Fair Housing Suit, the doctrine on Laches has taken over. You are locked out of suing because you attempted your suit after the one year allowance time to sue.)

30. When a brokerage does not predominately display the **Equal Housing Opportunity (EHO) Poster**, it is called **Prima Facie** Discrimination. (Prima Facie=Prime Face=in your face.)

31. Refusing to rent to someone based on race is a violation of the **Fair Housing Act**.

32. Landlord cannot segregate all the families with children in one area of the complex.

33. When three banks independently turn down a loan for a consumer based on the property's neighborhood economic factors, it is not **redlining**. Their decisions were not based on the protected classes. They were based on economic factors

34. Agents can- not steer people into neighborhoods where they believe people should live. It's called **steering**.

35. Agents can't go around the neighborhood inducing fear to get commissions. It is called **panic peddling** and **blockbusting**.

36. Dogs are allowed to live in non-pet apartments for handicap purposes including "**comfort pets**". **Americans with Disability Act**. A landlord cannot charge an extra pet fee for a comfort dog.
Student Gifts to Students

Part Eleven

1. REIT: A conglomerate of investors who pool their money to buy investments such as residential income property, high rises, malls, commercial building.

2. The disadvantage of a corporation is double taxation. When a corporation owns a shopping mall or high-rise or income property, double taxation still exists.

3. A notary The MOST important thing for a notary to do is to make sure the person is who he or she says they are and that the signing is not under duress or undue influence. (Voluntary)

4. A real estate licensee with many years of practice may become a real estate counselor to help people make real estate decisions.

5. A first-year real estate agent should not take a complicated listing such as a 200-unit apartment complex.

6. Know what 1099 S and 1099 MISC.

7. E and O Insurance will not cover an agent who makes a deliberate falsehood or tries to deceive someone on purpose.

8. It is illegal for a broker to supply health insurance or a retirement plan to an independent contractor. And 90% (a high percentage) of his income has to come from sales or commission.

9. Franchises like Century 21, Tarbell and Prudential have Volume Advertising. It is an advantage.

10. Capital gains exclusion- single at 250,000 and married 500,000.

11. Co-operative owners are shareholders of the corporation. Their ownership interest is personal property.

12. Desk Cost- An office with a Desk Fee is most likely to be found in a 100% commission office.

13. Company dollar- Gross income minus all commissions. (Basically, it's what's left over after the agents are paid.) After finding the Company Dollar, then the bills are paid.

14. Employee- At least 90% of his income must come from salary and wages. Can be told what to do and exactly how to do it.

15. Independent Contractor- At least 90% of his income must be made by commissions and sales. Has an agreement with his broker to produce certain results without being told how to do the job? The broker cannot offer a health insurance or a retirement plan. Will get a 1099misc from his broker yearly with the amount of commission received from the broker in order to pay his taxes.

16. 100% commission plan-is a landlord broker that makes his money on desk fees. A landlord broker is renting out the space in the office but in exchange to the agent, the agent is allowed to keep 100% of his earned commissions.

17. Franchise- Examples are Century 21, Tarbell, Keller Williams, and Prudential. Members pay a percentage of their earning to the franchise for expertise and/or advertising and branding.

18. S. Corporation- Ownership is limited to 35 shareholders. "A Pass-through Company."

19. Corporation- A legal entity that never dies. "Double Taxation."

20. General Partnership- Every partner has a personal liability.

21. Limited Partnership- The Limited Partners has limited liability in the amount of their investment. The General Partners have unlimited liability. The General Partners run the business.

22. Capital Gains-Exclusion Used for your personal residence. Must have lived there for at least two years out of the last five. Capital Gains exclusion is: $250,000 for a single person and $500,000 for a married couple. Capital Gains are computed on the difference between the net adjusted basis (cost) and the selling price.

23. UCC- Uniform Commercial Code regulates the sale of personal property apart from the real estate being sold when a business transfers ownership. Personal property should be transferred with a Bill of Sale.

24. Mission Statement- "To exceed our customer's expectations."

25. A Tie In - Tying Arrangement (tie-in): Requiring a buyer to list his or her current home with the same agent in order to purchase the desired new home the buyer really wants.

26. A beneficiary right to a property is personal property. It's a will. A will can be picked up and moved like a lease. The real estate itself is real property.

27. A building constructed off site is a modular home.

28. Standard Accounting Practices are used for keeping records.

29. Whenever money is transferred into a client's trust account, accurate records must be kept
30. A husband and wife own a property and when the husband died, one third of his interest went to each of his children and one third went to his wife. What form of ownership did he and his wife most likely have? In Common. (unequal interests)

31. A husband and wife own property as Joint Tenants. The husband's will give his interest to his property to his son. Upon his passing, how is title held? The wife owns the property In Severalty. The last surviving person owns the property by himself or herself. JTWROS (Joint Tenancy With Rights O Survivorship)

32. A husband and wife took title as joint tenants so that when one passes away the title to the real estate will avoid probate.

33. Title insurance extends to unrecorded instruments.

34. Joint tenancy: Time, title, possession and interest are the common components.

35. Tenancy in Common only has possession as the common component.

36. Spanish Common Law is usually found in the western states. They are community property states. Property a couple acquires after marriage is the property of both husband and wife. (Does not include inheritance)

37. Age 62 is the exemption age for familial status.

38. A 55+ community is excluded from the violation of familial status. A woman can be turned down on the rental because she has children younger than 18 years old.

39. Private Clubs can be excluded from Fair housing laws as long as they don't operate commercially. (They don't advertise or hire a real estate broker.)

40. Religious organizations may be excluded from fair housing rules.

41. Single family housing owned by one individual owning less than three such homes may sell or rent without being subject to the federal Fair Housing Act if no more than one such house is sold within a two-year period.

42. A one to four residential home is excluded from the federal Fair Housing Act if the owner lives on the property.

43. A single mother with two children applied to live in a singles complex. Her friend lives there and recommended the property. The single mother's rental application was rejected based on her having children. When the complex management found out her friend that lives in an apartment on the property recommended the rental, the friend got evicted. The mother's rejection and the friend's eviction violate federal fair housing laws.

44. A property management company can't demand that a person with a comfort pet pick up and carry the pet if she wants to ride in the elevator.

45. For blockbusting to exist there has to be some indication the agent is giving discounts on the listings in a particular neighbor based on the entry of a minority group in the area.

46. Redlining is when a bank refuses to give loans in a neighborhood because of a concentration of a protected class.

47. If three banks independently refuse to give a loan to person because the economic factors of the property neighborhood are deteriorating, it is not redlining. The decision was not based on a protected class.

48. Steering is directing a client into a property or neighborhood based on his belief that it is where the client belongs.

49. A landlord can discriminate if the property is a two to four-unit residential property and the landlord lives there.

50. A borrower is entitled to a three day right of rescission if his loan is on the residence where he lives.

51. Airborne asbestos is friable.

52. PCBs (polychlorinated biphenyls0 are found near electrical equipment.

53. A property manager was given permission by the owner to have an air conditioner repaired. The owner gave the property manager $1000. The repair ended up costing only $600. The property manager cannot keep the balance.

54. Fixed expenses in a property management agreement are things that occur regularly such as gas, electrical and maintenance expenses. It does not include repairs.

55. A property management agreement does not contain the legal address of the property. It contains terms and condition of employment, outline of expected duties and scope of authority.

56. Real estate agents cannot practice law. They cannot draw up legal agreements. They cannot practice accounting.

57. If rent is not paid by the due date, the property manager should first find out the problem and then if needed pursue an eviction. They shouldn't go straight to eviction.

58. During a time of inflation, a property manager would not wish to have long-term leases.

59. The landlord holds a reversionary interest when his property is rented.

60. The long-term lease of the land where the tenants expects to build an office is a ground lease.

61. When Joe rents the ski lodge from November 2nd to March 1st, it is an estate for years. It has a definite beginning and a definite end.

62. When Joe buys the commercial property with three existing leases, he has to honor those leases.

63. A renter's security deposit is to cover any repairs needed once the tenant vacates. It is not the last month's rent.

64. State laws that regulate real estate securities are called blue-sky laws.

65. A Purchase Agreement is still valid even if it doesn't contain a closing date.

66. The Buyer may rescind his offer and get his earnest money deposit back if done before the seller accepts the offer.

67. A broker must present all offers.

68. A seller is not forced to accept an offer less than asking price.

69. In an option the optionor is forced into seller the property if the optionee decides to purchase it.

70. The accepted ethical behaviors in the real estate profession are the Code of Ethics.

71. Brownfields help resurrect toxic, defunct and deserted industrial waste sites.

72. In investor will buy time in the purchase of an investment property through the use of an option contract.

73. If the bank cannot recover the amount due in a foreclosure, they may sue the mortgagor with a deficiency judgment.

74. The secondary mortgage market does not originate loans.

75. To find the medium household size or medium income, use a demographics report.

76. If a lease vacates before the end of the lease, he can be held responsible for the rents till the end of the lease.

77. The owner in a ground lease is the lessor. (or or givor)

78. Land contracts, installment contracts and purchase money mortgage are seller financing.

79. In a seller financing, the lessor will most likely use a Trust Deed because it's easier to foreclose.

80. A lender bases the amount they will loan on the appraised value.

81. The listing agent cannot tell the buyers the lowest price a seller will accept.

82. Delivery of a deed to a vendee completes the contract.

83. Bob executed a deed to Sally and then put it into a box. When he died, the property went to his heirs because the deed was not recorded.

84. A quitclaim deed gives the less protection in a deed. A General Warranty deed gives the most protection.

85. A deed that is not recorded is valid only between the parties.

86. A deed that is not dated is still valid between the parties.

87. An easement to a dominant tenement is an appurtenance.

88. An easement to a servient tenement is an encumbrance.

89. Riparian rights are found on a small waterway, creek or small stream.

90. Littoral water rights are found on navigable waterways. The Mississippi River is littoral.

91. When a person dies with no will and no heirs, the property become owned by the government. Land cannot be ownerless.

92. One cannot will a life estate.

93. Personal property is transferred by bill of sale.

94. A Chattel Mortgage is used to finance personal property.

95. Restrictions in a deed that only the grantor benefits can be removed by a quitclaim deed.

96. In a Cooperative, if one or more stockholders do not pay their mortgage, the other stockholders have to pay it for them so that the corporation does not default.

97. Owner in a cooperative own their units through stock. It is personal property because stock is a piece of paper. The amount of stock determines location and size of their units.

98. In a condominium, the owners own real estate.

99. If a broker establishes a company policy of charging a 6% commission, he is not in violation of the Sherman Antitrust Act. If that broker got together with another broker and they decided to do it together (price fix), it is illegal.

100. If a person doesn't pay their property tax, the taxing authority can foreclose.

101. It is permissible for a lending institution to refuse a loan based on income.

102. The chain of title is the history of a property's recorded ownership.

103. A landlord can refuse to rent to a person with a violent criminal history.

104. Lead abatement is not mandatory in a lead based paint disclosure.

105. Tenancy in Common allows for unequal interest in property. In Joint tenancy, ownership is always equal interests.

106. All liens are encumbrances.

107. Not all encumbrances are liens. (easements, encroachments)

108. A shared driveway is an encumbrance.

109. In a promissory note the purchase price does not appear.

110. An easement by necessity is used for a landlocked property.

111. When money is deposited into a broker's trust account, accurate records must be kept.

112. Recording a document gives constructive notice to the world.

113. If a seller changes his mind before the closing date, the broker must return the earnest money deposit to the buyer and look toward the seller for compensation.

114. A listing agreement terminates immediately upon the death of the seller or listing agent.

115. An Abstract of Title is the history of the property's recorded instruments.

116. An attorney will read the Abstract and Opinion.

117. The Purchase price is a debit to the buyer.

118. A credit score contains 3 digits.

119. A Suit to Partition can only be done in a Tenancy in Common and a Joint Tenancy.

120. Laws that prohibit monopolies are antitrust laws.

121. If a tenant in common tries to convey 100% interest in a property without the knowledge of the other investors, he has violated the Covenant of Seisen. The deal will be voided because of Impossibility of Performance.

122. A valid bill of sale does not have to include the date.

123. A mortgage banker lends his own money. He cannot prepare an appraisal for a fee.

124. VA and FHA loans are for owner occupied properties.

125. Before buying a property for a home-based business, check for zoning.

126. Before you extend a patio in the front yard, check set back limits.

127. VA is a guarantee company. They do not lend money. You need to go to a qualified lender.

128. FHA is an insurance company. They do not lend money. You need to go to a qualified lender.

129. Novation is the substitution of one party for another on a loan.

130. Pur Autrie Vie is a life estate based on the life of another.

Added: 2016

1. When a buyer pays discount points, the bank yield increases.

2. When a woman remolded her old home to look like an antebellum home, the listing agent should advertise the home as "an Antebellum Styled" home.

3. A buyer made an offer which matched the terms of the listing agreement between the seller and his agent. The seller accepted the offer but scratched out the close of escrow and extended the closing 30 extra days. The offer became voided. (A counter offer voids the original offer.)

4. An agent was sitting at a model home when after closing hours a buyer knocked on the door. The agent let the buyer in and the buyer made a written offer on a property. The agent should deliver the offer to the developer.

5. Land can never be a fixture.

6. Appurtenant easements run with the land.

7. Zoning regulations regulate and control the height of buildings, the population density and use of a building.

8. Moving a chain link fence closer to the street than is allowed by law may require a variance.

9. If a house has mold, the seller's agent must disclose it. (Seller, Seller's Agent and Buyer's Agent must disclose.)

10. Performance is not value.

11. The date of sale of a comparable property in a CMA or appraisal is very important.

12. Banks buy and sell from each other on the secondary mortgage market.

13. The change of position between two lenders requires a subordination agreement.

14. If a Special Agent becomes a property manager, she becomes a General Agent. New contracts are needed.

15. The broker must deposit an earnest money deposit into his checking account even if he receives it over the weekend.

16. The Chain of Title is the history of ownership.

17. A buyer's agent knows his buyer has bad credit. What should the agent have the buyer do before making an offer? See a loan broker or loan banker.

18. When a brokerage is advertising for "Veterans Only" because they specialize in veteran's loans, it is not discrimination.

19. When a developer finishes his subdivision plat map, he will record it.

20. When a seller built a bookcase that fit perfectly into an alcove in the home, it is considered personal property. It was not attached to the property. The seller can take it with him.

21. The seller can be held responsible to return the window boxes he removed from the home after the meeting of the minds. He can be sued for specific performance.

22. The seller may take the two oversized planters on the outside of his front door even if he needed a forklift to remove them. They were not attached to the property. They were personal property.

23. A seller and an agent discussed a contract for the agent to be the listing agent. There was no contract and the property was sold by the agent. The agent had no contract and does not have to be paid.

Know:
1031 Tax Deferred Exchange
Steering
Judicial Foreclosure
Blanket Loan
Package Loan
Title Insurance
Discount Points
Boycotting
Commingling
Unilateral option contracts
Bundle of Rights

Quizzes

Exam One

1.   A written agreement or contract between a buyer and seller when the buyer wants to buy and the seller wants to sell, after a meeting of the minds is called?
1.   A BPO.
2.   An appraisal.
3.   A contract.
4.   A disclosure agreement.

2.   An appraiser must be licensed or certified to handle federally related work on residential, residential income, commercial and all other real estate properties valued at
1. $1,000,000.
2. $550,000.
3. $250,000.
4. $525,000.

3.   Which of the following homeownership costs and expenses may be deducted on Federal Income Taxes?
1.   Repairs to the exterior building, assessments and purchasing fees.
2.   Cost of purchase including commissions paid premiums on title insurance and deed encumbrances.
3.   Mortgage loan origination fees, mortgage loan interest and local property taxes.
4.   Repairs, insurance premiums and interest.

4.   Which type of ownership is most often used for a timeshare?
1.   Stock Cooperative.
2.   Tenancy in common.
3.   Tenancy in severalty.
4.   Joint.

5.   How is title held when a person owns a cooperative?
1.   Tenancy in common.
2.   Tenancy by the entirety.
3.   Joint tenancy.
4.   Stock.

6.   The sellers and buyers have a contract in which the seller will convey title to the buyer if the buyer comes up with $35,000 before February 1st. What type of contract is this?
1.   Installment.
2.   Option contract.
3.   Variable.
4.   A buy - sell contract.

7.   The closing agent must give information as to the sales price and seller's social security number to the
1.   Bank in which the new mortgage is.
2.   HUD office.
3.   National Home Mortgage Association.
4.   IRS.

8.   A broker has supplied the money for a developer to build a new neighborhood with the stipulation that the broker becomes the sole agent for the builder when the properties are ready for sale. This is a
1.   Specific agency.
2.   Riparian rights.
3.   Agency coupled with an interest.

4.   Open agency.

9.   A Real Estate Broker has given a developer the money to build a new community in return for the developer to give the broker an Exclusive Right to Sell Agreement. This is a/an
1.   open agency coupled with financing.
2.   agency coupled with financing.
3.   open Listing Agreement.
4.   agency coupled with an interest.

10.   In a transaction what type of legal description is used in most cases?
1.   The street address only.
2.   The same one used in prior transactions, verified by a surveyor.
3.   The metes and bounds if the property is west of the Mississippi River.
4.   The one the seller guesses are correct.

11.   Assuming all factors are the same, which location would probably bring the highest price for a parking lot for sale?
1.   Business district zoned for one story small businesses.
2.   Recreational area.
3.   Residential area zoned for single-family homes.
4.   Business zoned for 20 story high rises.

12. **An arrangement in which an elderly homeowner borrows against the equity in his home and in return receives a regular monthly tax free payment from the lender is a**
1. Back Load Mortgage.
2. Front Load Mortgage.
3. Reverse Annuity.
4. Inverse Annuity.

13. **A mentally disabled person that was declared incompetent can't enter into a contract unless**
1. a person appointed by a parent can sign legal contracts for the disabled person.
2. a disabled person can under no circumstances enter into a contract without the written certification acquired while in school.
3. a person appointed by the court may enter into the contract on the disabled person's behalf.
4. All of the above under certain conditions.

14. **In a situation where state water rights are automatically conveyed with property is (*hint- best answer answer)**
1. prior appropriation.
2. prior subjective conditions.
3. a condition stated on all loan documents.
4. alluvial.

15. **A client would like to sell his house after owning it for one year. The client let the agent know that the property was treated for termites 14 months ago. What should the agent do?**
1. Tell the client not to disclose the information so the agent's husband can re - treat the property and make money.
2. Tell the client to keep his car out of the garage so not to attract any new termites.
3. Tell the client that radon is nothing to be afraid of.
4. Tell the client to disclose that information.

16. **Radon**
1. enters the house through the roof vents.
2. is nothing to be concerned about?
3. enters the house through the basement floor.
4. is caused by friable asbestos.

17. **Radon is**
1. a colorless, odorless and tasteless gas occurring naturally from the decay of substances.
2. colorless, odorless and tasteless friable asbestos.
3. a lead by product.
4. a black mold infestation that has become airborne.

18. **Friable asbestos**
1. airborne asbestos.
2. airborne asbestos coupled with lead.
3. is addictive and must be avoided.
4. can be found in paint on windowsills.

19. **When a judgment on a property has been properly recorded. The world has been given**
1. substantive written notice.
2. construed notice.
3. construction notice.
4. constructive notice.

20. **Two lots owned by the same seller and of the same size were sold two days apart. The lot directly on the sand beach was sold for $100,000 more than the lot across the highway which will have a peek a boo look at the water. What characteristic was taking effect?**
1. Permanence.
2. Streetus.
3. Situs.

4.   Situational indestructability.

21.   The FHA is best associated with
1.   a qualifying tool for mortgages.
2.   a banking entity with assets.
3.   a secondary market mortgage based interest indicator.
4.   an insurance company.

22.   Ana, a property manager, may legally refuse to rent to
1.   a person unable to live alone without help.
2.   a person convicted of selling drugs.
3.   a person who wants to adjust the apartment and pay for it in order to fit her wheelchair.
4.   Both 1 and 2.

23.   Discount points
1.   are the points paid on the sales price in order to reduce the price of a property.
2.   are the points paid on the full price offer with a 20% down payment in order to reduce a loan.
3.   are points paid on the amount of the loan in order to buy down interest rate.
4.   Can be any of the above.

24.   Each discount point is
1.   based on 1% of the loan.
2.   based on 1% of the purchase price.
3.   based on 1% of the cost of repairs made by the seller.
4.   based on 1% of each friable asbestos particle inhaled.

25.   Ana, a property manager and who under usual circumstances would not have to give notice to vacate to a person whose one-year lease will be coming to an end in 10 days. Ana has discovered that the tenant whose situation is mentioned above has been convicted of illegal drug dealing and knows she can legally not rent to the convicted drug dealer. Ana decided to give the convicted drug dealer a Notice to Vacate just in case. The drug dealer stayed in the property for 45 more days after the expiration of the lease and attempted to pay rent in which Ana refused. The tenant has
1.   a periodic tenancy.
2.   tenancy in common with other tenants.
3.   a tenancy in sufferance.
4.   a radar problem.

26.   A foremost reason for buying a condo over a luxury single family home on the ocean is
1.   the back yard.
2.   price.
3.   loan terms.
4.   discount points.

27.   A woman bought a house subject to her getting approval to run her beauty shop from the city. The city refused her request. The contract was canceled because of
1.   inability to pay.
2.   financing based on homes rather than businesses.
3.   impossibility of performance.
4.   her mother.

28.   A woman bought a house subject to her getting approval to run her business from her home. The city rejected her request. The woman was able to get her deposit money back because of a
1.   noncompliance clause.
2.   liquidated damages contingency.
3.   contingency in the offer.
4.   noncompliance of zoning.

29.   When taking a listing, the agent should verify

1. radon.
2. lead.
3. square footage.
4. the original purchase price.

30.   For federal tax purposes, the form a broker will give an agent to file their taxes is a
1. 5024 – misc.
2. 1099 misc.
3. 1099 – s.
4. 940.

Answers Exam One

1. A written agreement or contract between a buyer and seller when the buyer wants to buy and the seller is wanting to sell, after a meeting of the minds is called?
3. A contract.

2. An appraiser must be licensed or certified to handle Federally related work on residential, residential income, commercial and all other real estate properties valued at
3. $250,000.

3. Which of the following costs of homeownership may be deducted on Federal Income Taxes?
3. Mortgage loan origination fees, mortgage loan interest and local property taxes.

4. Which type of ownership is most often used for a timeshare?
2. Tenancy in common.

5. How is title held when a person owns a cooperative?
4. Stock.

6. The sellers and buyers have a contract in which the seller will convey title to the buyer if the buyer comes up with $10,000 before July 1st. What type of contract is this?
2. Option contract.

7. The closing agent must give information as to the sales price and seller's social security number to the
4.   IRS.

8. A broker has supplied the money for a developer to build a new neighborhood with the stipulation that the broker becomes the sole agent for the builder when the properties are ready for sale. This is a
3. agency coupled with an interest.

9. A Real Estate Broker has given a developer the money to build a new community in return for the developer to give the broker an Exclusive Right to Sell Agreement. This is
4. agency coupled with an interest.

10.   In a transaction what type of legal description is used in most cases?
2. The same one used in prior transactions, verified by a surveyor.

11.   Assuming all factors are the same, which location would probably bring the highest price for a parking lot for sale?
4. Business zoned for 20 story high rises.

12.   An arrangement in which an elderly homeowner borrows against the equity in his home and in return receives a regular monthly tax-free payment from the lender is
3. reverse annuity.

13.   **A mentally disabled person that was declared incompetent can't enter into a contract unless**
3. a person appointed by the court may enter into the contract on the disabled person's behalf.

14.   **In a situation where state water rights are automatically conveyed with property is**
1. prior appropriation.

15.   **A client would like to sell his house after owning it for one year. The client let the agent know that the property was treated for termites 14 months ago. What should the agent do?**
4. Tell the client to disclose that information.

16.   **Radon**
3.   enters the house through the basement floor.

17.   **Radon is**
1. a colorless, odorless and tasteless gas occurring naturally from the decay of substances.

18.   **Friable asbestos**
1. airborne asbestos.

19.   **When a judgment on a property has been properly recorded. The world has been given**
4. constructive notice/eviction.

20.   **Two lots owned by the same seller and of the same size were sold two days apart. The lot directly on the sand beach was sold for $100,000 more than the lot across the highway which will have a peek a boo look at the water. What characteristic was taking effect?**
3. Situs.

21.   **The FHA is best associated with**
4. an insurance company.

22.   **Ana, a property manager, may legally refuse to rent to**
2. a person convicted of selling drugs.

23.   **Discount points**
3. are points paid on the amount of the loan in order to buy down interest rate.

24.   **Each discount point is**
1. based on 1% of the loan.

25.   **Ana, a property manager and who under usual circumstances would not have to give notice to vacate to a person whose one-year lease will be coming to an end in 10 days. Ana has discovered that the tenant whose situation is mentioned above has been convicted of illegal drug dealing and knows she can legally not rent to the convicted drug dealer. Ana decided to give the convicted drug dealer a Notice to Vacate just in case. The drug dealer stayed in the property for 45 more days after the expiration of the lease and attempted to pay rent in which Ana refused. The tenant has**
3. a tenancy in sufferance.

26.   **A foremost reason for buying a condo over a luxury single family home on the ocean is**
2. price.

27.   **A woman bought a house subject to her getting approval to run her beauty shop from the city. The city refused her request. The contract was canceled because of**
3. impossibility of performance.

28.   **A woman bought a house subject to her getting approval to run her business from her home. The city rejected her request. The woman was able to get her deposit money back because of a**
3. Contingency in the offer.

29. **When taking a listing, the agent should verify**

3. square footage.

30. **For federal tax purposes, the form a broker will give an agent to file their taxes is a**

2. 1099 misc.

Exam Two

1. **The escrow agent or attorney at the close of escrow will file which tax form to be sent to the IRS?**
   1. 1099 - misc.
   2. 1099 - s
   3. 1040
   4. 360

2. **When a "trigger term" is used in an ad, The Truth in Lending Act requires the following disclosures except**
   1. amount of loan or cash price.
   2. pre-payment penalties.
   3. number, amount and frequency of payments.
   4. amount of the down payment required.

3. **Earnest money deposits should be**
   1. deposited into the broker's business account.
   2. deposited into a safe deposit box.
   3. deposited into a trust account by the end of the next business day.
   4. be given to the agent to hold.

4. **When a borrower defaults on a loan which has an acceleration clause it permits the lender**
   1. seize the personal assets of the borrower.
   2. force the borrower to vacate his home immediately.
   3. demand the entire note be paid immediately.
   4. All of the above.

5. **When a buyer of a four-plex refers to the property renting for 1000 dollars a month therefore the property is worth $100,000, the buyer is using the**
   1. IRS.
   2. HUD.
   3. GRM.
   4. NOAA.

6. **An Environmental Impact Statement**
   1. projects the dollar amount of an entire project.
   2. summarizes the neighborhood in general terms.
   3. projects the impact on the environment of a proposed project.
   4. is used only for state projects.
   5.

7. **A buyer wants to make an offer based on complex financing. The agent should**
   1. give legal advice.
   2. call his broker at home.
   3. suggest the buyer consult an attorney to furnish the wording.
   4. drop the client.

8. **The purpose of collecting an earnest money deposit is to**
   1. display the buyer has intention to carry out the deal.
   2. insure a commission will be paid.
   3. set aside funds for prorated taxes.
   4. All of the above.

9. **Usury laws are**
   1. intended to protect an agent from his broker.
   2. intended to supply fair housing information.
   3. intended to provide the FHA with down payment assistance.
   4. intended to regulate interest charged by lenders.

10. **Real Property is converted to personal property by**
    1. annexation.
    2. severance.
    3. novation.
    4. laches.

11. **Inducing panic selling in a neighborhood is**
    1. redlining.
    2. steering.
    3. friable asbestos.
    4. blockbusting.

12. **One day after a broker's listing on a property expired, the seller hired a new agent and that agent put the property on the MLS. A third agent called the broker with the expired listing and asked to see the property. The broker should respond by**
    1. telling the third agent who called to see the property that he no longer is the agent for the seller.
    2. setting up an appointment with the seller to show the property.
    3. hanging up.
    4. talking bad about the seller's property.

13. **Which of the following investors would like a property manager that emphasizes income and cash flow over maintenance?**
    1. The Dept. of Housing and Urban Development.
    2. A bank owning foreclosed property.
    3. An entrepreneur who owns several apartment buildings.
    4. All of the above.

14. **A buyer depended on his agent's information that the property the buyer is considering making an offer on is in a tax area of the lowest taxes in the city. Based on that information, an offer was made. Before the transaction closed the buyer found out the taxes in that area are some of the highest in the state. The buyer may seek to rescind the contract based on**
    1. redlining.
    2. blockbusting.
    3. misrepresentation.
    4. puffing.

15. **The document the buyer and seller sign to establish their legal rights is the**
    1. deed.

    2.   purchase contract.
    3.   listing agreement.
    4.   buyer's agreement.

16. Ownership of common stock in a corporation
    1.   can be real estate.
    2.   is a deed.
    3.   is considered personal property.
    4.   is required to purchase a home.

17. A homeowner paid his neighbor $10,000 in order to have access to cross over the southeast portion of his property to reach a new road. This is an easement
    1.   by prescription.
    2.   in gross.
    3.   appurtenant.
    4.   for safety.

18. Which of the following would cancel a listing agreement?
    1.   salesperson transferring to a new broker.
    2.   property owner's divorce.
    3.   property owner's marriage.
    4.   property owner's death.

19. A competitive market analysis (CMA) considers
    1.   demographics.
    2.   unknown friable asbestos.
    3.   original price of the property.
    4.   square footage of the subject property.

20. Under the Comprehensive Environmental Response, Compensation and Liability Act (CERCLA) who is liable for damages from the dumping hazardous waste on the property being sold?
    1.   The state government.
    2.   The federal government.
    3.   The buyer.
    4.   The seller.

21. Methods to calculate the reproduction or replacement cost of a building include all of the following except
    1.   quantity survey method.
    2.   straight line method.
    3.   unit in place method.
    4.   square foot method.

22. The best example of a buffer zone is
    1.   a warehouse between a neighborhood and strip mall.
    2.   garden homes between a single-family residential neighborhood and a shopping center.
    3.   an office building between a commercial strip mall and a school.
    4.   All of the above.

23. Antitrust Laws prohibit all except
    1.   dual representation.
    2.   setting commission fees with other brokers.
    3.   boycotting other brokers.
    4.   restricting competition.

24. Private homes built before 1978 may contain potentially dangerous levels of lead. The FHA
    1.   will not lend money on these properties.
    2.   require the buyer to acknowledge a disclosure of the presence of any known lead paint.

    3.   require the seller to remove the lead before selling.

    4.   require testing before the property can be sold.

25. Inverse (Reverse) Condemnation may be brought by

    1.   the city government.

    2.   the homeowner.

    3.   the federal government.

    4.   the state government.

26. The responsible broker is responsible for
1. all actions of salespeople.
2. all actions of unlicensed salespeople.
3. real estate activities of associated salespeople.
4. no acts of employees.

27. A salesperson told a customer that his listing has the best view of the ocean. The customer noticed that the property has a peek a boo view of the ocean. This is an example of
1. blockbusting.
2. a violation of Truth in Lending Laws.
3. puffing.
4. intentional fraud.

28. When does a lender require flood insurance?
1. When the property was flooded by a busted water line.
2. When the property is located in a Flood Hazard Zone.
3. When the seller puts down more than 20%.
4. When the buyer is using an out of state lender.
1. None of the above.

Answers Exam Two
1. The escrow agent or attorney at the close of escrow will file which tax form to be sent to the IRS?
2. 1099 – s

2. . When a "trigger term" is used in an ad, The Truth in Lending Act requires the following disclosures except
2. pre-payment penalties.

3. Earnest money deposits should be
3. deposited into a trust account by the end of the next business day.

4. When a borrower defaults on a loan that has an acceleration clause it permits the lender
3. demand the entire note be paid immediately.

5. When a buyer of a four-plex refers to the property renting for 1000 dollars a month therefore the property is worth $100,000, the buyer is using the
3. GRM.

6. An Environmental Impact Statement
3. projects the impact on the environment of a proposed project.

7. A buyer wants to make an offer based on complex financing. The agent should
3. suggest the buyer consult an attorney to furnish the wording.

8. The purpose of collecting an earnest money deposit is to
1. display the buyer has intention to carry out the deal.

9. Usury laws are
4. intended to regulate interest charged by lenders.

10. Real Property is converted to personal property by
2. severance.

11. Inducing panic selling in a neighborhood is
4. blockbusting.

12.   One day after a broker's listing on a property expired, the seller hired a new agent and that agent put the property on the MLS. A third agent called the broker with the expired listing and asked to see the property. The broker should respond by
1. telling the third agent who called to see the property that he no longer is the agent for the seller.

13.   Which of the following investors would like a property manager that emphasizes income and cash flow over maintenance?
3. An entrepreneur who owns several apartment buildings.

14.   A buyer depended on his agent's information that the property the buyer is considering making an offer on is in a tax area of the lowest taxes in the city. Based on that information, an offer was made. Before the transaction closed the buyer found out the taxes in that area are some of the highest in the state. The buyer may seek to rescind the contract based on
3. misrepresentation.

15.   The document the buyer and seller sign to establish their legal rights is the
2. purchase contract.

16. Ownership of common stock in a corporation
3. is considered personal property.

17.   A homeowner paid his neighbor $10,000 in order to have access to cross over the southeast portion of his property to reach a new road. This is an easement
3. appurtenant.

18.   Which of the following would cancel a listing agreement?
4. Property owner's death.

19.   A competitive market analysis (CMA) considers
4. square footage of the subject property.

20.   Under the Comprehensive Environmental Response, Compensation and Liability Act (CERCLA) who is liable for damages from the dumping hazardous waste on the property being sold?
4. The seller.

21.   Methods to calculate the reproduction or replacement cost of a building include all of the following except
2. straight line method.

22.   The best example of a buffer zone is
2. garden homes between a single-family residential neighborhood and a shopping center.

23.   Antitrust Laws prohibit all except
1. dual representation.

24.   Private homes built before 1978 may contain potentially dangerous levels of lead. The FHA
2. require the buyer to acknowledge a disclosure of the presence of any known lead paint.

25.   Inverse (Reverse) Condemnation may be brought by
2. the homeowner.

26.   The responsible broker is responsible for
3. real estate activities of associated salespeople.

27.   A salesperson told a customer that his listing has the best view of the ocean. The customer noticed that the property has a peek a boo view of the ocean. This is an example of
3. puffing.

28.   When does a lender require flood insurance?

2. when the property is located in a Flood Hazard Zone.

Exam Three

1. Under a land contract who retains equitable title?
1. Vendee.
2. Vendor.
3. Grantee.
4. Grantor.

2. Under a land contract who retains fee ownership of the property? (Title)
1. Vendor
2. Vendee
3. Grantor
4. Grantee

3. A buyer made an offer and the seller responded with a counter offer. When the buyer was reviewing the counter offer the seller received a better offer from another buyer. The seller can accept the second offer
1. if the second offer is coupled with a higher down payment.
2. if the seller withdraws the counter offer before the buyer accepts it.
3. if the first buyer has been informed in writing that the seller is going to accept the second offer.
4. the seller is forced to wait for the response of the first buyer.

4. A broker received a commission of 6% of the selling price from his client. The commission was $9720. The sales price of the property was
1. $160,000.
2. $158,000.
3. $162,000.
4. None of the above.

5. John listed his property with sales agent Tracy. John sold his own home to his cousin. John did not have to pay a commission to Tracy. The type of listing most likely was a/an
1. net listing.
2. gross listing.
3. exclusive Right to sell listing.
4. exclusive listing.

6. A broker has decided to buy his client's house, which the broker has listed. The broker should
1. wait six weeks.
2. buy the property through a straw man.
3. not accept any offers on the property to protect his interest.
4. make his true intention known to his client.

7. The gross rent multiplier for a duplex is calculated by dividing the sales price by
1. its gross yearly rent.
2. its gross monthly payment.
3. its gross monthly rent.
4. its net yearly income.

8. Depreciation is based on
1. land and the building.
2. land only.
3. building only.
4. economic obsolescence.

9.   A minority couple asked a salesperson to find them a property worth around $500,000. The salesperson showed the couple lower priced property in integrated neighborhoods only. This may be an example of
    1.   blockbusting.
    2.   redlining.
    3.   steering.
    4.   puffing.

10.   Mary died without a will. She has one daughter and three granddaughters. Mary's estate will be distributed by
    1.   statute of novation.
    2.   statute of reverse condemnation.
    3.   statute of escheat.
    4.   statute of descent.

11.   Real Estate transactions are reported to the IRS. Required information includes
    1.   sales price and buyer's name and social security number.
    2.   seller's name, social security number(s) and price.
    3.   buyer's name and method of payment.
    4.   seller's name and address only.

12.   If conditions for purchase are included in the deed and those conditions are violated
    1.   the violator may face jail and a fine.
    2.   the violator will serve jail time.
    3.   an injunction can be placed on the property.
    4.   the property reverts back to the original grantor/owner.

13.   When a seller gives her broker authorization to perform a single act, it causes
    1.   special agency.
    2.   dual agency.
    3.   universal agency.
    4.   uncommon lawful agency.

14.   When the government establishes legislation to preserve order, protect the public health and safety and promotes the general welfare of the public, it is called
    1.   lawful power.
    2.   police power.
    3.   inverse condemnation.
    4.   All of the above.

15.   If one party in a contract does not live up to their part of the contract there is money set aside that will serve as full compensation to the aggrieved party. This is called
    1.   earnest money.
    2.   liquidated damages.
    3.   arbitration clause.
    4.   agreement pay.

16.   When two parties have a verbal and a written contract and the contracts conflict, which contract takes precedent?
    1.   The oral agreement if it was made first.
    2.   The written contract.
    3.   Neither, new contracts must be drawn.
    4.   The oral agreement in all cases.

17.   Usury Laws protect
    1.   the lender.
    2.   the seller.
    3.   the borrower.

4. the agent.

18. **Which is the best method to appraise a single-family home?**
    1. Cost comparison.
    2. Depreciated method.
    3. Market data.
    4. Tax assessment method.

19. **A single woman has applied to rent an apartment in a community where 95% of the residents are over the age of 55. She has two children. One is eight and the other is three. The Federal Fair Housing Law**
    1. makes it mandatory that she be rented to.
    2. protects the apartment owner from being forced to rent to her because over 80% of the residents are over the age of 55.
    3. protects the children for familiar status.
    4. All of the above could happen.

20. **An agent told the buyer that the property the buyer wanted was connected to the city's sewer system. After the purchase the buyer found out that the property had a septic tank and was not connected to the city's sewer system. What protects the agent from financial loss?**
    1. The National Association of Realtors national protection fund.
    2. E and O insurance coverage.
    3. The homeowner's insurance policy.
    4. Title insurance.

21. **A position of trust and confidence a client puts into an agent is called**
    1. implied or expressed.
    2. fiduciary.
    3. customer loyalty.
    4. It can be any of the above.

22. **The owner of the property you have listed is**
    1. the customer.
    2. the subagent.
    3. the prospect.
    4. the client.

23. **The following is considered prima facie evidence of discrimination by a broker;**
    1. Failure for a customer to qualify for a loan.
    2. Failure of the lender not to grant.
    3. Failure to display the equal opportunity poster at the broker's office.
    4. Failure to keep appointments.

24. **Termination of an easement can happen**
    1. with a fire on the dominant property.
    2. when the owner of the easement dies.
    3. with the merger of titles.
    4. when one property sells.

25. **A contract to purchase that has not closed is**
    1. null.
    2. void.
    3. an executory contract.
    4. an implied assessment.

26. **An adjustable mortgage contains all of the following except**
    1. life of loan cap.
    2. margin.
    3. depreciation.

4.   index.

27.   Zoning Ordinances primarily
1.   implements a city master plan.
2.   implement the quality of workmanship.
3.   control business.
4.   control water quality.

28.   Economic characteristics of land include
1.   the metes and bounds.
2.   situs or area preference, scarcity and durability.
3.   the plot plan.
4.   palm trees.

29.   A tenant's lease expired last week. The tenant went ahead and paid next month's rent and the landlord gave him a receipt. This is a
1.   net lease.
2.   tenancy in common.
3.   holdover tenancy.
4.   tenancy at sufferance.

30.   A neighbor allowed his next-door neighbor to fish from his pond in the month of July only. The neighbor with the lake granted
1.   an easement appurtenant.
2.   a restriction.
3.   a gross easement.
4.   a license.

Answers Exam Three

1.   Under a land contract who retains equitable title?
1. Vendee

2.   Under a land contract who retains fee ownership of the property? (Title)
1. Vendor

3.   A buyer made an offer and the seller responded with a counter offer. When the buyer was reviewing the counter offer the seller received a better offer from another buyer. The seller can accept the second offer if
2. the seller withdraws the counter offer before the buyer accepts it.

4.   A broker received a commission of 6% of the selling price from his client. The commission was $9720. The sales price of the property was
3. $162,000.

5.   John listed his property with sales agent Tracy. John sold his own home to his cousin. John did not have to pay a commission to Tracy. The type of listing most likely was a/an
4. exclusive listing.

6.   A broker has decided to buy his client's house that the broker has listed. The broker should
4. make his true intention known to his client.

7.   The gross rent multiplier for a duplex is calculated by dividing the sales price by
3. its gross monthly rent.

8.   Depreciation is based on
3. building only.

9.   A minority couple asked a salesperson to find them a property worth around $500,000. The salesperson showed the couple lower priced property in integrated neighborhoods only. This may be an example of
3. steering.

10.   Mary died without a will. She has one daughter and three granddaughters. Mary's estate will be distributed by
4. statute of descent.

11.   Real Estate transactions are reported to the IRS. Required information includes
2. seller's name, social security number(s) and price.

12.   If conditions for purchase are included in the deed and those conditions are violated
4. the property reverts back to the original owner.

13.   When a seller gives her broker authorization to perform a single act, it causes
1. special agency.

14.   When the government establishes legislation to preserve order, protect the public health and safety and promotes the general welfare of the public, it is called
2. police power.

15.   If one party in a contract does not live up to their part of the contract there is money set aside that will serve as full compensation to the aggrieved party. This is called
2. liquidated damages.

16.   When two parties have a verbal and a written contract and the contracts conflict, which contract takes precedent?
2. The written contract.

17.   Usury Laws protect
3. the borrower.

18.   Which is the best method to appraise a single-family home?
3. Market data.

19.   A single woman has applied to rent an apartment in a community where 95% of the residents are over the age of 55. She has two children. One is eight and the other is three. The Federal Fair Housing Law
2. protects the apartment owner from being forced to rent to her because over 80% of the residents are over the age of 55.

20.   An agent told the buyer that the property the buyer wanted was connected to the city's sewer system. After the purchase the buyer found out that the property had a septic tank and was not connected to the city's sewer system. What protects the agent from financial loss?
2. E and O insurance coverage.

21.   A position of trust and confidence a client puts into an agent is called
2. fiduciary.

22.   The owner of the property you have listed is
4. the client.

23.   The following is considered prima facie evidence of discrimination by a broker.
3. Failure to display the equal opportunity poster at the broker's office.

24.   Termination of an easement can happen
3. with the merger of titles.

25.   A contract to purchase that has not closed is
3. an executory contract.

26.   An adjustable mortgage contains all of the following except
3. depreciation.

27.   Zoning Ordinances primarily
1. implements a city master plan.

28.   Economic characteristics of land include
2. Situs, scarcity and durability.

29.   A tenant's lease expired last week. The tenant went ahead and paid next month's rent and the landlord gave him a receipt. This is a
3. holdover tenancy.

30.   A neighbor allowed his next-door neighbor to fish from his pond in the month of July only. The neighbor with the lake granted
4. a license.

Exam Four

1.   A violation of The Federal Fair Housing law can be heard by either within the Dept. of Housing and Urban Development or by a Federal Judge. The Federal Court hearing has an advantage to the complaining party because
    1.   it's faster.
    2.   there is no dollar limit on damages paid.
    3.   it's fairer.
    4.   there is no advantage.

2.   When a property owner dies without a will or heirs, the property
    1.   become at sufferance.
    2.   is executory.
    3.   becomes the property of the closest neighbor.
    4.   escheats to the state.

3.   Ana, John and Jim bought together a property worth $675,000. John put up $337,500, Ana put up 25%. How much ownership interest does Jim have?
    1.   15%
    2.   25%
    3.   35%
    4.   45%

4.   Ana, John and Jim bought together a property worth $675,000. John put up $337,500, Ana put up 25%. How much money did Jim have to come up with?
    1. $172,564.
    2. $158,943.
    3. $168,750.
    4. $89,500.

5.   The amount of commission is
    1.   set by the Board of Realtors.
    2.   negotiable.
    3.   set by multiple brokers.
    4.   set by law.

6.   A doctor built a five-bedroom house with five bathrooms on a lot in a neighborhood where all the homes are three bedrooms and one bath. The doctor's home will most likely suffer from
    1.   subrogation.
    2.   novation.
    3.   progression.
    4.   regression.

7. **Which of the following owners of an apartment building would emphasize maintenance of value over income?**
1. An entrepreneur who owns several income properties.
2. HUD
3. FCC
4. Dept. of the Interior

8. **When several approaches of value are applied to a property, the appraiser will do which of the following?**
1. Plottage
2. Reconciliation
3. Ascension
4. Round off to the highest value

9. **Elevation Benchmark?**
1. A seat in the community park zoned recreational.
2. Horizontal Plain used to find the legal description in high rises.
3. A mark used in a rectangular survey system measurement.
4. The measurement point as the point of beginning.

10. Jim wants to open a grocery store on a lot that is zoned for residential. Jim
1. will need to obtain a variance or a conditional use permit.
2. will need to petition the local courts to change the zoning.
3. will be able to open if the people in the neighborhood write letters to the mayor.
4. All of the above can happen.

11. The Equal Credit Opportunity Act does not address
1. factors for borrower's analysis.
2. written credit denial letters.
3. interest rates.
4. discrimination in lending.

12. A property went into foreclosure with a first mortgage of 158,000 and a second mortgage of 33,000. The second mortgagee most likely will receive
1. the entire 33,000.
2. whatever is left over after paying off all other property liens.
3. one half of the amount owed.
4. nothing .

13. The government survey system is not generally used in
1. states west of the Mississippi River.
2. the southern states.
3. the original 13 states.
4. the northern states.

14. Violating Fair Housing practices, an agent
1. will lose their license only.
2. will get probation.
3. will get arrested immediately.
4. will have his license revoked and will be criminally prosecuted.

15. A very old oak tree!
1. Metes and Bounds
2. Rectangular Survey
3. Straight Line Method
4. North America

16. A CMA benefits?
1. The Buyer

    2.   The Seller
    3.   The Agent
    4.   The Broker

17. A contour map is used for which of the following locations?
1. Flat low-lying areas
2. Desert towns
3. A very hilly location
4. They are never used.

18. A Trustee may?
1. Sell the property
2. Lien the property
3. Do whatever is permitted in the trust agreement
4. Keep the deed after final payment

19. Prior Appropriation will most likely be found in what type of area?
1. Mountains
2. Deserts - Dry areas
3. Islands
4. Jungles

20. An Environmental Impact Statement is used for?
1. A proposed project
2. An outdated project
3. A private company
4. A quitclaim deed

21. **An environmental Impact Statement is considered police power because it deals with which of the following?**
   1. Fish
   2. Boats
   3. Health and Safety
   4. Pets

22. **When a person dies without a will and no heirs can be found, the property**
   1. escheats to the state.
   2. gets condemned.
   3. gets reverted.
   4. becomes part of the heir's estate.

23. **Escheat happens**
   1. because property – land cannot be ownerless.
   2. when the heirs reject the property.
   3. land reverts back to the original grantor.
   4. All of the above.

24. **Inverse – Reverse Condemnation may be brought by the**
   1. state.
   2. county.
   3. feds.
   4. homeowner.

25. **Deed restrictions pertain to**
   1. the seller only.
   2. the buyer only.
   3. the future and current owners.
   4. the previous grantee only.

26. **Determinable and defeasible are best described as**
   1. ownership with a condition.
   2. ownership with a deed.
   3. dual representation.
   4. single representation.

27. **When a condition is violated in a deed**
   1. it becomes a brownfield.
   2. the property becomes unusable.
   3. the property reverts back to the original grantor.
   4. the owner gets escheated.

28. **All of the following terms deal with appraisal except?**
    1. Reproduction costs
    2. Replacement costs
    3. Straight line method of depreciation
    4. Valuation

29. **Usury laws**
    1. protect the lender.
    2. protects the borrower.
    3. protects the bank.
    4. protects trade.

30. **The clause in a contract that allows the bank to call the entire note due and payable is?**
    1. Acceleration Clause
    2. Protection Clause
    3. Defeasible Fee Clause
    4. Santa Clause

Answers Exam Four

1. **A violation of The Federal Fair Housing law can be heard by either within the Dept. of Housing and Urban Development or by a Federal Judge. The Federal Court hearing has an advantage to the complaining party because**
2. there is no dollar limit on damages paid.

2. **When a property owner dies without a will or heirs, the property**
4. escheats to the state.

3. **Ana, John and Jim bought together a property worth $675,000. John put up $337,500, Ana put up 25%. How much ownership interest does Jim have?**
2. 25%

4. **Ana, John and Jim bought together a property worth $675,000. John put up $337,500, Ana put up 25%. How much money did Jim have to come up with?**
3. $168,750.

5. **The amount of commission is**
2. negotiable.

6. **A doctor built a five-bedroom house with five bathrooms on a lot in a neighborhood where all the homes are three bedrooms and one bath. The doctor's home will most likely suffer from**
4. regression.

7. **Which of the following owners of an apartment building would emphasize maintenance of value over income?**
2. HUD

8. **When several approaches of value are applied to a property, the appraiser will do which of the following?**
2. Reconciliation

9. **Elevation Benchmark?**
2. Horizontal Plain used to find the legal description in high rises.

10. **Jim wants to open a grocery store on a lot that is zoned for residential. Jim**
1. will need to obtain a variance or a conditional use permit.

11. The Equal Credit Opportunity Act does not address
3. interest rates.

12. A property went into foreclosure with a first mortgage of 158,000 and a second mortgage of 33,000. The second mortgagee most likely will receive
4. nothing.

13. The government survey system is not generally used in
3. The original 13 states.

14. Violating Fair Housing practices, an agent
4. will have his license revoked and will be criminally prosecuted.

15. A very old oak tree!
1. Metes and Bounds

16. A CMA benefits?
2. The Seller

17. A contour map is used for which of the following locations?
3. A very hilly location

18. A Trustee may?
3. Do whatever is permitted in the trust agreement.

19. Prior Appropriation will most likely be found in what type of area?
2. Deserts - Dry areas

20. An Environmental Impact Statement is used for?
1. A proposed project

21. An environmental Impact Statement is considered police power because it deals with which of the following?
3. Health and Safety

22. When a person dies without a will and no heirs can be found, the property
1. escheats to the state.

23. Escheat happens
1. because property – land can-not be ownerless.

24. Inverse – Reverse Condemnation may be brought by the
4. homeowner

25. Deed restrictions pertain to
3. the future and current owners

26. Determinable and defeasible are best described as
1. ownership with a condition.

27. When a condition is violated in a deed
3. the property reverts back to the original grantor.

28. All of the following terms deal with appraisal except?
3. straight line method of depreciation

29. Usury laws
2. protect the borrower.

30. The clause in a contract that allows the bank to call the entire note due and payable is?
1. Acceleration Clause

Exam Five

1. Who would have the most options for loans and loan programs?
1. Mortgage Banker
2. Mortgage Broker
3. Mortgage Servicer
4. Mortgage Repo Guy

2. An agent brought a ready, willing and able buyer that met the terms of the contract. The broker has earned her commission
1. when the seller gives a counter offer.
2. when the buyer gives a counter offer.
3. when the seller accepts the offer.
4. when the buyer accepts the counteroffer.

3. The term "Remainder" is most like?
1. When an owner conveys a life estate to one party and the remainder to another.
2. When the owner conveys ½ the estate to a relative and the remainder to a friend.
3. The remainder of the Offer to Purchase that needs to be completed.
4. The remainder of the rejected offers.

4. Tenancy for years is?
1. A leasehold for at least 5 years.
2. A lease for at least two years with a definite end.
3. A lease with a definite beginning and a definite ending.
4. A lease for the remainder of a person's life.

5. Real estate contracts must be in writing to be enforceable in court according to
1. prima facie laws.
2. statue of frauds.
3. moveable chattel.
4. because Jim says so.

6. The term "Duress" is most like;
1. Durability
2. Attainability
3. Undue Influence
4. Escheat

7. **When a renter finds the rental to be dangerous or unsafe to live in and the landlord refuses to make repairs needed to bring the property to a safe condition, the tenant may vacate and not be responsible for the remainder of the lease. When the tenant moves, the tenant has given the landlord**
    1. condemnation.
    2. association.
    3. constructive notice/eviction.
    4. construction notice.

8. **A lease on an apartment has ended yet the tenant keeps paying a monthly rent and the landlord keeps accepting the rent. This type of leasehold would be considered**
    1. a holdover tenancy.
    2. an illegal contract.
    3. unacceptable.
    4. void.

9. **The Civil Rights Act of 1968 was meant as a follow-up to the Civil Rights Act of 1964. It is called the**
    1. Fair Act.
    2. Fair Housing Act.
    3. Fair Housing Enactment.
    4. Fair Rental Housing Act.

10. **The Civil Rights Act of 1866 prohibited discrimination based on?**
    1. National Origin
    2. Familial Status
    3. Race
    4. Pregnancy

11. **The definition of subletting is most like?**
    1. The leasing of a premise by a lessee to a third party.
    2. The lease leasing to the lessor.
    3. The lessor leasing to a relative.
    4. The least lease the lessor leased to the lease.

12. **Which of the following is true for both VA Loans and FHA Loans?**
    1. They are both insured.
    2. Both are guaranteed.
    3. The buyer is insured by FHA with both.
    4. Both loans could have discount points to buy down the loan.

13. Public Assistance is considered
1. lawful income.
2. income not used in calculating income for a mortgage.
3. income not used in calculating income for a rental.
4. All of the above.
5.

14. When a landlord owns a four-plex in a FEMA designated flood plain and decides not to buy insurance but instead raise the air conditioners and heaters on high platforms, the owner
1. has forced insurance companies to accept his decision and pay him for new equipment in case of flood.
2. violated FEMA laws.
3. is said to be "Controlling his Risk".
4. is said to be "eliminating his risk".

15. A liquor store on the main highway was enjoying brisk business and substantial profits. The county decided to move the main highway ¼ mile away to the north of the store. This caused traffic to be re-routed and profits dropped significantly. This would be an example of?
1. Substantial misrepresentation
2. External or Economic obsolescence
3. Interior obsolescence
4. Functional Obsolescence

16. Which term describes a loan with the loan payment is less than the interest charged resulting in the outstanding balance of the loan increasing?
1. Straight Mortgage
2. Fully Amortized
3. Negative Amortization
4. Partial Payment and Interest

17. An Abstract of Title is
1. the history of the property.
2. the future recorded documents of the property.
3. the history of the recorded documents on a property.
4. an ownership title.

18. Into which bank account would a broker deposit commissions?
1. personal account
2. business account
3. escrow account
4. cash account

19. The cheapest way to handle asbestos is
1. to pull it from the floor with no protection.
2. scrap it off a building.
3. hire someone to take it out of a building.
4. encapsulation.

20. Radon
1. is an odorless colorless (radioactive) gas that may cause lung cancer.
2. is easily mitigated.
3. should be inspected and verified by a real estate broker before taking a listing.
4. Both one and two.

21. A buyer is purchasing a home in a neighborhood that has a homeowner's association. At the closing, what additional documents should the buyer receive?
1. The Neighborhood CC and R's (The covenants, conditions and restrictions) and bylaws.
2. The neighborhood nuisance disclosures.

3. The city tax disclosure and 6-month retroactive bill.
4. All of the above.

22. After the close of an escrow, who would keep for three years the Listing Agreement?
1. The customer and the client
2. The buyer and the Selling Agent
3. The Seller and the customer
4. The Client and the Seller's Agent

23. After the close of escrow, who would for three years keep the Purchase Agreement?
1. The Client
2. The Client, the Customer, the Selling Agent and the Seller's Agent
3. The Seller and the Buyer
4. The Customer and the Buyer's Agent

Answers: Exam Five

1. Who would have the most options for loans and loan programs?
2. Mortgage Broker

2. An agent brought a ready, willing and able buyer that met the terms of the contract. The broker has earned her commission
3. when the seller accepts the offer.

3. The term "Remainder" is most like?
1. When an owner conveys a life estate to one party and the remainder to another.

4. Tenancy for years is?
3. A lease with a definite beginning and a definite ending.
5. Real estate contracts must be in writing to be enforceable in court according to
2. Statue of Frauds.

6. The term "Duress" is most like
3. undue influence.

7. When a renter finds the rental to be dangerous or unsafe to live in and the landlord refuses to make repairs needed to bring the property to a safe condition, the tenant may vacate and not be responsible for the remainder of the lease. When the tenant moves, the tenant has given the landlord
3. constructive notice/eviction.

8. A lease on an apartment has ended yet the tenant keeps paying a monthly rent and the landlord keeps accepting the rent.   This type of leasehold would be considered
1. a holdover tenancy.

9. The Civil Rights Act of 1968 was meant as a follow-up to the Civil Rights Act of 1964. It is called the
2. Fair Housing Act.

10. The Civil Rights Act of 1866 prohibited discrimination based on?
3. Race

11. The definition of subletting is most like?
1. The leasing of a premise by a lessee to a third party

12. Which of the following is true for both VA Loans and FHA Loans?
4. Both loans could have discount points to buy down the loan

13. Public Assistance is considered

1. lawful income.

14. When a landlord owns a four-plex in a FEMA designated flood pain and decides not to buy insurance but instead raise the air conditioners and heaters on high platforms, the owner
3. is said to be "Controlling his Risk".

15. A liquor store on the main highway was enjoying brisk business and substantial profits. The county decided to move the main highway ¼ mile away to the north of the store. This caused traffic to be re-routed and profits dropped significantly. This would be an example of?
2. External or Economic obsolescence

16. Which term describes a loan with the loan payment is less than the interest charged resulting in the outstanding balance of the loan increasing?
3. Negative Amortization

17. An Abstract of Title is
3. the history of the recorded documents on a property.

18. Into which bank account would a broker deposit commissions?
2. Business account

19. The cheapest way to handle asbestos is
4. encapsulation.

20. Radon
4. Both one and two.

21. A buyer is purchasing a home in a neighborhood that has a homeowner's association. At the closing, what additional documents should the buyer receive?
1. The Neighborhood CC and R's (The covenants, conditions and restrictions) and bylaws.

22. After the close of an escrow, who would keep for three years the Listing Agreement?
4. The Client and the Seller's Agent

23. After the close of escrow, who would for three years keep the Purchase Agreement?
2. The Client, the Customer, the Selling Agent and the Seller's Agent

Exam Six

1. An Environmental Impact Statement is used for what?
1. A proposed project.
2. An outdated project.
3. A private company project only.
4. A governmental project only.

2. An Environmental Impact Statement is considered a Police Power because it deals with
1. bridges.
2. boat docks.
3. health and safety.
4. animals.

3. When a person dies without a will and no heirs can be found, the property
1. escheats to the state.
2. condemnation occurs.
3. a suit for specific non-action is filed.
4. inverse condemnation occurs.

4. Escheat happens
1. because property can - not be ownerless.
2. because there are more than two people involved.
3. because local governments want to build a real estate portfolio.
4. All of the above.

5. Inverse (Reverse) Condemnation may be brought by
1. the state.
2. the city.
3. the seller.
4. the homeowner.

6. Which of the following persons would most likely seek a Conditional Use Permit or Variance?
1. A person wanting to build an addition to their home.
2. A school.
3. A property owner whose property is zoned for single family residences but wants to open a small grocery store on the property.
4. A government agency.

7. Which of the following pertain to the present and the future owners?
1. Family size.
2. Home Designs.
3. Deed Restrictions.
4. All of the above.

8. Determinable Fee or Defeasible Fee are
1. ownership with a condition.
2. ownership without any conditions.
3. fee Simple Ownership.
4. a property owned by a corporation.

9. When a condition in a deed is violated, what happens to the property?
1. Nothing.
2. It reverts back to the original grantor.
3. The deed gets given to a public party.
4. All of the above.

10. All of the following deal with appraisal except
1. reproduction cost.
2. replacement cost.
3. straight line method of depreciation.
4. valuation.

11. Usury Laws
1. protects the lender.
2. protects the borrower.
3. protects the government.
4. protects China.

12. When a borrower defaults on a payment, the lender will call the entire note due and payable. The clause in the contract that allows for this is called
1. Acceleration Clause.
2. Protection Clause.
3. Defeasible Fee Clause.
4. Santa Claus.

13. Who would have the most options for loans and loan programs?
1. Mortgage Banker.
2. Mortgage Broker.
3. Mortgage Servicer.
4. Mortgage Repo Guy.

14. Another term for a Straight Mortgage (interest only) is a
   1. variable mortgage.
   2. amortized mortgage.
   3. term mortgage.
   4. reverse negative mortgage.

15. An agent brought a ready, willing and able buyer to the seller. The agent has earned her commission when which of the following happens?
   1. The seller gives a counter offer.
   2. The buyer withdraws the offer.
   3. The seller accepts the offer.
   4. The broker withholds all other offers.

Answers Exam Six

1. An Environmental Impact Statement is used for what?
1. A proposed project.

2. An Environmental Impact Statement is considered a Police Power because it deals with
3. health and safety.

3. When a person dies without a will and no heirs can be found, the property
1. escheats to the state.

4. Escheat happens
1. because property can - not be ownerless.

5. Inverse (Reverse) Condemnation may be brought by
4. the homeowner.

6. Which of the following persons would most likely seek a Conditional Use Permit or Variance?
3. A property owner whose property is zoned for single family residences but wants to open a small grocery store on the property.

7. Which of the following pertain to the present and the future owners?
3. Deed Restrictions.

8. Determinable Fee or Defeasible Fee are
1. ownership with a condition.

9. When a condition in a deed is violated, what happens to the property?
2. It reverts back to the original grantor.

10. All of the following deal with appraisal except
3. straight line method of depreciation.

11. Usury Laws
2. protects the borrower.

12. When a borrower defaults on a payment, the lender will call the entire note due and payable. The clause in the contract that allows for this is called
1. Acceleration Clause.

13. Who would have the most options for loans and loan programs?
2. Mortgage Broker.

14. Another term for a Straight Mortgage (interest only) is

3.   term mortgage.

15. An agent brought a ready, willing and able buyer to the seller. The agent has earned her commission when which of the following happens?

3.   The seller accepts the offer.

Exam Seven

1. In trying to find the value of a subject home, if the subject home has a fireplace worth $5000. and the comparable doesn't, where would an appraiser make an adjustment?
1. Add $5000 to the comparable property.
2. Add $5000 to the subject property.
3. Add $2500 to the comparable.

2. Allen was making payments of principle and interest but at the end of the term, he will be paying a balloon payment to pay off the outstanding balance. What type of loan does Allen have?
1. Straight
2. Negative
3. Partially Amortized

3. The term that best describes the effect on a property when there are six bedrooms on the second story and one bathroom of the first floor would most closely be?
1. Functional Obsolescence
2. External Obsolescence
3. Economic Obsolescence

4. Bob, a professional truck driver has been granted a right of way over Dwayne's property for ingress and egress so that he can park his large commercial truck on his own property when he is not working. Which of the following could terminate the easement?
1. When Dwayne sells his property to Samuel.
2. When Dwayne installs a fence to block Bob from using it.
3. When Bob sells his truck and retires.

5. Broker Sally has an Exclusive Buyer Agreement with potential buyer Towana. Broker Sally would like to show Towana a property listed by another company. What does Sally owe the Seller?
1. Fair and Honest Dealings
2. The seller is your client.
3. You are the subagent of the seller.

6. If Broker Tommy has an Exclusive Listing Agreement with his seller, he may have a relationship with the buyer in all of the following ways except
1. A dual agency
2. Exclusively represent the Buyer
3. The buyer may be your customer.

7. Which of the following would be a violation of federal fair housing laws?
1. Refusing to rent to a person who has a comfort dog because you own a non-pet building.
2. A 55+ community refused to rent to a woman with under-aged children based on familial status.
3. The owner lives in his four-unit apartment building and refuses to rent to families.

8. A landlord may do which of the following without being in violation of federal fair housing laws?
1. Demand that a vacating tenant remove the wheelchair ramp they installed before they move out.
2. Segregating families with children into specific areas of his complex.
3. Refusing to rent to a person because he does not want to install a wheel chair ramp.

9. A very old oak tree or a very large boulder
1. Lots and Blocks
2. Rectangular Survey System
3. Metes and Bounds

10. Who do Usury Laws protect?
1. Banks
2. The consumer
3. Mortgage Brokers

11. Bob is selling his mid-century modern home. He has built a free-standing wall with bookshelves on one side to separate the dining room from the living room. When Bob sells the property, this free-standing wall will be considered?
1. Personal property
2. Real property
3. Trade Fixtures

12. Billy and Scott were recently married. Both of them have never owned real estate. They decided to purchase their home with a FHA loan. What would be the advantage for them in choosing the FHA loan?
1. Buyer insurance with the FHA.
2. Their down payment could be as low as 3.5%.
3. FHA insuring the bank will get their money.

13. It is meant to protect an owner's or a lender's financial interest in real property against loss due to title defects.
1. FHA Insurance
2. Homeowners Insurance
3. Title Insurance

14. To what date does title insurance insure up to?
1. The date that it's issued.
2. The date of the transaction.
3. The date the purchase agreement was accepted.

15. An agent was showing a potential buyer a home. As they were walking up the driveway, the agent noticed that the property has nine missing roof tiles. The agent notified the Seller's Agent. The Seller's Agent and the Client denied there were missing tiles. What should they agent do?
1. Inform the buyer that you were wrong about the missing tiles.
2. Inform the buyer that the seller said tiles were not missing.
3. Disclose in writing to the Buyer that there are tiles missing.

16. Two months after a buyer moved into his new home, he noticed there were several roof tiles missing. The missing tiles allowed rain to damage the interior walls. He asked his agent to repair the damage. Would his agent be allowed to keep his commission?
1. No, because he is responsible for damages after the transfer.

    2.   Yes. The purchase agreement is between the Seller and buyer.

    3.   Yes but he is obligated to help the new owner make repairs.

17. An agent knowingly misleads the purchaser of a property as to where his property lines were. The new owner discovered the misrepresentation when he hired a contractor to build a fence on his property line. What could the agent be responsible for?

    1.   Actual Damages or Financial Damages.

    2.   Nothing. The buyer should have hired a surveyor before he made the offer to purchase.

    3.   He will be forced to buy the property.

18. The listing broker failed to disclose to the buyer's agent that a felony was committed on the property. Is he required to disclose that information?

    1.   No because the property has been renovated

    2.   Yes because a felony is a material fact.

    3.   No because a felony is not a material fact.

19. Brokers from Lazy Realty were in their weekly meeting. They were discussing how Ripped Realty charges a fee for a service that both companies do at a much higher price. What should the brokers do?

    1.   Reduce their fee to match Ripped Realty

    2.   Nothing

    3.   Raise their fee.

20. Sellers and landlords must disclose known lead - based paint and lead - based paint hazards and provide available reports to buyers or renters for homes built before what year?

    1.   1978

    2.   1866

    3.   1986

21. The Lead Based Paint Disclosure Act allows a buyer or renter of a property built before 1978 to inspect the property in ten days. What else is the buyer or renter required to be given?

    1.   A three day right of rescission.

    2.   The government booklet "Protect Your Family From Lead Based Paint.

    3.   Estoppel Certificates.

22. What is the most prevalent latent lead product found on a property?

    1.   Lead paint.

    2.   Lead based cleaners.

    3.   Lead pipes.

23. During the final inspection, the buyer noticed that the seller had removed the built in stereo speakers in the den. There are now large holes in the walls. Was the seller allowed to remove them?

    1.   Yes because they were connected to the seller's stereo which was not annexed onto the real property.

    2.   No because the property must be delivered to the buyer in the same condition as when the contract was signed. (in place)

    3.   Yes because it was the seller's personal property.

24. While moving her furniture into her new home, Suong realized that the seller had removed the window boxes containing perennial roses. Is the seller responsible for returning them?

    1.   Yes, because they were fixtures attached to the home.

    2.   No, because they were personal property.

    3.   No, because her agent told her to take them.

25. Bob and Rick owned a liquor store and were experiencing brisk business. The county built a main highway diverting traffic away from their store. What term best describes this situation?

    1.   Internal obsolescence

    2.   Depreciation

3. External obsolescence

26. **What is the best example of a "Less Than Arm's Length" transaction?**
    1. A conveyance between two strangers.
    2. A broker purchased a listing he had with a client.
    3. A mother sold her daughter the family home for 75% of the true market value.

Answers Exam Seven

1. **In trying to find the value of a subject home, if the subject home has a fireplace worth $5000. and the comparable doesn't, where would an appraiser make an adjustment?**
1. Add $5000 to the comparable property.

2. **Allen was making payments of principle and interest but at the end of the term, he will be paying a balloon payment to pay off the outstanding balance. What type of loan does Allen have?**
3. Partially Amortized

3. **The term that best describes the effect on a property when there are six bedrooms on the second story and one bathroom of the first floor would most closely be?**
1. Functional Obsolescence

4. **Bob, a professional truck driver has been granted a right of way over Dwayne's property for ingress and egress so that he can park his large commercial truck on his own property when he is not working. Which of the following could terminate the easement?**
3. When Bob sells his truck and retires.

5. **Broker Sally has an Exclusive Buyer Agreement with potential buyer Towanda. Broker Sally would like to show Towanda a property listed by another company. What does Sally owe the Seller?**
1. Fair and Honest Dealings

6. **If Broker Tommy has an Exclusive Listing Agreement with his seller, he may have a relationship with the buyer in all of the following ways except**
2. Exclusively represent the Buyer at the detriment to the seller

7. **Which of the following would be a violation of federal fair housing laws?**
1. Refusing to rent to a person who has a comfort dog because you own a non-pet building.

8. **A landlord may do which of the following without being in violation of federal fair housing laws?**
1. Demand that a vacating tenant remove the wheelchair ramp they installed before they move out.

9. **A very old oak tree or a very large boulder**
3. Metes and Bounds

10. **Who do Usury Laws protect?**
2. The consumer

11. **Bob is selling his mid-century modern home. He has built a free-standing wall with bookshelves on one side to separate the dining room from the living room. When Bob sells the property, this free-standing wall will be considered?**
1. Personal property

12. **Billy and Scott were recently married. Both of them have never owned real estate. They decided to purchase their home with a FHA loan. What would be the advantage for them in choosing the FHA loan?**
2. Their down payment could be as low as 3.5%.

13. **What is meant to protect an owner's or a lender's financial interest in real property against loss due to title defects.**
3. Title Insurance

14. To what date does title insurance insure up to?
1. The date that it's issued.

15. An agent was showing a potential buyer a home. As they were walking up the driveway, the agent noticed that the property has nine missing roof tiles. The agent notified the Seller's Agent. The Seller's Agent and the Client denied there were missing tiles. What should they agent do?
3. Disclose in writing to the Buyer and Seller's Agent that there are tiles missing.

16. Two months after a buyer moved into his new home, he noticed there were several roof tiles missing. The missing tiles allowed rain to damage the interior walls. He asked his agent to repair the damage. Would his agent be allowed to keep his commission?
2. Yes. The purchase agreement is between the Seller and buyer.

17. An agent knowingly misleads the purchaser of a property as to where his property lines were. The new owner discovered the misrepresentation when he hired a contractor to build a fence on his property line. What could the agent be responsible for?
1. Actual Damages or Financial Damages.

18. The listing broker failed to disclose to the buyer's agent that a felony was committed on the property. Is he required to disclose that information?
3. No because a felony is not a material fact.

19. Brokers from Lazy Realty were in their weekly meeting. They were discussing how Ripped Realty charges a much higher fee for the same services. What should the brokers do?
2. Nothing Brokers cannot price fix.

20. Sellers and landlords must disclose known lead - based paint and lead - based paint hazards and provide available reports to buyers or renters for homes built before what year?
1. 1978

21. The Lead Based Paint Disclosure Act allows a buyer or renter of a property built before 1978 to inspect the property in ten days. What else is the buyer or renter required to be given?
2. The government booklet "Protect Your Family from Lead Based Paint.

22. What is the most prevalent latent lead product found on a property?
3. Lead pipes.

23. During the final inspection, the buyer noticed that the seller had removed the built in stereo speakers in the den. There are now large holes in the walls. Was the seller allowed to remove them?
2. No because the property must be delivered to the buyer in the same condition as when the contract was signed. (in place)

24. While moving her furniture into her new home, Al realized that the seller had removed the window boxes containing perennial roses. Is the seller responsible for returning them?
1. Yes, because they were fixtures attached to the home.

25. Bob and Rick owned a liquor store and were experiencing brisk business. The county built a main highway diverting traffic away from their store. What term best describes this situation?
3. External obsolescence

26. What is the best example of a "Less Than Arm's Length" transaction?
3. A mother sold her daughter the family home for 75% of the true market value.

Exam Eight

1. A CMA is based on which appraisal technique?
1. Market Data
2. Cost Approach.
3. GRM

2. A CMA is predominately utilized by an agent to help a seller determine a listing range. What do the initials CMA stand for?
1. Complementary Market Analysis
2. Complete Monetary Action
3. Comparative Market Analysis

3.What are the four stages of a neighborhood?
1. growth, stability, decline, revitalization.
2. stability, growth, decline, revitalization.
3. growth, decline, revitalization, stability.

4. Outdated cabinets and fixtures would be an example of which of the following?
1. Incurable functional obsolescence.
2. Curable functional obsolescence.
3. Curable external obsolescence.

5. Which of the following would be used as a comparable when an appraiser is determining the value of a single-family residence?
1. The home that just closed yesterday and located one street over.
2. The same home floor plan built by the same contractor using the same materials three towns over.
3. The home for sale next door.

6. What is a deed restriction?
1. A police power
2. A zoning ordinance.
3. A limitation on use.

7. What is a good example of a buffer zone?
1. A large park between an office building and a single-family residence neighborhood.
2. A coffee shop between office buildings and a park.
3. A subway station between a city and the suburbs.

8. Which of the following is a material popular in the 1970's and 1980's used for insulation? It was pumped between the walls.
1. Pesticides
2. UFFI Urea Formaldehyde Foam Insulation (UFF or UFFI)
3. Brownfields

9. Which of the following is not a police power?
1. deed restrictions
2. eminent domain
3. environmental protection laws

10. How many square feet in an acre?
1. 43,560
2. 55,000
3. 640

11. A developer would like to arrange for a loan on a large piece of land he plans to subdivide, record and develop.

   1. Subdivision Mortgage
   2. Blanket Mortgage
   3. Package Mortgage

12. A commercial tenant has a triple net lease. What expenses will he be paying?
   1. The landlord's property taxes.
   2. His rent and the landlord pays all of his electric and gas payments.
   3. His rent plus some of the landlord expenses.

13. Is a Judicial Foreclosure a legal event?
   1. No
   2. It depends on factors leading to the foreclosure.
   3. Yes

14. An agent told an older couple that he would show them the most beautiful house in the best neighborhood. When the couple got to the property, they felt it was nice but there were also equally nice properties in the area. What was the agent doing?
   1. Puffing
   2. Negligent Misrepresentation.
   3. He was not practicing Care.

15. What antitrust law would Tran and Bob be guilty of if they got together and decided not to do business with Arthur to stamp out the competition?
   1. CERCLA.
   2. RESPA
   3. Antitrust – Sherman Antitrust.

16. An agent showed a couple with 10 children properties only in neighborhoods where a bunch of other large families lived. The couple requested to see other neighborhoods as well but the agent declined their request. The agent may be guilty of what fair housing law?
   1. Blockbusting
   2. Steering
   3. Redlining

17. What is the minimum amount of time that a person or married couple needs to live in their primary residence in order to qualify for a capital gains exclusion?
   1. Three out of the last six years.
   2. Two of the last five years.
   3. Three out of the last five years.

18. What is the capital gains exclusion on a primary residence for a single person and a married couple?
   1. $250,000 for a single person and $500,000 for a married couple.
   2. $250,000 for both singles and married couples.
   3. $100,000 for a single person and $250,000 for a married couple.

19. Toyota will be opening an auto factory in Small Town, USA within 12 months and will be creating 3000 new jobs. Several sellers decided to wait and sell their homes after the construction is complete because they believe their value will increase. What real estate theory do they believe?
   1. Anticipation
   2. Alienation
   3. Novation

20. An investor wished to sell one of his town homes. What type of account should be set up for him to be able to reinvest his profit while deferring taxes?
   1. 1099 misc. account
   2. 1031 tax deferred exchange
   3. Capital Gains Exclusion Account

21. **When an attorney reads and interprets a Chain of Title, what is it called?**
    1. Abstract and Testimonial
    2. Opinion and Guarantee
    3. Abstract and Opinion

22. **It protects an owner of a property or the mortgagee's financial interest in real estate against loss due to title defects, blemishes and liens.**
    1. Title Insurance
    2. FHA Insurance
    3. VA Guarantees

23. **What is the recorded history of a property called?**
    1. Title Insurance
    2. Chain of Title
    3. Abstract and Opinion

24. **What is the legal concept that gives the owner of real estate all legal rights such as possession, disposition and exclusion?**
    1. Power of Attorney
    2. Reverse Condemnation
    3. Bundle of Rights

25. **If the closing attorney and both agents disagree as to where an earnest money deposit should go, who is it given to?**
    1. It's turned over to the court to decide.
    2. It always goes back to the buyer.
    3. It's split three ways.

26. **Bob the Broker is a laissez faire manager. Instead of training his new agents, he provides them with manuals. An agent in Bob's office accidently disclosed some wrong information to a potential buyer. Whose responsible for the mistakes?**
    1. The agent
    2. Bob the Broker and the agent
    3. Bob the Broker only.

27. **An agent and her client noticed mold around the plumbing at several locations on the property. Who should disclose this to potential buyers?**
    1. The buyer's agent.
    2. The Seller, his agent and the buyer's agent.
    3. The Seller's Agent.

28. **A buyer gave an earnest money check to his Broker on Friday and the Broker deposited the check into his personal bank account on Saturday. What did the broker do?**
    1. Comingling
    2. Negligent Misrepresentation
    3. Arbitration

29. **Which of the following may not necessarily cancel a contract?**
    1. Death of the Broker
    2. The property burns down.
    3. Insanity of the Broker

30. **Sam and Al were in escrow. Sam was to buy Al's home. After the contract was executed and before the transaction was completed, Al's Broker called Sam's Broker to inform Sam that the property had a terrible fire last night and the entire structure is destroyed. Will Sam be forced into completing the contract to purchase Al's now destroyed property?**
    1. No, when the deed is conveyed everything with the property must be "in place" as it was when the offer was accepted.
    2. No, because Al didn't have insurance on the home since there was no mortgage. Insurance will not replace the home before closing.
    3. Yes, because Sam already started paying a pre-insurance on the property.

31. **What antitrust law would Tran and Bob be guilty of if they got together and both brokers decided not to do business with Arthur?**
    1. Laches
    2. Sherman Antitrust Act.
    3. Regulation Z.

32. **Carol represented Derrick in the purchase of Derrick's 20-unit apartment building. When the transaction was completed, Derrick asked Carol if she would like to manage the property for him. Carol accepted. What type of agent is Carol?**
    1. Special
    2. General
    3. Universal

33. **Bob could not afford a mortgage payment presented by his loan banker. The loan banker suggested that Bob should buy down the interest rate. What was the banker suggesting Bob to pay?**
    1. Principle and Commission Only
    2. P & I
    3. Discount Points

34. **Alice gave a small loan to Betty and recorded the note. After two years, Betty decided she would like to take out a larger mortgage. Betty asked Alice if she would sign a document to put her smaller loan into a second (junior lien position) position so that the bank would lend her $200,000. What document was Betty asking Alice to sign?**
    1. Superfund - CERCLA – Brownfield Agreement
    2. Subordination Agreement.
    3. Purchase Agreement

35. **What is the secondary mortgage market?**
    1. Banks buying and selling loans to each other.
    2. A Consumer who applies for a loan at a credit union.
    3. FHA lending a consumer a guaranteed loan.

36. **Which of the following could be considered a balloon payment?**
    1. Party Payments
    2. The largest payment is paid as points.
    3. A large balance due on a mortgage at a predetermined future date.

37. **To find the value of a library, an appraiser would use which of the following to determine value?**
    1. Research the market data of sold buildings within a ten-mile radius of the library.
    2. Find the replacement cost of the building and then add in the value of the land.
    3. Find a comparable library that sold in the last six Months.

38. **Which approach to value would an appraiser use to determine the value of Graceland?**
    1. Replacement Cost with new materials and add in the land.
    2. Comparable Method.
    3. Market Data and Reconciliation

39. **In which of the following would the Cost Approach likely to be used?**

1. A six-year-old SFR within a gated Community.
2. A five-year-old condo.
3. New construction.

40. An older woman decided not to list her home with Broker Carl because she believes the value of her home will increase when the new proposed highway is expanded into her area. What best describes her decision?
1. Alienation
2. Anticipation
3. Reverse Condemnation.

41. What does not contribute to value?
1. locations, situs and area preference
2. supply and demand and permanence.
3. Performance.

42. A developer built a new home community where the demand for his homes was great. Which home would most likely be sold for the least?
1. The last one.
2. The first one.
3. The one best negotiated

43. What does a home warranty cover?
1. Quality of workmanship.
2. It covers the seller against any latent defects that may show up to the new owner.
3. Plumbing and heating.

Answers Exam Eight

1. A CMA is based on which appraisal technique?
1. Market Data

2. A CMA is predominately utilized by an agent to help a seller determine a listing range. What do the initials CMA stand for?
3. Comparative Market Analysis

3.What are the four stages of a neighborhood?
1. growth, stability, decline, revitalization.

4. Outdated cabinets and fixtures would be an example of which of the following?
2. Curable functional obsolescence.

5. Which of the following would be used as a comparable when an appraiser is determining the value of a single-family residence?
1. The home that just closed yesterday and located one street over.

6. What is a deed restriction?
3. A limitation on use.

7. What is a good example of a buffer zone?
1. A large park between an office building and a single-family residence neighborhood.

8. Which of the following is a material popular in the 1970's and 1980's used for insulation? It was pumped between the walls.
2. UFFI Urea Formaldehyde Foam Insulation (UFF or UFFI)

9. Which of the following is not a police power?

1. deed restrictions

10. How many square feet in an acre?
1. 43,560

11. A developer would like to arrange for a loan on a large piece of land he plans to subdivide, record and develop.
2. Blanket Mortgage

12. A commercial tenant has a triple net lease. What expenses will he be paying?
3. His rent plus some of the landlord expenses.

13. Is a Judicial Foreclosure a legal event?
3. Yes

14. An agent told an older couple that he would show them the most beautiful house in the best neighborhood. When the couple got to the property, they felt it was nice but there were also equally nice properties in the area. What was the agent doing?
1. Puffing

15. What antitrust law would Tran and Bob be guilty of if they got together and decided not to do business with Arthur to stamp out the competition?
3. Antitrust – Sherman Antitrust.

16. An agent showed a couple with 10 children properties only in neighborhoods where a bunch of other large families lived. The couple requested to see other neighborhoods as well but the agent declined their request. The agent may be guilty of what fair housing law?
2. Steering

17. What is the minimum amount of time that a person or married couple needs to live in their primary residence in order to qualify for a capital gains exclusion?
2. Two of the last five years.

18. What is the capital gains exclusion on a primary residence for a single person and a married couple?
1. $250,000 for a single person and $500,000 for a married couple.

19. Toyota will be opening an auto factory in Small Town, USA within 12 months and will be creating 3000 new jobs. Several sellers decided to wait and sell their homes after the construction is complete because they believe their value will increase. What real estate theory do they believe?
1. Anticipation

20. An investor wished to sell one of his town homes. What type of account should be set up for him to be able to reinvest his profit while deferring taxes?
2. 1031 tax deferred exchange

21. When an attorney reads and interprets a Chain of Title, what is it called?
3. Abstract and Opinion

22. It protects an owner of a property or the mortgagee's financial interest in real estate against loss due to title defects, blemishes and liens.
1. Title Insurance

23. What is the recorded history of a property called?
2. Chain of Title

24. What is the legal concept that gives the owner of real estate all legal rights such as possession, disposition and exclusion?

3. Bundle of Rights

25. If the closing attorney and both agents disagree as to where an earnest money deposit should go, who is it given to?
1. It's turned over to the court to decide.

26. Bob the Broker is a laissez faire manager. Instead of training his new agents, he provides them with manuals. An agent in Bob's office accidently disclosed some wrong information to a potential buyer. Whose responsible for the mistakes?
2. Bob the Broker and the agent

27. An agent and her client noticed mold around the plumbing at several locations on the property. Who should disclose this to potential buyers?
2. The Seller, his agent and the buyer's agent.

28. A buyer gave an earnest money check to his Broker on Friday and the Broker deposited the check into his personal bank account on Saturday. What did the broker do?
1. Comingling

29. Which of the following may not necessarily cancel a contract?
2. The property burns down.

30. Sam and Al were in escrow. Sam was to buy Al's home. After the contract was executed and before the transaction was completed, Al's Broker called Sam's Broker to inform Sam that the property had a terrible fire last night and the entire structure is destroyed. Will Sam be forced into completing the contract to purchase Al's now destroyed property?
1. No, when the deed is conveyed everything with the property must be "in place" as it was when the offer was accepted.

31. What antitrust law would Tran and Bob be guilty of if they got together and both brokers decided not to do business with Arthur?
2. Sherman Antitrust Act.

32. Carol represented Derrick in the purchase of Derrick's 20-unit apartment building. When the transaction was completed, Derrick asked Carol if she would like to manage the property for him. Carol accepted. What type of agent is Carol?
2. General

33. Bob could not afford a mortgage payment presented by his loan banker. The loan banker suggested that Bob should buy down the interest rate. What was the banker suggesting Bob to pay?
3. Discount Points

34. Alice gave a small loan to Betty and recorded the note. After two years, Betty decided she would like to take out a larger mortgage. Betty asked Alice if she would sign a document to put her smaller loan into a second (junior lien position) position so that the bank would lend her $200,000. What document was Betty asking Alice to sign?
2. Subordination Agreement.

35. What is the secondary mortgage market?
1. Banks buying and selling loans to each other.

36. Which of the following could be considered a balloon payment?
3. A large balance due on a mortgage at a predetermined future date.

37. To find the value of a library, an appraiser would use which of the following to determine value?
2. Find the replacement cost of the building and then add in the value of the land.

38. Which approach to value would an appraiser use to determine the value of Graceland?
1. Replacement Cost with new materials and add in the land.

39. In which of the following would the Cost Approach likely to be used?

3. New construction.

40. An older woman decided not to list her home with Broker Carl because she believes the value of her home will increase when the new proposed highway is expanded into her area. What best describes her decision?

2. Anticipation

41. What does not contribute to value?

3. Performance.

42. A developer built a new home community where the demand for his homes was great. Which home would most likely be sold for the least?

2. The first one.

43. What does a home warranty cover?

3. Plumbing and heating.

Exam Nine

1. Bob and Patty have a verbal long term lease. According to the statute of frauds, If Bob breaches the agreement, Patty

1. Could not sue Bob in court because verbal agreements are unenforceable.
2. Would be successful in a court of law because Bob breached the contract.
3. Could sue Bob but an arbitration board would hear the case.
4. Could not sue Bob because the arbitration committee would refer the case to HUD.

2. At closing, which fees are prorated between the Seller and the Buyer?

1. Homeowners insurance.
2. Repair fees
3. Taxes
4. The mortgage late payments.

3. Patty acquired a loan from Mega Bank USA. The loan was secured on her new home and the furniture that was inside. The type of loan that Patty has is an?

1. Blanket Loan
2. Balloon payment loan.
3. Equity loan
4. Package loan.

4. Broker Bob received an offer on Seller Carl's home. The offeror gave Carl six days to decide if he would accept the offer. On day four, the offer wasn't accepted and the offeror instructed Broker Bob to withdraw his offer. In this case.

1. The offeror is entitled to his earnest money deposit because he withdrew the offer before the seller accepted the offer.
2. The offeror is not entitled to a refund of his earnest money deposit because the seller had planned to accept the offer later that afternoon.
3. The offeror's earnest money deposit is given to the seller because the offeror breached the contract.
4. Under no circumstances is the offeror entitled to an earnest money deposit once the offer is made.

5. Real Property includes all of the following except

1. water rights.
2. oak trees.
3. chattel.
4. rose bushes.

6. Two years ago the market was hot in City Ville. Homes were selling as fast as builders could build them. Several developers purchased land, got the required permits and built as many homes as they felt the market could handle. Now there are complete communities of vacant homes. The price of new homes in City Ville most likely will
1. Increased in value.
2. Decreased in value.
3. Values will remain the same.
4. Older home values will increase.

7. What section in a township is set aside for schools?
1. section 6
2. section 12
3. section 16
4. section 14

8. Metes and Bounds is associated with
1. point of beginning.
2. Meridians.
3. Baselines
4. Rectangles.

9. The family of an established farm is afraid the new farm upstream will divert water away from their farm. What water right may the established farm owners have?
1. littoral
2. riparian
3. encroachment
4. prior appropriation.

10. Bob, a truck driver, has an easement where he benefits. It allows him to have a wide ingress and egress so that he can store his very large truck when he is not driving it. How could this easement be terminated?
1. The servient tenement holder rejects Bob's right for ingress and egress.
2. Bob retires from truck driving, sells his truck and wants to end the easement.
3. When the servient tenement holder buys a bigger truck and access for Bob's truck is narrowed.
4. When Bob sells his truck.

11. Sally wants to have the highest protection of ownership when she purchases a new home. Sally should request what type of deed?
1. General Warranty Deed
2. Special Warranty Deed
3. Quitclaim Deed
4. Title Insurance

12. From the first day of ownership, four college students could not agree how to proceed the best way for their 400-unit apartment complex they purchased as Joint Tenants. They would like to divide the property so that each of them can do what they think is best. The four college students could go to court to dissolve the Joint Tenancy by requesting a?
1. Manager
2. Home Owners Association
3. Trustor
4. Partition

13. What are the two most important duties of a notary public?
1. To make sure the person signing is not a felon and to report to the police if the signer has a criminal record.
2. To make sure that the person signing is who they are and that the document is properly dated.
3. To make sure the person is who they are and to make sure they have a witness to their signing.
4. To make sure the person is who they claim to be and that their signing is voluntary.

14. The type of ownership known for double taxation is which of the following?
   1. LLC
   2. S Corporation
   3. Corporation
   4. REIT

15. When no specific type of co-ownership is stated in a deed, what type deed is presumed to be granted?
   1. General Warranty Deed
   2. Joint Tenancy
   3. Tenant in Common
   4. Tenants by the Entirety.

16. Investor have decided to create a limited partnership. What would be the benefit?
   1. Their losses are limited up to their investment.
   2. They would like to actively participate in the venture.
   3. The tax consequences are favorable.
   4. All of the above.

17. Corporations may take title in which of the following ways?
   1. Tenants by the Entirety or Joint Tenants
   2. Joint tenants and tenants in common
   3. In Severalty or joint Tenants
   4. in Severalty

18. Three Tenants in Common would like to dissolve their relationship on the ownership of a large commercial property. The best way to dissolve their ownership relationship would be to?
   1. Go to court and obtain a partition.
   2. Will their interests to their heirs?
   3. Write up a codicil.
   4. Turn the property over to a trustee.

19. What is the effect of recording a deed into public record?
   1. Letting the world acknowledge a warranty forever.
   2. Giving the world constructive notice.
   3. Title certification
   4. Intentional Notice

20. When a potential buyer inspects the recorded documents of a property and inspects the actual property, what type notice is he given?
   1. Constructive notice
   2. Intentional notice
   3. Accrued Notice.
   4. Actual Notice

Answers Exam Nine

1. Bob and Patty have a verbal long term lease. According to the statute of frauds, If Bob breaches the agreement, Patty
1. Could not sue Bob in court because verbal agreements are unenforceable.

2. At closing, which fees are prorated between the Seller and the Buyer?
3. Taxes

3. Patty acquired a loan from Mega Bank USA. The loan was secured on her new home and the furniture that was inside. The type of loan that Patty has is an?

4. Package loan.

4. Broker Bob received an off on Seller Carl's home. The offeror gave Carl six days to decide if he would accept the offer. On day four, the offer wasn't accepted and the offeror instructed Broker Bob to withdraw his offer. In this case.
1. The offeror is entitled to his earnest money deposit because he withdrew the offer before the seller accepted the offer.

5. Real Property includes all of the following except
3. chattel.

6.. Two years ago the market was hot in City Ville. Homes were selling as fast as builders could build them. Several developers purchased land, got the required permits and built as many homes as they felt the market could handle. Now there are complete communities of vacant homes. The price of new homes in City Ville most likely will
2. Decreased in value.

7. What section in a township is set aside for schools?
3. section 16

8. Metes and Bounds is associated with
1. point of beginning.

9. The family of an established farm is afraid the new farm upstream will divert water away from their farm. What water right may the established farm owners have?
4. prior appropriation.

10. Bob, a truck driver, has an easement where he benefits. It allows him to have a wide ingress and egress so that he can store his very large truck when he is not driving it. How could this easement be terminated?
2. Bob retires from truck driving, sells his truck and wants to end the easement.

11. Sally wants to have the highest protection of ownership when she purchases a new home. Sally should request what type of deed?
1. General Warranty Deed

12. From the first day of ownership, four college students could not agree how to proceed the best way for their 400-unit apartment complex they purchased as Joint Tenants. They would like to divide the property so that each of them can do what they think is best. The four college students could go to court to dissolve the Joint Tenancy by requesting a?
4. Partition

13. What are the two most important duties of a notary public?
4. To make sure the person is who they claim to be and that their signing is voluntary.

14. The type of ownership known for double taxation is which of the following?
3. Corporation

15. When no specific type of co-ownership is stated in a deed, what type deed is presumed to be granted?
3. Tenants in Common

16. Investor have decided to create a limited partnership. What would be the benefit?
1. Their losses are limited up to their investment.

17. Corporations may take title in which of the following ways?
4. in Severalty

18. Three Tenants in Common would like to dissolve their relationship on the ownership of a large commercial property. The best way to dissolve their ownership relationship p would be to?
1. Go to court and obtain a partition.

19. What is the effect of recording a deed into public record?
2. Giving the world constructive notice.

20. When a potential buyer inspects the recorded documents of a property and inspects the actual property, what type notice is he given?
4. Actual Notice

Exam Ten

1. Power of a government to take private property for public use; the U.S. Constitution gives national and state governments this power. Just compensation is paid to the owner. Condemnation.

1. acceleration clause
2. leasehold estate
3. designated agency
4. eminent domain

2. A will that is written, dated, and signed in the handwriting of the maker.

1. novation
2. riparian rights
3. acceleration clause
4. holographic will

3. The rate of return a property will produce on the investors investment.

1. condemnation
2. assumption of mortgage
3. Defeasible fee
4. capitalization rate

4. A document acknowledging the payment of a debt. Given to the mortgagor when the mortgage has been paid.

1. Appurtenant easements
2. condemnation
3. Subdivision plats
4. Deed of Satisfaction

5. The business of buying and selling as agents for others and for a commission.
1. Net lease
2. progression
3. tax sale
4. brokerage

6. Incomplete right, such as a wife's dower interest in her husband's property during his life.
1. marketable title
2. inchoate right
3. periodic estate
4. benchmark

7. A legal description that starts and ends at a point of beginning.
1. holographic will
2. inchoate right
3. amortized loan
4. Metes and bounds

8. A written instrument given to pass title to personal property.

1. specific lien
2. brownfields
3. Equal Credit Opportunity Act (ECOA)
4. bill of sale

9. Limited in durations to life of a life tenant or life or lives of some other designated person or persons.
1. Eminent Domain
2. progression
3. condemnation
4. Life estate

10. A one sided contract by which one party makes a promise to induce a second party to do something.

1. executory contract
2. bilateral contract
3. personal property
4. unilateral contract

11. The party that grants or gives an option.

1. optionor
2. life tenant
3. agent
4. Novation

12. A regulation of the Federal Reserve Board designed to ensure that borrowers and customers in the need of consumer credit are given meaningful information with respect to the cost of credit. Includes advertising and trigger terms. Gives a homeowner a three day right of recession when acquiring a loan based on his personal residence.

1. Regulation Z
2. cost approach
3. rescission
4. amortization loan

13. The pledge of property as security of a loan in which the borrower maintains possession of the property while it is pledged as security.
1. blockbusting
2. hypothecation
3. actual eviction
4. Appreciation

14. A sudden tearing away of land by the action of natural forces. The two ends of a barrier island got washed away during a hurricane.
1. affidavit
2. Fee simple
3. assignment
4. avulsion

15. Usually take priority over all other liens.
1. capital gain
2. Comprehensive Loss Underwriting Exchange
3. testate
4.`Real estate taxes and special assessments

16. The result of legal action originated by a lessor by which a defaulted tenant is physically ousted from the rented property pursuant to a court order.
1. proration
2. estate in land
3. accretion
4. actual eviction.

17. The imposition of a tax, charge or levy, usually according to established rates.
1. assessment

2. arbitrage
3. Defeasible fee
4. Attachment

18. A horizontal plane from which heights and depths are measured.
1. REALTOR®☐
2. usury
3. Novation
4. datum

19. Amount of ownership.
The degree, quantity, nature, and extent of interest a person has in real property.
1. township lines
2. Tenancy in common
3. marketable title
4. estate in land

20. One who is prepared to buy property on the seller's terms and is ready to take positive steps to consummate the transaction.
1."ready, willing, and able" buyer
2. agreement of sale
3. Federal Home Loan Mortgage Corporation (FHLMC)
4. General lien

21. The voluntary and permanent cessation of use or enjoyment with no intention to resume or reclaim one's possession or interest. May pertain to an easement of a property.
1. Abandonment
2. condemnation
3. escheat
4. police power

22. An acceptance by parties to an agreement to replace an old debtor with a new one.
1. novation
2. buy-down
3. intestate
4. Appreciation

23. The land and the improvements there-on designated by the owners as his or her homestead.
1. Freehold estates
2. Real property
3. tenancy by the entirety
4. homestead protection

24. The horizontal lines running at six mile intervals parallel to the baseline in the rectangular survey system.
1. Inchoate right
2. township lines
3.steering
4. Tenancy in common

25. Carelessness and inattentiveness resulting in a violation of trust. Failure to do what is required.
1. gross lease
2. redlining
3. emblements
4. negligence

24. Highest type of interest in real estate recognized by law. The holder is entitled to all rights incident to the property. Continues for indefinite period and is inheritable by heirs of owner.
1.Fee simple
2. Regulation Z

3. Attachment
4. Abandonment

25. Run north and south
1. Meridian
2. Baseline
3. Friable
4. Alluvion

26. A tenancy by which a lessee retains possession of leased property after her or his lease has expired and the landlord, by continuing to accept rent from the tenant, agrees to the tenant's continued occupancy as defined by state law. Could also lead to a tenancy in Sufferance.
1. package mortgage
2. notary public
3. holdover tenancy
4. habendum clause

27. The succession of conveyances of real property.
1. intestate
2. appraised value
3. chain of title
4. periodic estate

28. The land and the improvements there-on designated by the owners as his or her homestead.
1. fee simple estate
2. homestead protection
3. accrued depreciation
4. Freehold estates

29. A written or oral agreement in which all terms are explicitly stated. "pay first"
1. encroachment
2. commingling
3. expressed contract
4. Tenancy in common

30. The transfer of title to property to a grantee, by which the grantee assumes liability for payment of an existing note secured by a mortgage against the property.
1. Easement of necessity
2. homestead protection
3. designated agency
4. assumption of mortgage

31. The rate of return a property will produce on the investors investment.
1. attorney in fact
2. fee simple estate
3. consideration
4. capitalization rate

32. The holder of a power of attorney.
1. ground lease
2. attorney in fact
3. Real property
4. tenancy by the entirety

33. A procedure by which property of a debtor is placed in the custody of the law and is held as security, pending the disposition of a creditors suit.
1. Attachment
2. Fee simple
3. hypothecation
4. Encroachments

34. A person to whom a grant is conveyed (the person receiving the interest).
1. mechanic's lien
2. life tenant
3. general lien
4. grantee

35. The law designed to preserve the free enterprise of the open marketplace by making illegal certain private conspiracies and combinations formed to minimize competition such as price fixing or group boycotting.
1. easement by necessity
2. tenancy at sufferance
3. antitrust laws
4. constructive eviction

36. A listing contract under which the owner appoints a real estate broker as the exclusive agent for a designated period of time to sell the property, on the owner's stated terms, for a commission. The owner reserves the right to sell without paying anyone a commission if the owner sells to a prospect who has not been introduced or claimed by the broker.
1. Alienation clause(due on sale clause)
2. exclusive-agency listing
3. purchase money mortgage
4. percentage lease

37. The process of estimating the value of a property by adding the appraiser's estimate of the reproduction or replacement cost of the building less depreciation. The final step is to add in the value of the land.
1. Abstract of title
2. arbitration
3. cost approach
4. hypothecation

38. An item installed by commercial tenant and removable by tenant before expiration of lease
1. negligence
2. buffer zone
3. Trade fixture
4. "time of the essence"

39. A listing contract under which the owner appoints a real estate broker as the exclusive agent for a designated period of time to sell the property, on the owner's stated terms, for a commission. The owner reserves the right to sell without paying anyone a commission if the owner sells to a prospect who has not been introduced or claimed by the broker.
1. Abstract of title
2. Inchoate right
3. exclusive-agency listing
4. secondary mortgage market

Exam Ten Answers

1. Power of a government to take private property for public use; the U.S. Constitution gives national and state governments this power. Just compensation is paid to the owner. Condemnation.

4. eminent domain

2. A will that is written, dated, and signed in the handwriting of the maker.
4. holographic will

3. The rate of return a property will produce on the investors investment.
4. capitalization rate

4. A document acknowledging the payment of a debt. Given to the mortgagor when the mortgage has been paid.
4. Deed of Satisfaction

5. The business of buying and selling as agents for others and for a commission.
4. brokerage

6. Incomplete right, such as a wife's dower interest in her husband's property during his life.
2. inchoate right

7. A legal description that starts and ends at a point of beginning.
4. Metes and bounds

8. A written instrument given to pass title to personal property.
4. bill of sale

9. Limited in durations to life of a life tenant or life or lives of some other designated person or persons.
4. Life estate

10. A one sided contract by which one party makes a promise to induce a second party to do something.
4. unilateral contract

11. The party that grants or gives an option.
1. optionor

12. A regulation of the Federal Reserve Board designed to ensure that borrowers and customers in the need of consumer credit are given meaningful information with respect to the cost of credit. Includes advertising and trigger terms. Gives a homeowner a three day right of recession when acquiring a loan based on his personal residence.
1. Regulation Z

13. The pledge of property as security of a loan in which the borrower maintains possession of the property while it is pledged as security.
2. hypothecation

14. A sudden tearing away of land by the action of natural forces. The two ends of a barrier island got washed away during a hurricane.
4. avulsion

15. Usually take priority over all other liens.
4. Real estate taxes and special assessments

16. The result of legal action originated by a lessor by which a defaulted tenant is physically ousted from the rented property pursuant to a court order.
4. actual eviction.

17. The imposition of a tax, charge or levy, usually according to established rates.
1. assessment

18. A horizontal plane from which heights and depths are measured.
4. datum

19. Amount of ownership.
The degree, quantity, nature, and extent of interest a person has in real property.
4. estate in land

20. One who is prepared to buy property on the seller's terms and is ready to take positive steps to consummate the transaction.

1."ready, willing, and able" buyer

21. The voluntary and permanent cessation of use or enjoyment with no intention to resume or reclaim one's possession or interest. May pertain to an easement of a property.
1. Abandonment

22. An acceptance by parties to an agreement to replace an old debtor with a new one.
1. novation

23. The land and the improvements there-on designated by the owners as his or her homestead.
4. homestead protection

24. The horizontal lines running at six mile intervals parallel to the baseline in the rectangular survey system.
2. township lines

25. Carelessness and inattentiveness resulting in a violation of trust. Failure to do what is required.
4. negligence

24. Highest type of interest in real estate recognized by law. The holder is entitled to all rights incident to the property. Continues for indefinite period and is inheritable by heirs of owner.
1.Fee simple

25. Run north and south
1. Meridian

26. A tenancy by which a lessee retains possession of leased property after her or his lease has expired and the landlord, by continuing to accept rent from the tenant, agrees to the tenant's continued occupancy as defined by state law. Could also lead to a tenancy in Sufferance.
3. holdover tenancy

27. The succession of conveyances of real property.
3. chain of title

28. The land and the improvements there-on designated by the owners as his or her homestead.
2. homestead protection

29. A written or oral agreement in which all terms are explicitly stated. "pay first"
3. expressed contract

30. The transfer of title to property to a grantee, by which the grantee assumes liability for payment of an existing note secured by a mortgage against the property.
4. assumption of mortgage

31. The rate of return a property will produce on the investors investment.
4. capitalization rate

32. The holder of a power of attorney.
2. attorney in fact

33. A procedure by which property of a debtor is placed in the custody of the law and is held as security, pending the disposition of a creditors suit.
1. Attachment

34. A person to whom a grant is conveyed (the person receiving the interest).
4. grantee

35. The law designed to preserve the free enterprise of the open marketplace by making illegal certain private conspiracies and combinations formed to minimize competition such as price fixing or group boycotting.
3. antitrust laws

36. A listing contract under which the owner appoints a real estate broker as the exclusive agent for a designated period of time to sell the property, on the owner's stated terms, for a commission. The owner reserves the right to sell without paying anyone a commission if the owner sells to a prospect who has not been introduced or claimed by the broker.
2. exclusive-agency listing

37. The process of estimating the value of a property by adding the appraiser's estimate of the reproduction or replacement cost of the building less depreciation. The final step is to add in the value of the land.
3. cost approach

38. An item installed by commercial tenant and removable by tenant before expiration of lease
3. Trade fixture

39. A listing contract under which the owner appoints a real estate broker as the exclusive agent for a designated period of time to sell the property, on the owner's stated terms, for a commission. The owner reserves the right to sell without paying anyone a commission if the owner sells to a prospect who has not been introduced or claimed by the broker.
3. exclusive-agency listing

MATCH

Quizlet Quizzes

1. Panic peddling_____	**A.** Sellers, Ex. you should sell your house since they are about to move into town
2. Novation	**B.** owner sells agent gets nothing
	C. Sellers, same as panic peddling
3. 1968_____	**D.** government takes over your land and pays you for it
	E. same as truth in lending act
4. condemnation_____	**F.** Buyers, steering them away from communities to preserve even though they are qualified
	G. federal fair housing law
5. appraisal___	**H.** must be hired for property over 250,000
	I. New contract releases liability "nova"="new"
6. Exclusive Agency Listing_____	**J.** regulates settlement services, Ex. agent refers customer to certain lender that pays agent for referral
7. Steering_____	**K.** resale marketplace
	L. goes with the person
8. real property_____	**M.** agreement between both parties to terminate all remaining duties and contract and go back to before contract
9. secondary market_____	**N.** transfer of contract rights from one party to another
	O. money you physically have after you sell your house
10. regulation Z_____	**P.** real property turns into personal property
	Q. goes with the real estate
11. equity_____	**R.** must be in writing to be enforceable
	S. limits on interest rates
	T. can take everything to settle debt
12. assignment_____	

13. severance_____

14. RESPA_____

15. Rescission_____

16. Blockbusting_____

17. general lien_____

18. personal property_____

19. statue of fraud_____

20. Usury laws_____

ANSWERS

1. **Panic peddling**
   A. Sellers, Ex. you should sell your house since they are about to move into town

2. **Novation**

   I. New contract releases liability "nova"="new"

3. **1968**

   G. federal fair housing law

4. **condemnation**

   D. government takes over your land and pays you for it

5. **appraisal**

   H. must be hired for property over 250,000

6. **Exclusive Agency Listing**

   B. owner sells agent gets nothing

7. **Steering**

   F. Buyers, steering them away from communities to preserve even though they are qualified

8. **real property**

   Q. goes with the real estate

9. **secondary market**

   K. resale marketplace

10. **regulation Z**

    E. same as truth in lending act

11. **equity**

    O. money you physically have after you sell your house

12. **assignment**

    N. transfer of contract rights from one party to another

13. **severance**

    P. real property turns into personal property

14. **RESPA**

J. regulates settlement services, Ex. agent refers customer to certain lender that pays agent for referral

15. **rescission**

M. agreement between both parties to terminate all remaining duties and contract and go back to before contract

16. **Blockbusting**

C. Sellers, same as panic peddling

17. **general lien**

T. can take everything to settle debt

18. **personal property**

L. goes with the person

19. **statue of fraud**

R. must be in writing to be enforceable

20. **Usury laws**

S. limits on interest rates

1. A difference between an individual's ownership interest in a cooperative and a condominium is that in a cooperative, the owner_____

2. A broker was listing a man's house for sale when the man informed her that he was Catholic and could not sell the house to anyone who was not Catholic. The broker should_____

3. You have listed your house with only one licensed broker but reserved the right to sell the property yourself without owing a commission. This relationship is called a(n)_____

4. Which of the following statements does NOT correctly describe the relationship of a salesperson working for a broker as an employee?_____

5. Keeping which of the following types of funds in a broker's trust account is MOST likely to be illegal?_____

6. Standing timber is legally considered to be_____

7. A CORRECT statement about agency relationships when a salesperson lists a property is that_____

8. A property manager renting units for an apartment owner is an example of a_____

A. a general partnership.

B. general agent.

C. real property.

D. regression.

E. The broker may not tell salespeople how to list property.

F. exclusive-agency listing.

G. Regulation Z

H. a tenant in common, owning an undivided 1/2 interest.

I. the licensee's broker becomes the agent of the seller.

J. holds a personal property interest, whereas a condominium owner holds a real property interest.

K. hypothecation.

L. not take the listing

M. income.

N. the lending institution.

O. equitable title.

P. a broker/employer.

Q. No, because she is not living in the

apartment building.

9. A salesperson may legally accept a cash bonus directly from_____

R. is a nonconforming use.

S. The seller has AIDS.

10. You have pledged your home as security for a mortgage without giving up possession. This is called_____

T. Commission earned on previous sales.

11. You own a home on a block that is zoned residential; however, there is a retail store on the lot next door to you. The retail store_____

12. Under their mother's will, a woman and her brother inherited title to a house as tenants in common. The woman married and had title to her share put in joint tenancy with her husband. Her brother is now_____

13. You purchased a home with an FHA-insured loan. At closing, the seller was charged the five discount points for the loan. This money will be paid to_____

14. A broker has met with a customer and declined to work with the person in finding a home. It is legal for the broker to decline the opportunity, if the decision is based on the customer's_____

15. A doctor built a $400,000 home in a neighborhood of $200,000 homes. This situation reflects the principle of_____

16. Which of the following facts would NOT need to be disclosed by a

broker?_____

17. A woman owns a four-unit apartment building but does not live there. She is currently advertising for Lutheran tenants only. Is her advertising policy legal?_____

18. You own a defeasible fee estate and sell it on a land contract. Until the land contract has been paid in full, the buyer will hold a(n)

19. Ownership is freely transferable in all of the following forms of ownership EXCEPT_____

20. Which of the following governs the disclosures required when advertising financing terms for real estate?_____

ANSWERS

1. difference between an individual's ownership interest in a cooperative and a condominium is that in a cooperative, the owner

   J. holds a personal property interest, whereas a condominium owner holds a real property interest.

2. A broker was listing a man's house for sale when the man informed her that he was Catholic and could not sell the house to anyone who was not Catholic. The broker should

   L. not take the listing

3. You have listed your house with only one licensed broker but reserved the right to sell the property yourself without owing a commission. This relationship is called a(n)

   F. exclusive-agency listing.

4. Which of the following statements does NOT correctly describe the relationship of a salesperson working for a broker as an employee?

   E. The broker may not tell salespeople how to list property.

5. Keeping which of the following types of funds in a broker's trust account is MOST likely to be illegal?

    T. Commission earned on previous sales.

6. Standing timber is legally considered to be

    C. real property.

7. A CORRECT statement about agency relationships when a salesperson lists a property is that

    I. the licensee's broker becomes the agent of the seller.

8. A property manager renting units for an apartment owner is an example of a

    B. general agent.

9. A salesperson may legally accept a cash bonus directly from

    P. a broker/employer.

10. You have pledged your home as security for a mortgage without giving up possession. This is called

    K. hypothecation.

11. You own a home on a block that is zoned residential; however, there is a retail store on the lot next door to you. The retail store

    R. is a nonconforming use.

12. Under their mother's will, a woman and her brother inherited title to a house as tenants in common. The woman married and had title to her share put in joint tenancy with her husband. Her brother is now

    H. a tenant in common, owning an undivided 1/2 interest.

13. You purchased a home with an FHA-insured loan. At closing, the seller was charged the five discount points for the loan. This money will be paid to

    N. the lending institution.

14. A broker has met with a customer and declined to work with the person in finding a home. It is legal for the broker to decline the opportunity, if the decision is based on the customer's

    M. income.

15. A doctor built a $400,000 home in a neighborhood of $200,000 homes. This situation reflects the principle of

    D. regression.

16. Which of the following facts would NOT need to be disclosed by a broker?

    S. The seller has AIDS.

17. A woman owns a four-unit apartment building but does not live there. She is currently advertising for Lutheran tenants only. Is her advertising policy legal?

    Q. No, because she is not living in the apartment building.

18. You own a defeasible fee estate and sell it on a land contract. Until th land contract has been paid in full, the buyer will hold a(n)

    O. equitable title.

19. Ownership is freely transferable in all of the following forms of ownership EXCEPT

    A. a general partnership.

20. Which of the following governs the disclosures required when advertising financing terms for real estate?

    G. Regulation Z

1. assumption of mortgage_____

2. trust deed_____

3. alienation clause_____

4. mortgage_____

5. interest-only loan_____

6. discount rate_____

7. satisfaction of mortgage_____

8. due-on-sale clause_____

9. deficiency judgment_____

10. Comprehensive Loss Underwriting Exchange (CLUE)_____

11. Trustor_____

12. automated underwriting_____

13. fully amortized loan_____

14. beneficiary_____

15. reverse mortgage_____

16. hypothecation_____

17. amortized loan_____

18. variable rate mortgage_____

19. discount point_____

20. mortgage banker_____

A. provision in the mortgage stating that the entire balance of the note is immediately due and payable if the mortgagor transfers (sells) the property

B. to pledge property as security for an obligation or loan without giving up possession of it

C. the person for whom a trust operates or in whose behalf the income from a trust estate is drawn; a lender in a deed or trust loan transaction

D. mortgage loan in which the interest rate varies depending on market conditions

E. acquiring title to property on which there is an existing mortgage and agreeing to be personally liable for the terms and conditions of the mortgage, including payments

F. the clause in a mortgage or deed of trust stating that the balance of the secured debt becomes immediately due and payable at the lender's option if the property is sold by the borrower; in effect, this clause prevents the borrower from assigning the debt without the lender's approval

G. a mortgage loan company that originates, services, and sells loans to investors

H. a borrower in a deed of trust loan transaction; one who places property in a trust; also, called a grantor or settler

I. an instrument used to create a mortgage lien by which the borrower conveys title to a trustee, who holds it as security for the benefit of the note holder (the lender)

J. a database of consumer claims history that allows insurance companies to access prior claims information in the underwriting and rating process

K. a loan consisting of equal, regular payments satisfying the total payment of principal and interest by the due date

L. a document acknowledging the payment of a mortgage debt

M. a loan in which the principal, as well as the interest, is payable in monthly or other periodic installments over the term of the loan

	N. a loan by which a homeowner receives a lump sum, monthly payments, or a line of credit based on the homeowner's equity in the property secured by the mortgage; loan must be repaid at a prearranged date, upon the death of the owner, or upon the sale of the property
	O. interest rate set by the Federal Reserve that member banks are charged when they borrow money through the Fed
	P. a personal judgment levied against the borrower when a foreclosure sale does not produce sufficient funds to pay mortgage debt in full
	Q. conditional transfer or pledge of real estate as security for the payment of a debt; document creating a mortgage lien
	R. a loan that only requires the payment of interest for a stated period of time with the principal due at the end of the term
	S. computer systems that permit lenders to expedite the loan approval process and reduce lending costs
	T. a unit of measurement used for various loan charges; one point equals 1 percent of the amount of the loan

ANSWERS

1. **assumption of mortgage**

   E. acquiring title to property on which there is an existing mortgage and agreeing to be personally liable for the terms and conditions of the mortgage, including payments

2. **trust deed**

   I. an instrument used to create a mortgage lien by which the borrower conveys title to a trustee, who holds it as security for the benefit of the note holder (the lender)

3. **alienation clause**

   F. the clause in a mortgage or deed of trust stating that the balance of the secured debt becomes immediately due and payable at the lender's option if the property is sold by the borrower; in effect, this clause prevents the borrower from assigning the debt without the lender's approval

4. **mortgage**

   Q. conditional transfer or pledge of real estate as security for the payment of a debt; document creating a mortgage lien

342

5. **interest-only loan**

    R. a loan that only requires the payment of interest for a stated period of time with the principal due at the end of the term

6. **discount rate**

    O. interest rate set by the Federal Reserve that member banks are charged when they borrow money through the Fed

7. **satisfaction of mortgage**

    L. a document acknowledging the payment of a mortgage debt

8. **due-on-sale clause**

    A. a provision in the mortgage stating that the entire balance of the note is immediately due and payable if the mortgagor transfers (sells) the property

9. **deficiency judgment**

    P. a personal judgment levied against the borrower when a foreclosure sale does not produce sufficient funds to pay mortgage debt in full

10. **Comprehensive Loss Underwriting Exchange (CLUE)**

    J. a database of consumer claims history that allows insurance companies to access prior claims information in the underwriting and rating process

11. **trustor**

    H. a borrower in a deed of trust loan transaction; one who places property in a trust; also, called a grantor or settler

12. **automated underwriting**

    S. computer systems that permit lenders to expedite the loan approval process and reduce lending costs

13. **fully amortized loan**

    K. a loan consisting of equal, regular payments satisfying the total payment of principal and interest by the due date

14. **beneficiary**

    C. the person for whom a trust operates or in whose behalf the income from a trust estate is drawn; a lender in a deed or trust loan transaction

15. **reverse mortgage**

    N. a loan by which a homeowner receives a lump sum, monthly payments, or a line of credit based on the homeowner's equity in the property secured by the mortgage; loan must be repaid at a prearranged date, upon the death of the owner, or upon the sale of the property

16. **hypothecation**

B. to pledge property as security for an obligation or loan without giving up possession of it

17. **amortized loan**

M. a loan in which the principal, as well as the interest, is payable in monthly or other periodic installments over the term of the loan

18. **variable rate mortgage**

D. mortgage loan in which the interest rate varies depending on market conditions

19. **discount point**

T. a unit of measurement used for various loan charges; one point equals 1 percent of the amount of the loan

20. **mortgage banker**

G. a mortgage loan company that originates, services, and sells loans to investors

1. negative amortization_____

2. loan-to-value ratio (LTV)_____

3. deed or reconveyance_____

4. debt to income (DTI)_____

5. fully amortized loan_____

6. nonconforming loan_____

7. participation mortgage_____

8. hypothecation_____

9. discount point_____

10. annual percentage rate (APR)_____

11. computerized loan origination (CLO)_____

12. deed in lieu of foreclosure_____

13. adjustable-rate mortgage (ARM)_____

14. novation_____

15. release deed_____

16. due-on-sale clause_____

17. reverse mortgage_____

18. first mortgage_____

19. Comprehensive Loss Underwriting Exchange (CLUE)_____

20. promissory note_____

A. an electronic network for handling loan applications through remote computer terminals linked to various lenders' computers

B. information about an applicant's gross income and total debt that lenders generally look at as a percentage to determine qualification for a loan

C. a loan by which a homeowner receives a lump sum, monthly payments, or a line of credit based on the homeowner's equity in the property secured by the mortgage; loan must be repaid at a prearranged date, upon the death of the owner, or upon the sale of the property

D. the relationship of the total finance charges associated with a loan; must be disclosed to borrowers by lenders under the Truth in Lending Act

E. a database of consumer claims history that allows insurance companies to access prior claims information in the underwriting and rating process

F. a mortgage loan wherein the lender has a partial equity interest in the property or receives a portion of the income from the property

G. a document, also known as a deed of reconveyance, that transfers all rights given a trustee under a deed of trust loan back to the grantor after the loan has been fully repaid

H. a financing instrument that states the terms of the underlying obligation, is signed by its maker, and is negotiable (transferable to a third party)

I. a unit of measurement used for various loan charges; one point equals 1 percent of the amount of the loan

J. a mortgage that has priority over all other mortgages

K. a loan characterized by a fluctuating interest rate, usually one tied to a bank or savings and loan association cost-of-funds index

L. to pledge property as security for

	an obligation or loan without giving up possession of it
	M. a deed given by the mortgagor to the mortgagee when the mortgagor is in default under the terms of the mortgage
	N. the relationship between the amount of the mortgage loan and the value of the real estate being pledged as collateral
	O. substituting a new obligation for an old one or substituting new parties to an existing obligation
	P. a provision in the mortgage stating that the entire balance of the note is immediately due and payable if the mortgagor transfers (sells) the property
	Q. process by which the amount of the loan increases; the mortgagor sets a payment cap, but the difference between the payment made and the full payment amount is added to the remaining mortgage balance
	R. a loan consisting of equal, regular payments satisfying the total payment of principal and interest by the due date
	S. a loan that exceeds the Federal Housing Finance Agency (FHFA) loan limits; also, called a jumbo loan
	T. a document that a trustee uses to transfer the title back to the trustor (borrower) when the note is repaid

ANSWERS

1. **negative amortization**

   Q. process by which the amount of the loan increases; the mortgagor sets a payment cap, but the difference between the payment made and the full payment amount is added to the remaining mortgage balance

2. **loan-to-value ratio (LTV)**

   N. the relationship between the amount of the mortgage loan and the value of the real estate being pledged as collateral

3. **deed or reconveyance**

T. a document that a trustee uses to transfer the title back to the trustor (borrower) when the note is repaid

4. **debt to income (DTI)**

B. information about an applicant's gross income and total debt that lenders generally look at as a percentage to determine qualification for a loan

5. **fully amortized loan**

R. a loan consisting of equal, regular payments satisfying the total payment of principal and interest by the due date

6. **nonconforming loan**

S. a loan that exceeds the Federal Housing Finance Agency (FHFA) loan limits; also **called a jumbo loan**

7. **participation mortgage**

F. a mortgage loan wherein the lender has a partial equity interest in the property or receives a portion of the income from the proerty

8. **hypothecation**

L. to pledge property as security for an obligation or loan without giving up possession of it

9. **discount point**

I. a unit of measurement used for various loan charges; one point equals 1 percent of the amount of the loan

10. **annual percentage rate (APR)**

D. the relationship of the total finance charges associated with a loan; must be disclosed to borrowers by lenders under the Truth in Lending Act

11. **computerized loan origination (CLO)**

A. an electronic network for handling loan applications through remote computer terminals linked to various lenders' computers

12. **deed in lieu of foreclosure**

M. a deed given by the mortgagor to the mortgagee when the mortgagor is in default under the terms of the mortgage

13. **adjustable-rate mortgage (ARM)**

K. a loan characterized by a fluctuating interest rate, usually one tied to a bank or savings and loan association cost-of-funds index

14. **novation**

O. substituting a new obligation for an old one or substituting new parties to an existing obligation

15. **release deed**

G. a document, also known as a deed of reconveyance, that transfers all rights given a trustee under a deed of trust loan back to the grantor after the loan has been fully repaid

16. **due-on-sale clause**

P. a provision in the mortgage stating that the entire balance of the note is immediately due and payable if the mortgagor transfers (sells) the property

17. **reverse mortgage**

C. a loan by which a homeowner receives a lump sum, monthly payments, or a line of credit based on the homeowner's equity in the property secured by the mortgage; loan must be repaid at a prearranged date, upon the death of the owner, or upon the sale of the property

18. **first mortgage**

J. a mortgage that has priority over all other mortgages

19. **Comprehensive Loss Underwriting Exchange (CLUE)**

E. a database of consumer claims history that allows insurance companies to access prior claims information in the underwriting and rating process

20. **promissory note**

H. a financing instrument that states the terms of the underlying obligation, is signed by its maker, and is negotiable (transferable to a third party)

Key Real Estate Terms

Study online at quizlet.com/_2ucddw

1. 1031 exchange: "under Internal Revenue Code section 1031, a tax-deferred exchange of "like kind" properties."

2. 1099-S Reporting: "a report to be submitted on IRS Form 1099-S by escrow agents to report the sale of real estate, giving the seller's name, Social Security number, and the gross sale proceeds."

3. abandonment: failure to occupy or use property that may result in the extinguishment of a right or interest in the property.

4. abatement: a legal action to remove a nuisance.

5. abendum clause: "a clause in a deed, usually following the granting clause and beginning with the words "to have and to hold," that describes the type of estate being transferred."

6. abstract of judgment: judgment that can be recorded in which the debtor owns property and to create a judgment lien against such properties.

7. abstract of title: summary of all grants, liens, wills, judicial proceedings, and other records that affect the property's title. 8. abstractor: the person who prepares an abstract of title.

9. acceleration clause: "a clause in either a promissory note, a security instrument, or both that states that upon default the lender has the option of declaring the entire balance of outstanding principal and interest due and payable immediately."

10. acceptance: consent (by an offeree) to an offer made (by an offeror) to enter into and be bound by a contract.

11. accession: "the acquisition of additional property by the natural processes of accretion, reliction, or avulsion, or by the human processes of the addition of fixtures or improvements made in error."

12. accretion: a natural process by which the owner of riparian or littoral property acquires additional land by the gradual accumulation of soil through the action of water.

13. accrued depreciation: depreciation that has happened prior to the date of valuation.

14. acknowledgment: "a written declaration signed by a person before a duly authorized officer, usually a notary public, acknowledging that the signing is voluntary."

15. acknowledgment of satisfaction or satisfaction of mortgage: "a written declaration signed by a person before a duly authorized officer, usually a notary public, acknowledging that a lien has been paid off in full and that the signing is voluntary."

16. adjustable-rate mortgage (ARM): a mortgage under which interest rates applicable to the loan vary over the term of the loan.

17. administrator: a person appointed by a probate court to conduct the affairs and distribute the assets of a decedent's estate when there was no executor named in the will or there was no will.

18. ad valorem: a Latin phrase meaning "according to value." The term is usually used regarding property taxation.

19. advance fee: a fee charged in advance of services rendered.

20. adverse possession: the process by which unauthorized possession and use of another's property can ripen into ownership of that other's property without compensation.

21. agency: "an agency in which the agent is employed by the principal, either by express agreement, ratification, or implication."

22. agent: a person who represents another.

23. alienation clause: a due-on-sale clause

24. alluvium: addition to land acquired by the gradual accumulation of soil through the action of water.

25. Americans with Disabilities Act: "a federal act that prohibits discrimination against persons with disabilities, where "disability" is defined as "a physical or mental impairment that substantially limits a major life activity.""

26. amortization: "in general, the process of decreasing or recovering an amount over a period of time; as applied to real estate loans, the process of reducing the loan principal over the life of the loan."

27. annual percentage rate (APR): "expresses the effective annual rate of the cost of borrowing, which includes all finance charges, such as interest, prepaid finance charges, prepaid interest, and service fees."

28. appraisal: an estimate of the value of property resulting from an analysis and evaluation made by an appraiser of facts and data regarding the property.

29. appreciation: an increase in value due to any cause.

30. appurtenance: "an object, right or interest that is incidental to the land and goes with or pertains to the land."

31. asbestos: "a naturally occurring mineral composite that once was used extensively as insulation in residential and commercial buildings, in brake pads, and in fire-retardant products, such as furniture. As asbestos ages, it breaks down to small fibers that, if inhaled in sufficient quantity over sufficient time, can cause a variety of ailments, including a type of cancer known as mesothelioma."

32. assignment: the transfer of the rights and obligations of one party (the assignor) to a contract to another party (the assignee); a transfer of a tenant's entire interest in the tenant's leased premises.

33. assumption: "an adoption of an obligation that primarily rests upon another person, such as when a purchaser agrees to be primarily liable on a loan taken out by the seller."

34. attachment lien: "a prejudgment lien on property, obtained to ensure the availability of funds to pay a judgment if the plaintiff prevails."

35. attorney in fact: a holder of a power of attorney.

36. average price per square foot: the average price per square foot for a given set of properties is arrived at by adding the per- square-foot cost of each property in the set by the number of properties in the set.

37. avulsion: "a process that occurs when a river or stream suddenly carries away a part of a bank and deposits it downstream, either on the same or opposite bank."

38. balloon payment: "significantly greater" generally being considered as being more than twice the lowest installment payment paid over the loan term.

39. beam: "a horizontal member of a building attached to framing, rafters, etc., that transversely supports a load."

40. bearing wall: "a wall that supports structures (such as the roof or upper floors) above it. In condominiums, non-bearing walls are owned by the individual condominium owners, whereas bearing walls usually are property owned in common.

41. bilateral contract: a contract in which a promise given by one party is exchanged for a promise given by the other party.

42. bill of sale: a written document given by a seller to a purchaser of personal property.

43. blanket mortgage: a mortgage used to finance two or more parcels of real estate.

44. blight: "as used in real estate, the decline of a property or neighborhood as a result of adverse land use, destructive economic forces, failure to maintain the quality of older structures, failure to maintain foreclosed homes, etc."

45. blind ad: an advertisement that does not disclose the identity of the agent submitting the advertisement for publication.

46. blockbusting: "the illegal practice of representing that prices will decline, or crime increase, or other negative effects will occur because of the entrance of minorities into particular areas."

47. bona fide: in good faith; authentic; sincere; without intent to deceive.

48. boot: cash or other not like-kind property received in an ex c hange.

49. bridge loan: a short-term loan (often referred to as a swing loan) that is used by a borrower until permanent financing becomes available.

50. broker: "a person who, for a compensation or an expectation of compensation, represents another in the transfer of an interest in real property. "

51. brownfields: "as defined by the EPA, "real property, the expansion, redevelopment, or reuse of which may be complicated by the presence or potential presence of a hazardous substance, polluted, or contaminant.""

52. buffer zone: "in zoning, a strip of land to separate, or to ease the transition from, one use to another, such as a park separating a residential zone from a commercial zone, or a commercial or industrial zone separating residential zones from busy streets or highways."

53. bundle of rights: rights the law attributes to ownership of property.

54. buyer's agent: a real estate broker appointed by a buyer to find property for the buyer.

55. capital gain: the amount by which the net sale proceeds from the sale of a capital asset exceeds the adjusted cost value of the asset.

56. capitalization rate: The rate of return for an investor. "the annual net income of a property divided by the initial investment in, or value of, the property; the rate that an appraiser estimates is the yield rate expected by investors from comparable properties in current market conditions."

57. CC& Rs: often used to refer to restrictions recorded by a developer on an entire subdivision.

58. certificate of occupancy: "a written document issued by a local governmental agency, stating that a structure intended for occupancy has been completed, inspected, and found to be habitable."

59. chain of title: a complete chronological history of all of the documents affecting title to the property.

60. Civil Rights Act of 1866: "a federal law enacted during Reconstruction that stated that people of any race may enjoy the right to enforce contracts, to sue, be parties, and give evidence, to inherit, purchase, lease, sell, hold, and convey real and personal property, and to full and equal benefit of all laws."

61. Civil Rights Act of 1968: "a federal law (often referred to as the Fair Housing Act) that prohibited discrimination in housing based on race, creed, or national origin.

62. client: an agent's principal

63. closing: "in reference to an escrow, a process leading up to, and concluding with, a buyer's receiving the deed to the property and the seller's receiving the purchase money."

64. cloud on title: "any document, claim, lien, or other encumbrance that may impair the title to real property or cast doubt on the validity of the title."

65. coastal zone: a region where significant interaction of land and sea processes occurs.

66. Coastal Zone Management Act (CZMA): "a federal act intended to protect coastal zones, including the fish and wildlife that inhabit those zones, of the Atlantic, Pacific, and Arctic oceans, the Gulf of Mexico, Long Island Sound, and the Great Lakes from harmful effects due to residential, commercial, and industrial development."

67. commingling: "regarding trust fund accounts, the act of improperly segregating the funds belonging to the agent from the funds received and held on behalf of another; the mixing of separate and community property."

68. commission: "an agent's compensation for performance of his or her duties as an agent; in real estate, it is usually a percent of the selling price of the property or, in the case of leases, of rentals."

69. community property: "property owned jointly by a married couple or by registered domestic partners, as distinguished from separate property. As a general rule, property acquired by a spouse or registered domestic partner through his/her skills or personal efforts is community property."

70. comparable property: "a property similar to the subject property being appraised that recently sold at arm's length, where neither the buyer nor the seller was acting under significant financial pressure."

71. comparative market analysis (CMA): "a comparison analysis made by real estate brokers using recent sales, and current listings, of similar nearby homes to determine the list price for a subject property."

72. condemnation proceeding: a judicial or administrative proceeding to exercise power of eminent domain.

73. conditional use: "a zoning exception for special uses such as churches, schools, and hospitals that wish to locate to areas zoned exclusively for residential use."

74. condominium: "a residential unit owned in severalty, the boundaries of which are usually walls, floors, and ceilings, and an undivided interest in portions of the real property, such as halls, elevators, and recreational facilities."

75. conflict of interest: "a situation in which an individual or organization is involved in several potentially competing interests, creating a risk that one interest might unduly influence another interest."

76. consideration: "anything of value given or promised, such as money, property, services, or a forbearance, to induce another to enter into a contract."

77. construction mortgage: a security instrument used to secure a short-term loan to finance improvements to a property.

78. constructive eviction: a breach by the landlord of the covenant of habitability or quiet enjoyment.

79. constructive notice: "(1) notice provided by public records; (2) notice of information provided by law to a person who, by exercising reasonable diligence, could have discovered the information."

80. contingency: "an event that may, but is not certain to, happen, the occurrence upon which the happening of another event is dependent."

81. contract: a contract is an agreement to do or to forbear from doing a certain thing.

conventional loan: a mortgage loan that is not FHA insured or VA guaranteed.

82. cooperating broker: a broker who attempts to find a buyer for a property listed by another broker.

83. cost approach: an appraisal approach that obtains the market value of the subject property by adding the value of the land (unimproved) of the subject property to the depreciated value of the cost (if currently purchased new) of the improvements on subject property.

84. counteroffer: a new offer by an offeree that acts as a rejection of an offer by an offeror.

85. coupled with an interest: "an aspect of an agency that refers to the agent's having a financial interest in the subject of the agency, which has the legal effect of making the appointment of the agent irrevocable."

86. covenant: "a contractual promise to do or not do certain acts, such as on a property, the remedy for breach thereof being either monetary damages or injunctive relief, not forfeiture."

87. crawlspace: the space between the ground and the first floor that permits access beneath the building.

88. debits: "in reference to an escrow account, items payable by a party. This definition of a debit does not conform to its use in double-entry bookkeeping or accounting."

89. deed: a document that when signed by the grantor and legally delivered to the grantee conveys title to real property.

90. deed in lieu of foreclosure: a method of avoiding foreclosure by conveying to a lender, title to a property in lieu of the lender's foreclosing on the property.

91. deferred maintenance: any type of depreciation that has not been corrected by diligent maintenance.

92. deficiency judgment: a judgment given to a lender in an amount equal to the balance of the loan minus the net proceeds the lender receives after a judicial foreclosure.

93. demand: the level of desire for a product.

94. deposit receipt: a written document indicating that a good-faith deposit has been received as part of an offer to purchase real property; also, called a purchase and sale agreement.

95. depreciation: the loss in value due to any cause.

96. depreciation deduction: an annual tax allowance for the depreciation of property.

97. designated agent: "an agent authorized by a real estate broker to represent a specific principal to the exclusion of all other agents in the brokerage. This designated agent owes fiduciary responsibilities to the specified principal, but other agents in the brokerage may represent other parties to the same

transaction that the specified principal is a party to without creating a dual agency situation. Where this practice of designated agency is allowed, disclosure of the designated agency relationship is required."

98. devise: (1) (noun) a gift of real property by will; (2) (verb) to transfer real property by a will.

99. devisee: a recipient of real property through a will.

100. divisor: the receiver of the will

103. discount points: "a form of prepaid interest on a mortgage, or a fee paid to a lender to cover cost the making of a loan. The fee for one discount point is equal to 1% of the loan amount."

104. documentary transfer tax: a tax imposed by counties and cities on the transfer of real property within their jurisdictions. 105. dominant tenement: land that is benefited by an easement appurtenant.

106. down payment: the amount of money that a lender requires a purchaser to pay toward the purchase price.

107. drywall: prefabricated sheets or panels nailed to studs to form an interior wall or partition.

108. dual agent: a real estate broker who represents both the seller and the buyer in a real estate transaction.

109. due diligence: the exercise of an honest and reasonable degree of care in performing one's duties or obligations. A real estate agent's due diligence involves investigating the property to ensure that the property is as represented by the seller and to disclose accurate and complete information regarding the property.

110. due-on-sale clause: "a clause in the promissory note, the security instrument, or both that states that the lender has the right to accelerate the loan if the secured property is sold or some other interest in the property is transferred."

111. duress: unlawful force or confinement used to compel a person to enter into a contract against his or her will.

112. earnest money deposit: a deposit that accompanies an offer by a buyer and is generally held in the broker's trust account.

113. easement: "a non-possessory right to use a portion of another property owner's land for a specific purpose, as for a right-of- way, without paying rent or being considered a trespasser."

114. easement appurtenant: "an easement that benefits, and is appurtenant to, another's land."

115. easement by necessity: "easement by necessity —arises as a creation of a court of law in certain cases were justice so demands, as in the case where a buyer of a parcel of land discovers that the land he or she just purchased has no access except over the land of someone other than from the person from whom the parcel was purchased."

116. easement in gross: an easement that benefits a legal person rather than other land.

117. eaves: the overhang of a roof that projects over an exterior wall of a house.

118. economic life: the period of time that the property is useful or profitable to the average owner or investor.

119. emancipated minor: "a minor who, because of marriage, military service, or court order, is allowed to contract for the sale or purchase of real property."

120. emblements: "growing crops, such as grapes, avocados, and apples, that are produced seasonally through a tenant farmer's labor and industry."

121. eminent domain: "right of the state to take, through due process proceedings (often referred to as condemnation proceedings), private property for public use upon payment of just compensation."

122. encroachment: "a thing affixed under, on, or above the land of another without permission."

123. encumber: To place a lien or other encumbrance on property. 124. encumbrance: "A right or interest held by someone other than

the owner the property that affects or limits the ownership of the property, such as liens, easements, licenses, and encroachments."

125. Environmental Impact Statement (EIS): " a written document that federal agencies must prepare for any development project that a federal agency could prohibit or regulate, and any development project for which any portion is federally financed. An EIS can include comments on the expected impact of a proposed development on such things as air quality, noise, population density, energy consumption, water use, wildlife, public health and safety, and vegetation."

126. Equal Credit Opportunity Act (ECOA): "a federal law that prohibits a lender from discriminating against any applicant for credit on the basis of race, color, religion, national origin, sex, marital status, or age (unless a minor), or on the grounds that some of the applicant's income derives from a public assistance program."

127. equitable title: the right to possess or enjoy a property while the property is being paid for. An insurable interest for the buyer.

128. escalator clause: "a provision in a lease that provides for periodic increases in rent in an amount based on some objective criteria not in control of either the tenant or the landlord, such as the Consumer Price Index."

129. escheat: "a process whereby property passes to the state if the owner of the property dies intestate without heirs, or if the property becomes abandoned."

130. escrow: a neutral depository in which something of value is held by an impartial third party (called the escrow agent) until all conditions specified in the escrow instructions have been fully performed.

131. escrow agent: an impartial agent who holds possession of written instruments and deposits until all of the conditions of escrow have been fully performed.

132. escrow instructions: "the written instructions signed by all of the principals to the escrow (buyers, sellers, and lenders) that specify all of the conditions that must be met before the escrow agent may release whatever was deposited into escrow to the rightful parties."

133. estate: "the degree, quantity, nature, duration, or extent of interest one has in real property."

134. estate at sufferance: "a leasehold that arises when a lessee who legally obtained possession of a property remains on the property after the termination of the lease without the owner's consent. Such a holdover tenant can be evicted like a trespasser, but if the owner accepts rent, the estate automatically becomes a periodic tenancy."

135. estate at will: "an estate (or tenancy) in which a person occupies a property with the permission of the owner; however, the tenancy has no specified duration, and, in most states, may be terminated at any time by either the tenant or the owner of the property upon giving proper notice. "

136. estate for years: "a leasehold that continues for a definite fixed period of time, measured in days, months, or years."

137. estate from period to period: "a leasehold that continues from period to period, whether by days, months, or years, until terminated by proper notice."

138. estoppel: "a legal principle that bars one from alleging or denying a fact because of one's own previous actions or words to the contrary. Ostensible agency can be created by estoppel when a principal and an unauthorized agent act in a manner toward a third-party that leads the third party to rely on the actions of the unauthorized agent, believing that the actions are authorized by the principal."

139. exclusive agency listing: a listing agreement that gives a broker the right to sell property and receive compensation (usually a commission) if the property is sold by anyone other than the owner of the property during the term of the listing.

140. exclusive right to sell listing: "a listing agreement that gives a broker the exclusive right to sell property and receive compensation (usually a commission) if the property is sold by anyone, including the owner of the property, during the term of the listing."

141. executed contract: a contract that has been fully performed; may also refer to a contract that has been signed by all of the parties to the contract.

142. executor: a person named in a will to carry out the directions contained in the will.

143. executory contract: a contract that has not yet been fully performed by one or both parties.

144. express contract: "a contract stated in words, written or oral." 145. external obsolescence: "depreciation that results from things

such as (1) changes in zoning laws or other government restrictions, (2) proximity to undesirable influences such as traffic, airport flight patterns, or power lines, and (3) general neighborhood deterioration, as might result from increased crime."

146. false promise: a promise made without any intention of performing it.

147. Fannie Mae: a U.S. government conservatorship originally created as the Federal National Mortgage Association 8 to purchase mortgages from primary lenders.

148. fee simple absolute estate: the greatest estate that the law permits in land. The owner of a fee simple absolute estate owns all present and future interests in the property.

149. fee simple defeasible estate: "a fee estate that is qualified by some condition that, if violated, may "defeat" the estate and lead to its loss and reversion to the grantor."

150. FHA: "the Federal Housing Administration is a federal agency that was created by the National Housing Act of 1934 in order to make housing more affordable by increasing home construction, reducing unemployment, and making home mortgages more available and affordable."

151. FICO score: a credit score created by the Fair Isaac Corporation that ranges from 300 to 850 and is used by lenders to help evaluate the creditworthiness of a potential borrower.

152. fiduciary relationship: "a relationship in which one owes a duty of utmost care, integrity, honesty, and loyalty to another."

153. first mortgage: a security instrument that holds first-priority claim against certain property identified in the instrument.

154. fixture: "an object, originally personal property, that is attached to the land in such a manner as to be considered real property."

155. flashing: sheet metal or other material used in roof and wall construction to prevent water from entering.

156. flat fee listing: a listing in which the broker's compensation is a set amount rather than a percentage of the sale price.

157. floodplain: "an area of low, flat, periodically flooded land near streams or rivers."

158. flue: a channel in a chimney through which flame and smoke passes upward to the outer air.

159. footing: "concrete poured on solid ground that provides support for the foundation, chimney, or support columns. Footing should be placed below the frost line to prevent movement."

160. foreclosure: "a legal process by which a lender, in an attempt to recover the balance of a loan from a borrower who has defaulted on the loan, forces the sale of the collateral that secured the loan."

161. four unities in Joint tenancy: "refers to the common law rule that a joint tenancy requires unity of possession, time, interest, and title."

162. Freddie Mac: a U.S. government conservatorship originally created as the Federal Home Loan Mortgage Corporation to purchase mortgages from primary lenders in the private mortgage money market.

163. freehold estate: an estate in land whereby the holder of the estate owns rights in the property for an indefinite duration.

164. fully amortized loan: a loan whereby the installment payments are sufficient to pay off the entire loan by the end of the loan term.

165. functional obsolescence: "depreciation that results (1) from deficiencies arising from poor architectural design, out-dated style or equipment, and changes in utility demand, such as for larger houses with more garage space, or (2) from over- improvements, where the cost of the improvements was more than the addition to market value."

166. general agent: an agent who is authorized by a principal to act for more than a particular act or transaction. General agents are usually an integral part of an ongoing business enterprise. A property manager.

167. general lien: a lien that attaches to all of a person's nonexempt property.

168. general partnership: a partnership in which each partner has the equal right to manage the partnership and has personal liability for all of the partnership debts.

169. gift deed: "a deed used to convey title when no tangible consideration (other than "affection") is given. The gift deed is valid unless it was used to defraud creditors, in which case such creditors may bring an action to void the deed."

170. Ginnie Mae: the Government National Mortgage Association is a wholly owned U.S. government corporation within HUD to guarantee pools of eligible loans that primary lenders issue as Ginnie Mae mortgage-backed securities.

171. graduated lease: "a lease that is similar to a gross lease except that it provides for periodic increases in rent, often based on the Consumer Price Index."

172. grantee: one who acquires an interest in real property from another.

173. grantor: one who transfers an interest in real property to another.

174. gross income: total income from a property before any expenses are deducted.

175. gross income multiplier (GIM): a number equal to the estimated value of a property divided by the gross yearly income of the property.

176. gross lease: "a lease under which the tenant pays a fixed rental amount, and the landlord pays all of the operating expenses for the premises."

177. gross rent multiplier (GRM): a number equal to the estimated value of a property divided by the gross monthly rental income of the property.

178. ground lease: a lease under which a tenant leases land and agrees to construct a building or to make other significant improvements on the land.

179. group boycott: "in antitrust law, the action of two or more brokers agreeing not to deal with another broker or brokers."

180. heir: a person entitled to obtain property through intestate succession.

181. hip roof: a sloping roof that rises from all four sides of the house.

182. holographic will: "a will written, dated, and signed by a testator in his or her own handwriting."

183. home equity line of credit (HELOC): a revolving line of credit provided by a home equity mortgage.

184. home equity mortgage: a security instrument used to provide the borrower with a revolving line of credit based on the amount of equity in the borrower's home.

185. homestead: a homestead exemption that applies to a homeowner's principal residence and that provides limited protection for the homeowner's equity in that residence against a judgment lien foreclosure.

186. homestead exemption: the amount of a homeowner's equity that may be protected from unsecured creditors.

187. HUD-1 Uniform Settlement Statement: an escrow settlement form mandated by RESPA for use in all escrows pertaining to the purchase of owner-occupied residences of 1-4 dwelling units that use funds from institutional lenders regulated by the federal government.

188. implied contract: "a contract not expressed in words, but, through action or inaction, understood by the parties."

189. income approach: "an appraisal approach that estimates the value of an income-producing property as being worth the present value of the future income of the property through a three-step process: (1) determine the net annual income, (2) determine an appropriate capitalization rate, and (3) divide the net income by the capitalization rate to obtain the estimate of value."

190. incurable depreciation: depreciation that results from (1) physical deterioration or functional obsolescence that cannot be repaired at a cost that is less than or equal to the value added to the property and (2) economic obsolescence (which is beyond the control of the property owner).

191. independent contractor: "a person who performs work for someone, but does so independently in a private trade, business, or profession, with little or no supervision from the person for whom the work is performed."

192. index: "under an adjustable-rate mortgage, the benchmark rate of interest that is adjusted periodically according to the going rate of T-bills, LIBOR, or the like."

193. innocent landowner defense: "a defense to liability for cleanup of toxic waste under CERCLA (the Superfund Law) by one who acquires contaminated property after the contamination occurred and who acquired the property by inheritance or bequest or who, prior to purchasing the property, performed "all appropriate inquiries" to determine that the property had not been contaminated."

194. installment note: "a promissory note in which periodic payments are made, usually consisting of interest due and some repayment of principal."

195. intentional misrepresentation: "the suggestion, as a fact, to a party that which is not true committed by another party who does not believe it to be true and who makes the suggestion with the intent to deceive the first party, who was deceived to his or her detriment, such as by being induced to enter into a contract."

196. interest: the compensation fixed by the parties for the use of money.

197. interest-rate cap: "interest-rate cap —under an adjustable-rate mortgage, the maximum that the interest rate can increase from one adjustment period to the next or over the life of the entire loan."

198. interpleader: "an action that allows for a neutral third party (such as a real estate agent) to avoid liability to two or more claimants (such as a seller and buyer) to the same money or property (such as an earnest money deposit) by forcing the claimants to litigate among themselves, letting the court determine who deserves what while not enmeshing the neutral third party in the litigation."

199. Interstate Land Sales Full Disclosure Act: a federal consumer protection act that requires that certain land developers register with the Consumer Financial Protection Bureau if they offer across state lines parcels in subdivisions containing 100 or more lots. Subdivisions where each lot in the subdivision contains at least 20 acres are exempt from this registration requirement. A developer must provide each prospective buyer with a Property Report that contains pertinent information about the subdivision and that discloses to the prospective buyer that he or she has a minimum of 7 days in which to rescind the purchase agreement.

200. intestate: "not having made, or not having disposed of by, a will."

201. intestate succession: transfer of the property of one who dies intestate.

202. inverse condemnation: a judicial or administrative action brought by a landowner to force the condemnation of the landowner's land where nearby condemned land or land used for public purposes (such as for noisy airports) severely reduces the value of the landowner's land.

203. involuntary lien: "a lien created by operation of law, not by the voluntary acts of the debtor."

204. joint tenancy: "joint tenancy —a form of joint ownership which has unity of possession, time, interest, and title."

205. joist: one of a series of parallel heavy horizontal timbers used to support floor or ceiling loads.

206. judgment: a court's final determination of the rights and duties of the parties in an action before it.

207. judicial foreclosure: "a foreclosure carried out not by way of a power-of-sale clause in a security instrument, but under the supervision of a court."

208. junior mortgage: "a mortgage that, relative to another mortgage, has a lower lien-priority position."

209. land installment contract: a real property sales contract. The Seller retains legal title and the buyer is given equitable title until the loan is paid in full. During the time of the contract, the buyer has possession of the property.

210. leasehold estate: a less-than-freehold estate.

211. lease-option: "a lease (also referred to as a lease with an option to purchase) that provides the tenant with the right, but not the obligation, to purchase the leased property at a specified price within a specified period of time."

212. lease-purchase: an agreement (also referred to as a lease with an obligation to purchase) that provides for the purchase of property preceded by a lease under which a portion of each lease payment is applied to the purchase price.

213. lease renewal: a continuation of tenancy under a new lease. 214. lessee: a person (the tenant) who leases property from another.

215. lessor: a person (the landlord) who leases property to another. 216. less-than-freehold estate: an estate in which the holder has the exclusive right to possession of land for a length of time. The holder of a less-than-freehold estate is usually referred to as a lessee or tenant.

217. leverage: a method of multiplying gains (or losses) on investments by using borrowed money to acquire the investments.

218. lien: "lien —an encumbrance against real property that is used to secure a debt and that can, in most cases, be foreclosed."

219. lien priority: the order in which lien holders are paid if property is sold to satisfy a debt.

220. lien theory: "a legal theory of mortgage: the mortgagor retains both legal and equitable title of the property, including exclusive possession and use of the property. The mortgagee simply possesses a lien against the property (usually a lien of higher priority than certain other liens, such as judgment liens). Upon default, the mortgagee must go through a formal (judicial) foreclosure proceeding to obtain legal title and possession."

221. life estate: "either by the life of the person holding the estate, or by the life or lives of one or more other persons."

222. limited liability partnership: a partnership in which there is at least one general partner and one or more limited partners. The limited partners have no liability beyond their investment in and pledges to the partnership.

223. liquidated damages: "a sum of money that the parties agree, usually at the formation of a contract, will serve as the exact amount of damages that will be paid upon a breach of the contract."

224. lis pendens: (Latin for "action pending") a notice of pendency of action.

225. listing agreement: "a written contract between a real estate broker and a property owner (the principal) stipulating that in exchange for the real estate broker's procuring a buyer for the principal's property, the principal will compensate the broker, usually with a percentage of the selling price."

226. loan modification: a restructuring or modification of a mortgage or deed of trust on terms more favorable to the buyer's ability (or desire) to continue making loan payments.

227. loan-to-value ratio (LTV): the amount of a first mortgage divided by the lesser of (1) the appraised value of the property or (2) the purchase price of the property.

228. long-term capital gain: "the capital gain on the sale of a capital asset that was held for a relatively long period of time, usually more than one year."

229. margin: "a number of percentage points, usually fixed over the life of the loan, that is added to the index of an adjustable-rate mortgage to arrive at the fully indexed rate."

230. market allocation: "in antitrust law, the process of competitors agreeing to divide up geographic areas or types of products or services they offer to customers."

231. market price: the price actually paid for a particular property. 232. market value: "as defined for appraisal purposes by HUD/FHA is: "The most probable price which a property should bring in a competitive and open market under all conditions requisite to a fair sale, the buyer and seller, each acting prudently, knowledgeably and assuming the price is not affected by undue stimulus.""

233. material fact: a fact that is likely to affect the decision of a party as to whether to enter into a transaction on the specified terms.

234. mechanics lien: a specific lien claimed by someone who furnished labor or materials for a work of improvement on real property and who has not been fully paid.

235. median price per square foot: the median price per square foot of a set of properties is the price per square foot of the property whose price per square foot is such that half of the properties in the set have an equal or lower price per square foot and half have an equal or higher price per square foot.

236. Megan's Law: an informal name for various federal and state laws that provide for the registration of sex offenders and for the making available to the public information regarding the location of these offenders.

237. metes and bounds land description: "a method of describing a parcel of land that uses physical features of the locale, along with directions and distances, to define the boundaries of the parcel."

238. moldings: "patterned strips, usually of wood, used to provide ornamental finish to cornices, bases, windows, and door jambs."

239. mortgage banker: a primary lender that uses its own money in creating a mortgage loan.

240. mortgage broker: an individual or company that finds borrowers and matches them with lenders for a fee.

241. mortgagee: a lender or creditor to whom a mortgagor gives a mortgage to secure a loan or performance of an obligation.

242. mortgage loan originator (MLO): "a person who takes, or offers to take, a residential mortgage loan application or offers or negotiates terms of a residential mortgage application for compensation or gain or in expectation of compensation or gain."

243. mortgagor: the borrower who gives a mortgage on his or her property to secure a loan or performance of an obligation.

244. multiple listing service: an organization (MLS) of real estate brokers who share their listings with other members of the organization.

245. mutual consent: refers to the situation in which all parties to a contract freely agree to the terms of the contract; sometimes referred to as a "meeting of the minds."

246. National Association of Real Estate Brokers: a real estate trade association whose members are called Realtists®. They subscribe to a code of ethics.

247. National Association of Realtors®: "the largest real estate trade association in the United States, founded in 1908, whose members are called Realtors®." They subscribe to a code of ethics.

248. National "Do Not Call" Registry: a registry established by the Federal Trade Commission to protect consumers from unwanted commercial telephone solicitations.

249. negative amortization: a loan repayment scheme in which the outstanding principal balance of the loan increases because the installment payments do not cover the full interest due.

250. negative amortized loan (NegAm loan): "the unpaid part of the interest due being tacked onto the principal, thereby causing the principal to grow as each month goes by."

251. negligent misrepresentation: "an assertion not warranted by the information of the party making the assertion that an important fact was true, which was not true, relied on by another party to that party's detriment."

252. net income: income from a property remaining after expenses are deducted from gross income.

253. net lease: a lease under which the tenant pays a fixed rental amount plus some of the landlord's operating expenses.

254. net listing: a listing agreement providing the broker with all proceeds received from the sale over a specified amount. Net listings are not legal in many states.

255. nonconforming loan: a loan not in conformance with FHFA guidelines .

256. nonconforming use: "a zoning exception for areas that are zoned for the first time or that are rezoned and where established property uses that previously were permitted to not conform to the new zoning requirements. As a general rule, such existing properties are "grandfathered in," allowing them to continue the old use but not to extend the old use to additional properties or to continue the old use after rebuilding or abandonment."

257. non-judicial foreclosure: "a foreclosure process culminating in a privately conducted, publicly held trustee's sale. The right to pursue a non-judicial foreclosure is contained in the power-of- sale clause of a mortgage or deed of trust, which, upon borrower default and the beneficiary's request, empowers the trustee to sell the secured property at a public auction."

258. notice of completion: "a written form that notifies that a work of improvement on real property has been completed, and that limits the time in which mechanic's liens may be filed against the property."

259. notice of default (NOD): a document prepared by a trustee at the direction of a lender to begin a non-judicial foreclosure proceeding.

260. notice of sale: a document prepared by a trustee at the direction of a lender that gives notice of the time and place of sale of an identified foreclosed property.

261. novation: "a substitution of a new obligation or contract for an old one, or the substitution of one party to a contract by another, relieving the original party of liability under the contract."

262. nuisance: "anything that is indecent or offensive to the senses, or an obstruction to the free use of property, so as to interfere with the comfortable enjoyment of life or property."

263. offer: a proposal by one person (the offeror) to enter into a contract with another (the offeree).

264. offeree: one to whom an offer to enter into a contract is made.

265. offeror: one who makes an offer to enter into a contract.

266. open listing: "a listing agreement that gives a broker the nonexclusive right to sell property and receive compensation (usually a commission) if, but only if, the broker is the first to procure a buyer for the property. "

267. opinion of title: a written rendering of an opinion on the condition of ownership of title in a real estate transaction prepared by an attorney after examination of an abstract of title.

268. option contract: a contract that gives the purchaser of the option the right to buy or lease a certain property at a set price any time during the option term.

269. origination fee: "the fee a lender charges to cover expenses of processing a loan, such as purchasing credit reports, inspection reports and appraisals, and paying office expenses and salaries of personnel who interview borrowers and analyze the reports and appraisals."

270. partially amortized loan: "an installment loan under which monthly payments pay all of the interest due but not enough of the principal to fully pay off the loan at the end of the loan term. In such a case, a balloon payment would be due at the end of the loan term."

271. partial release clause: "a clause in a blanket mortgage that allows a developer to sell off individual parcels and pay back, according to a release schedule, only a proportionate amount of the blanket loan."

272. partition: partition —a court-ordered or voluntary division of real property held in joint ownership into parcels owned in severalty.

273. passive income: "in general, income from either rental activity or from a business in which the taxpayer does not materially participate."

274. passive investor: an investor who does not actively contribute to the management of the business invested in.

275. payee: the person to whom a promissory note is made out. 276. payment cap: "payment cap — under an adjustable-rate

mortgage, the maximum amount that installment payments may increase from one adjustment period to the next or over the life of the loan."

277. percentage lease: "a lease, often used in shopping centers, under which the tenant typically pays a base rent amount plus a percentage of the gross receipts of the tenant's business."

278. periodic tenancy: an estate from period to period.

279. period of redemption: a period of time after a sheriff's sale in a judicial foreclosure proceeding during which the borrower may redeem his or her property by paying off the entire debt plus costs.

280. physical deterioration: depreciation that results from wear and tear of use and from natural causes.

281. physical life: the period of time that the property lasts with normal maintenance.

282. pitch: the degree of inclination or slope of a roof.

283. plaintiff: the one who brings a lawsuit.

284. plaster: "a mixture of lime or gypsum, sand, water, and fiber that is applied to walls and ceilings and that hardens into a smooth coating."

285. point: "in finance, a point is equal to 1% of the loan amount.

The term is used by lenders to measure discount charges and other costs such as origination fees and private mortgage insurance premiums."

286. point of beginning: the fixed starting point in the metes and bounds method of land description.

287. police power: "the power of a government to impose restrictions on private rights, including property rights, for the sake of public welfare, health, order, and security, for which no compensation need be made."

288. power of attorney: a special written instrument that gives authority to an agent to conduct certain business on behalf of the principal. The agent acting under such a grant is sometimes called an attorney in fact.

289. power-of-sale clause: "a clause contained in most trust deeds that permits the trustee to foreclose on, and sell, the secured property without going to court."

290. preapproval: preapproval —an evaluation of a potential borrower's ability to qualify for a loan that involves a credit check and verification of income and debt of the potential borrower.

291. predatory lending: "the imposition of unfair, deceptive, abusive, or fraudulent loan terms on borrowers."

292. prepayment penalty: a fee charged to a borrower for paying off the loan faster than scheduled payments call for.

293. prequalification: an initial unverified evaluation of a potential borrower's ability to qualify for a mortgage loan.

294. prescription: a method of acquiring an interest in property by use and enjoyment for five years.

295. prescriptive easement: an easement acquired by prescription.

296. price fixing: an agreement between competitors to set prices or price ranges.

297. price per square foot: the price per square foot of a specific property is determined by dividing the price (either selling or listing) by the property's square footage. Appraisers determine the square footage of a property by using the outside measurement of the property.

298. primary financing: first mortgage property financing.

299. primary mortgage market: the market where mortgage loans are originated.

300. principal: the one whom an agent represents.

301. principle of anticipation: "principle that value is derived from a calculation of anticipated future benefits to be derived from the property, not from past benefits, though past benefits may inform as to what might be expected in the future."

302. principle of conformity: "principle that the maximum value of land is achieved when there is a reasonable degree of social, economic, and architectural conformity in the area. "

303. principle of contribution: "principle that improvements made to a property will contribute to its value or that, conversely, the lack of a needed improvement will detract from the value of the property."

304. principle of four-stage life cycle: "principle that property goes through a process of growth, stability, decline, and revitalization."

305. principle of plottage: states that assembling two or more parcels of land into one parcel results in the larger parcel having a greater value than the sum of the values of the smaller parcels.

306. principle of progression: principle that the value of a residence of less value tends to be enhanced by proximity to residences of higher value.

307. principle of regression: principle that the value of a residence of higher value tends to be degraded by the proximity to residences of lower value.

308. principle of substitution: principle that the value of a property will tend toward the cost of an equally desirable substitute property.

309. principle of supply and demand: "principle that the value of property in a competitive market is influenced by the relative levels of supply and demand: the greater level of demand in relation to the level of supply, the greater the value."

310. principle of the highest and best use: principle that the best use of a property in terms of value is the use most likely to produce the greatest net return (in terms of money or other valued items).

311. private mortgage insurance (PMI): mortgage insurance that lenders often require for loans with an LTV more than 80%. 312. probate: a legal procedure whereby a superior court in the county where the real property is located or where the deceased resided oversees the distribution of the decedent's property.

313. procuring cause: "a common law legal concept developed by the courts to determine the proportioning of commissions among agents involved in a real estate transaction In general, an agent who is a procuring cause of a sale originated a chain of events that resulted in the sale and is thereby entitled to at least some part of the total commission generated by the sale."

314. promissory note: "a contract whereby one person unconditionally promises to pay another a certain sum of money, either at a fixed or determinable future date or on demand of the payee."

315. property disclosure statement: "a statement filled out by the seller of residential property consisting of 1 to 4 dwelling units, disclosing to potential purchasers defects in the property that are known to the seller, or that should be known to the seller upon reasonable inspection."

316. proration: an adjustment of expenses that either have been paid or are in arrears in proportion to actual time of ownership as of the closing of escrow or other agreed-upon date.

317. protected class: a group of people protected from discrimination by federal or state law.

318. public dedication: "a gift of an interest in land to a public body for public use, such as for a street, a park, or an easement to access a beach."

319. public grant: "public land conveyed, usually for a small fee, to individuals or to organizations, such as to railroads or universities."

320. puffing: the act of expressing a positive opinion about something to induce someone to become a party to a contract.

321. purchase money loan: "a deed of trust or mortgage on a dwelling for not more than four families given to a lender to secure repayment of a loan which was in fact used to pay all or part of the purchase price of that dwelling, occupied entirely or in part by the purchaser."

322. pyramid roof a hip roof that has no ridge.: pyramid roof a hip roof that has no ridge.

323. quantity survey method: " the most detailed method of estimating the replacement or reproduction cost of a structure, in which an estimate is made of the cost of all of the raw materials needed to replace the building. Such material-cost information is available in construction cost handbooks"

324. quiet title action: "see, suit to quiet title"

325. quitclaim deed: "a deed that contains no warranties of any kind, no after-acquired title provisions, and provides the grantee with the least protection of any deed; it merely provides that any interest (if there is any) that the grantor has in the property is transferred to the grantee."

326. rafter: "one of a series of parallel sloping timbers that extend from the ridge-board to the exterior walls, providing support for the roof."

327. real estate investment trust (REIT): "a company that invests in and, in most cases operates, income-producing real estate and that meets numerous criteria, such as the necessity of being jointly owned by at least 100 persons."

328. real estate owned (REO): property acquired by a lender through a foreclosure sale.

329. Real Estate Settlement Procedures Act (RESPA): "a federal law designed to prevent lenders, real estate agents, developers, title insurance companies, and other agents (such as appraisers and inspectors) who service the real estate settlement process from providing kickbacks or referral fees to each other, and from facilitating bait-and-switch tactics."

330. real property sales contract: an agreement in which one party agrees to convey title to real property to another party upon the satisfaction of specified conditions set forth in the contract and that does not require conveyance of title within one year from the date of formation of the contract.

331. Realtist®: a member of the National Association of Real Estate Brokers. Subscribe to a code of ethics.

332. Realtor®: a member of the National Association of Realtors®. Subscribe to a code of ethics.

333. reconciliation: the process of ascertaining value by comparing and evaluating values obtained from comparables or from different valuation approaches; the process of comparing what is in a trust fund account with what should be in the account.

334. reconveyance deed: "a deed executed by the trustee of a deed of trust after the promissory note is paid off in full by the borrower and the lender instructs the trustee to so execute the reconveyance deed, which reconveys legal title to the borrower"

335. recorded map or plat system: "a method of land description that states a property's lot, block, and tract number, referring to a map recorded in the county where the property is located. "

336. rectangular survey system: a method of land description based on a grid system of north-south lines ("ranges") and east- west lines ("tier" or "township" lines) that divides the land into townships and sections.

337. red flag: "a condition that should alert a reasonably attentive person of a potential problem that warrants further investigation. Examples include stains on ceilings or walls, the smell of mold, and warped floors or walls."

338. redlining: the illegal practice of refusing to make loans for real property in particular areas.

339. Regulation Z: the set of regulations that implement the Truth- in-Lending Act (TILA).

340. reinforced concrete: "concrete poured around steel bars or metal netting to increase its ability to withstand tensile, shear, and compression stresses."

341. rejuvenation: "the phase when a property is rebuilt, remodeled, or otherwise revitalized to a new highest and best use."

342. reliction: a natural process by which the owner of riparian or littoral property acquires additional land that has been covered by water but has become permanently uncovered by the gradual recession of water.

343. remainder: "the residue of a freehold estate where, at the end of the estate, the future interest arises in a third person."

344. remainderman: a person who inherits or is entitled to inherit property held as a life estate when the person whose life determines the duration of the life estate passes away.

345. replacement cost: "the cost of replacing improvements with those having equivalent utility, but constructed with modern materials, designs, and workmanship."

346. reproduction cost: the cost of replacing improvements with exact replicas at current prices.

347. rescission: the cancellation of a contract and the restoration of each party to the same position held before the contract was entered into.

348. reserve account: "in reference to loan servicing, the escrow account from which the loan servicer typically pays, on behalf of the borrower, property taxes, hazard insurance, and any other charges (such as mortgage insurance) with respect to the loan."

349. retaliatory eviction: an eviction action brought to retaliate against a tenant for making a habitability complaint or for asserting other of the tenant's legal rights.

350. return on investment (ROI): an investor's cash flow (net income minus financing charges) divided by the investor's actual cash investment (as distinct from the purchase price).

351. reverse mortgage: "a security instrument for a loan for homeowners over the age of 62 who have a large amount of equity in their homes, usually designed to provide such homeowners with monthly payments, often over the lifetime of the last surviving homeowner who either moves out of the house or dies."

352. reversion: "the residue of a freehold estate where at the end of the estate, the future interest reverts to the grantor."

353. revocation: the withdrawal of an offer by the person who made the offer.

354. rezoning amendment: an amendment to a zoning ordinance that property owners may request if they feel that their area has been improperly zoned.

355. ridge-board: a horizontal board placed on edge at the apex of a roof to which the upper ends of the rafters are attached.

356. right of first refusal: "the right to be given the first chance to purchase a property at the same price, terms, and conditions as is offered to third parties if and when the property is put up for sale."

357. right of survivorship: "the right to succeed to the interest of a joint tenant or, if community property with right of survivorship, to succeed to the interest of a spouse or registered domestic partner. Right of survivorship is the most important characteristic of joint tenancy."

358. riparian rights: "the rights of a landowner to use water from a stream or lake adjacent to his or her property, provided such use is reasonable and does not injure other riparian owners."

359. robocall: "a pre-recorded, auto-dialed telephone call."

360. R-value: "a measure of the resistance of insulation to heat

transfer. The FTC requires sellers of new homes to disclose the R-value of each home's insulation. The higher the R-value, the greater is the effectiveness of the insulation."

361. safety clause: "a provision in a listing agreement, providing that the broker will earn the full commission if the property is sold within a specified number of days after the termination of the listing to a buyer with whom the broker has dealt in certain specified ways regarding the property."

362. sales comparison approach: an appraisal approach that compares recent sales of similar properties in the area to evaluate the market value of the subject property.

363. salesperson: a natural person who is employed by a licensed real estate broker to perform acts that require having a real estate license.

364. sandwich lease: a leasehold interest that lies between a primary lease and a sublease.

365. sash: frames that contain one or more windowpanes.

366. scarcity: a lack of abundance.

367. secondary financing: second mortgage and junior mortgage property financing

368. secondary mortgage market: the market where mortgages are sold by primary mortgage lenders to investors.

369. second mortgage: a security instrument that holds second- priority claim against certain property identified in the instrument.

370. secret profit: any compensation or beneficial gain realized by an agent not disclosed to the principal. Real estate agents must always disclose any interest that they or their relatives have in a transaction and obtain their principals' consent.

371. section: "one square mile, containing 640 acres."

372. security instrument: the written instrument by which a debtor pledges property as collateral to secure a loan.

373. seller carry back loan: a loan or credit given by a seller of real property to the purchaser of that property.

374. seller's agent: a real estate broker appointed by the seller to represent the seller.

375. selling agent: the real estate agent who sells or finds and obtains a buyer for the property in a real estate transaction.

376. senior mortgage: "a mortgage that, relative to another mortgage, has a higher lien-priority position."

377. separate property: "property that is owned in severalty by a spouse or registered domestic partner. Separate property includes property acquired before marriage or the registering of domestic partnership, and property acquired as a gift or by inheritance during marriage or registered domestic partnership."

378. servient tenement: land that is burdened by an easement.

379. setback: "a designation of a governing body as to how far a structure must be situated from something else, such as a curb or a neighboring property."

380. severalty: ownership of property by one person.

381. severance: "the act of detaching an item of real property that changes the item to personal property, such as the cutting down of a natural tree. Also, the act of terminating a relationship, such as the act of partitioning by court order for the transfer of an interest that changes a joint tenancy into a tenancy in common."

382. severance damages: damages paid to an owner of land partially taken by eminent domain where the value of the remaining portion of the owner's land is severely reduced by the severance of the condemned a portion of owner's land.

383. Sherman Act: "the federal law passed in 1890 that prohibits agreements, verbal or written, that have the effect of restraining free trade."

384. short sale: a pre-foreclosure sale made by the borrower (usually with the help of a real estate agent) with lender approval of real estate for less than the balance due on the mortgage loan.

385. short-term capital gain: "the capital gain on the sale of a capital asset that was held for a relatively short period of time, usually one year or less."

386. sill: "the board or metal forming the lower side of the frame for a window or door; the lowest part of the frame of a house, resting on the foundation and providing the base for the studs."

387. single agent: an agent who represents only one party in a given transaction.

388. situs: "the legal location of something; also refers to the preference for a particular location to live, work, or invest in"

389. special agent: an agent for a particular act or transaction.

390. special assessment: "a tax levied against properties in a particular area that are benefited by improvements such as for streets, water, and sewers."

391. specific lien: a lien that attaches only to specific property.

392. specific performance: a court order that requires a person to perform according to the terms of a contract.

393. spot zoning: "spot zoning —refers to the zoning of isolated properties for use different from the uses specified by existing zoning laws. To spot zone a particular property may, in some cases, be a violation of the requirement that police power apply similarly to all property similarly situated, which in turn arises from the constitutional guarantee of equal protection under the law."

394. square-foot method: "the most widely used method of estimating reproduction or replacement cost of a building, involving the collection cost data on recently constructed similar buildings and dividing the total cost by the square footage to obtain cost per square foot"

395. statute of frauds: "a law that requires certain types of contracts, including most real estate contracts, to be in writing and signed by the party to be bound in order for the contract to be enforceable."

396. statute of limitations: a law that requires particular types of lawsuits to be brought within a specified time after the occurrence of the event giving rise to the lawsuit.

397. steering: "the illegal practice of directing people of protected classes away from, or toward, housing in particular areas."

398. stigmatized property: a property having a condition that certain persons may find materially negative in a way that does not relate to the property's actual physical condition.

399. stock cooperative: a corporation formed or availed of primarily for the purpose of holding title to improved real property either in fee simple or for a term of years.

400. straight-line depreciation: "the expensing of a property by equal amounts over the useful life of the property, determined by subtracting from the cost of the property the estimated residual value of the property and dividing that amount by the useful life of the property measured in years."

401. straight-line method: a method of calculating annual depreciation of an improvement by dividing the cost of the improvement by the estimated useful life of a typical such improvement.

402. straight note: a promissory note under which periodic payments consist of interest only.

403. strict foreclosure: full title simply passes to the lender. 404. subagent: an agent of an agent.

405. subject to: acquiring real property that is burdened by a mortgage without becoming personally liable for the mortgage debt.

406. sublease: a transfer of a tenant's right to a portion of the leased premises or to the entire premises for less than the entire remaining lease term.

407. subordination clause: a provision in a mortgage or deed of trust that states that the mortgage or deed of trust will have lower priority than a mortgage or deed of trust recorded later.

408. suit to quiet title: "a court proceeding intended to establish the true ownership of a property, thereby eliminating any cloud on title."

409. tax deed: "the deed given to the successful buyer at a tax sale. A tax deed conveys title free and clear from private liens, but not from certain tax liens or special assessment liens, or from easements and recorded restrictions."

410. tenancy by the entirety: "recognized in some states, a special form of joint tenancy between a married couple, in which, as in a joint tenancy, there is the right of survivorship, but in which, unlike in a joint tenancy, neither spouse may convey his or her interest in the property during the lifetime of the other spouse without the consent of the other spouse."

411. tenancy in common: "a form of joint ownership that is presumed to exist if the persons who own the property are neither married nor registered domestic partners and they own undivided interests in property. Tenants in common may hold unequal interests; however, if the deed does not specify fractional interests among the tenants, the interests will be presumed to be equal."

412. tenancy in partnership: a form of joint ownership in which the partners combine their assets and efforts in a business venture.

413. testament: a will.

414. testator: one who dies leaving a will.

415. time-share estate: an estate in real property coupled with the right of occupancy for certain periods of time.

416. time-share use: "a right to occupancy during certain periods of time, not coupled to an estate in real property."

417. title search: "an examination of all relevant public documents to determine whether there exist any potential defects (such as judicial liens, lis pendens, or other encumbrances, including tax liens and special assessments) against the title."

418. title theory: "a legal theory of mortgage, holding that a mortgage transfers legal title to the mortgagee (the lender) while the mortgagor (the borrower) retains equitable title to the property, which permits the mortgagor exclusive possession and use of the property. Upon default, the mortgagee is entitled to immediate possession and use (such as to collect rents) of the property."

419. townhouse: "a form of condominium in which the individual units are connected by a common wall and, in general, (unlike in a high-rise condominium complex) a deed to the land beneath the townhouse is granted to the townhouse owner."

420. township: "six square miles, containing 36 sections."

421. trade fixtures: "objects that a tenant attaches to real property for use in the tenant's trade or business. Trade fixtures differ from other fixtures in that, even though they are attached with some permanence to real property, they may be removed at the end of the tenancy of the business."

422. transactional broker: "a non-agent middleman who brings the parties to a real estate transaction together and lets the parties do all of the negotiating among themselves. States that permit this kind of non-agent-facilitator status impose an obligation on the transactional broker to act fairly, honestly, and competently to find qualified buyers or suitable properties, but the transactional broker does not owe fiduciary legal obligations to any of the parties."

423. transferability: the ability to transfer some interest in property to another.

424. triggering term: any of a number of specific finance terms stated in an advertisement for a loan that triggers Regulation Z disclosure requirements in the advertisement.

425. triple net lease: "a lease under which the tenant pays a fixed rent plus the landlord's property taxes, hazard insurance, and all maintenance costs."

426. trust account: "an account set up by a broker at a bank or other recognized depository in the state where the broker is doing business, into which the broker deposits all funds entrusted to the broker by principles or others."

427. trust deed: "a three-party security device, the three parties being the borrower (trustor), the lender (beneficiary), and a third- party (trustee) to whom "bare legal title" is conveyed."

428. trustee: "a person who holds something of value in trust for the benefit of another; under a deed of trust, a neutral third-party who holds naked legal title for security."

429. trustor: a borrower who executes a deed of trust.

430. Truth-in-Lending Act (TILA): "a federal consumer protection law that was enacted in 1968 with the intention of helping borrowers understand the costs of borrowing money by requiring disclosures about loan terms and costs (in particular, the APR) and to standardize the way in which certain costs related to the loan are calculated and disclosed."

431. tying arrangement: occurs in antitrust law when the seller conditions the sale of one product or service on the purchase of another product or service.

432. underwriter: "one who analyzes the risk of, and recommends whether to approve, a proposed mortgage loan."

433. undivided interest: an ownership interest in property in which an owner has the right of possession of the entire property and may not exclude the other owners from any portion by claiming that a specific portion of the property is his or hers alone.

434. undivided interest subdivision: a subdivision in which owners own a partial or fractional interest in an entire parcel of land. The land in an undivided interest subdivision is not divided; its ownership is divided.

435. unenforceable contract: a contract that a court would not enforce.

436. Uniform Commercial Code (UCC): a set of laws that established unified and comprehensive regulations for security transactions of personal property and that superseded existing laws in that field.

437. unilateral contract: a contract in which one party gives a promise that is to be accepted not by another promise but by performance.

438. unit-in-place method: unit-in-place method — a method of estimating the replacement or reproduction cost of a structure by calculating the unit cost of components of the structure.

439. unlawful detainer: a legal action to regain possession of real property.

440. useful life: "the estimated period during which a property generates revenue (if the property is an income property) or usefulness (if the property, such as a private residence, has value other than income value)."

441. usury: the charging of interest in excess of that allowed by law.

442. utility: "the usefulness of property; its ability to satisfy a potential buyer's need or desire, such as to provide shelter or income."

443. VA: the Department of Veterans Affairs is a federal agency designed to benefit veterans and members of their families.

444. valid contract: a contract that is binding and enforceable in a court of law.

445. value: "the present worth to typical users or investors of all rights to future benefits, arising out of property ownership."

446. variance: an exception that may be granted in cases where damage to the value of a property from the strict enforcement of zoning ordinances would far outweigh any benefit to be derived from enforcement.

447. vendee: the purchaser in a real property sales agreement

448. vendor: the seller in a real property sales agreement.

449. vicarious liability: "liability imposed on a person not because of that person's own acts but because of the acts of another.

450. voidable contract: "a contract that, at the request of one party only, may be declared unenforceable, but is valid until it is so declared."

451. void contract: a purported contract that has no legal effect.

452. voluntary lien: a lien obtained through the voluntary action of the one against whose property the lien attaches.

453. warranty deed: "a deed in which the grantor warrants that the title being conveyed is good and free from defects or encumbrances, and that the grantor will defend the title against all suits."

454. wetlands: "as defined by the EPA, "areas that are soaked or flooded by surface or groundwater frequently enough or for sufficient duration to support plants, birds, animals, and aquatic life. Wetlands generally include swamps, marshes, bugs, estuaries, and other inland and coastal areas, and are federally protected.""

455. will: a document that stipulates how one's property should be distributed after death; also called a testament.

456. writ of attachment: a writ ordering the seizure of property belonging to a defendant to ensure the availability of the property to satisfy a judgment if the plaintiff wins.

457. writ of execution: a writ directing a public official (usually the sheriff) to seize and sell property of a debtor to satisfy a debt 458. zoning: laws of a city or county that specify the type of land-use that is acceptable in certain areas.

Made in the USA
Columbia, SC
12 June 2021